Investing

DeMYSTiFieD®

DeMYSTiFieD® Series

The Demystified Series publishes over 125 titles in all areas of academic study. For a complete list of titles, please visit www.mhprofessional.com.

Investing
DeMYSTiFieD®

Second Edition

Paul J. Lim

New York   Chicago   San Francisco   Lisbon   London   Madrid   Mexico City
Milan   New Delhi   San Juan   Seoul   Singapore   Sydney   Toronto

1 2 3 4 5 6 7 8 9 10 DOC/DOC 1 9 8 7 6 5 4 3 2 1 0

ISBN 978-0-07-174912-1
MHID   0-07-174912-8

This publication is designed to provide accurate and authoritative information in regard to the subject matter covered. It is sold with the understanding that neither the author nor the publisher is engaged in rendering legal, accounting, securities trading, or other professional services. If legal advice or other expert assistance is required, the services of a competent professional person should be sought.

> —From a Declaration of Principles Jointly Adopted by a Committee of the American Bar Association and a Committee of Publishers and Associations

McGraw-Hill books are available at special quantity discounts to use as premiums and sales promotions or for use in corporate training programs. To contact a representative, please e-mail us at bulksales@mcgraw-hill.com.

About the Author

Paul J. Lim is a senior editor at *MONEY* magazine, where he oversees the publication's investing section. Lim has also written for *The New York Times, The Los Angeles Times,* and *U.S. News & World Report,* where he headed up the magazine's coverage of the markets and personal finance.

Lim is a graduate of Princeton University, where he earned his bachelor's degree in politics in 1992, and the University of Pennsylvania, where he earned his master's degree in 1994 from the Fels Center of Government.

Contents

Introduction

If the last decade has taught us anything, it's the importance of getting back to the basics when it comes to our understanding of investing.

In the late 1990s, in what now seems like a bygone era—before Wall Street's numerous bubbles burst—many investors thought trading stocks was a simple road to riches. Well, as it turned out, that road was full of unexpected twists and turns, and potholes and detours that have taken many households off the path of being able to meet their long-term financial goals. Indeed, after returning nearly 20 percent a year throughout the 1990s, equities actually lost ground between 2000 and the start of 2010. This period of time was so difficult for investors that it got its own name: "The Lost Decade."

Of course, as soon as the stock market soured, investors moved onto other investments, such as the real estate market in 2000 and 2001. And sure enough, throughout the early part of the 2000s, our homes had supplanted stocks as the preferred alternative route to riches. And just as "day traders" thought they could make it rich trading stocks in a fast-and-furious fashion in the late 1990s, home flippers thought they could get into and out of residential real estate— at a tidy profit. Of course, a problem arose: the epic collapse in the mortgage market that sent home prices sinking and millions of homes into foreclosure.

You can blame timing for some of this. If you look back at history, the essential asset classes that make up one's investment portfolio—stocks, bonds, cash, real estate and commodities—all go through cycles of ups and downs. And as it just so happened, stocks and real estate (and to a lesser extent, commodities) all went up and down at just about the same time. This made it next to impossible for investors to hide out from market troubles in recent years.

But investors themselves weren't blameless either. In the late 1990s and again in the early 2000s, many investors thought that the powerful gains they were enjoying in the stock and housing markets changed the rules of investing. For instance, many investors thought that investment gains could take the place of good old-fashioned savings. As it turned out, they were wrong. And many incorrectly assumed that powerful bull markets in stocks and houses made concepts like moderation and diversification outmoded. They were wrong as well.

The enduring lesson of the Lost Decade for investors isn't that investing is pointless—everyone must learn how to invest for their financial security, as we'll explain later on. Rather, the enduring lesson of this roller-coaster ride of a decade is that the essential rules of investing never change—no matter how much we want them to.

For every reward you might receive in your investment portfolio, you have to accept a commensurate level of risk. And sometimes, risk means losing more money than you're willing (or capable) of losing.

That's why now more than ever, it's vital that you truly understand what it takes to invest in a safe and sound manner to make it possible to achieve all of your financial goals.

How to Use this Book

This book is geared for all those investors and would-be investors out there who know the importance of managing their money for the future but who aren't entirely certain how to go about it. That's probably the majority of the general population. Public opinion polls tell us that today more Americans think and worry about money—and how to invest it—than any generation in this country's history. Part of this worry, as I'll explain, is due to the fact that more of us are responsible for our own financial futures than ever before. Yet fewer than 20 percent of us feel that we're doing very well at this incredibly important task, which explains why baby boomers and members of Generation X worry more about their financial well-being than their own mortality.

This book is also geared for those of you who aren't entirely interested in investing but who realize its importance. Again, that's probably the majority of you. But who can blame you? After a series of bear markets and roller coaster rides in a variety of investment vehicles between 2000 and 2010, the once-unshakable faith that investors had in stocks, real estate, and even commodities has been tested thoroughly. Yet at the end of the day, investors in this modern age, when the security of government and corporate pensions is under threat, realize that learning to invest on their own—and to secure their own financial security—is as unavoidable today as paying taxes.

Finally, this book will be particularly useful for those of you who are just getting started in your careers or who are still in school. Why? It boils down to the basic laws of compound interest. The so-called time value of money tells us that the younger you start saving and investing for your future, the easier it will be to meet your long-term goals. Consider this simple but ubiquitous example: If you want to have $1 million saved up for your golden years and you start putting away a portion of your income starting at age 20, all you would need to set aside annually would be around $3,500 (assuming your investments returned around 7 percent annually). However, if you were to wait until you turned 35, you would have to sock away nearly $11,000 a year to reach that same goal—just because of the later start you got.

It just goes to show how easy, in theory, it can be to make your investments work for you. Unfortunately, even though investing has become a daily part of our lives—and a daily part of our national conversation—the language of investing and some basic investing concepts are still foreign to many of us.

The sad reality is, no one really teaches us how to become investors. Few high schools these days even offer economics courses, let alone lessons in personal finance or investing. And unless your parents were investors themselves and taught you the ins and outs of the stock and bond markets, you were probably left to figure it out on your own.

What happens if you don't pick it up? Chances are, you'll be thrown head first into the markets—with little clue about how to stay afloat—the minute you start a new job and enroll in your employer's 401(k) retirement plan. Those enrollment papers not only ask you if you want to participate but what investments you want to put money into and how much money you want to invest in each. Terms like "small-cap growth funds" and "long-term government bonds" and "annual expense ratios" will be thrown at you as if you somehow intuitively understand what it all means. Yet in this day and age, you have to know what these things mean to take control of your financial futures.

Hopefully, this book will answer some of your basic questions and take some of the mystery out of investing. When you boil it down, learning to invest is really a four-step process. First, you have to figure out who you are and what kind of investor you plan to be. Then, you have to become familiar with the assets that serve as the building blocks to an investment portfolio.

Then you have to figure out how to research and select those assets.

And finally, you have to learn how to mix and organize those assets into a comprehensive and diversified portfolio that will serve your specific set of needs.

I'll outline how I hope to address these topics in the coming chapters.

Getting Ready

In Part I, "Getting Ready," I want to familiarize you not only with the basic concepts of investing—like risk and returns—but also investing jargon. I begin in Chapter 1 with a discussion on "Why We Invest." That's followed in Chapter 2 with laying the groundwork. Here, I address all the things you have to consider "Before You Get Started." In Chapter 3 the focus is on "Demystifying the Language of

Investing," in order to expedite our conversation about key investing terms and concepts. And then, in Chapter 4, "What Kind of Investor Are You?" I discuss what strategies may work well with your sensibilities as a saver and investor.

Some investors find success by investing directly in the stock market by buying shares of individual companies. Others prefer to go through professionally managed mutual funds. Some have built nice nest eggs by buying and holding a diversified basket of stocks and funds. Others have done well by concentrating their bets on only their best ideas. Some make money by focusing on those investments that offer the greatest growth. Still others focus not on the best investments but the best-priced investments. In other words, they go bargain hunting. History has shown that money can be made in all sorts of ways, and I'll outline some of those different schools of investing for you.

Your Assets

In Part II, "Your Assets," I turn the attention to the building blocks of investing. You can make money, as was just discussed, in stocks and bonds, just as you can in real estate and gold. So I'll discuss the basic types of investments you can choose from, outlining their risks and rewards. In Chapter 5, I'll focus on "Demystifying Stocks." In Chapters 6 and 7, I'll turn the focus on "Demystifying Bonds" and "Demystifying Cash." And in Chapters 8 and 9, I'll spend time with perhaps the most popular investment for most households, mutual funds, in "Demystifying Mutual Funds I and II." Then, in Chapter 10, I'll turn our attention to "Demystifying Other Assets," including real estate, commodities, and a new class of fund-like investments we call "unmutual funds."

Selecting Your Assets

In Part III, I focus on "Selecting Your Assets." Here, I'll outline some basic ways investors can research and sort through the thousands of choices before them, starting with stocks and bonds. Then, I'll cover the most popular investment vehicles, mutual funds. I'll cover those topics in Chapters 11 through 13.

Organizing Your Assets

In Part IV, I address issues surrounding "Organizing Your Assets." In Chapter 14, "Demystifying Asset Allocation," I'll discuss the importance of creating an asset allocation strategy and talk about ways to determine what the right mix of stocks, bonds, and cash is for you. And finally, in Chapter 15, "Demystifying Asset Location," I'll go into the different types of asset accounts in which you can hold your stocks and bonds, and the strategies you might employ.

Again, just as there is no single investment that's right for everyone, there is no single investment account that's best for all investors. Some may find it more appropriate to invest primarily in a Roth IRA. Others will find traditional IRAs better. Still others may decide that it's beneficial to invest some money in a regular, taxable brokerage account.

By the end of this book, no matter who you are or what kind of investments you choose, I hope you will feel more comfortable as an investor—and I hope you will start to invest in a manner that is both appropriate for your circumstances and suitable to your sensibilities.

Part I

Getting Ready

chapter 1

Why We Invest

CHAPTER OBJECTIVES

In this chapter, you will learn the following:

- Why a majority of Americans invest
- How the shift from pensions to 401(k) plans is driving this trend
- Why you need to plan for at least a 30-year retirement
- The difference between investing and saving

In this age of Roth IRAs, 401(k)s, 403(b)s, 457s, and 529 savings plans, all of us are investors—or at least we're bound to be. Yet this wasn't always the case.

Not so long ago, Americans could be classified into two distinct groups. On the one hand, there were workers. On the other, there were investors. The difference being: The working class worked long hours and often earned little pay, while the investor class worked few hours but earned great sums. The advantage the investor class had, of course, was access to *capital*. In other words, they had money. And that money worked on their behalf so they didn't have to. Of course, back then, investors didn't invest because they had to. They invested because they wanted to—and because they could.

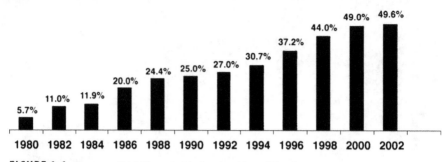

FIGURE 1-1 • Percent of U.S. Households Owning Mutual Funds.

The number of Americans who invest in mutual funds has grown by leaps and bounds since the start of the 1980s. Today, nearly half of all households have some exposure to the stock market through mutual funds.

Source: Investment Company Institute

But times have changed, in all sorts of ways. Today, nearly 90 million Americans in more than 51 million homes—representing around half of all households—own shares of at least one mutual fund. That means that at the very least, half of the country invests directly or indirectly in the stock and bond markets.

This is a far cry from just a half a century ago, when only around 6 million people invested. Even as recently as 1980, less than 6 percent of American families owned shares of a single mutual fund. By 1990 that number had grown to around a quarter of all American households. And by the mid- to late 1990s, more than a third of all households got into the investing game (Figure 1-1).

As big as today's numbers are, they're bound to grow in the coming years, since more and more Americans are getting an early start investing. Today, nearly a third of all workers age 24 or younger have money working for them in the stock or bond markets. By the time we hit age 35, nearly half of us invest, primarily through mutual funds and company-sponsored retirement accounts (Figure 1-2). Even low incomes aren't stopping us. Around one out of eight of us who are earning less than $35,000 a year manage, somehow, to invest a portion of our annual incomes in the stock market. And around half of all mutual fund shareholders have incomes of less than $75,000 a year—hardly Rockefeller territory (Figure 1-3).

Why Are We Investing?

You can thank the advent of so-called **self-directed retirement accounts** like 401(k)s and Roth IRAs, along with the rise of low-minimum brokerage accounts and

Age	1999	2000	2001	2002	2003
24 or younger	28%	23%	32%	27%	27%
25–34	47%	49%	50%	48%	44%
35–44	55%	58%	60%	57%	54%
45–54	58%	59%	60%	59%	57%
55–64	50%	54%	54%	55%	59%
65 or older	34%	32%	41%	37%	34%

FIGURE 1-2 · Mutual Fund Ownership by Age.

It's not just older investors who invest in mutual funds. A large percentage of investors of all age groups invest in funds, including twenty-somethings.

Source: Investment Company Institute

cheap online commissions—all of which helped democratize Wall Street in the 1980s and 1990s—for this investing boom. A record 46 million of us invest through individual retirement accounts, while another nearly 50 million of us invest through company-sponsored retirement plans. These include 401(k) plans, to which private-sector employees typically have access; 403(b) accounts, which are 401(k)-like accounts for nonprofit workers and teachers; and 457s, which are 401(k)-like savings plans for municipal workers. Collectively, workers have around $2 trillion of their savings invested in these plans. The recent rise of 529 college savings plans—and the exorbitant cost of sending kids to universities—is another force driving more Americans to invest.

Figures 1-4 and 1-5 graphically illustrate the increasing number of Americans investing in 401(k)s and the billions in assets they are investing.

Age	1999	2000	2001	2002	2003
$24,999 or less	15%	17%	21%	14%	15%
$25,000–$34,999	30%	37%	38%	36%	33%
$35,000–$49,999	49%	49%	49%	48%	41%
$50,000–$74,999	62%	66%	66%	67%	59%
$75,000–$99,999	78%	77%	78%	79%	77%
$100,000 or more	78%	79%	85%	82%	83%

FIGURE 1-3 · Mutual Fund Ownership by Income.

A large percentage of investors of all income levels invest in funds. But as this chart indicates, Americans tend to invest in funds aggressively once their household incomes rise above $50,000.

Source: Investment Company Institute

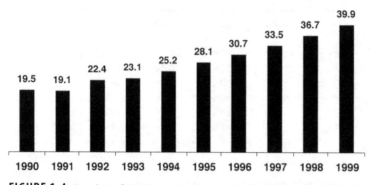

FIGURE 1-4 · Number of Americans Participating in 401(k) Plans (in Millions).

As the bull market roared throughout the 1990s, an increasing number of American workers took advantage of their 401 (k) tax-deferred retirement accounts.

Source: Department of Labor and Cerulli Associates

Why We Can't Afford *Not to* Invest

Now, some of you may be wondering whether all this effort is necessary, especially since stocks wound up losing value in the entire decade of the 2000s. Indeed, the Dow Jones Industrial Average, the most recognized index of U.S. stocks, entered January 1, 2000, at a level of 11,497. A decade later, the index had fallen by around 1,000 points. This is hardly the recipe for investment success.

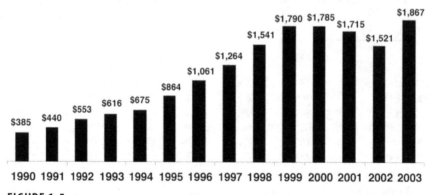

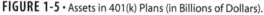

FIGURE 1-5 · Assets in 401(k) Plans (in Billions of Dollars).

Not only have more and more workers taken advantage of their 401 (k) retirement accounts, they are putting a staggering amount of money into these tax-deferred plans, which hold nearly $2 trillion in assets.

Source: Investment Company Institute

But it's important to note that investing isn't all about stocks. In fact, if you invested $100,000 on December 31, 1999, in a portfolio consisting of 60 percent stocks and 40 percent bonds, and you kept investing $1,000 a month for the next decade—and if you annually readjusted your portfolio so that it remained consistently at around a 60-40 mix—you would have earned about 4.3 percent a year on your investments throughout the 2000s. And over longer stretches of time, investing in a diversified mix of stocks and bonds has done even better than that.

Indeed, according to the investment research group Ibbotson Associates, a portfolio consisting of 50 percent stocks and 50 percent bonds (which is generally considered a conservative approach, especially for younger investors) returned an average of around 8 percent a year since 1926.

And as you can see in the chart in Figure 1-6, it's returns like these—which only stocks and bonds can consistently deliver over extremely long stretches of time—that give you the better chance of being able to meet your long-term financial goals. Those include retirement, college education costs for your children, continuing education expenses for yourself or your spouse, the purchase of a new home, etc.

Okay, but couldn't you have at least come close by staying on the sidelines and keeping your money safe in cash accounts?

Let's check the numbers. If you had decided that investing wasn't worthwhile and instead stuck all of your money in cash, you would have earned only 2.6 percent a year between the start of 2000 and the start of 2010. Today, it's even worse.

At the beginning of this decade, a typical bank checking account, for example, was yielding less than 1 percent in interest income a year. At this percentage rate, guess how long it will take to turn $1 into $2. Seventy years. Yet if you were to invest that money in, say, the bond market and earned 5 percent a year on average (and that's a conservative figure) over 70 years,

No. Years	1.5X	2X	3X	5X	10X
3	14.5%	26.0%	44.2%	80.0%	115.4%
5	8.4%	14.9%	24.6%	38.0%	58.5%
7	6.0%	10.4%	17.0%	25.8%	38.9%
10	4.1%	7.2%	11.6%	17.5%	25.9%
25	1.6%	2.8%	4.5%	6.6%	9.6%

FIGURE 1-6 · Rates of Return Needed to Reach Goals.

This table indicates the average annual returns investors would need to generate to grow their money by these various factors. For example, if you had 25 years to invest, you could turn $1 into $3 by earning 4.5 percent a year on your money. This would indicate that you could invest in bonds to achieve your goal. But if you only had 10 years to achieve the same goal, you would need to earn 11.6 percent a year on average. This would indicate that you would need equities in your portfolio.

you could easily grow that $1 into $30. And if you were to invest that money in the stock market and earned 7 percent a year, on average, you'd turn that same buck into $114. That's the power of *compound interest*. That's the power of investing.

A generation ago, we didn't need to concern ourselves with these matters because many workers were guaranteed income in retirement through traditional pension plans. These investment funds were run by employers who bore all of the investment burden, decision making, and risk. But as pension costs have risen, and as Corporate America moved to cut expenses to improve profitability in the 1980s and 1990s, fewer and fewer companies offered workers pension coverage. This trend was exacerbated in the financial crisis and global recession that took place in 2008, when companies were forced to make record amounts of cost-cutting moves to remain in business during the credit crunch. Instead, more and more workers have been pushed into 401(k) or 401(k)-like retirement plans, which require *the worker* to make all of his or her own investment decisions. And the worker, in this arrangement, must bear all the risk of investing incorrectly.

This shift couldn't have come at a worse time, as more of us are living longer in retirement, which means the stakes are higher. Obviously, living longer is a good thing. But the concern that arises from a long life is: Who's going to pay for it? The average American man is now expected to live to age 75, while the average woman lives to over 80. Just a quarter-century ago, the average man lived to 70 while the average woman lived to 77. And a half-century ago, the average life expectancy for all Americans was just 68 (Figure 1-7).

The typical age for retirement, meanwhile, is between 62 and 65 (though this too may go up if our health improves and if changes are made to age requirements for Social Security and other benefits). This means that instead of having to save and invest enough money to cover another handful of years, we now have to invest well enough to pay for at least another 15 to 20 years' worth of living expenses.

Actually, the challenge is even bigger because those averages are just that: averages. Once a person makes it to 65 and retires, the odds of living a much longer life are that much greater. In fact, the average woman who makes it to age 65 can expect to live another 20 years, bringing the life expectancy figure up to 85. If you're lucky enough to make it to age 75, you can expect to live another 12½ years, according to the actuarial tables. That would bring you to nearly 88. That's a whole lot of years of bills to pay.

Now more than ever, we are a nation of workers *and* investors because we have to be. This trend is only going to continue because future generations will live even longer (thank you, modern medicine!) and because the cost of living will continue to rise (thank you, inflation!). In fact, at this rate, virtually all working adults will be investors of some kind or another a generation

At Birth	All	Male	Female
1900	47.3	46.3	48.3
1950	68.2	65.6	71.1
1960	69.7	66.6	73.1
1970	70.8	67.1	74.7
1980	73.7	70.0	77.4
1990	75.4	71.8	78.8
2000	77.0	74.3	79.7
2005	77.8	75.2	80.4
At 65	**All**	**Male**	**Female**
1950	13.9	12.8	15.0
1960	14.3	12.8	15.8
1970	15.2	13.1	17.0
1980	16.4	14.1	18.3
1990	17.2	15.1	18.9
2000	18.0	16.2	19.3
2005	18.8	17.2	20.0
At 75	**All**	**Male**	**Female**
1980	10.4	8.8	11.5
1990	10.9	9.4	12.0
2000	11.4	10.1	12.3
2005	11.5	10.2	12.4

FIGURE 1-7 · Life Expectancy in America.

Figures represent how many additional years a person can expect to live after reaching a certain age.

Source: Centers for Disease Control and Prevention

from now. Don't forget: Nearly 70 percent of us are already homeowners, which is a record level of property ownership in the history of this and most other countries. And buying property is one of the oldest forms of investing over long periods of time. So we're much closer to achieving this goal than you might think.

Investor, Educate Thyself

The upshot of this is, we all need to prepare and educate ourselves—and our children—to the new realities of being members of the investing class. For some of us that means seeking the help of qualified professionals, such as certified financial planners, certified public accountants, brokers, or investment consultants. There is absolutely nothing wrong with seeking advice, provided that the help you receive is sound and reasonably priced.

While there was a flurry of do-it-yourself investing activity in the late 1990s, surveys have shown that a growing percentage of Americans are seeking professional financial advice. For example, before the bear market of the early 2000s, around two out of five investors sought the advice of a professional planner. After that bear, more than half of us did. And after the debacle in the real estate market in 2005, and yet another bear market in stocks in 2008, that figure has grown even more. Studies today show that upwards of two-thirds of investors now use or plan to use the help of a professional adviser or planner. This is to be expected, especially in a world where the rules for investing are getting ever more complicated.

For other investors, the prospect of finding a good and affordable financial consultant may seem just as daunting as finding good, affordable investments. So this group might choose not to seek professional investment advice at all. After all, how do you know you can trust the person advising you? And how can you tell if the advice is (a) good and (b) worth the fee?

Still other investors may want the help of a professional but might not be able to afford such services. As the financial services industry focuses on their most profitable clients—the so-called high-net-worth crowd—fees for small accounts have risen while services are being cut back. Finally, there's yet another category of investors: those who like managing their own money and who are good at it.

Regardless of which group you fall within, it is still important to absorb as much information as you can about the principles—and pitfalls—of executing an investment plan. Even if you're paying a professional to construct your portfolio for you, it's important to at least know enough to be able to tell whether that professional advisor is working in your best interest. Educating yourself might mean reading the *Wall Street Journal* religiously. It could mean tuning into financial television networks like CNBC. Hopefully, this book will play some role in your journey.

But What Does It Mean to Invest?

You'll often hear the phrase "invest for the future." Not only is this a cliché but it is also redundant. That's because the act of investing *necessarily* involves the future, on a couple of levels. Obviously, the reason we invest is to be able to meet certain goals in the future—be it going on vacation, buying a house, sending children to college, or building up a nest egg. But investing also takes time. That means, by definition, it's a future-oriented endeavor.

While spending involves instantaneous gratification—you're giving up something today in exchange for something else immediately—investing is just the opposite. It's all about delaying one's gratification. It involves giving up something today (i.e., the use of your money) in hopes of getting something greater back in the future. That "something greater," of course, is more money.

The interesting thing is, there is a relationship between spending money and investing it. When you invest, you are often interacting with would-be spenders. For example, if you are a stock investor and buy shares of a company, you are giving the firm your capital (i.e., your cash), which it will use to spend on various projects. The hope is that the company will not only survive but also thrive to the point where its value (and the value of your shares) will increase substantially down the road.

Investing in bonds works the same way. When you buy a U.S. Treasury bond, for example, you are handing over your money—and all the potential uses you might have for that cash—so the government can gratify its needs by spending your money. In return, you are making a calculated bet that the federal government will not only survive but will also be able to pay you back your investment at a future date, along with an agreed-upon amount of interest.

The greater the length of time you're willing to delay that gratification, the greater the odds of being rewarded for your patience. Sometimes, to invest properly and safely, you may need to tie up your money for months, if not years, if not decades—if not longer. Indeed, a recent study by the asset management firm T. Rowe Price found that to be assured that stocks will work in your favor, you really have to have a 15-year time horizon. In other words, to be absolutely sure that equities will be worthwhile, you have to be willing to stick it out with stocks for a decade and a half. Similarly, anyone who has purchased a home with a 30-year mortgage will appreciate just how long some investments are designed to ripen. But rewards are often well worth the wait.

In many ways, the greatest lie perpetrated by the Internet bubble of the 1990s and the real estate bubble of the early 2000s was the sense that we could somehow get rich overnight by putting money into the market. But an overnight investment in any market—be it the stock market, bond market, real estate market, or whatever—is not investing. That's gambling.

Now, for a brief, shining moment in the late 1990s, when the stock market was routinely returning 20, 25, or even 30 percent a year, investors truly felt that things had somehow changed, and that the rules that govern investing had somehow gone away. But the rules of investing change about as often as the rules of physics do. The 2000-2002 bear market should have reminded us of that. So too should have the slump in housing that started in 2006 and continued through 2010. And so too should have the equally grisly 2007-2009 bear market in equities that was technically worse than the bursting of the Internet bubble. This most recent bear cut the S&P 500 index of stocks by around 56 percent.

What Investing Isn't

Before we start discussing what investing is, it's important to understand what it isn't. The bear markets of 2000–2002 and 2007–2009 showed us that investing is not about getting rich quick. Here are some other important lessons to keep in mind:

- *Investing is not just about stocks.* For several years in the 1990s people associated investing exclusively with the stock market. That's because stocks were generating returns in excess of 20 percent a year for several years. Bonds, by comparison, were producing only single-digit gains. Given the choice between earning, say, 6 percent a year on your money and earning 26 percent, obviously, most of us preferred the latter. This would explain why a generation of investors was beginning to think that you didn't need to own bonds in your portfolio. Some believed that putting all your money in stocks, in fact, was preferable to investing even a sliver of it in real estate.

  But when the bear market struck in 2000, we were reminded of two things: first, that risk must be factored into all of our investing decisions; and second, that when one investment asset falls, another typically rises. True to form, when blue-chip stocks lost nearly half of their value in the bear market of 2000–2002, and when technology stocks lost more than three-quarters, bonds saw tremendous gains. A basic bond portfolio gained 6.2 percent in 2000, 6 percent in 2001, and another 6.5 percent in 2002.

  Similarly, in 2008, when stocks lost more than a third of their overall value, U.S. Treasury bonds soared more than 25 percent. That's because in that market storm, investors sought the safety that U.S. bonds traditionally provide. In fact, because bonds have performed so consistently well over the past two decades—and because equities have been rocked by two severe bear markets recently—these two assets have delivered very similar gains over the past 20 years. According to Ibbotson Associates, both U.S. stocks and U.S. government bonds have delivered returns of around 8 percent a year since 1990.

  To be sure, that's not always likely to be true. Historically, stocks do better than other assets over time. But it just goes to show that equities should never be considered the only game in town.

- *Investing is not just about "financial assets" like stocks or bonds.* If you owned or purchased a home in the early 2000s, you know that there are times when tangible assets like real estate can perform better—sometimes much better—than financial assets can.

Often, when one type of investment zigs, the other tends to zag. Consider that in 2000, when stock prices tumbled, investors who moved money out of the equity markets and into real estate saw big gains because the housing market boomed just as the equity market ebbed. But by 2005, when the stock market had recovered from its tech bubble losses, home values across the country began to sink.

Another way to measure the value of investing in real estate is to measure the performance of **real estate investment trusts (REITs)**, which are shares of companies that either invest in or operate real estate properties—ranging from office buildings to apartment complexes to shopping malls to hospitals to hotels and warehouses. Mutual funds that invest in REITs rose 27 percent in value in 2000, nearly 10 percent in 2001, and more than 4 percent in 2002 when stocks faltered. But in 2007, by which time stocks had fully healed from the 2000 bear, real estate stocks sank by double digits.

Beyond real estate, another asset investors have historically put a portion of their portfolio into are commodities. These so-called real assets range from oil to copper to agricultural products like wheat and corn. But the commodity that investors are most familiar with—and comfortable owning—tends to be gold. After decades of underperforming stocks, gold investments have delivered double-digit gains in the 2000s, at a time when stocks have lost value.

- *Investing is not the same thing as savings.* While it is true that you need to save money to invest it, investing and saving are completely different exercises. When you save money, the ultimate goal is to protect every last penny of that pot. On Wall Street they have a fancy expression for this. It's called **capital preservation.**

  When you invest, you hope that your money is protected. But your goal, ultimately, is to grow the pot of money. Wall Street has a fancy term for this too. It's called **capital appreciation.** To reach that goal, the rules of investing say you have to expose yourself to some risk. But over time, and in a well-diversified portfolio of different types of investments, that risk can be minimized. Saving and investing work in cycles.

  For instance, say your goal is to invest money to buy a house. For the sake of argument, let's assume that you and your spouse are hoping to make a down payment on your first home five years from now. First, you have to save money from your day-to-day income to get started. This money might be set aside in a bank savings or checking account—or in a money market account. All of these are considered "cash" investments. And they happen to be federally insured against losses. As you accumulate enough savings to cover your daily expenses and rainy day funds, you can start investing that money in higher-yielding (and higher-risk) investments like a stock mutual fund or bonds. Now, as your investments grow over the next five years, you will soon approach your deadline for actually making that down payment on the house. As you get within a year or two of that goal, you will probably want to shift back into savings mode. That's because in any short-term window of time, your stock or bond investments could lose value. And you don't want your investments to lose value just as you're going to need the cash. So, this is the time to start shifting back into "savings" or "capital preservation" mode.

Confused? Don't worry. Once we get going on the basics of investing, all of this will seem like second nature.

QUIZ

1. **The majority of Americans have been investing in stocks and bonds for several generations.**
   A. True
   B. False

2. **More and more workers are becoming investors because . . .**
   A. More and more companies offer corporate pensions.
   B. Fewer and fewer companies offer corporate pensions.
   C. The Internet makes investing easier than in the past.

3. **Compound interest means . . .**
   A. The younger you are, the less you have to invest.
   B. The younger you are, the more you have to invest.
   C. It is interest that compounds your losses.

4. **With the average age of retirement at 65, you have to prepare for a retirement that lasts . . .**
   A. 5-10 years
   B. 20-30 years
   C. 65 years

5. **Stocks and bonds deliver the same returns over time.**
   A. True
   B. False

6. **If you want to double your money in 10 years, you will need to earn this much annually:**
   A. 14.9 percent
   B. 11.6 percent
   C. 7.2 percent

7. **Which of the following assets move in perfect lock step with one another?**
   A. Stocks and bonds
   B. Stocks and commodities
   C. Commodities and real estate
   D. None of the above

8. **Which of the following investments are designed for short-term money gains?**
   A. Stocks
   B. Bonds
   C. Cash

9. **The longer you live, the more you have to invest.**
    A. True
    B. False

10. **The reason why you need to learn how to invest is that . . .**
    A. Most Americans have to secure their own financial futures.
    B. Most households seek professional investment advice.
    C. Most households don't need to learn how to invest.

chapter 2

Before You Get Started . . .

In this chapter, you will learn the following:

- What it takes to invest on your own
- What you need to know before you invest
- How to set up a financial safety net
- How to know how much you can invest
- How to set your investing goals

Investing is a lot like running a marathon. Just as you don't wake up one morning and decide to run 26.2 miles on a whim, you shouldn't invest without preparing for the challenge. In both cases, failing to adequately train for your goal could lead to major injuries. The difference is, your body may only need weeks to heal from a pulled muscle or strained back. It could take years, if not decades, to overcome investment errors you make in your portfolio. This is something that investors who failed to prepare in 2000 are only now coming to grips with.

Still, it's a useful exercise to embrace this analogy. Running a race of this length takes months of training to build necessary endurance. It requires a strategy that factors in the length of the course, the nature of the path, and an assessment of external forces like the weather or even one's own health. And it takes a commitment to stay the course, no matter how painful this exercise may be.

Investing, which is also a lengthy journey, requires similar steps. Your challenges include the following:

- **To set aside enough time to plan your financial future.** Studies have shown, for instance, that people spend far more time planning family vacations than they do planning their financial futures. In fact, one well-known study of workers and retirees found that three-quarters of Americans spend about four hours or more planning for upcoming holidays. Less than half, however, spend as much time in a given year planning for retirement. Yet family vacations last for a few short days. Your future, as we discussed in the previous chapter, could entail 30 or 40 years of living. So spend at least two or three months studying up on the various investment options—and deciding which ones are right for you.

- **To set aside enough time to analyze and reassess your investment decisions at least once every quarter.** Chances are, you won't have to do anything to your investment portfolio every three months. In fact, you probably want to show more patience than that. But one of the lessons of the past few years is that at the very least, you must constantly monitor your progress to see if your original assumptions are unfolding as planned. For example, if you decided to be ultra-aggressive by loading up on risky stocks and then the market plummets, as it did in 2008, you have to set aside the time to revisit your strategy to make sure it's the course you still want to take.

  Another reason to check on your portfolio quarterly is to consider any changes that have taken place in your life that may require altering your investment strategy as time goes forward. For example, if you recently got married or divorced, had a child, or discovered that your child is bound for Harvard, you may need to factor those things into your overall plan. But if you recently suffered a pay cut or lost your job, those are also reasons to revisit your investment plans.

  Unfortunately, studies show that a majority of investors rarely make any adjustments to their investment portfolios. In fact, only about one in six retirement investors make any changes to their 401(k) in a given year. That's not being an investor. That's being a bystander.

- **To become familiar enough with your investment options to make wise and informed decisions.** Or, conversely, to recognize that you don't have the time or desire to tend to such matters and need the help of a professional advisor.

- *To figure out what type of investor you plan to be.* (We'll discuss this at length in the following chapter.) For example, what is your investment philosophy? Do you plan to invest for the long term, or will you concentrate mostly on meeting short-term needs?

- *To figure out what types of investments to own (for instance, stocks, bonds, or real estate) and how much of each.* It's not good enough simply to decide to invest in stocks and bonds. Figuring out the right mix of stocks and bonds and other assets—which investment experts refer to as an **asset allocation strategy**—is critical. The list in Figure 2-1, which follows, will give you some idea of the return on certain investments.

Two portfolios that consist of the exact same investment choices, for example, can deliver wildly different results, depending on what percentage of your money you put into each. For instance, if you put 90 percent of your money in U.S. stocks and 10 percent in U.S. bonds, historically, you stand a decent chance of earning an average of 9.6 percent a year (that's based on actual historical results from 1926 to 2009), according to Ibbotson Associates.

But if you flipped the mix and put 10 percent in stocks and 90 percent in bonds, there's a good chance you'll earn just 6 percent a year.

However, it's important to note that these are only averages. And in any given year, the numbers could vary yet more. For example, had you

Small-capitalization stocks	+11.9%
Large-capitalization stocks	+9.8%
Long-term corporate bonds	+5.9%
Long-term government bonds	+5.4%
Intermediate-term government bonds	+5.3%
30-day Treasury bills	+3.7%
Average 30-year fixed rate mortgage	−4.3%
Stafford student loans	−5.6%
Average 4-year car loan	−6.0%
Average credit card interest rate	−14.4%

FIGURE 2-1 • Rates of Return.*

As this table indicates, the positive returns investors enjoy in their stock and bond portfolios are often eroded by interest they owe on loans and credit card balances.

*Data as of September 2010.

Sources: Ibbotson Associates, Bankrate.com, Cardweb.com

invested only 10 percent in stocks and 90 percent in bonds in the 2000s, you'd have earned 7 percent a year, versus just 0.1 percent annually for a 90 percent stock and 10 percent bond portfolio between 2000 and the start of 2010. So as you can see, your overall exposure to certain types of assets—rather than simply the individual stocks and bonds you pick—can often have a tremendous impact on your overall portfolio.

- *To figure out how to choose individual securities that will go into your portfolio.* For example, should you invest in shares of Microsoft or Apple? Keep in mind that the timing of such a determination can also make a huge impact. For instance, if you bet on Microsoft between 1986 and 2000, you'd have been right since its shares soared around sixfold while Apple's shares pretty much went nowhere. But between 2000 and 2010, it was Microsoft's stock that treaded water, while Apple's shares soared more than 20 times in value.

   Similarly, is a 10-year Treasury security better than a municipal bond put out by the state of California? Another challenge is to figure out how much money to invest in each of your securities once you've selected them.

- *To figure out what type of account you will use to invest in these securities.* In other words, should you invest in stocks through your tax-deferred 401(k) account, or should you use that account to invest in bonds?

How Much Should You Invest?

In addition to dealing with these investment-related matters, there are some more basic considerations to weigh before getting started. One question all investors need to ask themselves before diving into the investing pool, for instance, is: How much money do you have to invest in the first place?

It's not as simple as figuring how much you bring home every year and how much you spend—and investing the remainder. Calculating how much you can invest will not only depend on your annual income, but your level of savings as well.

Say you earn $50,000 after taxes and are left with around $25,000 after paying off your monthly mortgage, car loans, utilities, and other bills. This doesn't mean you can—or should—invest all $25,000. You may have other needs to take care of that aren't routine. For instance, this may be the year or even the month that you'll need to repair your home's roof, replace a water heater, or buy a new car. In that case, a good portion of that $25,000 should go to building up your savings accounts to meet those and other potential short-term needs.

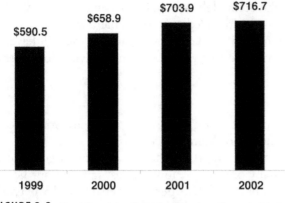

FIGURE 2-2 • Total Revolving Debt for American Households (in Billions of Dollars).

While stock prices fell during the bear market years of 2000 through 2002, household debt continued to soar.

Source: Federal Reserve

Remember, short-term goals require capital preservation. And capital preservation means saving money—in a savings instrument like a money market fund or a certificate of deposit—not investing it in stocks, bonds, or real estate.

Another major issue to contend with is debt. No doubt you've heard a lot about this subject, usually when the growing indebtedness of Americans is discussed or cited. The charts in Figures 2-2 and 2-3 graphically illustrate the truth of these concerns. If you happen to be debt-free and have savings, then of course you can go ahead and invest most of the money left over from your income after covering your essential living expenses. (In fact, you probably should, rather than spending it on discretionary purchases.) But if you're one

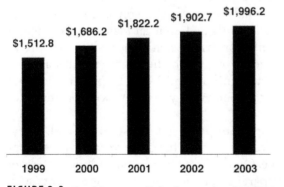

FIGURE 2-3 • Total Consumer Debt Outstanding (in Billions of Dollars).

Source: Federal Reserve

of those oft-cited Americans who are in debt—even if you can easily handle the monthly minimum obligations—you're faced with that challenge first.

If you're sitting on $15,000 in credit card debt, for example, you will have to consider which is the better move: investing your free cash or paying down debt.

Pay Down Debt First

For most investors, paying down debt first makes sense before investing. Here, we're talking about consumer debt, not home mortgages.

In the grand scheme of things, home mortgage debt is a relatively good form of indebtedness. For starters, many of us enjoy low interest rates on our home mortgages (perhaps in the neighborhood of 5 percent, versus the 15 percent mortgages that homeowners were paying a generation ago) thanks to record low interest rates at the start of this decade. Even better, interest payments on mortgages of up to $1 million are tax deductible in most cases. Even interest on home equity loans, which many of us use to upgrade our kitchens or even pay off our credit card balances, is deductible in many cases, provided the loan itself does not exceed a certain amount.

Moreover, taking on home mortgage debt is actually a form of investing, in the sense that you are borrowing money to buy an asset that will likely appreciate over time. In the case of a home mortgage, investors are making two calculations: First, they are betting that the mortgage payments, based on their interest rate, will allow them to live comfortably enough at a monthly price that is competitive with the home rental market. And second, investors are also making a longer-term bet that the home mortgage interest they are losing to a bank will be made up, in the future, by the rising value of the underlying asset—the home and land beneath it. In a low-mortgage-rate environment, such as the one that Americans enjoyed in the late 1990s and the start of the 2000s, the bar for meeting this challenge was relatively low.

But when it comes to relatively bad forms of debt—revolving debt on department store charge cards, or credit cards, and even car loans—it's a different story. Credit card interest payments, for instance, are not deductible. Credit card companies also tend to charge among the highest interest rates around. Typically, that means a rate that starts off around 14 to 16 percent but that gets jacked up to as much as 21 or 29 percent if you're late with payments or exceed your spending limit.

In addition, credit card debt helps you spend, not invest. In the end, everything that is purchased through plastic—clothes, furniture, vacations, electronics, etc.—lessens in value over time. On the other hand, homes appreciate over time—as do stocks (for the most part) and bonds and other investments such as precious metals like gold or silver.

The fact is, credit card debt will work against you as an investor. Think about it: When you invest in the stock market, your goal is to earn around 8 percent on your money—or more—a year over time. But what good is it to invest, say, $25,000 earning 8 percent a year if you owe $25,000 on credit cards charging 21 percent interest? No matter how successful you might be in picking stocks and other investments, you will invariably fall deeper into the hole under this scenario, which is why you should pay off that debt first.

Here's another way to think about it: Paying off a credit card charging 21 percent a year is a form of investing. It is the equivalent of owning a stock portfolio that grows 21 percent a year. The only difference is, instead of growing your nest egg, you are ensuring that it does not keep shrinking over time. Even better, there is absolutely no risk in paying off credit card debt. In fact, you wind up lowering your overall financial risk by paying off debt, since it improves your credit score and frees up money for other, more productive uses.

Investing, on the other hand, comes with all sorts of risks. The question you have to ask yourself is: What are the chances of earning credit-card-like interest rates—say, 21 percent—in the stock, bond, or real estate markets in any given year? The simple answer, of course, is slim to none. Even in the late 1990s, for example, when stocks were returning more than 20 percent annually, those results were negated by the following decade, when equities lost ground. And since 1929, stocks have returned more than 21 percent less than a third of the time. More importantly, what are the odds of earning 21 percent in the stock or bond market risk free? The answer to that is zero. Unfortunately, most investors don't get this. Though the majority of us are investors, the average American household carries credit card balances of around $8,000, spread out among 10 or more credit cards. That means that, even though many Americans are investing, they're creating vicious cycles for themselves by overusing credit and paying interest at far higher rates than they're earning on their investments.

Start a Rainy Day Fund

In addition to paying down debt, it's important for all would-be investors to establish an emergency savings fund before beginning their marathon. This rainy day stash will help you lay the financial groundwork to invest safely and successfully.

Conventional wisdom has historically said we should all save at least three months' worth of expenses before doing anything else with our money, including investing it. But there's a good reason to boost that to at least six months' worth of expenses today.

Why even have an emergency fund to begin with? Well, what happens if the water heater explodes or your refrigerator dies? Many families have the wherewithal to cover such short-term needs. But if you were forced to sell an investment, like stocks or, harder still, real estate, to pay your emergency bills, it could take you out of the market just when you needed to be in it. Moreover, you could be forced to sell your investments at a price that doesn't fully reflect their true value. For example, imagine you were forced, by family circumstances, to sell out of the stock market when equities were plummeting in September 2008, at the height of the global financial crisis? If that were the case, you might have been forced to lock in losses of 25 percent or more based on the market's perception of equities in a panic. Since that time, the value of those shares has largely recovered, but that wouldn't matter to you had you been forced to sell back then. So in a sense, having a rainy day emergency fund actually improves your odds of investment success.

Plus, selling even a small portion of your investment portfolio to meet basic needs is likely to trigger two things: brokerage commissions and capital gains taxes. And your goal as an investor is to minimize fees and delay paying taxes, since they eat into your portfolio, reducing the ability of compound interest to work its magic (we'll discuss this in a moment).

Now, why should you set aside *six months'* worth of expenses, rather than the old conventional wisdom of three months'? Well, another big reason for having an emergency fund is in case you were to lose your job. In the 1990s, when the job market was robust, it typically took about three months' time to find a new job if you were laid off. But in the ever-changing economy, where job growth slowed dramatically in the 2000s, it can easily take six months—or longer—to find new work if you're laid off. So it makes sense to adjust your need for emergency funds accordingly.

To be certain, some investors who don't have rainy day funds may regard their investment portfolio as their emergency pot of money. But again, if you invest without an emergency stash of cash, you may be forced to sell your investments at inopportune moments to pay your bills. Moreover, selling your investments may mean losing out on another source of income—your investment income (this includes the interest that your bonds pay out as well as the dividends that your stocks throw off)—at the same time you've lost your employment income. Unfortunately, this too is another concept that most investors fail to appreciate. Three out of five households don't have emergency savings to speak of.

To figure out how much you'll need, run through this basic exercise:

Step 1: Tally up your total gross monthly income. Include not only your weekly or semimonthly paychecks, but also any other routine money you might have coming in, be it from rental properties, investment portfolios, alimony checks, etc.

Step 2: Add up all the money you lose every month to local, state, and federal taxes. Also consider the money that gets deducted from your paychecks through Social Security and payroll taxes. And if you typically make quarterly tax payments to the Internal Revenue Service, calculate how much you need to set aside each month to cover those checks.

Step 3: Start a monthly budget (Figure 2-4). For three months, keep a pencil and paper with you at all times. Write down everything you buy on any

Incoming Money
Monthly salary
Other sources of work income
Government-related income
Investment income
Inheritance/estate-related income
    Total Monthly Income

Outgoing Money
Mortgage payment and/or rent
Electricity
Heat/heating oil
Water and other utilities
Car loan/car repair/car maintenance
Car insurance
Homeowners' insurance (or renters' insurance)
Life insurance
Health insurance
Home repair/maintenance
Home improvement
Gasoline costs
Food/groceries
Food/dining out
Gasoline and other transportation costs
Clothing
Coffee
Phone
Cellular phone(s)
Cable
Internet service provider
Other cable/Internet subscriptions
Newspaper/magazine subscriptions
Movies
Other entertainment
Haircuts and personal care
Out-of-pocket health-care/dental costs
Set-asides for taxes (property, income, etc.)
Incidentals
    Total Monthly Expenses

    Total Monthly Income—Total Monthly Expenses

FIGURE 2-4 · Budgeting Your Expenses.

given day, be it a cup of coffee, a stick of gum, a newspaper, or something bigger like groceries or gas for your car. Add in any bigger-ticket items you purchased too, like furniture or appliances. And don't forget monthly bills like mortgages or rent, car loan payments, student loan payments, cable bills, phone bills, cellular phone bills, monthly charges for your Internet service provider, utilities, and subscriptions. Factor in your entertainment costs as well, whether dinners out or movie tickets. Finally, throw in your car insurance, home insurance, health insurance, and life insurance payments. (Here's a tip: Take whatever you owe for health and life insurance each month and double it. If your emergency is that you just lost your job, chances are you will probably lose access to employer-sponsored health care. Moreover, many companies provide employees with a minimum level of life insurance. So if you lose your job, these monthly bills will probably increase greatly.) After doing this for three months, divide your entire total by three to get an average monthly bill.

Step 4: Add your answers for Steps 2 and 3 together. This is how much you typically need every month. Depending upon your circumstances, set aside at least six times your monthly bills to seed your emergency fund. If you're the sole breadwinner in the family, you might want to set aside an additional three months' of expenses on top of that. If you're a parent, you'd also probably want to go out to at least nine months for the sake of your children.

Step 5: Subtract your Step 4 answer from your Step 1 total. So, assume that you earn $5,000 a month but lose $1,500 a month to taxes and spend another $2,500 on mortgage, utilities, and necessities. That leaves you with $1,000 each month. This is what investment officials would regard as your *free cash flow*, the money left over after obligations are met that isn't earmarked for anything specific. Now, if $2,500 of your after-tax money is earmarked for basic bills, your emergency fund will need to be at least $15,000.

How to Start a Savings Plan

In addition to building an emergency fund, there's another good reason to save. You can't invest money until you have saved enough money to invest. To gain access to a mutual fund, for example, you may need to start off with at least $2,000 before the company will let you in the door. At some fund companies like Vanguard, the minimum initial investment for many funds is typically $3,000 (Figure 2-5).

If you plan on opening a brokerage account, you may need even more—that is, if you want to invest in an account that doesn't charge you steep fees or monthly service charges, for example, or higher trading commissions. Many financial services firms levy extra charges on small investors, since they're less profitable to these firms than high-net-worth clients.

Fund Company	Minimum Investments Required to Start an Automated Savings Plan
Vanguard	$3,000
American Funds	$ 50
Fidelity	$2,500
American Century	$2,500
Janus	$ 500
Templeton	$ 50
Dodge & Cox	$2,500
Putnam	$ 25
T. Rowe Price	$ 100
Franklin	$ 50
AIM	$ 50

FIGURE 2-5 · Automated Savings Plans.

Source: Morningstar.com

But even though most of us want to be investors, a quarter of us don't save at all. And more than 60 percent of us don't save regularly. See Figure 2-6.

Ironically, most of us can afford to set aside another $20 a week, over and above what we're currently saving. A group called the Employee Benefit Research Institute helps oversee an annual study called the Retirement Confidence Survey. Every year, around two-thirds of workers polled say they can easily afford to save another $80 a month. Eighty dollars a month works out to another $960 a year. If you were to invest that amount every year for the next 25 years and earned 7 percent interest annually, you'd have around $65,000.

% of Americans Who . . .	All Households	Households with Assets of Less Than $10,000
Don't save at all	23%	41%
Don't save regularly	61%	78%
Spend more than they earn	14%	22%
Spend less than they earn	56%	36%

FIGURE 2-6 · Americans' Savings Behavior.

As these figures indicate, the majority of American households don't save money on a regular basis. This is particularly true among households with few assets to speak of.

Source: Consumer Federation of America

Savings Method	Somewhat or Very Useful
Utilizing a 401(k)	80%
Saving a fixed amount each month	79%
Developing a long-term savings plan	69%
Paying off mortgage before retirement	68%
Saving a fixed amount each month through an automated savings plan	68%
Paying off credit card debt	67%

FIGURE 2-7 · Americans' Savings Attitudes.

The figures represent the percent of Americans who said in surveys that they found these savings somewhat or very useful.

Source: Consumer Federation of America

This would seem to imply that inertia—not our incomes—is the problem. The solution: Set your savings plan on autopilot. The good news is that there are plenty of ways to save automatically. For example, when we invest in a 401(k) retirement plan, we are automatically deducting a certain amount of money from each paycheck into our account. Savers can do the same thing outside a 401(k). Many financial institutions will allow you to set up an **automated savings plan**, in which a portion of your paycheck is automatically sent each week or month to a money market fund or some other savings vehicle. More than two-thirds of Americans think that saving a fixed amount of money each month through an automated savings plan is one of the best ways to build up savings (Figure 2-7).

Set Your Investing Goals

Before you get started, there's yet another question you need to ask yourself: "How much *should* I invest?" At first blush, this may seem like the same question we asked earlier. But there's a big difference between figuring out how much money you can potentially put in the market versus how much money you ought to put at risk. *Risk* is the operative word.

The whole point of investing is finding a financial way to reach a set of **intermediate-term** and **long-term goals**. These are goals that won't arise for at least five years, though they could be 30 or 40 years in the making. But to meet these goals, you have to expose your money to risks, such as short-term stock or bond market losses. It makes no sense whatsoever to expose yourself to more risk than is required.

The only way to figure out how much risk is required—in other words, how much you *must* invest—is to take an inventory of your needs. They may include:

paying for college, buying a bigger house, retiring early, retiring well, or start-ing a business and quitting your job. Each of these goals comes with a general time frame. You may know, for example, that retirement won't be for another 27 years. College expenses for your children might not roll around for 12 years. But the bigger house may be something you want in six years. Your daughter's wedding may be coming up in two years.

Contrary to popular belief, it's not how much you want something or need something that dictates the level of risk you should expose your portfolio to. It's the length of time you have to invest—in Wall Street, this is referred to as your **time horizon**—that dictates how much risk you can expose yourself to.

Why is that? There is a basic relationship in investing: The greater the risk, the greater the reward. The corollary to this rule is that the lower the risk you take, the lower the reward you are likely to receive. This makes sense. After all, when you are investing money, you are entering into a transaction, and some-one else is on the other side of that trade. That someone else may be another investor selling stock you want to buy. Your trading partner may be a company issuing a bond that it wants to sell you to help raise funds.

If the person on the other side of the transaction knows that this financial arrangement you're about to enter into exposes you to no risks—in other words, there's no downside for you—then he or she would have little incentive to compensate you for your business. On the other hand, if the person knows you could lose everything by entering into this arrangement, he or she might sweeten the pot to make it worth your while. This basic relationship explains why a company with poor credit has to pay investors high interest rates on their bonds (another name for a **high-yield bond** is a **junk bond**). On the other hand, the U.S. government, which for all intents and purposes has perfect credit because it controls the nation's Treasury, often pays among the lowest inter-est rates on its bonds because investors know that there is absolutely no way the federal government can or will default on its debt. If push comes to shove, Uncle Sam can simply print more money.

Now, there are myriad ways investors can reduce some of these risks. One is to **diversify** a portfolio by owning many individual securities, so that if one stock (say, shares of Enron) fails, the others in their holdings can keep them from losing too much money. Another is to diversify a portfolio by owning different types of assets, so that if the stock market fails, the real estate market may protect you—or vice versa. A third way involves time.

We will discuss this point at greater length later on, but time has a way of re-ducing investing risks. That's because over time, most investments have a way of making money. If they didn't, they wouldn't be classified as investments—they'd be considered gambling. Take stocks, for example. In any one-year period of time, there is about a 27 percent chance that you will lose some of your money in the broad stock market, according to one study that looked at the equity markets from 1926 to 2002. However, if you have a three-year window of time, the odds of losing money fall to just 14 percent. If you have a whole decade, it goes down to 4 percent (Figure 2-8). While that's extremely low, you no doubt realize that it's not zero. Anyone who invested in stocks between 2000 and 2010 knows that there is still a chance of losing money in equities over a long period of time.

Nevertheless, this means a couple of things. If you have long periods of time to invest, at least 10 years but actually more like 15 or 20 years, then you can afford a riskier mix of investments that tilts more toward equities than bonds. On the other hand, if you have only a few years to invest, the odds of losing money with riskier investments is extremely high. So you would likely want to tilt your portfolio more heavily toward safer bonds and cash.

So, to figure out how much you *should* invest, you need to figure out when your goals come due. If most of the money you need is required this year and next, don't invest it. Save that money. For instance, if you have $100,000 worth of financial needs, but $75,000 of that is earmarked for goals that come due in two years or less, don't invest 100 percent of your money. Save 75 percent of your money in a savings account of some sort or in some financial instrument that guarantees—or at least promises—capital preservation. The rest, you can think about investing.

Remember, the whole point of investing is to undertake a long-term journey with your money. But it makes no sense to start this journey if you aren't totally prepared. That means saving up enough money to make this journey worthwhile. It means taking care of other financial obligations so you won't be distracted over time. And it means plotting out a proper course before you get started.

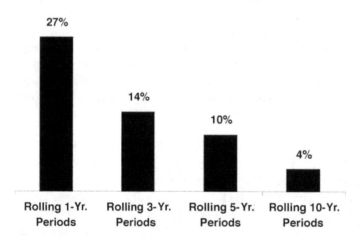

FIGURE 2-8 · Odds of Losing Money in Stocks.

As this chart indicates, the longer your time horizon, the lower the odds of losing money in the equity markets. If you have only one year to invest, for example, the odds are greater than one in four of losing money in equities. But over 10-year periods of time, the odds of losing money drop to just 4 percent.

Source: T. Rowe Price

QUIZ

1. **The decision between investing or paying down credit card debt comes down to . . .**
   A. How much you want to invest in stocks.
   B. Whether you plan to invest in stocks or bonds.
   C. What interest rate your cards are charging.
   D. How big your overall credit card balances are.

2. **You should pay off all your debt before investing a single cent in stocks.**
   A. True
   B. False

3. **Your rainy day fund depends on which of the following:**
   A. How much you make
   B. How much you owe in monthly expenses
   C. Whether you have dependents or not
   D. All of the above
   E. None of the above

4. **The better you are at investing, the smaller your emergency fund needs to be.**
   A. True
   B. False

5. **What are the odds of earning 21 percent or more in the stock market annually risk free?**
   A. 50 percent
   B. 33 percent
   C. 10 percent
   D. 0 percent

6. **Your risk tolerance is a matter of . . .**
   A. Time.
   B. The size of your portfolio.
   C. How much money you want to make.

7. **The riskier an investment is . . .**
   A. The more you are guaranteed of making.
   B. The greater the likelihood you can lose money in it.
   C. The lower its expected long-term return.

8. **You can reduce the amount of investment risk you're exposing yourself to by doing the following:**

    A. Diversifying the number of investments you own
    B. Diversifying the types of investments you own
    C. Lengthening the time you own an investment
    D. None of the above
    E. All of the above

9. **If you own stocks for 10 years or more, you are guaranteed of making money in your investments.**

    A. True
    B. False

10. **The more time you have to invest . . .**

    A. The more you are guaranteed of making in equities.
    B. The less you will make in equities.
    C. The greater the likelihood of making money in equities.
    D. The less the likelihood of making money in equities.

chapter **3**

Demystifying the
Language of Investing

CHAPTER OBJECTIVES

In this chapter, you will learn the following:

- Different ways to value stocks
- Risks associated with owning equities
- The fundamental relationship between bonds and interest rates
- Different ways to own stocks and bonds
- The importance of compound interest

The Dow. The Nasdaq. Compound interest. Dividend income. Media commentators and financial experts often throw out these terms casually, overlooking the fact that some of these phrases, while common on Wall Street, may not come secondhand to everyone. Yet it's vital for all investors and would-be investors to become familiar with the language of investing, if only to figure out what they're investing in and why. So before we get too far ahead of ourselves, it may be useful to go over some of the basic terms and concepts involved in investing.

If you don't know what some commonly used financial terms mean—or if you think you know but aren't entirely sure—don't be embarrassed to ask. You can always talk to your financial advisor, if you have one. Or anyone who invests in a mutual fund, a 401(k) account, or an IRA with a major financial services company—like Fidelity, Charles Schwab, or E*TRADE—can call the 1-800 numbers at these firms and ask someone in customer service. Many of the people who man these call centers are required to have a basic knowledge and understanding of investing and must pass certain exams to qualify for their jobs. Moreover, that's what these people are there for—to help you become a better investor.

Educational Web Sites

There are a number of free (or mostly free) Web sites that offer information about investing-related topics. Some of the best include www.morningstar.com, which is run by the mutual fund-tracking organization Morningstar; www.mfea.com, the Mutual Fund Education Alliance's Web site; www.fool.com, an entertaining site belonging to the investing gurus at The Motley Fool; and www.bankrate.com, which is great for bond and cash-related information. The finance section of the popular Web portal Yahoo! offers good educational information as well.

Of all of these sites, I would go ahead and bookmark Morningstar.com and Bankrate.com. Morningstar is among the most comprehensive sites when it comes to mutual fund and stock information. You can also get a tremendous amount of information on bond mutual funds through this site. Bankrate.com is a great resource for anyone interested in saving money, as it routinely surveys banks and cash-related securities, like bank certificates of deposit and loans.

I also find that some of the best sites are run by specific financial services firms. The good news is, many of these firms' sites don't require you to be a client to take advantage of the basic educational and research tools on their Web pages. In fact, many of these companies use their sites as carrots to draw in would-be investors. While you don't have to bite, there's no harm in nibbling on the freebies. Among the best in the group are www.fidelity.com, run by the mutual fund giant Fidelity; www.troweprice.com, run by the Baltimore-based fund company T. Rowe Price; www.schwab.com, run by the brokerage Charles Schwab; and www.etrade.com, run by the brokerage E*TRADE Financial.

Fidelity's Web site is particularly good at discussing issues surrounding the various types of investment accounts at your disposal, such as 401(k)s, IRAs, 529 college savings plans, Uniform Gift to Minors Act accounts (known as

UGMAs), and traditional brokerage accounts. The T. Rowe Price site is exceptional for retirement-related matters. It is also quite good at helping investors formulate strategies surrounding income-related investing plans.

While www.vanguard.com, the site run by the low-cost mutual fund company Vanguard, isn't the most technically sophisticated, it's always good to keep tabs on what Vanguard is doing and saying, since the firm is an ethical and low-cost leader in the financial industry. Often, Vanguard's site will issue statements or warnings to investors about not getting too euphoric about particular investments, be it Internet stocks or high-yield bonds. (An expansive list of helpful Web sites is presented in Figure 3-1.)

So, let's get started. Perhaps the best place to begin is with the basic investment vehicles that you can choose from, since that's what most of us are interested in talking about.

Demystifying Stock Lingo

We all know what the stock market is. Well, sort of. We know it's an arena in which we can invest our money and often do quite well over long periods of time. We also understand that over time, investors are likely to do better in stocks than in many other assets. But what does it mean to *own stock?*

The term simply refers to partial ownership—in fact, a specific unit of ownership—of a company. In other words, when you purchase stock, either directly through your brokerage account or indirectly through a mutual fund, you are a part owner of that firm. This is why stocks are also referred to as equities, since you are building an equity position in that business, giving you certain rights and benefits that you ought to be aware of.

Unfortunately, not all stock investors appreciate this fact. In fact, some would argue that in the modern era, investors don't act like owners so much as they act like renters, flipping into and out of different stocks in rapid-fire fashion without really knowing what the underlying businesses are all about.

For all intents and purposes, when we discuss stock investing, we are referring to partial ownership of a publicly traded company—in other words, a company whose shares are not held exclusively by a single person or family, but rather, shares that trade freely among members of the general public on an open exchange. Moreover, by and large, when we say stock, we mean common shares.

Common Stock

Common stock is the most basic (and therefore "common") share of ownership of a business. As an owner of common stock, you will probably receive a portion

For Stock Research and Basic Education	
URL	**Run by**
www.morningstar.com	Morningstar Inc.
www.fool.com	Motley Fool
www.schwab.com	Charles Schwab
www.etrade.com	E*Trade Financial
www.marketwatch.com	Marketwatch
www.cnnmoney.com	CNNMoney, *Money* magazine
finance.yahoo.com	Yahoo!
www.zacks.com	Zacks
www.thomsonfinancial.com	Thomson Financial
www.aaii.com	American Association of Individual Investors
www.betterinvesting.org	National Association of Investors Corp.
www.investopedia.com	Investopedia
www.standardandpoors.com	Standard & Poor's
www.nyse.com	New York Stock Exchange
www.nasdaq.com	Nasdaq
For Bond Research and Basic Education	
URL	**Run by**
www.investinginbonds.com	The Bond Market Association
www.treasurydirect.gov	U.S. Treasury Department
www.bankrate.com	Bankrate.com
www.federalreserve.gov	Federal Reserve Board
For Mutual Fund Research and Basic Education	
URL	**Run by**
www.morningstar.com	Morningstar Inc.
www.mfea.com	Mutual Fund Education Alliance
www.troweprice.com	T. Rowe Price
www.vanguard.com	The Vanguard Group
www.fidelity.com	Fidelity Investments
www.ici.org	Investment Company Institute
www.lipperweb.com	Lipper Inc.
www.standardandpoors.com	Standard & Poor's

FIGURE 3-1 · Useful Investing Web Sites.

of the firm's earnings back through **dividend payments**, which are typically made quarterly, though some companies pay out semiannually. Companies issue dividends for two basic reasons: to reward their owners, and to attract new would-be shareholders who may be interested in receiving a steady stream of dividend income.

Historically, dividends represented a huge chunk—around 40 percent—of the total returns that an investor enjoyed. That is not necessarily true today. The average **dividend yield** on the S&P 500 index of blue-chip stocks, for example, has recently fallen under 2 percent. This means that if you were to invest $100, you're likely to see $2 in dividend income annually.

To calculate a stock's dividend yield, take the annual dividend income per share generated by the stock and divide by the current price per share:

Dividends per share/Current price per share

So, if Stock X threw off $1.25 in annual dividends per share, and its shares were currently trading at $25 a share, its dividend yield would be 5 percent:

Dividends per share ($1.25)/Price per share ($25)

$1.25/$25 = 5 percent

It's important to note that not all companies pay dividends. Some businesses, as a policy, do not issue any dividends, preferring instead to use their earnings to reinvest in the business. In the 1990s some companies also chose to use their profits to buy back stock, or to invest in other companies, rather than to send the money back to their owners.

Of course, as an owner of common stock, you have some say in what your company does with its earnings. That's because common stock holders can vote for who will serve as directors of the company, who in turn hire the company's managers, who in turn decide on how earnings are handled.

Though you are technically a part owner of the business as a common stock holder, you are disadvantaged in one way. In the event the company you invest in goes under, you are pretty much last in line to recoup any losses. Ahead of you in court will be lenders to the company—including secured and unsecured creditors—along with bondholders. Also ahead of common stock holders are investors in so-called **preferred stock**.

Preferred Stock

What is preferred stock? Like common stock, preferred shares represent an ownership unit of a company. However, preferred stock is considered a slightly less risky investment than common stock. For one thing, preferred stock holders typically receive bigger dividend payouts than common stock investors; for another, in many cases those dividends are fixed or guaranteed by the company. In fact, some companies that pay dividends to preferred stock holders don't return any of their earnings back to common stock holders through such payouts. Moreover, some companies choose to slash dividends paid to common stock holders when times are tough but protect the dividends of preferred share holders.

This tends to make preferred stock attractive to high-net-worth and income-oriented investors, who are looking for dependable but not necessarily sky-high returns. Another aspect of preferred stock that makes this investment attractive to risk-averse investors is that, in the event of a liquidation, preferred stock holders have greater legal standing to make claims against the failed company than common stock holders.

But as we mentioned, in investing, the more risk you're willing to expose yourself to, the bigger the potential reward; the less risk, the smaller the reward. In the case of preferred stock, investors typically don't see the type of **price appreciation** in these shares that they might in common stock. Moreover, preferred stock does not normally give the investor voting rights in the company's business.

Stock Ownership

How much does one share of a company's stock get you? That depends on the company. Every company that "goes public"—or starts issuing shares that can be traded by the general public through what's known as an **initial public offering**, or **IPO**—establishes a set number of shares. Over time, that number can grow.

After its IPO, for instance, the company might make an additional offering of shares, which is called a **secondary offering**. Or the company may decide to enter into what's known as a **stock split**, where it subdivides the shares outstanding to make each unit more affordable to small investors. After seeing their shares soar in price in the 1990s, many technology companies split their stock, for example, at two for one—meaning if you owned one share of Company X at $30, it then became two shares at $15 each. Conversely, in the global financial meltdown in 2008 and early 2009, the share prices of many banks and financial institutions fell so dramatically that companies were forced to entertain **reverse splits**, where two shares of a stock trading at, say, $4 a piece were combined to become one share priced at $8.

The number of shares a company has can also shrink a different way: if the company repurchases some of them through what's known as a **stock buyback**. Firms will do this from time to time to signal to other investors that their shares are trading at attractive prices. Or they may entertain a buyback to boost the price of the shares by taking some of the supply of shares off the market.

Since no two companies carve up the ownership of their business with the exact same number of shares, there are no rules that say each share of stock you own buys you x percent of that firm. Based on the total number of shares of stock a company has floating in public, 1 million shares of Company A might buy you a 1-percent ownership of that business, but 1 million shares of Company B may make you a 10-percent owner.

To find out what share of the company you own, you have to keep an eye on the **total shares outstanding**. This information can be found on various financial Web sites, as well as a company's own Web site (typically, this number can be found in the firm's annual report, which is available through the mail but also is found online on a company's homepage, usually under the heading: "Investor Information" or "Investor Relations").

The actual price of a stock is meaningless, unless you have other information. For example, you may own two investments, one stock trading at $1 a share, the other at $125. But your holdings in the $1 stock may ultimately be more "valuable" than the $125 stock depending on how many shares there are and what percentage of them you own.

Market Value

There are a couple of basic ways investors place a monetary value on a company. The first is its **market value**. If you know what a stock is trading for and how many shares there are, you can figure this out.

The term **market value** simply means the price that Wall Street collectively places on a company at a given moment in time, based on the company's stock price at that moment. It's simple to calculate:

Current price per share × Total shares outstanding = Market value

So for instance, if shares of Company X are trading at $10 a piece, and if the firm has 10 million shares outstanding, its market value would be $100 million:

Price = $10

Total shares outstanding = 10 million

$10 × 10 million = $100 million

Now, this is not a static number. The minute Company X's stock changes in price, its market value would change too. For example, if, after a bad piece of earnings news, Company X stock falls from $10 to $8 a share, its market value or worth would drop from $100 million down to $80 million. So, what seems like a small change in a company's stock price could represent millions of dollars of shareholder value.

Cap Size

Financial commentators will often use the terms **market value** and **market capitalization** interchangeably. They may even use shorthand and refer to a company's **market cap**. This simply means its market value.

Type of Stock	Capitalization Range	Examples	Best-Fit Index
Mega-cap	$25 billion or higher	GE, Microsoft	Dow Jones Industrial Average
Large-cap	$10 billion or higher	Clorox, Kodak	S&P 500
Mid-cap	$1 billion to $10 billion	Williams-Sonoma, Delta Airlines	S&P 400
Small-cap	$250 million to $1 billion	Micromet, B&G Foods	S&P 600 or Russell 2000
Micro-cap	$250 million or lower	Exactech, Weyco Group	Wilshire Micro Cap Index

FIGURE 3-2 · Breaking Down the Stock Universe.

Loosely speaking, large stocks, or **large-caps**, as they are sometimes called, are considered shares of companies with market values of $10 billion or more. Medium-sized stocks, or **mid-caps**, are those with market caps of $1 billion to $10 billion. And **small-caps** are those that are valued by the market at less than $1 billion. There is even a subset of the small-cap stock universe known as *micro-caps*, which generally refers to stocks with market capitalization of $250 million or less, though some people set the threshold at $300 million. Figure 3-2 lists the types of stocks, their capitalization ranges, the indexes that best reflect their activity, and an example of each.

Small-cap and micro-cap stocks are typically shares of young, growing companies. As a result, these investments tend to be more volatile than shares of large-cap stocks (since you never can tell if a young start-up is going to be the next Microsoft or is headed for bankruptcy). Shares of large stocks are considered safer and more stable, which is one reason they are sometimes referred to as **blue-chip stocks**. But over long periods of time, they have not delivered the big returns on average that small shares have.

As we will discuss in a later chapter, micro-caps, small-caps, mid-caps, and large-caps tend to run in cycles. When one type of stock is doing well, some others tend to be out of favor in the markets. So it is important, if you plan on being a stock investor, to own a diversified mix of large-, mid-, small-, and even, perhaps, micro-cap stocks.

Still Confused?

The terms large-cap and small-cap have nothing to do with the number of employees a company has, or the sales or profits the firm generates. Instead, these terms refer to the value that investors collectively assign a firm at a given moment in time. Of course, investors could have things wrong. So don't confuse market capitalization with the intrinsic worth of a firm.

Book Value

There are a number of other ways to value a company. One option, popular among some mutual fund managers, is to consider a company's *intrinsic value*, which takes into account all the tangible and intangible value that a company possesses, including its perceived worth. Another is to consider what a potential private buyer might bid for the company—lock, stock, and barrel—to buy it out.

But perhaps the most popular way to assess a company's value, aside from considering its market cap, is to consider its **book value**. Book value tries to assess what a company is really worth by weighing all of the assets on its balance sheet, or books. The fact of the matter is, your fellow investors could be wrong in gauging the market value of a business, as they might have been wrong in assessing the true value of Internet stocks in the late 1990s. Sometimes, emotions get the better of us, and we are willing to value a stock for more than it is really worth.

To figure out a company's book value, follow this simple formula:

Total assets − Intangible assets − Liabilities = Total net assets = Book value

A company's book value reflects what the company is literally worth, based on things it owns, including its inventory, properties, and facilities. At times, a business's book value and market value could be wildly divergent, depending on whether a stock is in favor or out of favor among investors. Think of it this way: In assessing the value of your home, you can put it on the market and start receiving bids. That would measure the market value of your home. But another way to assess the true value of your house is to calculate how much money was put into it in the form of materials, construction costs, labor, appliances, decorations, etc. That would be akin to assessing its book value.

Valuations

Knowing a company's book value can come in handy when assessing whether a stock is trading at a reasonable or fair price. For instance, investors may feel hesitant to purchase a stock whose price per share is 10 times its book value per share. They may feel much more comfortable investing in a stock that is trading at only around four times its book value per share. To figure out a company's so-called **price-to-book ratio**, or **P/B ratio**, consider the following formula:

Total net assets (or Book value)/Total shares outstanding

= Book value per share

Stock price/Book value per share = Price-to-book ratio

This would be one way to judge a company's **valuation**, a term that refers to the cheapness or priceyness of a stock. Depending on the company and the industry, you can get a fairly reasonable sense of whether a stock is over- or undervalued based on its price-to-book ratio. For example, you can go to Web sites such as www.morningstar.com to find out the P/B ratio of a specific stock along with the P/B ratio of other companies in that industry. If your stock's price-to-book ratio is lower than that of its peers, that's one clue that it probably is undervalued.

Another so-called valuation measure is to consider a stock's price relative to the earnings generated by the underlying company. This is referred to as a stock's **price-to-earnings ratio** or **P/E ratio**. To figure out a company's P/E **ratio**, use the following formulas:

Earnings/Total shares outstanding = Earnings per share (EPS)

Stock price/Earnings per share = Price-to-earnings ratio

So, assume that you are considering investing in the Smith Phone company. And assume that Smith Phone generated earnings of $1.20 per share. If the stock is trading at $25 per share, its P/E would be just under 21:

Price per share = $25

Earnings per share = $1.20

Price per share ($25)/Earnings per share ($1.20) = 20.8

The chart in Figure 3-3 shows the P/E ratios for the S&P 500 from 1972 to 2004.

It's important to keep in mind that a stock has more than one P/E ratio. Some investors, for example, believe it's important to gauge a stock's price versus its *forward earnings*. So, assuming that Smith Phone is expected to earn $1.50 a share over the next four quarters, its **forward P/E**, based on estimated earnings for the next 12 months, may be 16.67.

Other investors hate using estimates, so they focus instead on actual earnings numbers. So let's say that over the prior 12 months Smith Phone earned $0.95 per share. Its **trailing P/E**, then, would be 26.3.

There is yet another type of price-to-earnings ratio that is commonly used on Wall Street. And that is the P/E ratio that relies not just on past earnings but 10 years' worth of historic earnings that have been averaged. This method of valuing a company was popularized by Yale economist Robert Shiller, who is famous for having predicted the stock market crash in 2000 and the decline in real estate shortly thereafter. Why do many investors favor the **10-year averaged P/E**? By averaging out profits over a lengthy period of time, this method smooths out any

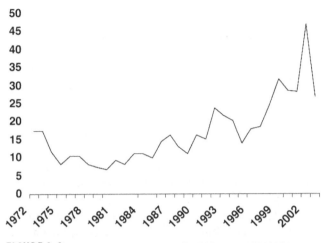

FIGURE 3-3 · Price-to-Earnings Ratios for S&P 500, 1972–2004.

Price-to-earnings ratios measure the price that investors are willing to pay for corporate earnings. During different periods of time, that price has fluctuated.

Source: InvesTech Research

anomalies that may take place in earnings during booms and busts. To find out the current 10-year averaged P/E, as well as historic figures, using this method, you can go to Professor Shiller's Web site: www.econ.yale.edu/~shiller/data.htm.

Regardless of which P/E ratio you favor, make sure you're comparing apples to apples. If you want to invest in Smith Phone based on how cheap its trailing P/E is, compare its valuation to the trailing P/Es of its peers.

Why is it important to even be looking at P/E ratios in the first place? For starters, it's always good to know if you're overpaying for a stock, or if you're getting your shares at bargain prices.

But the single best reason to pay attention to a stock's price-to-earnings ratio is that this gauge is often a good predictor of how well equities will perform over time. Indeed, if you look at the market's past performance based on its 10-year average P/E ratios, you will find that the higher the market's P/E ratio, the greater the likelihood that your investments will deliver lower-than-average gains. Conversely, the lower the market's P/E ratio, the greater the anticipated returns.

Consider this: Since 1929, the stock market has gained more than 15 percent a year on average in the 10 years after it trades at a P/E ratio of less than 8. When that P/E ratio rises to 8 to 16 (16 is the market's long-term average), your expected returns are closer to around 13 percent. When that P/E ratio climbs to between 16 and 24, projected gains fall to just 7 percent or so. And when P/E ratios soar above 24, returns are likely to be only around 3 percent annually.

Still Confused?

Forget stock prices. The price-to-earnings and price-to-book ratios for stocks are the best reflection of the value of a company at a particular moment in time. The good news is, most Web sites that offer price quotes for equities—including Morningstar.com and CNNMoney.com—also provide basic P/E and P/B data that's updated daily.

Stock Returns

There are two ways stock investors can make money, just as there are two ways bond investors can profit (which we'll get to in a moment). The first, as we mentioned, is through occasional payouts of earnings known as **dividend income**.

The other way—and in fact the more glamorous way—to make money in stocks is through **price** or **capital appreciation**. This is a fancy way of saying that you make money when the price of the stock you hold rises over time. It's simple to figure out the capital appreciation of a stock. Let's say that on January 1, 2010, you bought shares of Jones Building Materials for $20 a piece. And assume that by January 1, 2011, those shares had jumped to $27. The formula to gauge capital appreciation consists of the following:

New price − Original price/Original price = Price appreciation

In our example, the new price was $27. Our original purchase price was $20. So, $27 − $20 = $7. You take that profit of $7 and divide it by the original price of $20. So, $7 divided by $20 = 35 percent. In other words, your return was 35 percent in 2010.

This basic formula also works in situations where your stock doesn't rise in value but rather, falls. Going back to our example, assume that you bought shares of Jones Building Materials not for $20 a piece, but for $37 on January 1, 2008. And assume again that by January 1, 2010, the stock was at $27. Over this two-year period, we can say that the Jones stock lost 27 percent of its value:

Original value = $37

New value = $27

Original value − New value = −$10

−$10/Original value ($37) = −27 percent

By combining a stock's dividend income and capital appreciation, you can assess its **total return** over a given period of time. Total return is an important figure, since it represents what you really made—or lost—as an investor. Only by comparing the total returns of all your investments, including your stocks, bonds, and real estate, will you know where you've been successful and where you've lagged as an investor.

Stock Risks

The risk in owning stock is self-evident. On one level, the most basic risk you face as a stock investor is that the value of your shares will decline. Unlike bond investments or cash accounts, there are no guarantees or even implied promises that you'll receive your original investment back in full. If you buy a stock trading at $10 a share today and it falls to $7 tomorrow and you have to sell, you're out $3 per share.

One reason why your stock may be down might be because the entire market is suffering through a bad patch. This is referred to as **market risk**. Just as a rising tide of a **bull market** lifts most stocks, the waves caused by a **bear market** will probably send most stocks crashing, even if the fundamental health of the specific company you're investing in is strong. If the overall stock market, measured by such benchmarks as the Dow Jones Industrial Average or the S&P 500 Index, falls 10 percent, it is often referred to as a **market correction**. If it falls more than 20 percent, it is considered a **bear market**, though different investors have different specific definitions for what a true bear market is.

Of course, there are times when your stock falls not because the overall market is shaky but because of turmoil in the underlying business. This is referred to as **stock-specific risk**. When the energy giant Enron, for example, went under at the start of the past decade, it had nothing to do with the conditions of the market, even though we were technically in a bear market. It had to do with accounting improprieties at the company. Stock-specific risk can be dealt with through **diversification**. That is, you can easily minimize this risk by owning shares of multiple companies. Thus, if one stock in your portfolio blows up on you, it will only represent a fraction of your holdings. Meanwhile, gains among the other stocks in your portfolio could mask your losses from that one bad stock.

There are ways that investors measure risks associated with stocks. While you don't necessarily have to know how to calculate these measures, since many financial Web sites and services crunch the numbers for you, it might be useful to quickly discuss what they are.

One classic measure of risk is known as **beta**. Beta gauges an investment's volatility relative to the overall market. A stock with a beta of 1 is said to be as volatile as the overall market. A stock with a beta less than 1 is said to be less volatile than the market. But a stock with a beta exceeding 1 will be more erratic. For example, if a stock has a beta of 1.7, it would be considered 70 percent more volatile than the S&P 500. In the short term, the higher your beta, the greater the likelihood of losing money. But over very long periods of time, high-beta stocks could end up doing much better than the overall market.

Another measure of risk is called **standard deviation**. Instead of measuring volatility relative to the overall stock market, standard deviation measures a specific stock's volatility over a particular period of time, relative to the average volatility of that same stock during this time.

There's a technical way of gauging a stock's standard deviation that requires you to jump through some mathematical hoops involving square roots. But for the purposes of our discussion, think of the following example: Say you invest in a stock that rises 10 percent in the first year, 8 percent in the second, and 12 percent in the third. Its average performance over these three years would have been 10 percent:

$$(10 \text{ percent} + 8 + 12)/3 \text{ years}$$

But in achieving that 10 percent average annual return, this stock showed tremendous stability, which is desirable from the standpoint of being an investor. In the first year the stock hit its 10 percent average. In the second it fell just 2 percentage points shy of its 10 percent average. And in the third year it did 2 percent better than its average. Its standard deviation, then, roughly speaking, would be around 2.

On the other hand, if your stock rose 10 percent in the first year, rose 40 percent in the second, but fell 20 percent in the third, it too would have generated 10 percent average annual returns. But in so doing, its standard deviation would have been closer to 30. All things being equal, the lower the standard deviation, the less risky an investment may be.

Still Confused?

The concepts of beta and standard deviation are similar, in that they measure how volatile a particular investment is. But think of standard deviation as a seismic reading for a stock: It measures how shaky that investment is on its own. On the other hand, standard deviation measures the potential ripple effects a volatile stock market can have on a specific stock. In either case, the lower the measures, the more stable the investment is likely to be. The good news is that you can look up the standard deviation and beta readings for most stocks at Morningstar.com.

Demystifying Bond Lingo

Stocks and bonds are entirely different animals. When you invest in a stock, you are assuming the role of an owner. When you invest in a bond, however, you're playing the part of a bank. Bond investors in effect loan money to companies or governments or other entities that issue this form of debt to raise money for particular purposes.

These loans come with specific terms. For instance, bonds have **fixed maturity dates**, at which point the bond issuer promises to pay you back your **principal**, or original investment, in full. So, if you are investing in a 10-year Treasury security, the federal government promises to pay you back your original investment a decade from now.

In addition, the bond issuer promises to compensate investors for the loan by paying a fixed amount of interest along the way. This is one reason why bonds are casually referred to as **fixed-income instruments**. If you purchase a new 10-year bond at **par value**, or face value, promising a 6 percent **coupon**, you can expect a 6 percent yield or return on the bond based on your purchase price.

Government Bonds

Just because the bond issuer promises to pay you interest—and to pay you back in full—does not mean that bonds are risk-free. Far from it. A company that issues a bond may go belly up before your bond comes due. Even before that, it may **default** on its promise and withhold your interest payments.

The risk that a bond issuer will default is referred to as **credit risk**.

One type of bond where investors face minimal risk is with federal government debt. This is especially true with **Treasury bonds**, since they are backed by the full faith and credit of Uncle Sam. Never has the federal government defaulted on its bonds. Nor will it. This is because Uncle Sam controls the national treasury, and if the government ever gets in a fiscal bind, it can literally print more money to meet its obligations.

Why does the government issue debt to begin with? For starters, it doesn't have shares of ownership to dole out to raise capital, like a corporation does with stock. More important, the federal government, like American households, from time to time requires loans to pay its bills. For instance, for years the government has been running budget deficits, sometimes in the hundreds of billions of dollars. Those deficits have been financed, in part, by the issuance of Treasury bonds, which allow Uncle Sam to pay his creditors in small increments over time, rather than all at once. This is akin to a household using credit cards to finance short-term gaps in its household budget. While it's not necessarily the best fiscal policy for the government to spend more than it takes in, it's often needed.

One advantage to owning Treasuries over corporate bonds is that income generated by these bonds is state and local tax free. However, you will still have to pay federal taxes on Treasuries.

In addition to traditional Treasury bonds there are other flavors of government bonds. For example, there are now inflation-indexed Treasury bonds, which protect investors from the deleterious effects of inflation (which is defined as "the gradual loss of purchasing power of your money over time").

Other bonds that fall under the "government" category include mortgage-backed bonds issued not by the Treasury but by quasigovernment agencies like Freddie Mac or Fannie Mae, two organizations that purchase mortgages on the secondary market to boost the mortgage market. However, there's a big difference between these bonds, which are popular among professional investors like mutual fund managers, and good old-fashioned Treasury debt. While the federal government helped start Freddie Mac and Fannie Mae to boost home ownership throughout the country, the government does not technically back these bonds with its full faith and credit. Unfortunately, many investors assume that Uncle Sam does.

Corporate Bonds

Companies also issue bonds to raise capital, when doing so is more cost effective than issuing more shares of stock. But because corporations can—and do—go bankrupt from time to time, the level of credit risk associated with corporate debt is substantially higher than on government bonds. This is why bond investors often fixate on the **credit quality** of the companies that issue this type of debt.

The landscape of corporate bonds can be broken down into two groups: so-called **investment-grade bonds** and, at the other end of the spectrum, **high-yield bonds**.

Investment-grade bonds are debt instruments issued by companies with strong credit histories and ratings, as graded by the major credit-rating agencies. You might have heard of the two biggest such agencies: Moody's and Standard & Poor's. An investment-grade bond is considered relatively safe, and as a result, companies that issue these bonds are not typically forced to promise investors fat yields to attract investments. This goes back to what we were saying earlier—the higher the risk, the more the investor is likely to be compensated; the lower the risk, the lower level of compensation required. Of course, it's important to remember that just because a corporate bond receives an investment-grade rating doesn't mean it's guaranteed to be safe, like a Treasury bond. Investors learned this lesson the hard way in the financial crisis of 2008 when many mortgage-backed securities that were rated triple-A by many rating agencies actually turned "toxic," leading to troubles all around Wall Street.

High-yield bonds, often referred to as **junk bonds**, are issued by companies with poor credit ratings; they must make bigger interest payments to lure risk-averse investors. To reduce some of this credit risk, investors are often reminded to diversify their holdings of corporate bonds.

Municipal Bonds

Municipal bonds are issued by a different form of government—states, counties, municipalities, local agencies, and school districts—to pay for such things as construction projects, highways, or basic obligations. But **munis**, as they are often called, are not typically grouped in with federal government debt. That's because, unlike Uncle Sam, local and state governments can pose real credit risks to investors. One need only recall the bankruptcy filing of Orange County, California, in the early 1990s, due to bad investments decisions.

To be sure, defaults are rare in the municipal bond world—at least rarer than in the corporate world. But like corporate bonds, municipal debt tends to go through cycles. When the economy sours, fears of default rise; when times are good, those fears abate. As a result of this credit risk, municipal bond investors must always be mindful of the credit rating of the state or municipal government whose bonds they are thinking of purchasing.

The muni bond universe can be bifurcated into two general groups: **general obligation bonds** and **revenue bonds**. General obligation bonds are issued by states, counties, or cities for general purposes. Because they are issued by governments, which have the authority to raise taxes, there is a perception that these types of munis are relatively safe. Revenue bonds, on the other hand, are typically floated by an agency of state or local government for a specific project. While revenue bond holders are typically paid from the receipts generated from these projects—like highway or tunnel tolls—there is no explicit promise that the state or municipality will bail out the bond issuers should the projects run into financial difficulties.

There's another reason why muni bonds are classified in a group unto themselves: From a tax standpoint, many of them are treated beneficially, relative to other bonds. Muni income is federal tax free. Moreover, if you invest in a muni bond issued by your home state, interest on that bond is also likely to be state tax free for residents. This is why muni bonds are often a favorite investment for investors in high tax brackets, especially in high tax states.

However, the downside to this favorable tax treatment is that muni bond yields are typically much lower than interest thrown off by Treasury bonds. That's because of their tax advantage.

To figure out whether a muni is more or less attractive relative to ultrasafe Treasuries, you have to calculate its so-called **taxable equivalent yield**. The formula is simple:

Muni bond yield/(1 − Your tax bracket)

= Taxable equivalent yield

Muni Bond	Your Tax Bracket				
Yield	15%	25%	28%	33%	35%
2%	2.35%	2.67%	2.78%	2.99%	3.08%
3%	3.53%	4.00%	4.17%	4.48%	4.62%
4%	4.71%	5.33%	5.56%	5.97%	6.15%
5%	5.88%	6.67%	6.94%	7.46%	7.69%
6%	7.06%	8.00%	8.33%	8.96%	9.23%
7%	8.24%	9.33%	9.72%	10.45%	10.77%

FIGURE 3-4 · Municipal Bond Taxable Equivalent Yields.

Figures represent the comparable taxable yield of a municipal bond, compared with Treasury securities. If your muni bond, for example, is yielding 3 percent, it is the equivalent of a Treasury yielding 4 percent for an investor in the 25-percent tax bracket.

Let's plug some basic numbers into this formula to see how it works. Assume that muni bonds are yielding 4 percent. And say you fall in the 33-percent federal tax bracket:

$$\text{Muni bond yield} = 4 \text{ percent}$$

$$\text{Tax bracket} = 0.33$$

$$\text{Muni yield (4 percent)}/(1 - 0.33) = \text{Taxable equivalent yield}$$

$$1 - 0.33 = 0.67$$

$$4/0.67 = 5.97 \text{ percent}$$

This means that if your muni is yielding 4 percent but Treasury bonds are yielding less than 5.97 percent, it may well be worth it to consider that tax-free bond. However, if Treasuries are yielding more than that, you may be better off in safer Treasuries. (Some taxable equivalent yields are presented in Figure 3-4.)

Still Confused?

While municipal bonds are issued by governmental bodies—namely, states, counties, and municipalities—they are not considered as safe as other government bonds, particularly Treasury debt. Why not? Because municipalities don't have the power to print money to pay off their debts. And cities and counties can declare bankruptcy, which the federal government cannot.

Bond Returns

Bonds, like stocks, generate returns for investors in a combination of ways. First, there is the **yield** investors earn on the bond's coupon. Many bond investors fixate solely on the yield, because this often represents the biggest source of investment gains for bond investors. But like stocks, bonds can be traded on the secondary market.

Based on a combination of factors that include the financial health of the issuer, interest rate trends, inflation trends, and the relative attractiveness of alternative investments, the underlying value of a bond that gets traded in the open market may fluctuate. In this sense, bonds function much like stocks. If your bond falls in price more than it is yielding, the bond investment could lose money. If the bond rises in price, those gains can be tacked onto the yield to give you an even bigger **total return** (again, *total return equals an investment's yield plus or minus its price appreciation*).

There is one huge difference, though, when it comes to bonds. A bondholder can choose to either trade the security in the open market, in which case he or she would make or lose money based on market trends. Or the bondholder can elect to hold the loan to maturity, at which point the bond issuer promises to pay back the investor's principal value in full. There is no equivalent concept—or safeguard—to maturity in the stock market.

Credit and Interest-Rate Risk

We touched upon this earlier, but it's too important not to talk about at length. Bond investors face two basic types of risk, which are important to understand. The first, as we discussed, is **credit risk**. Again, this simply refers to the possibility that the bond issuer, despite its promises and best intentions, may default on its obligations to pay you a certain coupon or to return your principal back to you at maturity.

The second type of risk bond investors face is called **interest-rate risk**. This refers to a basic principle of bond investing, which all investors must memorize: *Bond prices move in the opposite direction of market interest rates*. So, if market interest rates rise, bond prices will fall. If interest rates fall, bond prices will rise:

Interest rates ▲ Bond prices ▼

Interest rates ▼ Bond prices ▲

It's easy to see why. Let's say you're holding a Treasury bond yielding 5 percent. Now, assume that since the time you bought the bond, market interest rates rose dramatically, to the point where new bonds are yielding 7 percent. Why would another investor want to purchase your 5-percent bond when he or she can simply buy a new one yielding 7 percent? Obviously, he or she wouldn't want to, which means that the price of your fixed-income investment is likely to fall.

Conversely, say you bought that same Treasury bond yielding 5 percent. But this time imagine that market interest rates have fallen, to the point where new bonds are yielding only 4 percent. All of a sudden the price of your old, higher-yielding bond is likely to rise since other investors may want the opportunity to earn bigger yields.

If you plan to hold your individual bond to maturity, you do not have to worry about interest-rate risk, since you won't be trading your security on the open market. But if you invest in a bond fund, which has no single maturity date because it's a portfolio of hundreds of different securities, you do have to worry about this form of risk.

Duration

According to a dictionary definition, the term **duration** refers to the "weighted average of the present values for all cash flows" of your fixed-income invest-ments. But while that may be the technical definition, it's one that most inves-tors can't seem to relate to. Who can blame them?

For the purposes of our discussion, duration is simply "a measure of the amount of exposure an investment has to interest-rate risk." This is particularly useful in discussions surrounding bond mutual funds.

Let's assume you are investing in a bond fund with a duration of five years. Roughly translated, this means that should interest rates rise 1 percent, the bond fund is likely to lose about 5 percent of its value. A bond fund with a higher duration, say, seven years, would lose even more under these circum-stances: 7 percent. On the flip side, should interest rates fall 1 percent, a bond fund with a seven-year duration would be expected to rise 7 percent in value.

Generally speaking, a bond fund that invests in longer-term maturities is likely to have a higher duration. The average maturity of bonds in a short-term bond fund, as can be seen in Figure 3-5, is roughly 3 years, and its duration is around 2 years. Meanwhile, a long-term bond fund's duration is more than 9 years. This means that if you want to reduce your exposure to interest-rate risk, you should stick with **short-term** or **ultra-short-term bond funds**, which invest in fixed-income securities that mature in about 2 or 3 years or less.

Demystifying Other Terms

Mutual Fund

A **mutual fund** is not a security, but rather, a company that exists solely to in-vest in securities such as stocks, bonds, and cash instruments. Hence, funds are referred to as **investment companies**. Mutual funds pool their investors' assets

Category	Average Maturity	Average Duration
Long-term general	14.9 years	9.2 years
Intermediate-term general	7.3 years	4.4 years
Short-term general	3.0 years	2.0 years
Ultra-short-term general	3.2 years	0.9 years
Long-term government	21.7 years	13.9 years
Intermediate-term government	6.8 years	3.6 years
Short-term government	3.2 years	2.0 years

FIGURE 3-5 · Average Durations of Various Types of Bond Funds.*

*Data through December 2009.

Source: Morningstar

together to create a single, diversified portfolio, of which each investor owns a particular number of shares (based on how much money he or she puts into the fund).

Mutual funds come in many flavors. There are **stock funds**, which invest in equities; **bond funds**, which invest in fixed-income securities; and **balanced funds**, which invest in a mix of stocks and bonds. These three categories of funds are referred to by some in the industry as **long-term funds**.

Within the realm of long-term stock funds, there are **general funds** that invest in various industries and sector funds that only invest in certain industries, like technology, health care, or financial services. There are also **international stock funds**, which only invest overseas, and **world stock funds**, which invest primarily overseas but can also invest some portion of their money in the United States too.

The bond fund universe is generally divided between **taxable bond funds** and **municipal bond funds**. And beyond the realm of long-term funds, there are also **money market mutual funds** that invest in money market accounts and other cash instruments.

Exchange-Traded Funds

An **exchange-traded fund**, or **ETF**, is a hybrid investment that looks and acts like a fund. For instance, an ETF represents a basket of different stocks or bonds that can be purchased in one trade and that offer instant diversification. However, an ETF can be traded like a stock multiple times during a day. Mutual funds, by comparison, can be bought or sold only once a day—at that trading day's closing prices.

Another difference between ETFs and mutual funds: You will need to open a brokerage account to trade ETFs. And every time you invest in an ETF, you'll have to pay brokerage commissions (though some brokerages have recently begun to lift those commissions in an effort to attract customers). Among mutual funds, there are many that charge no commissions when you buy or sell.

Similar to mutual funds, however, ETFs come in several different flavors. For example, there are ETFs that give you exposure to different types of stocks, bonds, commodities, and even investment strategies.

Indexes

An **index** is a benchmark of sorts that reflects a portion of the stock market and therefore is used by investors to judge how that segment of the market is performing. For example, the **S&P 500 index** is a list of 500 of the biggest companies in the U.S. market, as determined by Standard & Poor's. The **Dow Jones Industrial Average** is also an index, composed of 30 of the biggest companies in the U.S. market that reflect the industrial strength of the domestic economy. In the Dow's case, companies are added or deleted based on the judgments of the editors of the *Wall Street Journal*. Figure 3-6 contains a list of popular indexes.

Since indexes are supposed to measure the performance of the market, their composition does not change that often. However, individual stocks in an index occasionally do get replaced, as when companies get merged, acquired, or go out of business. It also happens when stocks grow or shrink to the point where they must be kicked out of one index and be moved into another. This happens often with small stocks in the Russell 2000 index. As some grow, they

Segment of Market	Indexes
Large Stocks	S&P 500, Russell 1000, Dow Jones Industrial Average
Total U.S. market	Wilshire 5000, Russell 3000, S&P Super 1500
Mid-cap stocks	S&P 400, Wilshire MidCap 500
Small-cap stocks	S&P 600, Russell 2000
Small- and mid-cap stocks	Wilshire 4500, Russell 2500
Foreign stocks (developed)	MSCI EAFE index
Emerging markets stocks	MSCI Emerging Markets index
Bond market	Barclays Aggregate Bond index
Technology stocks	Dow Jones U.S. Technology Sector index
Financial stocks	Dow Jones U.S. Financial Sector index
Health-care stocks	Dow Jones U.S. Healthcare Sector index
Energy stocks	Dow Jones U.S. Energy Sector index
Real estate stocks	Dow Jones U.S. Real Estate index

FIGURE 3-6 · Examples of Popular Indexes.

graduate into a bigger-stock index, like the S&P 400 mid-cap index or even the S&P 500 large-cap index. Indexes are not investments, but rather, yardsticks by which other investments can be judged.

However, in recent years mutual fund companies have developed funds that mimic the holdings in these indexes. These so-called **index funds**, such as the Vanguard 500 index fund, are investments you can put your money into. It's a bit confusing, but you should be aware of this distinction.

Still Confused?

Various types of stocks trade in the broad market. Those groupings are tracked by indexes. And you can invest in the types of stocks that those indexes represent through mutual funds or ETFs that track those different indexes.

Exchanges

Often, investors confuse indexes with exchanges. While an **index** represents a benchmark by which certain segments of the markets are measured, an **exchange** is the actual location at which stocks or bonds or other securities are traded. Examples of these are the **New York Stock Exchange**, which is sometimes referred to as "the Big Board," where some of the leading stocks in the U.S. market are traded, and the **Nasdaq National Market**, an electronic exchange where some of the leading technology and growth companies in the United States are listed.

In addition, there are exchanges that facilitate the trading of bonds, as well as commodities and financial contracts. You may have heard of these as well: The **New York Board of Trade** facilitates trading in commodities such as cocoa, coffee, cotton, ethanol, and sugar. The **Chicago Board Options Exchange** is a leading exchange in **futures** and **options contracts**, which are complex financial instruments used primarily by professionals to hedge their investment bets. And the **Chicago Mercantile Exchange** facilitates trading in a wide range of investments, from currencies such as Eurodollars to commodities like beef, dairy, fertilizer, and lumber.

Compound Interest

If you take anything away from this book, let it be this: *There is a time value of money.* The longer you delay spending money and the more time you give yourself to invest, the more your assets are likely to appreciate—and the greater the actual appreciation will be. This is a concept that many investors fail to grasp, because they don't quite understand the power of *compound interest*.

For instance, if you invest $10,000 and it earns 7 percent a year, you will have earned $700. But this does not mean that if you were to invest for three years, you'd earn $2,100 ($700 times 3). You'd actually earn a lot more. That's because each year you earn that 7 percent, you are growing your pot of money. So the next year that you earn 7 percent, you will be earning it off a bigger value. Here's how it works:

Year One

$$\$10,000 \times 7 \text{ percent} = \$ \quad 700$$

$$\$700 \text{ profit} + \text{original } \$10,000 = \$10,700$$

Year Two

$$\$10,700 \times 7 \text{ percent} = \$ \quad 749$$

$$\$749 \text{ profit} + \$10,700 = \$11,449$$

Year Three

$$\$11,449 \times 7 \text{ percent} = \$ \quad 801.43$$

$$\$801.43 \text{ profit} + \$11,449 = \$12,250.43$$

Since we started out with $10,000 and now have $12,250.43, our three-year profit is $2,250.43—not $2,100. The tables in Figures 3-7 through 3-10 show the power of compound interest, over time, under a variety of scenarios.

Interest Rate	10 Years	25 Years	30 Years	40 Years
5%	$16,290	$ 33,865	$ 43,220	$ 70,400
7%	$19,670	$ 54,275	$ 76,125	$149,745
10%	$25,940	$108,350	$174,495	$452,590

FIGURE 3-7 · Amount You Would Accumulate by Investing a Lump Sum of $10,000.

Interest Rate	10 Years	25 Years	30 Years	40 Years
5%	$40,720	$ 84,660	$108,050	$ 176,000
7%	$49,180	$135,685	$190,305	$ 374,360
10%	$64,845	$270,865	$436,235	$1,131,480

FIGURE 3-8 · Amount You Would Accumulate by Investing a Lump Sum of $25,000.

Interest Rate	10 Years	25 Years	30 Years	40 Years
5%	$33,750	$129,600	$181,100	$ 332,400
7%	$37,700	$176,550	$266,000	$ 573,200
10%	$44,700	$290,500	$495,600	$1,390,600

FIGURE 3-9 · Amount You Would Accumulate by Investing $50 a Week.

Interest Rate	10 Years	25 Years	30 Years	40 Years
5%	$67,500	$259,100	$362,300	$ 664,800
7%	$75,300	$353,100	$532,100	$1,146,300
10%	$89,400	$581,100	$991,200	$2,781,200

FIGURE 3-10 · Amount You Would Accumulate by Investing $100 a Week.

Using a Financial Calculator to Compound Interest

Calculating these figures over one or two years can be done easily by hand. But when dealing with compound interest calculations over decades, you're going to be better off relying on a financial calculator, such as the Hewlett-Packard (HP) 12C. These days, financial calculators can also be found in everything from your iPhone to the Internet. Using a financial calculator is quite simple. There are essentially five buttons to consider: *i, n, pv, fv, and pmt*.

> *i* = Interest rate
> *n* = Number of years
> *pv* = Present value
> *fv* = Future value
> *pmt* = Payment

Say you're dealing with a lump sum investment of $5,000. And let's assume that you know the interest rate is 6.4 percent. If you want to know what your investment will become in 10 years, punch in the following, in this order on your HP12C or an equivalent online financial calculator:

1. $5,000, then hit the *pv* button.
2. 6.4, then hit the *i* button.
3. 10, then hit the *n* button.
4. Then hit the *fv* button.

The answer will pop up $9,297.93. Actually, on a financial calculator, it will come up as negative $9,297.93. Disregard the negative sign in front of the figure—it's a foible of financial calculators.

You can also use your financial calculator to figure out what rate of return you will require to reach a certain goal, based on the principles of compound interest. For example, say your goal is to accumulate $450,000 by the time you retire. You currently have $105,000 invested in the market, and you know that you have 20 more years until retirement. Using your financial calculator, punch in the following, in the following order:

1. −$450,000, then hit the *fv* button.
2. $105,000, then hit the *pv* button.
3. 20, then hit the *n* button.
4. Then hit the *i* button.

The answer is 7.5 percent. This means you will have to construct a portfolio that can earn at least 7.5 percent a year, on average, over the next 20 years. (Again, the reason we punched in *negative* $450,000 was because of that foible we find in financial calculators.)

You can also find out how routine investments over time will grow. Take a simple example like an annual investment plan. Assume that you invest $2,000 in the stock market every year. And say you've been averaging annual returns of 6 percent. If you were to keep that up for 25 years, how much would you have? Here, we know the interest rate (6 percent), we know the number of years (25), and we know that we're investing $2,000 a year throughout this period (this is the payment). You can punch in the following:

1. $2,000, then hit the *pmt* button.
2. 6, then hit the *i* button.
3. 25, then hit the *n* button.
4. Then hit the *fv* button.

The answer is $116,312.77. That's the power of compound interest.

If you don't have access to a financial calculator, you can use the table in Figure 3-11. Just make a photocopy of it and keep it near your desk.

It may be a bit more cumbersome to use the table in Figure 3-11 than to use a calculator, since you'd have to keep it around, but these figures can be quite useful. To calculate how much a certain amount of money will grow at a certain interest rate over a certain number of years, just multiply the amount of money you're working with based on the factors listed in the table.

For example, if you're interested in knowing how much $33,000 will become if it earns 9 percent interest over 17 years, go to the table and look up the factor associated with 9 percent interest and 17 years. It indicates: 4.327633. So $33,000 multiplied by 4.327633 equals $142,811.89. And if you check with

Interest Rates

Yrs	1%	2%	3%	4%	5%	6%	7%	8%	9%	10%
1	1.010000	1.020000	1.030000	1.040000	1.050000	1.060000	1.070000	1.080000	1.090000	1.100000
2	1.020100	1.040400	1.060900	1.081600	1.102500	1.123600	1.144900	1.166400	1.188100	1.210000
3	1.030301	1.061208	1.092727	1.124864	1.157625	1.191016	1.225043	1.259712	1.295029	1.331000
4	1.040604	1.082432	1.125509	1.169859	1.215506	1.262477	1.310796	1.360489	1.411582	1.464100
5	1.051010	1.104081	1.159274	1.216653	1.276282	1.338226	1.402552	1.469328	1.538624	1.610510
6	1.061520	1.126162	1.194052	1.265319	1.340096	1.418519	1.500730	1.586874	1.677100	1.771561
7	1.072135	1.148686	1.229874	1.315932	1.407100	1.503630	1.605781	1.713824	1.828039	1.948717
8	1.082857	1.171659	1.266770	1.368569	1.477455	1.593848	1.718186	1.850930	1.992563	2.143589
9	1.093685	1.195093	1.304773	1.423312	1.551328	1.689479	1.838459	1.999005	2.171893	2.357948
10	1.104622	1.218994	1.343916	1.480244	1.628895	1.790848	1.967151	2.158925	2.367364	2.593742
11	1.115668	1.243374	1.384234	1.539454	1.710339	1.898299	2.104852	2.331639	2.580426	2.853117
12	1.126825	1.268242	1.425761	1.601032	1.795856	2.012196	2.252192	2.518170	2.812665	3.138428
13	1.138093	1.293607	1.468534	1.665074	1.885649	2.132928	2.409845	2.719624	3.065805	3.452271
14	1.149474	1.319479	1.512590	1.731676	1.979932	2.260904	2.578534	2.937194	3.341727	3.797498
15	1.160969	1.345868	1.557967	1.800944	2.078928	2.396558	2.759032	3.172169	3.642482	4.177248
16	1.172579	1.372786	1.604706	1.872981	2.182875	2.540352	2.952164	3.425943	3.970306	4.594970
17	1.184304	1.400241	1.652848	1.947900	2.292018	2.692773	3.158815	3.700018	4.327633	5.054470
18	1.196147	1.428246	1.702433	2.025817	2.406619	2.854339	3.379932	3.996019	4.717120	5.559917
19	1.208109	1.456811	1.753506	2.106849	2.526950	3.025600	3.616528	4.315701	5.141661	6.115909
20	1.220190	1.485947	1.806111	2.191123	2.653298	3.207135	3.869684	4.660957	5.604411	6.727500
21	1.232392	1.515666	1.860295	2.278768	2.785963	3.399564	4.140562	5.033834	6.108808	7.400250
22	1.244716	1.545980	1.916103	2.369919	2.925261	3.603537	4.430402	5.436540	6.658600	8.140275
23	1.257163	1.576899	1.973587	2.464716	3.071524	3.819750	4.740530	5.871464	7.257874	8.954302
24	1.269735	1.608437	2.032784	2.563304	3.225100	4.048935	5.072367	6.341181	7.911083	9.849733
25	1.282432	1.640606	2.093778	2.665836	3.386355	4.291871	5.427433	6.848475	8.623081	10.834706
26	1.295256	1.673418	2.156591	2.772470	3.555673	4.549383	5.807353	7.396353	9.399158	11.918177
27	1.308209	1.706886	2.221289	2.883369	3.733456	4.822346	6.213868	7.988061	10.245082	13.109994
28	1.321291	1.741024	2.287928	2.998703	3.920129	5.111687	6.648838	8.627106	11.167140	14.420994
29	1.334504	1.775845	2.356566	3.118651	4.116136	5.418388	7.114257	9.317275	12.172182	15.863093
30	1.347849	1.811362	2.427262	3.243398	4.321942	5.743491	7.612255	10.062657	13.267678	17.449402

FIGURE 3-11 • Compound Interest Factors—Growth of $1.

This table will help you calculate how much your investments will grow over time, assuming a particular rate of return and a set number of years. For example, say you wanted to figure out what a $10,000 investment would grow into if it earned 7 percent a year for 10 years. Go to the box that sits at the intersection of 10 years and 7 percent interest. The figure is 1.967151, and the answer is $19,671.51.

your financial calculator, you will see that this is indeed what $33,000 grows into based on these compound interest assumptions.

Final Thoughts

Confused yet? Don't worry. You'll have plenty of time to familiarize yourself with these terms and concepts as you read along. The purpose of this chapter was not to become an expert on any of these issues, but to get your feet wet. One of the difficulties of demystifying investing is that the world of stocks and bonds has its own quirky language. Hopefully, this chapter served as a cheat sheet of sorts to breaking the code. Feel free to refer back to this chapter as you get further along in the book.

QUIZ

1. **Preferred stocks give you higher returns than common stocks.**
   A. True
   B. False

2. **Which of the following will help you gauge a stock's valuation?**
   A. Its price per share
   B. Its earnings per share
   C. Its price-to-earnings ratio

3. **Which of these two terms represent the same idea?**
   A. Book value and intrinsic value
   B. Market value and market capitalization
   C. Book value and market value

4. **The most conservative way to gauge the valuation of a company is looking at its . . .**
   A. P/E ratio using 10-year averaged earnings.
   B. P/E ratio using projected profits.
   C. P/E ratio using past 12 months' earnings.
   D. P/B ratio.

5. **This term represents the risk that your stocks will fall due to volatility in the overall market:**
   A. Beta
   B. Standard deviation
   C. Market risk
   D. Duration

6. **This term represents the risk that your bonds will lose value due to rising interest rates:**
   A. Beta
   B. Standard deviation
   C. Market risk
   D. Duration

7. **Which of the following is not a type of government bond?**
   A. Municipal bonds
   B. Treasury inflation-protected bonds
   C. 10-year Treasury bonds

8. **AAA-rated corporate bonds are as safe as Treasury bonds.**
   A. True
   B. False

9. **The tax equivalent yield of a municipal bond compares the interest paid by municipal debt versus . . .**
   A. Treasury bonds.
   B. Corporate bonds.
   C. Stocks.
   D. Tax-free dividends.

10. **Mutual funds can be bought and sold . . .**
    A. Once a day.
    B. Once a month.
    C. Multiple times a day, like stocks.

What Kind of Investor Are You?

There is no single right way to invest.

Consider the two of the richest people in the world, Warren Buffett and Bill Gates. Buffett, known as "the Sage of Omaha" for his stock-picking prowess, built his fortune by putting his money into a multitude of different companies in various industries—and in various ways. In some cases, his investment company, Berkshire Hathaway, owns businesses outright. These are firms like the insurer Geico, the paint manufacturer Benjamin Moore, or the fast-food chain Dairy Queen. Though Buffett is most closely associated with the insurance business, he also owns companies in the furniture, jewelry, confectionery, publishing, clothing, and private transportation industries.

In other cases, Berkshire Hathaway doesn't own an entire company, but invests in the common stock of publicly traded companies. These firms also run the gamut of different industries. His well-publicized holdings include stakes in blue-chip leaders like American Express, Coca-Cola, Gillette, and the Washington Post Co. But he doesn't stick exclusively to large capitalization stocks. In still other cases, Buffett invests in shares of smaller, more obscure companies that he thinks can grow, if given time. This mix-and-match, hodge-podge strategy has allowed Buffett to become one of the world's richest people.

Then there's Bill Gates, founder of the software giant Microsoft Corp., who is also consistently ranked as one of the richest people in the world. Like Buffett, Gates is known as one of the smartest people in business, having built a fortune for the ages. But Gates amassed his wealth in a decidedly different manner than Buffett, whom, interestingly enough, Gates counts as a mentor and friend.

First and foremost, Gates is a classic entrepreneur, having dropped out of Harvard to start his own business. In fact, he helped found an industry—software. For years his company, which became the world's largest software concern and one of the biggest corporations in history, was Gates's sole source of wealth. It not only represented the main source of his income, it was virtually the sum total of his investment portfolio.

As the shares of Microsoft doubled in value and doubled once more, and again and again, Gates's personal stake in the business propelled him to his station as this generation's Andrew Carnegie. While Gates has since gone on to become a first-class investor in other companies—for instance, he has built himself a reputation for investing in biotechnology start-ups—his wealth still by and large rides with the fortunes of his company, Microsoft.

The different paths that Gates and Buffett took to investment success—the former through one big idea that turned into a whale of investment success, the latter through a lot of good little ideas—is common to Wall Street. If you looked at the most successful stock mutual funds between 1994 and 2004, you would find something interesting: Among the absolute best performers during this 10-year stretch, based on total returns, was a mid-cap stock fund, a healthcare fund, a small-cap stock fund, a technology-oriented portfolio, a couple of funds that focused on stocks in the financial services sector, a blue-chip stock fund, and what's known as a **balanced fund**, which is a portfolio that invests in a mix of stocks and bonds. It's all over the map (see Figure 4-1).

This is yet another reason why it's good to diversify your portfolio—so that your odds of finding these hidden gems improve. It also goes to prove that you can find many paths to investment success, just as you can find many ways to go broke.

Fund Name	Category	10-Year Annualized Return
Calamos Growth	Mid-cap growth	21.9%
Vanguard Health Care	Health-care sector	21.0%
Meridian Value	Mid-cap blend	19.6%
Wasatch Core Growth	Small-cap growth	18.8%
Bruce Fund	Balanced	18.7%
Fidelity Select Electronics	Technology sector	18.6%
Legg Mason Value	Large-cap blend	18.4%
Fidelity Select Insurance	Financial sector	18.3%
FPA Capital	Small-cap value	18.0%

FIGURE 4-1 • Best-Performing Funds, 1994–2004.*

*Data as of March 31, 2004.

Source: Morningstar

Deciding Who You Are

The single biggest challenge for new investors, then, is to find a strategy that not only provides decent odds for success, but that suits their sensibilities. If you have no stomach for risk and like the stability of knowing that you'll earn a set amount of dividend income every quarter, for instance, then placing your bets on risky start-ups in the volatile technology sector may not be your best move. Not only do technology stocks pay little in the way of dividends, their price can often fluctuate violently. Even if the tech stocks you end up picking do well, what are the odds that you'd have the stomach to ride the ups and downs?

The next biggest hurdle: finding sufficient fortitude to stick to a philosophy, even when things start to look bleak.

The history of investments is replete with good ideas that at some point or another ran into difficulties. At the turn of the twenty-first century, for example, the housing market was booming nationally as interest rates fell to lows not seen for decades and as credit flowed freely. But you have to remember that only a decade prior to that, real estate investors were scrambling to unload their properties amidst major downturns in the economies in places like New York and Los Angeles. And since 2006, those can't-miss bets on houses fell apart as the mortgage meltdown froze credit, deterring new potential homeowners from entering the market, which in turn sent home prices lower.

When it comes to stocks, pick any major success story and you'll find periods of severe underperformance. Microsoft used to be considered a "can't–miss" stock. But between 1999 and 2009 its stock went nowhere. Well, sort of. It went way up, and then way down, and then sputtered in between, in what's referred to as a **trading range**, meaning its share price seems stuck in a rut. Dell Computer is widely regarded as one of the best run companies in the world. But people often forget that in the early 1990s, when the computer industry was just getting going, Dell suffered through several missteps and its share price was beaten down as a result.

No investment strategy will work if investors give up midway into implementation. It's akin to flipping a coin 100 times and seeing it come up heads *every time.* You know that at some point the laws of probability will kick in and *your* coin will come up tails, at least a few times. But if you give up after the hundredth toss, you'll never see the laws of probability work their magic. The same goes for investing.

Be True to Yourself

In addition to knowing who you are and having fortitude, there is a third big challenge that all of us face in the stock, bond, and real estate markets, though it's one that few people talk about often. It involves not only being patient with your approach to investing, but consistent all the way through.

The process of investing is like writing a good novel. Like good literature, a good investing plan has a solid beginning, middle, and end. In investing, there are three distinct periods of owning any asset: buying it, holding it, and selling it.

No investment strategy can be deemed successful until the asset is eventually sold and the profits are booked. To be sure, it may appear as if you're on the right track. You may have built up hundreds of thousands of dollars in paper profits based on where your investment is trading at today. But until you actually realize those gains by selling the security, it's all hypothetical. That means it's just as important to be good at selling stocks as buying them.

Take a look at the primary reasons stock pickers sell stocks in Figure 4-2. When it comes to selling, it is still important to be true to your philosophy. If the reason you bought a stock was because you considered it underpriced, then why sell it if you still think it's cheap? Wasn't the whole point of buying the stock because eventually you thought other investors would realize the company's potential? If you wanted to be truly consistent with this philosophy, why not sell when you think the stock becomes overpriced?

Similarly, if the reason you bought a stock was because you felt its earnings would grow faster than those of its peers, then sell it when it stops growing that fast. Don't hang onto the stock as the earnings slow.

The same level of consistency is important in other avenues of investing. Let's say you bought a second home because you felt the tax laws were beneficial to

Fundamentals are deteriorating	46%
Stock is overvalued	37%
Stock has hit a preset target price	14%
Other stocks look more attractive	2%
Stock has fallen X percent	1%

FIGURE 4-2 · Primary Reasons Stock Pickers Sell Stock.

This study reflects the favored reasons for selling stocks among institutional money managers surveyed between 2000 and 2002.

Source: "Sell Discipline and Institutional Money Management," *Journal of Portfolio Management,* Spring 2004

such a holding. What would you do if Congress all of a sudden changed those laws? Some might consider hanging on to the investment for sentimental reasons. But emotions and sentiment are typically what get investors into trouble. Logic and consistency are important for keeping you on the right path, no matter which trail you chose to begin with.

So, now that we understand that, what kind of investor are you?

Do-It-Yourself versus Using an Advisor

It used to be that investors divided themselves into two distinct camps. On the one hand there were traditional, old-fashioned investors who were largely experienced in the ways of Wall Street. Like their parents before them, they relied on brokers, tax accountants, financial planners, and estate attorneys to help them formulate their investment approaches. This group consisted largely of the "monied" class, who inherited not only their portfolios, but long-standing ties with brokerage firms like Merrill Lynch, J.P. Morgan, and Goldman Sachs.

On the other side of the fence were relatively new investors, many of whom did not have such ties to full-service advisors. These were also independent-minded Baby Boomers and Gen Xers, who unlike their parents' generation felt more comfortable handling the major decisions concerning their stock and bond portfolios. For a while in the late 1990s this was not only fun, it was rewarding. These do-it-yourself investors who executed their trades through online brokerages like Charles Schwab, E*TRADE, and Ameritrade, were less interested in advice and more interested in costs and control.

Which camp would you place yourself in? Ask yourself the following, and the answer should start to become self-evident:

- Do you videotape CNBC during the day so you can watch the whole day's broadcast after work?

- Do you consider Ben Bernanke to be as much of a celebrity as Angelina Jolie?
- Do you harass your human resources department to add additional mutual funds to your 401(k) plan?
- Do you subscribe to multiple investing newsletters?
- Do you strap a Hewlett Packard 12c financial calculator to your belt instead of a cell phone?

If you answered yes to more than one of these questions, chances are you're a do-it-yourselfer. Or at the very least you're inclined to want to invest money on your own.

But the reality is, do-it-yourself investing is hard. And the dirty little secret of the 1990s was that many do-it-yourself investors never really did everything themselves. For it was shown, after the fact, that many investors who proclaimed to be do-it-yourselfers were actually getting some professional advice on the side.

Mutual fund industry figures tell the story. While many regarded the late 1990s as the era of do-it-yourself investing, the fact is, the percentage of fund investors who picked no-load funds on their own diminished during this period. In 1990 nearly a quarter of all fund shares were sold directly—without a financial advisor's recommendation. By 2003 this figure dropped to just 13 percent, as a greater percentage of us sought financial advice (Figure 4-3).

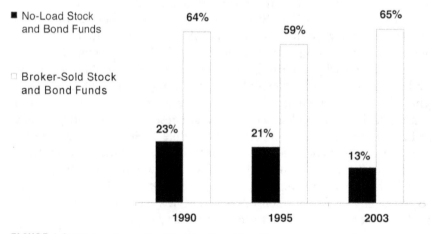

FIGURE 4-3 · Market Share of No-Load Stock and Bond Funds.

As this chart indicates, no-load funds, which hold a minority of mutual fund assets, have seen their market share dwindle.

Source: Investment Company Institute

It's not surprising. Consider all the decisions an investor has to make: They range from **investment selection** (which specific stocks, bonds, or real estate holdings to buy) to **asset allocation** (how much money should I put in each investment) to **asset location** (which accounts should those investments be held in) to **sell decisions** (which stocks, bonds, and real estate holdings to sell—and how much).

To ensure that you are indeed a do-it-yourself investor, ask yourself:

- Do I have the time—and interest—to consistently review all my financial goals and needs? This is likely to take at least an hour or even more every day. This involves sitting down with your entire family to assess plans for your children's college fund, your own retirement, and, more than likely these days, your parents' needs in old age.

- Do I feel confident enough about my knowledge of stocks, bonds, and real estate to know which investment options are the most appropriate to meet my goals?

- If not, do I have the time—and interest—to learn?

- Do I have the time—and interest—to research specific investments?

- Do I know when to invest in certain assets? It's not good enough to know to buy 100 shares of Microsoft. If you're doing everything on your own, you'll also have to determine when the best time to be purchasing 100 shares of Microsoft is.

- And finally, do I have the time—and interest—to execute my plan, which includes making periodic adjustments to my strategy as circumstances change?

Not surprisingly, the majority of investors seek help in one way or another. This assistance may come through a financial advisor who oversees your entire portfolio. It may come in the form of a broker, who only helps you with your stock or bond portfolios. It may come through a financial Web site that only helps you deal with your 401(k). These days, there are myriad online advisory services, such as the three listed in Figure 4-4, that seek to assist

Company	Web Site
Financial Engines	www.financialengines .com
Morningstar Associates	www.morningstar.com
Scarborough Group	www.401 kadvice.com

FIGURE 4-4 · Sources for Online Investing Advice.

novice investors or to help time-strapped investors deal with the headache of managing their investments while they're also managing their careers and personal lives.

Increasingly, investors are inclined to do a little bit of both—that is, invest a portion of their assets on their own, while handing the rest of their money over to a professional to oversee. But if you plan on being both a do-it-yourselfer and an advice seeker, be careful. Make sure that what you're doing on your own jibes with what your advisor is doing with your overall financial plan.

A Mix and Match Problem

Here's a classic example of what can go wrong by mixing and matching do-it-yourself techniques with an advisor's comprehensive financial plan:

Say you hire a financial planner who determines that the best approach to managing your money is to invest 60 percent of your assets in stocks and 40 percent in bonds. And within your equity allocation, he has you in a mix that's 80 percent large-cap stocks and 20 percent small-cap stocks.

But on your own you decide to switch out of the Fidelity Balanced fund in your 401(k) and to shift the money into Fidelity Low-Priced Stock fund, which is a well-known small-capitalization stock fund. In so doing, you make a switch that you feel comfortable with. But this tweaks your overall asset allocation. You now have only 65 percent of your stock holdings in large stocks and 35 percent in small stocks. And because Fidelity Balanced invests in a mix of blue-chip stocks and bonds, your stock and bond mix goes from 60 percent equities/40 percent fixed income to 75 percent stocks/25 percent bonds. While this may not sound like a radical departure, it may have thrown your advisor's plans way off course.

So if you do plan on mixing and matching approaches, make sure you keep your advisor fully informed of all of your decisions.

Value versus Growth

There is another big division in the world of investing, this one between the value and growth schools of investing. The distinctions between them are easy to describe. They can be summed up as the difference between investors who seek to remain true to the old investing adage, "Buy low and sell high," and those who are willing to buy at any price so long as they think they can sell it at an even higher level.

Value investors are bargain-basement shoppers. They care most about price, and less about quality. In fact, the merchandise can be scratched, dented, crushed, or defective in any number of ways. So long as the price is right, they'll take it. The philosophy of value investors is to buy stocks, bonds, or real estate that's trading at a price below what the actual asset is worth, even if that asset doesn't seem attractive right now.

Value investors may not even care why a stock is trading below its intrinsic value. The fall in price may have been caused by a mistake on the part of management. It may have been due to the arrival of a new competitor that's cutting in on the underlying company's earnings. It may be a mistake. Wall Street may have simply miscalculated the strengths and weaknesses of the company. It doesn't matter, so long as the value investor believes that over time the mistake will be rectified, and that over time the price will reflect the true value of the asset.

Because the types of assets that value investors put their money in may require time to repair themselves, value investors are typically willing to wait, sometimes for years, if not decades. Investing legends such as Warren Buffett and Benjamin Graham are among history's greatest value investors.

If value investors are the equivalent of building contractors who buy old housing stock, renovate it, wait, and sell it at a steep price down the road, growth investors are home buyers who want a property that's ready to move into today.

Growth investors are all about performance. They care about which stocks, in a universe of tens of thousands, are exhibiting the greatest levels of profit growth. Growth investors believe in another old investing adage: "Stock prices eventually reflect earnings." This is why they care most about earnings and less about price, since they believe that over time, higher earnings will push stock prices up.

To study an investment's earnings potential, a growth investor will often look both backward and forward. If dealing with equities, he or she will consider the historic earnings and revenue growth rates of a company. Then these investors will not only compare that to the earnings of the company's competitors, but also to the sector and broad stock market. Often, they will also consider a company's revenue growth. Revenue, or sales, reflects the ability of a company to attract customers. Earnings reflect the company's ability to take those sales and maximize profit generation.

In addition to growth and value investors, you will also hear terms "growth stocks" and "value stocks." The simple definition is that a growth stock is one that appeals to growth investors while a value stock appeals to value-oriented shareholders.

Another definition is that **growth stocks** are shares of companies that are growing their earnings (and to a lesser extent their sales) faster than the broad stock market. Historically, earnings for companies in the S&P 500 index have grown around 7 percent a year. So shares of companies with long-term earnings growth rates in the high single digits and low double digits are likely to be considered growth stocks.

Value stocks, on the other hand, are typically thought of as shares of companies whose valuations—their **price-to-earnings** or **price-to-book ratios**—are lower than the broad stock market. Since the long-term historic P/E ratio of the S&P 500 is roughly 16, stocks trading at 16 times their earnings or below are often thought of as value stocks.

It may be helpful to know that Standard & Poor's and other firms that run stock indexes have recently created separate indexes that track growth stocks and value shares. For instance, in addition to the S&P 500 stock index, there are the S&P 500 Growth index and the S&P 500 Value index. There are similar growth and value indexes for the S&P 400 mid-cap stock index and the S&P 500 small-cap index. The Russell family of indexes—you're probably most familiar with the Russell 2000 index of small stocks—does something similar. In the case of the S&P indexes, the world of stocks is broken into two equally sized groups, based on their valuation levels. Those trading at below-average valuations are considered value stocks; those trading at above-average valuations are considered growth.

Active versus Passive

The terms "active" and "passive" investing are mostly used in the world of mutual funds. An **actively managed fund** is a traditional portfolio that's managed by a professional stock picker who buys and sells securities as he or she sees fit, based on the parameters set by the fund. In the universe of more than 26,000 mutual funds, about 95 percent are classified as actively managed portfolios, according to the mutual fund tracking service Morningstar.

A **passively managed fund**, on the other hand, isn't really managed in traditional sense. These are so-called **index funds**. Unlike an actively managed fund, index funds are not led by stock pickers. While they do have managers who oversee them, index funds simply try to mirror the basic stock and bond market indexes that already exist, in an attempt to give their investors a taste of the entire market.

In an S&P 500 index fund, for example, the fund will simply buy and hold all of the 500 stocks that comprise the index, and will hold them in proportionate weightings, based on what percent of the index they represent. When S&P routinely kicks out one or two companies from the index and replaces them (perhaps because an existing company was acquired in a merger), then the index fund will mirror that move by removing that investment from its holdings and replacing it with the new stock or bond in the index.

It is important to note that in the past few years, exchange-traded funds have grown significantly in popularity and are starting to compete with mutual funds for individual investor dollars. Well, you should know that virtually all ETFs are index funds. Some ETFs, like the iShares S&P 500, track broad, recognizable market benchmarks like the S&P 500 index. But others track obscure indexes that represent a niche segment of the market. For instance, there's the Energy Select Sector SPDR, which tracks an index that represents a subset of energy firms in the S&P 500 index. There's also the iShares Dow Jones Select Dividend Index, which tracks a popular benchmark of stocks that pay out dividends.

Jack Bogle, founder of the mutual fund giant Vanguard Group, and a tireless advocate for shareholder rights, has described the difference between actively managed funds and passively managed funds this way: Active fund managers seek to find those needles in the haystack that lead to outsized results; passive fund managers simply buy the whole haystack.

By definition, then, an index fund investor can only obtain average results. That's because by buying an index fund, they are buying the whole stock market—and their performance will be the mathematical average of the performance of all those shares.

So why would a person want to be just average, by going with a passively run fund? While it's true that the fund industry has produced some fantastic stock pickers—people like Peter Lynch, formerly of Fidelity Magellan, or Bill Miller, manager of the Legg Mason Value fund, who beat the S&P 500 14 straight years between 1991 and 2004—the fact of the matter is, the majority end up underperforming the averages over time. For example, over the past 15 years through December 31, 2009, the average domestic stock fund has trailed the S&P 500 index. In fact, over the past 15 years, less than 15 percent of all domestic stock funds have outperformed the Vanguard 500 index, the largest and most popular index fund, which simply mirrors the S&P 500. And over longer periods of time, as Figures 4-5 and 4-6 show, the

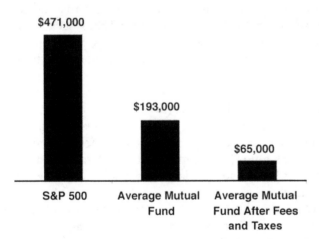

FIGURE 4-5 · Index versus Actively Managed Stock Funds (1950–1999).

This chart illustrates the growth of $1,000 invested in the S&P 500 versus actively managed stock funds between 1950 and 1999. Clearly, the low costs and low turnover of index funds have given them a distinct advantage over the past half century.

Source: Vanguard; The Bogle Financial Markets Research Center

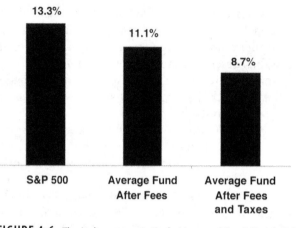

FIGURE 4-6 · The Index versus Actively Managed Stock Funds (1950–1999).

This chart indicates annualized rates of returns of the S&P 500 versus actively managed stock funds between 1950 and 1999.

Source: Vanguard; The Bogle Financial Markets Research Center

average gains earned in an actively managed fund trail the potential gains of simply investing in a broad stock market index. So, being average doesn't seem so bad.

Interestingly, many critics of index investing have made the case that indexing works only when the market is going higher and higher. That's because in theory, in bull markets rising tides are supposed to lift all boats, giving index funds an advantage. These critics have argued that investors would see the folly of indexing once the markets hit a rough patch.

As it turned out, the markets did hit a rough patch—the so-called Lost Decade—when stocks lost value over a 10-year stretch between December 31, 1999, and December 31, 2009. So were the critics right? Was indexing a flawed theory? The answer is no. In the 10-year period ending in December 2009, only about a third of all domestic stock funds (and only a third of all large-cap stock funds) wound up beating the S&P 500 index of large-cap stocks, despite what a tough time it was for the index.

So, your choice is clear: Do you seek to outperform the markets by taking a chance on an actively managed fund? Or do you settle for the averages and go with an index strategy? The former has a big upside and a big downside. In the case of the latter, you hedge your risks by owning a share of a broad swath of stocks. But at the same time, you run the risk of missing out on potentially big gains. The odds say it's safer to go with an index approach. But not all investors like to settle for being average.

Buy and Hold versus Pick and Roll

Are you the type of consumer who waits patiently for sales, even if they don't come around for months or years at a stretch? Do you hang onto antiques or memorabilia for years, allowing them to gather dust in the attic, in hopes that someday someone will want what you have?

If the answer is yes, then chances are, you're a **buy-and-hold investor**. Buy and hold is exactly what the name describes: someone who is willing to hang onto stocks, bonds, or real estate properties for years, even if they don't initially rise in value, so that they can sell them at a higher price down the road.

There was a time, not so long ago, when the majority of investors classified themselves as buy and holders. A few decades ago the average **holding period** (a fancy term for how long someone hangs onto an investment before selling) for a mutual fund investor was 20 years. That meant many of us invested in our funds for a generation, developing a loyalty to the fund and giving the manager time to do his or her work. In other words, we worried more about long-term gains than short-term fluctuations in our portfolios. Today, the average holding period is below three years.

The same is true for stock fund managers. A generation ago the average domestic stock fund had a **turnover rate** of around 30 percent. **Turnover** refers to the speed with which a fund manager sells out of all his holdings. A turnover rate of 100 percent means the fund is likely to replace all of its stocks in one year. A turnover rate of 33 percent means it may take more than three years for a fund to turn over all of its investments. Today, the average turnover rate for a stock fund is around 100 percent. (You can look up a fund's turnover rate and other statistics on www.morningstar.com.)

More and more, investors have become pick and rollers. This simply means that this group of investors is willing to sell out of an investment quickly if: (a) bad things start to happen; (b) its price falls sharply, say, 10 percent or more; (c) its price rises sufficiently to book a quick profit; or (d) a better investment comes along. In the heyday of the late 1990s Internet investing craze, **day traders**, who sold stock within minutes of buying in order to book intrahour profits, were the icons of this philosophy of investing. Today there are more moderate examples of pick and rollers, such as **swing traders**, a more reformed version of day traders who hang onto stocks for days and weeks before flipping out.

While buy and holders are willing to ride out short-term troubles, pick and rollers would rather cut their losses soon and move on to better choices. While buy and holders consider pick and rollers to be impatient, if not irresponsible, pick and rollers think their strategy makes a lot of sense. Why hang onto a stock for 10 years if you see something better to invest in now? Why hang onto an investment that's simply treading water for decades at a time? Why sit on dead money? Why not take that money and invest it elsewhere in something that is working?

Buy and holders would say such a strategy triggers capital gains taxes and brokerage commissions sooner rather than later. Pick and rollers on the other hand, would argue that these taxes and fees can be overcome by making better underlying investments. Political correctness says it's important to buy and hold. But even though conventional wisdom says buy and hold is the way to go, the majority of investors don't really practice buy-and-hold investing anymore.

Historical odds say it's harder to pick and roll, on average, than to buy and hold. For starters, by turning over your portfolio frequently with a pick-and-roll strategy, you create transactional costs such as brokerage commissions and fees (which we will address in greater detail later in the book). These costs make it that much harder for an active investor to beat the averages.

Moreover, it is difficult to time the market perfectly. Long-term studies of the performance of mutual fund investors would seem to bear this out. The financial research firm Dalbar studied the performance of fund investors (not mutual funds themselves) between January 1984 and December 2002 (Figure 4-7). It found that as a result of poor market timing decisions, the typical fund investor earned only 2.6 percent a year on average during this tremendous bull market period. By comparison, the S&P 500 rose 12.2 percent. Why did fund investors perform so poorly? Because many picked the wrong funds and rolled into and out of them at the worst possible times. Again, this is not to say that you can't do well with this strategy. But the odds of success are low.

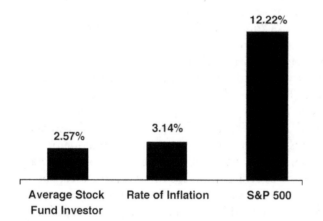

FIGURE 4-7 · Hazards of Picking and Rolling, 1984–2002.

This chart shows the annualized returns earned by stock fund investors between January 1984 and December 2002. Due to poor timing decisions, average stock fund investors have not only badly trailed the S&P 500, they have not even kept up with the historic rate of inflation.

Source: Dalbar

Fundamental versus Technical

The terms **fundamental analysis** and **technical analysis** refer to different ways in which people choose to research the investments they intend to put their money into. Perhaps the best way to describe the two approaches is with an analogy of shopping for a car.

Like all buyers, fundamentally oriented investors and technical investors are both looking for good deals. And at the end of the day, they are both interested in the potential resale value of their asset. They both realize that the only way to make a profit on their investment is if someone else is willing to pay a higher price for the asset than they themselves initially purchased it for. But there are competing schools of thought when it comes to determining ways to gauge when investments are good bets.

A fundamental investor will literally "kick the tires"—and "check under the hood" to see if there are any problems with the vehicle's engine. To determine the investment's strengths and weaknesses, this type of investor will pore over the company's financial statements, which includes its **balance sheet** (outlining the company's assets and its liabilities), **income statement** (revenues coming in and costs going out), and the **statement of cash flows** (which tracks the flow of money into and out of the company's coffers). They will pay particularly close attention to the investment's engines, which in the case of stocks is the company's earnings and earnings potential. At the end of the day, the stock will be chosen based on the merits. In our analogy, an investor will buy it if he or she thinks the car's strengths are worth the price tag and pass if the price tag is too high.

Technical analysis, on the other hand, focuses less on the car itself than on external trends, such as how other investors regard the car.

Followers of technical analysis recognize that trends in the market repeat themselves over time, and as a result, that stock market trends can be spotted—and therefore predicted—if investors learn how to read patterns that form in stock market charts. Instead of spending all day researching a company's books or competition, a technician, as they're sometimes called, might study patterns that form in the routine trading of that stock. They will literally see if they can spot shapes in the price charts of a given stock or stock index.

For instance, someone might look at a stock's recent trading pattern and see the outline of what looks like the letter *W*. This is referred to as a "double bottom," since it reflects shares falling in a short period of time, recovering, then falling some more, and then rising some more. In other cases, a technician might look at a stock chart and see what looks like the shape of a person's head and shoulders. Or, the pattern might be described as a cup with handle. This is no joke.

The point of this exercise is not to read charts like a palm reader reads palms, but to use these classic patterns to gauge the psychology of investors who are buying and selling a security. By reading and interpreting chart patterns, technical analysis tries to determine if other investors are more or less likely to buy or sell the stock in the future.

Take the classic W pattern. Technicians consider this a bullish indicator for a stock since the pattern reflects the fact that as a stock begins to fall, investors are stepping in to create a floor for the share price. This forms the left-hand side of the W. But then something else happens. As the stock's price begins to rise again, many investors start to sell again, just as the stock comes back up to their original purchase price. Academic research indicates that some investors often hang onto money-losing stocks not because they are bullish, but because they loathe the thought of selling at a loss. So, if a stock begins to rally, they will sell into the rally once they realize they can recoup their original investments.

Once these wishy-washy sellers are wrung out of the market, a second floor might emerge, and the genuinely bullish investors will hopefully step in, sending the stock up again, forming the final leg of the W. Technical analysts would see the W formation as a sign that this security is ready to rise further, or **break to the upside**, as they might say.

Trading volume is considered another key variable for technical investors to consider, since it speaks to the *conviction* that other investors have about current trends in the market. An upward rise in a stock, in conjunction with greater-than-usual trading volume, would indicate the strength of attitude among traders. An upward rise met with tepid trading volume might indicate that a certain trend is not strong enough to form a trend.

Another tool that technical investors often rely on is whether a stock is trading above or below its **historic moving average**. Some rely on a 50-day moving average, while others rely on 100-day or 200-day moving averages. Calculating these moving averages is simple: Add up the closing prices of the S&P 500, for example, for the past 50 days and divide by 50. Many financial Web sites that offer charting capabilities, such www.bigcharts.com, will indicate a stock's moving average for you. Typically, it is considered a bearish sign for a security if its price falls below 50- or 100-day moving averages. Conversely, it's considered bullish when a stock breaks out above its historic moving averages.

So, continuing with our car shopping analogy, a technical investor will focus less on the engine and brakes of the car and more on the emotional attachment that other would-be buyers may have on the vehicle. The technical investor realizes that while earnings and sales growth drive the health of a company over the long term, the psychological feelings that other investors have—or don't have—for that vehicle will influence how the market set its price too.

Various characteristics that separate fundamental and technical investors are listed on Figure 4-8. It can be said that fundamental investors care about profits,

Characteristics	Fundamental Investor	Technical Investor
Cares about corporate earnings	Yes	No
Cares about valuations	Yes	No
Cares about recent trading trends	No	Yes
Cares about trading volume	No	Yes
Cares what other investors think	No	Yes
Cares about emotions	No	Yes
Is momentum driven	No	Yes
Reads chart patterns	No	Yes

FIGURE 4-8 · Fundamental versus Technical.

profit margins, and sales trends, because at the end of the day earnings correlate with stock price. The technical analyst, on the other hand, cares about the supply-and-demand relationship of an investment. Technicians believe that a stock is like any other product in demand. There are a limited number of shares for that stock that float in the open market. So depending on how strong or weak demand is for that limited supply, you can gauge where the stock price will move.

Bottom line: Fundamental analysis is a logical exercise that concentrates on the head. Technical analysis is the study of emotions that gauges the heart. Both strategies make sense. But it's important to determine which makes more sense to you, since they do not work in unison.

Final Thoughts

As you can see, there are a number of different ways to make money as an investor. The trick is to find a style that suits your own sensibilities. Before you start researching the stock and bond markets, you need to do a little fundamental analysis on yourself.

Are you the type of person who will likely seek out the assistance of a financial adviser? Or do you really want to do everything yourself? When it comes to investing, are you a bargain-basement shopper, seeking out value-oriented investments? Or do you gravitate to high quality—and in some cases high-priced—investments? Do you plan on playing the odds and sticking with a low-cost, low-risk strategy of indexing the broad stock and bond markets? Or are you a bit of a risk taker, seeking out the potential for higher returns through active fund management? Answering these questions *before* you begin to invest will help build the foundation for a stronger investment plan.

QUIZ

1. It always makes sense to work with a financial advisor.
   A. True
   B. False

2. Your ability to invest on your own will depend on which key factor?
   A. Your skills
   B. Your time
   C. Your interest
   D. None of the above
   E. All of the above

3. Thanks to the Internet, more and more Americans are becoming do-it-yourself investors.
   A. True
   B. False

4. Because different types of investments come into and out of favor at different times, you should . . .
   A. Be a growth investor.
   B. Be a value investor.
   C. Be diversified.

5. Value investors care most about how fast a company's earnings are growing.
   A. True
   B. False

6. Growth investors care most about how fast a company's earnings are growing.
   A. True
   B. False

7. Index investing does well when in bull markets, but it has difficulties in bear markets.
   A. True
   B. False

8. The majority of actively managed funds managed to make money in the so-called Lost Decade.
   A. True
   B. False

9. **One of the dangers of frequent trading is that it ...**

   A. Leads to brokerage commissions.
   B. Leads to capital gains taxes.
   C. Leads to timing mistakes.
   D. All of the above.
   E. None of the above.

10. **Fundamental investors care more about the financial health of the company than short-term moves in its stock price.**

    A. True
    B. False

Part II

Your Assets

chapter 5

Demystifying Stocks

In this chapter, you will learn the following:

- Why stocks should be a core part of your long-term portfolio
- The nature of stock market returns
- The nature of stock market risks
- How you can minimize those risks
- Different types of equities to consider

The Stock Market

Though investors don't typically think about it this way, buying a stock is like starting your own business: There are limitless opportunities ahead of you, coupled with a seemingly endless list of risks.

Whereas bond investors enter into contractual relationships when they buy government or corporate debt, stock investors must take a leap of faith. Bond investors know exactly what they'll earn in interest income, when they'll get it, and precisely what date they're due to get their principal investment returned to them when the bond matures. It's impossible for stock investors, on the other hand, to know with any certainty how much they'll earn in profits, via dividends, or whether the company itself will ultimately survive or die.

To be sure, before you become part owner of a publicly traded company, you can research the investment to the point where you feel generally comfortable with the company's management, its products and services, its industry, and its growth forecasts. But the point is, you can never tell.

On the plus side, there is the possibility that the company you invest in will not only thrive, but that it will grow more than you ever imagined it could. And if that is the case, stock investors will earn far more on their money than any bond investor ever could. Indeed, the potential upside of a successful stock investment is virtually limitless, since it is tied to the earnings the company will accrue over time.

For instance, who could have predicted back in the late 1970s that when a skinny college dropout named Bill Gates and his friend Paul Allen started a tiny company out of a makeshift office in Albuquerque, New Mexico, it would grow to become the world's biggest software company. Today, Microsoft, now headquartered in Redmond, Washington, generates annual revenues in excess of $60 billion.

But for every Microsoft, there is an AIG. Or a Lehman Brothers. And that is ultimately the risk you face as an investor of common stock: that the company you invest in will falter or go bankrupt, and while in bankruptcy, common stock holders are last in line to make any claims to recoup losses from the failed firm. The fact is, there are no guarantees in the stock market, just as there are no assurances that if you were to open a dry cleaning store down the street or a fast-food stand at the local mall you wouldn't lose your shirt.

Stock Returns

Having said that, stocks are the best financial asset in which *long-term* investors can put their money (Figure 5-1). Consider this: Between 1926 and 2009 blue-chip equities delivered average returns of 9.8 percent a year. Remember, this figure includes the effects of the Lost Decade, when the stock market suffered two of the biggest bear markets in history, back-to-back. If you had invested $10,000 in 1926, your money would have grown to more than $23 million by 2003. Mind-blowing, isn't it? This means that if you were to invest just $10,000 for your child at birth—and never put another dime into stocks afterward—your child could retire with more than 2,000 times your original investment.

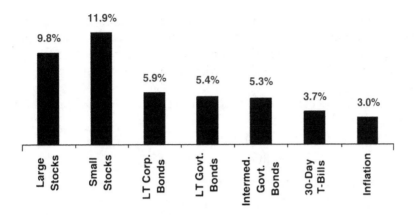

FIGURE 5-1 · Annualized Returns (1926–2009).

As this chart indicates, stocks have far outpaced the average annual returns of bonds and cash throughout the past century.

Source: Ibbotson Associates

Here's another way to think about it: The stock market, over this long period of time, has delivered nearly twice the 5.4 percent annual returns of long-term government bonds. And as for cash accounts, it's not even close. Equities have gained nearly three times as much as cash accounts on average, as measured by 30-day Treasury bills, on a yearly basis, over the past three-quarters of a century.

Compounding Stock Gains

But remember how we discussed the power of compound interest? Though the 9.8 percent returns of stocks is around *twice* the 5.4 percent returns of long-term government bonds, the gap grows even bigger in real terms—in actual dollars—as time marches forward. Let's plug the numbers into a financial calculator, as we did in Chapter 3, to see how. Let's start with stocks.

Assume we invest $10,000:

$$\text{Present value } (pv) = 10,000$$

Assume that we invest for 10 years:

$$\text{Number of years } (n) = 10$$

We know that stocks returned 10.4 percent:

$$\text{Interest rate } (i) = 9.8$$

We then hit the future value (*fv*) button. And we get:

$$fv = \$25,470$$

What this means is that a $10,000 investment grows to $25,470 over a 10-year stretch, assuming it grows at a rate of 9.8 percent a year. In other words, your investing gain would be $15,470 (remember, we started with $10,000 and that grew to $25,470—so we subtracted $10,000 from $25,470 to arrive at $15,470).

Now, let's do the same calculation, but with the **historic rate of return** for long-term government bonds.

Again, assume that we invest an initial $10,000:

$$\text{Present value } (pv) = 10,000$$

Again, assume that we invest for 10 years:

$$\text{Number of years } (n) = 10$$

We know that government bonds returned 5.4 percent:

$$\text{Interest rate } (i) = 5.4$$

We then hit the future value (*fv*) button. And we get:

$$fv = \$16,920$$

In the case of bonds, our investing gain was $6,920. What does this tell us? It says that while the long-term rate of return for stocks is less than double that of government bonds, over a 10-year stretch stocks delivered $2\frac{1}{3}$ times the paper profit of bonds (we arrived at this figure by dividing $15,470 by $6,920).

Now, to show how compound interest works over even longer periods of time, let's rerun the numbers, but with a 30-year time horizon.

Again, assume that we invest $10,000:

$$\text{Present value } (pv) = 10,000$$

Assume that we invest for 30 years this time:

$$\text{Number of years } (n) = 30$$

We know that stocks returned 9.8 percent:

$$\text{Interest rate } (i) = 9.8$$

We then hit the future value (*fv*) button. And we get:

$$fv = \$165,223$$

Given 30 years, our investing gains in stocks were $155,223. Now let's rerun the same assumptions for bonds, again using the 30-year time horizon.

Again, assume that we invest $10,000:

$$\text{Present value } (pv) = 10,000$$

Again, assume that we invest for 30 years:

$$\text{Number of years } (n) = 30$$

We know that bonds returned 5.4 percent:

$$\text{Interest rate } (i) = 5.4$$

We then hit the future value (*fv*) button. And we get:

$$fv = \$48,441$$

With a 30-year time horizon, bonds generated gains of $38,441 in pretax paper profits. That's fine, but stocks generated more than 4 times the paper profits generated by bonds over a three-decade-long period. (Again, we arrived at this by dividing the paper profits of stocks, $155,223, by the paper profits of bonds, $38,441.)

This confirms our original point: While stocks' rate of return is around twice that of bonds, over time the difference in real dollar terms could grow to five times, due to the power of compound interest. This is why one of the three pillars of an investment portfolio—and perhaps the most important asset for investors just starting out to own—is equities.

Stock Risks

The question is: Why doesn't everyone put every last cent that he or she has in the stock market if, over the long term, stocks do so well? Well, the experience of the past few years may help answer that question.

It's because, paradoxically, stocks can also be the worst financial asset for an investor in the **short term**. Anyone who was investing in the stock market between October 2007 and March 2009 can attest to that. During this bear market period, stocks, as measured by the S&P 500, lost more than 56 percent of their value.

How did we know that? Let's go back and see what the S&P 500 was trading at back then. On October 9, 2007, which marked the peak of the bull market for large stocks, the S&P 500 index closed at a level of 1,565.15. Over the next few years, stock prices drifted lower and lower, until the index fell as low as 676.53 on March 9, 2009. As we discussed earlier, the way to calculate the price appreciation (or in this case, depreciation) of a stock or index is simple:

$$\text{S\&P 500 closing value on Oct 9, 2007} = 1,565.15$$

$$\text{S\&P 500 closing value on March 9, 2009} = 676.53$$

$$1,565.15 - 676.53 = 888.62$$

$$888.62/1,565.15 = 0.568$$

You take the original value (in this case, 1,565.15) and subtract the new value (676.53). In our example, that leaves us with 888.62. Now, take that answer and divide by the original value (again, 1,565.15). The answer we get is 0.568, which means stocks lost 56.8 percent, or more than half, of their original value.

Market Risk

The bear market was no aberration. Since 1950 the stock market has experienced 12 major corrections or bear markets (Figure 5-2). **Corrections**, again, are loosely defined as losses of 10 percent or more, while bear markets are considered sustained downturns of 20 percent or more. On average, those downturns cost investors around a third of the value of their investments. And just as important, it typically took investors around two years to recoup their losses, according to a study of major stock market declines done by The Leuthold Group, an investment advisory firm.

In some cases it took considerably more time. A classic example was the 1973-74 bear market, which, until recently, used to be considered the worst bear market since the Great Depression. In that bear market, stocks lost around half of their value and it took nearly four years for investors to get back to where they were at the peak of the prior bull market.

Following the bear market that began in March 2000, it took roughly seven years for the major stock market indexes to climb back to their pre-Internet

Date of Market Peak	Date of Market Trough	Losses
October 9, 2007	March 9, 2009	−57%
March 24, 2000	October 9, 2002	−49%
July 17, 1998	August 31, 1998	−19%
July 16, 1990	October 11, 1990	−20%
August 25, 1987	December 24, 1987	−34%
November 28, 1980	August 12, 1982	−27%
September 21, 1976	March 6, 1978	−20%
January 11, 1973	October 3, 1974	−48%
November 29, 1968	May 26, 1970	−36%
February 9, 1966	October 7, 1966	−22%
December 12, 1961	June 26, 1962	−28%
August 2, 1956	October 22, 1957	−22%
Average Market Decline Since World War II		−32%

FIGURE 5-2 · Major Corrections in the Stock Market.*

*Data reflects losses suffered by the S&P 500 Index during major bear markets and corrections in history.

Source: The Leuthold Group

bubble peaks. But alas, within months of making it back to new highs, the stock market entered into yet another bear market in October 2007.

This is what's known on Wall Street as **market risk**: the risk that you happen to be in the stock market when the bear decides to come out of hibernation. And the fact of the matter is, since 1900 the Dow Jones Industrial Average has experienced a 10-percent short-term drop every one and a half years, a 20-percent drop every two and a half years; a 30-percent drop every four and a half years, and a 40-percent drop about once in every nine years. (These calculations come from InvesTech Research, a respected investing advisory and research firm.) For stockholders this is the reality—and the risk—of being an investor.

Minimizing Market Risk

There are four basic ways investors can reduce market risk while simultaneously remaining in the market:

1. *Invest in a multitude of asset classes.* For instance, put a portion of your money in bonds and cash to diversify your stock holdings. We will explore this more at length later in the book.

2. *Invest in multiple stock markets.* In other words, invest in foreign as well as U.S. stocks. We will explore this more at length later in this chapter.

3. *Stretch out the length of time investors plan to invest.* Over long periods of time, bear markets are balanced by roaring bull markets, such as the one investors enjoyed in the 1980s and the more recent one in the mid-to-late 1990s. The good news is, on average, bull markets last a lot longer than bear markets. Throughout the past century, the average bull market has lasted around three years, while the typical bear market has averaged just over a year and a half.

   This means that as your time horizon expands, the odds of surviving short-term troubles caused by market corrections diminish. The mutual fund company T. Rowe Price studied the odds of losing money in the broad stock market, relying on S&P 500 data. They not only looked at stock market performance in every calendar year between 1926 and 2002, they also studied rolling periods of time during this stretch, in an effort to be as comprehensive as possible. Their conclusion: If you have only one year to invest, there's a 27-percent chance of losing money in any 12-month stretch of time. But if you have three years to invest, those odds drop to 14 percent. Over rolling five-year periods, the S&P 500 lost money only 10 percent of the time, this study found. And over rolling 10-year periods, there's only a 4 in 100 chance of losing money by investing in the broad stock market.

4. *Diversify when investors invest in the market*, not just if and how they invest in equities. It's called **dollar cost averaging**. This term refers to a basic strategy that many investors practice without even realizing that they're practicing it.

To dollar-cost-average means not to invest every last penny you have in the market all at once. Instead, this conservative approach calls for putting small amounts of money to work each month, quarter, or at some other routine interval. This is exactly what we do with our 401(k)s, where a small amount of money is deducted automatically from our paychecks every week or month and is stuffed into the stock market.

While a **lump sum investor** would put $10,000 to work in the market all at once, a dollar cost averager may decide to put $2,500 into the stock market at the start of each quarter (January 1, April 1, June 1, and September 1), or $833.33 every month. By doing so, dollar cost averagers ensure that they never put all their money into the market at the worst possible time (when the market is peaking just before a crash). Instead, their **cost basis**—which is the price they paid for the stock—is spread out over intervals in time and averaged out. Hence the name.

It should be noted that Vanguard recently ran an interesting analysis showing the value of dollar cost averaging. Vanguard assumed that an investor put $100,000 into a mix of 60 percent stocks and 40 percent bonds on December 31, 1999. The firm further assumed that the investor continued to invest $1,000 a month in this mix every month for the next 10 years until December 31, 2009, much as an investor might through a 401(k) retirement account. If someone followed this strategy, and made sure on an annual basis that his or her investment portfolio continued to be roughly 60 percent stocks and 40 percent bonds, that person would have enjoyed annual returns of 4.3 percent during what was largely considered to be a lost decade for investing.

Keep in mind, though, that one does not dollar-cost-average to maximize gains. The whole purpose of this strategy is to minimize risks. In an up market, a lump sum investor will do far better than a dollar cost averager because he or she will have money in stocks just before equity prices begin to rise. In a falling market, however, the lump sum investor would also have all of his or her money in the market just in time for a correction.

Stock-Specific Risk

The other major risk associated with equities involves the specific companies you choose. This is often referred to as **stock-** or **company-specific risk**.

Take the fortunes of two investors who happen to make a bet on retailing stocks in the mid-1980s. One chooses Sears, a household name and an industry leader at the time, and the other chooses Wal-Mart, an upstart discounter based in a tiny town called Bentonville, Arkansas.

At the start of 1984, shares of Sears, which at the time was a major component of the Dow Jones Industrial Average, were going for $36.50 a pop. So if the first investor—let's call him John—bought 1,000 shares of the stock, his total initial investment was $36,500. Over the course of the next 20 years, John saw the stock price of Sears meander and fall. By the start of 2004, Sears wasn't just out of the Dow Jones Industrial Average (the editors of the *Wall Street Journal* kicked it out in 1999), its shares had fallen to $19.88. This means John's original $36,500 shrunk to under $19,880 over two decades. Despite two roaring bull markets—one in the 1980s and the other in the 1990s—John lost an annualized 3 percent a year, give or take, over the course of 20 years.

Meanwhile, on the other side of the block, Sarah decided to invest the same amount of money in Wal-Mart. Back in January 1984, shares of the Arkansas-based discounter were on discount themselves. They were selling for just $1.20 a pop. So Sarah put $36,500 into Wal-Mart stock, which got her 30,416 shares. (We arrived at that figure by dividing her $36,500 investment by the share price of $1.20.)

Over the course of the next 20 years, Wal-Mart supplanted Sears as the nation's biggest and most successful retailer. Its share price went from $1.20 to $52.30. And with 30,416 shares, this means Sarah's investment grew to $1.6 million. That works out to annualized returns of nearly 21 percent, far exceeding the overall market gains.

This is a perfect example of how company risk can affect your portfolio in the real world. In this illustration, the overall actions of the market did not affect the stock price of John's and Sarah's stocks. Instead, it was the actions of the management teams at Sears and Wal-Mart that affected their returns. This means there are actually two risks embedded in company-specific risk. There's the risk that you—the investor—are simply mediocre at picking winning stocks. And there's the risk that the management of the company you invest in—despite showing all the traditional signs of competence—fails to execute a winning strategy.

Minimizing Stock-Specific Risk

Obviously, the way to minimize stock-specific risk is to invest in a plethora of different companies. You can do this easily with a diversified stock mutual fund or ETF, since the average fund invests in hundreds of different stocks.

Conventional wisdom used to say investors needed to own about two dozen stocks to achieve adequate equity diversification. But new academic research seems to indicate that investors need exposure to around 50 stocks to adequately minimize company risk. Keep in mind also that those 50 or more stocks should be spread out among a multitude of sectors of the economy, since stocks within the same industries tend to move in relative correlation with one another. It's important also to balance your portfolio, if you do choose to diversify for defensive reasons, among different types of stocks— large and small, growth and value, and domestic and foreign—as we will discuss in a moment.

Risk of Not Being in the Market

With all of these risks, why does anyone invest in stocks? The first response goes back to what we discussed at the start of this chapter: Stocks, over the long run, are the best-performing asset you can put your money into.

But it's important to note that this won't necessarily be true if, fearing market risks, you pull your money out of stocks and miss even a handful of the best trading days in the market. Now, there are some talented investors who feel they can beat the market by timing these decisions and trading strategically and frequently. If you don't feel you can do that with success, then staying in the market—but in a diversified and conservative manner—would appear a decent alternative.

For example, between August 1982 and August 1987 the S&P 500 averaged annual gains of more than 26 percent. But if you were out of the stock market for just 20 of the best trading days that the S&P 500 enjoyed during that stretch, your returns fell to 13.1 percent. And if you missed out on the 40 best days during this bull market, you'd have generated returns of only 4.3 percent. Investors experienced the same results in the 1990s bull market. Those who were on the sidelines for the best six-month stretch between 1992 and 2001 enjoyed annual returns of only 8 percent, whereas equity investors who stayed in the market at all times enjoyed double-digit gains on average every year (Figure 5-3).

Being out of the market is particularly damaging during what are known as **inflection points** for stocks. These are those points in time when market trends reverse and we go from a bear market to a bull, or from a correction to a rally. Since the start of World War II, people who have been invested in the market during periods of market recoveries have enjoyed returns of more than 32 percent, on average, in the first year of such rallies. But if you were to miss just one quarter (three months' worth) of that first-year rally, your average gains would be cut by more than half.

Time Period	S&P 500 Annualized Returns
8/82 to 8/87	26.3%
8/82 to 8/87 minus 10 best days	18.3%
8/82 to 8/87 minus 20 best days	13.1%
8/82 to 8/87 minus 30 best days	8.5%
8/82 to 8/87 minus 40 best days	4.3%
1/92 to 12/01	12.9%
1/92 to 12/01 minus best month	12.2%
1/92 to 12/01 minus best 2 months	11.4%
1/92 to 12/01 minus best 3 months	10.5%
1/92 to 12/01 minus best 6 months	8.0%

FIGURE 5-3 · Risk of Not Being in the Market.

Investors who missed out on even a handful of the market's best days have wound up losing tremendous amounts of gains over the long run.

Sources: The University of Michigan, Crandall, Pierce & Co., *Straight Talk on Investing*

Stocks as an Inflation Hedge

But the second answer to the question, "Why do we invest in stocks at all, given their risks?" is, we generally have to, given the deleterious effects of inflation. The fact is, if you earn less than 3 or 4 percent on your money on average over time, you could actually be going backward, since inflation is constantly eating away at the future purchasing power of your money.

Inflation is an economic phenomenon in which prices rise over time. It's actually a healthy outgrowth of an expanding economy. Unfortunately, gradually rising prices means that over time the purchasing power of today's dollars diminishes. This means that you have to earn more than the rate of inflation just to stay even.

Since the 1990s, inflation has largely been kept in check, with the **consumer price index** (CPI) a closely followed gauge of trends in consumer prices, growing at around 3 or 4 percent or less a year. But investors who were in the market in the 1970s up through the early 1980s will recall a period in which inflation ran into the double digits. And there's no way to predict what the future rate of inflation will be with absolute certainty. So, many investors feel it's prudent to plan for the worst. Or at the least, it's best to plan for historic averages. And history says that the long-term average annual rate of inflation is around 3 percent.

Today's Dollars	10 Years	15 Years	20 Years	30 Years
$ 50,000	$ 36,900	$ 31,700	$ 27,200	$ 20,000
$100,000	$ 73,700	$ 63,300	$ 54,400	$ 40,100
$200,000	$147,500	$126,700	$108,800	$ 80,200
$300,000	$221,200	$190,000	$163,100	$120,300
$400,000	$295,000	$253,300	$217,500	$160,400
$500,000	$368,700	$316,600	$271,900	$200,500

FIGURE 5-4 · Effects of Inflation.*

*Figures reflect the real purchasing power of your financial assets over various lengths of time, based on a 3-percent annual rate of inflation.

Even a 3-percent inflation rate can damage a person's long-term investment plans. The chart in Figure 5-4 shows how much your investment accounts would suffer over time based on a 3-percent inflation rate.

While bonds have historically returned more than the rate of inflation—about 5.4 percent a year versus 3 percent—bonds barely grow your money in real terms in high-inflation periods. As for cash, it has historically grown at the rate of inflation, which means, in real terms, your money really isn't growing at all in checking or savings accounts, even if they are bearing interest. That leaves stocks as your only real alternative among the major asset classes to combat inflation.

Now, some would argue that in recent years, with the development of inflation-indexed bonds, which are sold by the Treasury Department, there is a way for bond investors to combat inflation too. And that is true. However, again, the point isn't simply to beat inflation, it's maximizing your total returns, net of inflation, over time at an acceptable level of risk.

Stocks, with their superior average long-term returns, can leverage compound interest like no other asset. For instance, say you're 45 years old and your goal as an investor is to turn your $100,000 nest egg into $500,000 by the time you retire.

How many years will it take you to turn $100,000 into $500,000 if you invested in a money market account? Let's be generous and assume that your money market account pays out nearly 4 percent annual interest over the long term. At that rate of return, it's going to take another 42 years for your money to reach its goal. And remember, this is before we factor in the impact of inflation. If inflation were to average 3 percent during this time, your net returns might only be 1 percent a year in a cash account, if that. At 1 percent interest, it would take 162 years for you to grow your investment portfolio big enough to live comfortably.

Choice of Stocks

Large Stocks versus Small Stocks

There are many distinctions in the types of stocks one can purchase. One of the biggest is between large and small stocks. The terms "large" and "small" refer to the *size of the company* you're investing in, not the price of the stock itself.

You can have a large stock trading for $5 a share and a small stock trading for more than $100 a pop.

Specifically, the terms "large" and "small" refer to the *market value*, or *market capitalization*, of the underlying company, as discussed earlier in the book. You'll recall that the way to calculate a company's **market cap**—which is the dollar value investors collectively place on a stock (not to be confused with its book value)—is to take its current stock price and multiply that by the total number of shares the company has outstanding.

So, a company could be trading at $5 a share, but if it has 10 billion shares outstanding, it would have a market cap of $50 billion, which would clearly make it a large stock. Conversely, a company could be trading at $100 a share, but if it only has 1 million shares outstanding, it would still be a small-cap stock with a market cap of $100 million.

Generally speaking, **large stocks** are those with market caps of above $10 billion. These are companies typically found in various large stock indexes like the S&P 500 index of blue-chip stocks, the Russell 1000 index, or even the Dow Jones Industrial Average (the Dow, however, only consists of 30 companies and is not as comprehensive as the S&P 500 or the Russell 1000).

Meanwhile, **small stocks** are those with market caps of under $1 billion. Major stock indexes that track small stocks include the Russell 2000 index of small stocks and the S&P 600 index. Within the universe of small-cap stocks, there is a subset of even smaller stocks referred to as **micro-cap stocks**, which are shares of companies valued by the market at around $250 million or less. These stocks can be found in the Wilshire micro-cap index.

In between large and small stocks there is another classification, called **mid-cap stocks**, examples of which are found in the S&P 400 mid-cap index. While this is a meaningful category of equities to consider—since mid caps offer some of the safety and stability of large caps but also some of the growth potential of small stocks—financial planners generally recommend that investors start off by diversifying first between large and small, to obtain some balance in one's overall portfolio. This is because large stocks and small stocks have historically acted so differently (Figure 5-5).

When you're investing in a small stock, you are making an entirely different wager than an investor purchasing a large blue-chip stock. **Small-cap stocks** are often shares of relatively young companies that are just getting started. Or

Year	Small Stocks	Large Stocks
2003	43.89%	27.49%
2002	−20.80%	−20.63%
2001	1.39%	−8.81%
2000	5.14%	1.40%
1999	36.44%	14.58%
1998	0.22%	17.77%
1997	22.71%	27.64%
1996	20.89%	20.82%
1995	30.48%	33.34%
1994	−1.42%	−0.84%

FIGURE 5-5 · Annual Returns: Small versus Large Stocks.*

*As measured by performance of large stock funds and small stock funds.

Source: Morningstar

these companies may have been around for some time, but for some reason the market has not come around to recognizing their full growth potential.

Either way, when you're investing in small companies, you're investing in **potential**. This means that your investment could potentially grow into something huge, or that potential could fizzle out. Ironically, both the risks and rewards are very large when it comes to small-cap stock investing. This would explain why a diversified basket of small stocks has actually outperformed blue chips over long periods of time. According to Ibbotson Associates, small stocks have gained 11.9 percent on average between 1926 and 2009, while large caps have returned 9.8 percent.

But the risks you face as a small-cap stock investor can be considerable. For starters, large stocks tend to be followed by dozens, if not hundreds, of Wall Street analysts who work for the major research and brokerage houses. Moreover, they are tracked closely by hundreds if not thousands of different money managers who either invest in these stocks or consider putting their money into them. This means that large stocks tend to be relatively well followed and that their financial situation is therefore relatively transparent. It would be difficult for a large stock to surprise investors with any unexpected news, since word of day-to-day developments flows through the analyst community.

Small stocks, on the other hand, may have only one or two analysts on Wall Street who really follow them on a day-to-day basis. And instead of thousands of money managers keeping tabs on them, it may be more like dozens. While small stocks must report their financial status to investors and federal regulators the same way that large stocks do, there are fewer professionals on Wall Street paying attention, so the potential for key bits of surprising news slipping through the cracks is higher.

There's a theory in stock investing, the **efficient market theory**, that says the stock market itself is ultimately rational and efficient. This theory states that one of the reasons why it's so difficult for professional managers to beat the major indexes is that stock prices fully reflect the sum total of all the relevant market information that exists to help price the stock. In other words, in this information age, anything you know about a stock, other investors are likely to know too. And that information is probably already priced into those shares.

Now, this is certainly true for large stocks. Because there is so much information and data floating around about them, they tend to be the most efficiently priced. But small stock investors would argue that because of the relative lack of Wall Street coverage, small caps are sometimes less efficiently priced than large caps, which means there are opportunities for small stock investors to outperform. Conversely, this also means there are greater opportunities for small stock investors to underperform, especially if they misinterpret information about these stocks.

There's another risk when it comes to small stocks. Some of them—in particular the micro caps—may be **illiquid** relative to bigger shares. **Liquidity** simply refers to the ease with which investors can buy and sell shares.

When you're buying or selling stocks, you require a partner—someone on the other side of the trade who is willing to buy the stocks you want to sell or to sell the stocks you want to buy. Unlike a mutual fund, where an investor can simply go to a fund company and ask to redeem their shares for cash, the stock market requires a matching up of buyers and sellers.

When dealing with large stocks, you're likely to find a bevy of individual or institutional investors who are willing to take your blue-chip shares off your hands at virtually any price. But when it comes to selling small stocks, the list of potential buyers may be significantly smaller, which means you may have difficulty selling shares of tiny companies quickly. Or more likely, for the smallest companies, you may have a hard time selling at a price you would like.

Small stocks, because of their faster growth potential but greater volatility, tend to do well when the economy is emerging from recessions and entering recoveries. (Figure 5-6 lists periods when small stocks outperformed large.) Meanwhile, large stocks tend to do well when the economy is already in expansion mode and also when there are signs of trouble. In times of heightened economic or geopolitical risks, investors often head for large-cap stocks in what's known as a classic "flight to quality."

The bottom line is, small stocks and large stocks take turns leading the market.

Years	Length in Years	Excess Annualized Returns*
1932–1937	4.8	16.0%
1940–1945	6.0	13.9%
1963–1968	6.0	10.8%
1975–1983	8.5	14.5%
1991–1994	3.3	11.3%
1999–2004	5.0	11.7%

FIGURE 5-6 · Periods of Small Stock Leadership.

* Reflects additional annualized total returns small stocks delivered over large stocks during these periods in time.

Source: Prudential Equity Group

Value Stocks versus Growth Stocks

Another big distinction among equities is between **value-oriented stocks** and **growth stocks**. As we discussed earlier, value-oriented investors are those who shop for investments based on price. Growth stock investors care more about the earnings and sales potential for the company down the road. Where a value investor might be willing to buy a broken-down company so long as its shares are priced cheaper than the company itself is worth, a growth investor only cares about performance. And growth investors are willing to pay for it.

A **growth company** is one whose earnings and sales growth exceed that of the overall market. Historically, the overall earnings growth rate for companies in the S&P 500 has been about 7 percent a year. So one would expect the annual earnings growth rate for a growth stock to exceed that. Indeed, the three-year average growth rate for growth stocks, according to Morningstar, was more than 16-percent a year at the start of 2010. Compare that to the 8-percent annual earnings growth rate for value stocks. Clearly, growth stocks are the best performers, in terms of profits and sales, in the equity universe (Figure 5-7).

But keep in mind that there is a big difference between **earnings performance** and **stock performance** in the short term. While there is in fact a longer-term correlation between overall earnings growth and stock price appreciation, in the short run there could be a huge disconnect. In fact, stocks will often times run-up in anticipation of future earnings improvement. So there are going to be many periods when value stocks outperform growth stocks, even though growth stocks may be outearning value stocks at a particular moment in time.

Consider the performance of growth and value stocks in the 10-year period of 1994 through 2003 (Figure 5-8). As you can see, they take turns leading the equity markets.

Type of Income	Value Stocks	Growth Stocks
1-year revenue	−1.4%	30.7%
1-year net income	29.7%	61.0%
1-year EPS	24.4%	51.6%
3-year revenue	2.3%	36.8%
3-year net income	7.4%	29.3%
3-year EPS	4.4%	21.1%

FIGURE 5-7 · Growth Characteristics: Value versus Growth Stocks.*

As this table indicates, value-oriented stocks exhibit slower growth rates when it comes to both earnings and revenues.

*As of March 31, 2004.

Source: Morningstar

This raises an interesting question: Why would anyone want to own a beaten down or overlooked company as opposed to one that's firing on all cylinders?

Again, it goes back to the price you're willing to pay for an asset, and at what stage of that growth you want to be a buyer.

Equity investing is all about anticipation. There's an old saying in the markets: "Buy on the rumor and sell on the news." Well, value investors buy in anticipation of a potential turnaround in a company and sell once the company gets its act together and starts to perform. In this sense, value investors are like contractors who are willing to buy dilapidated houses if the prices are right. They then step in, fix them, and sell them at far higher prices once the homes

Year	Value Stocks	Growth Stocks
2003	32.06%	34.66%
2002	−15.93%	−27.48%
2001	2.02%	−17.92%
2000	13.12%	−8.26%
1999	5.97%	51.29%
1998	7.74%	21.73%
1997	27.78%	22.64%
1996	20.51%	18.77%
1995	31.55%	33.06%
1994	−0.76%	−1.51%

FIGURE 5-8 · Annual Performance: Value versus Growth Stocks.

Source: Morningstar

are in good working condition. A growth investor, on the other hand, only wants stocks that are already in pristine condition.

This tells us a couple of things about value stocks and value investors: First, just as there is a continuum of sorts between small and large stocks—with small stocks eventually growing into large ones—value stocks, if successful, will eventually turn into growth stocks if management can turn things around.

This means value investors, like growth stock investors, enjoy capital appreciation based on earnings. The only difference is, value stock investors find earnings growth potential early and profit as the stock price appreciates in anticipation of that turn. Growth investors find growth stocks well after they've already shown signs of earnings performance—and as a result, they pay higher prices.

Going back to an earlier chapter, we discussed a couple of favorite ways that investors gauge the relative price of a stock. One is to judge its price based on the underlying company's earnings. This is called a stock's **P/E ratio**. The other is to consider a stock's price relative to the company's book value, which is referred to as a stock's **P/B ratio**. Consider how much cheaper value stocks can be, relative to growth, as shown in Figure 5-9.

Value investors tend to make money on this gap—buying something when it's down and out and getting out once the company is back on its feet. Value investors also tend to make money in a couple of different ways:

1. **On dividend income.** Value stocks, because they are down and out, often need to prove their worth to skeptical investors. One way they do that is by returning a greater portion of their profits back to shareholders in the form of dividend income. The average dividend yield of large growth stocks at the start of 2010 was 0.3 percent, while the average dividend yield of large-cap value stocks was 1.4 percent. (Large stocks, because they are established, also tend to pay out higher dividend yields than small stocks.) In contrast, the average dividend payout for growth stocks of all sizes was

	Large Value Stocks	Large Growth Stocks
Average price/earnings ratio	14.9	20.1
Average price/book ratio	1.8	2.8
Average price/sales ratio	1.0	1.6

FIGURE 5-9 · Valuations: Value versus Growth stocks.*

As this table indicates, growth stocks are far more expensive than value stocks when it comes to traditional valuation measures, such as price/earnings and price/book value ratios.

*As December 31, 2009.

Source: Morningstar

a paltry 0.2 percent. The **payout ratio** for value stocks—the percentage of profits that gets returned to shareholders—is about 50 percent. For growth stocks, it's barely around 10 percent, since growth companies tend to want to reinvest profits back into the firm to fund expansion.

2. ***During troubled markets.*** Typically, when the markets or economy are wobbly, investors naturally gravitate to value stocks. You saw that in the period between 2000 and 2009, when the economy suffered not one but two bear markets and two major recessions—the first stemming from the bursting of the technology stock bubble in 2000 as well as the 9/11 terrorist attacks on the United States, and the second stemming from the global financial contagion in 2007 and 2008. During this uncertain stretch, value stocks actually made investors money, to the tune of 1.2 percent a year, while growth stocks lost nearly 4 percent of their value annually throughout the decade. This represented a major change in fortune, as growth stocks trounced value stocks throughout the decade of the 1990s, when the U.S. economy experienced one of its strongest expansionary periods in recent memory.

   That said, value isn't always the safer play, even in troubled economic times. Investors who held a large portion of their portfolios in the financial sector during the global credit crisis of 2008 witnessed this firsthand, as shares of many banks, brokerages, and insurance companies that got caught up in the mortgage meltdown lost more than half their value in that panic. The fact that these stocks paid generous dividends was not enough, in that crisis, to prevent investors from fleeing. Still in general, investors often gravitate toward value in uncertain times.

   One reason value does better in such times is because value stocks pay dividends—and investors like to be paid to wait out a market storm. But in addition, it's because investors regard value stocks as having already been beaten down or overlooked. If times should get bad, then these stocks, in theory, would have less room to fall than high-flying growth stocks. After all, they tend to trade at deep discounts to growth stocks on a P/E and P/B and even price-to-sales ratio basis. Value stocks tend to do particularly well, relative to growth, when the so-called **equity risk premium**—the extra returns that investors demand from stocks during periods of high economic, geopolitical, or market risks—is high.

Figure 5-10 lists the traditional value and growth sectors of the economy.

Still Confused?

In the spectrum of investments, value stocks are thought to be the conservative investor's choice, because these stocks tend to be cheap, they're already beaten

Classic Value Sectors	Percentage of S&P 500*
Financial services	16.4%
Consumer staples	11.5%
Energy	10.8%
Industrials	10.6%
Utilities	3.6%
Materials	3.4%
Total	*56.0%*
Classic Growth Sectors	**Percentage of S&P 500***
Technology	18.8%
Health care	11.7%
Consumer cyclicals	10.5%
Telecommunications	2.9%
Total	*44.0%*

FIGURE 5-10 · Traditional Growth and Value Sectors of the Economy.

*Reflects sector weightings in the S&P 500 as of May 2010.

Source: Standard & Poor's

down (so they have less room to fall), and they pay generous dividends to keep investors patient. While you won't double your money quickly in these shares, you will reduce your odds of losing money. Growth stocks, meanwhile, are considered a more aggressive choice, because they're often pricey and pay little in the way of dividends. In other words, they operate without a safety net.

Domestic Stocks versus Foreign Stocks

The final major distinction in the equity markets is between domestic and foreign stocks. The fact is, U.S. stock-exchange-listed companies account for less than half of the total market capitalization of the world's equities. Some of the leading companies in the world aren't based in the United States, though their products and services are probably familiar to most American consumers and investors. They include such names as Sony, Nokia, Novartis, Toyota, Glaxo-SmithKline, Honda, Deutsche Telekom, HSBC, and the list goes on and on.

This means that by sticking only with U.S. stocks, you are potentially turning your back on half the opportunities that may present themselves to you as an investor. And the fact is, foreign and domestic stocks have historically taken turns outperforming one another, as can be seen in Figure 5-11. And in fact, had you turned your back on foreign stocks in the 2000s, you would have left a tremendous amount of gains on the table. True, over the past decade, the average foreign stock based in the developed economies of Western Europe and Japan also lost ground, just as the S&P 500 index of U.S. stocks did. But foreign stocks based in emerging economies like China and India soared more than 7 percent a year for the decade ending December 31, 2009. In other words, if you invested $10,000 solely in U.S. stocks over the past decade, you would be left with around $9,090 today. But had you invested that money overseas in emerging markets, it would have doubled to more than $20,000 over the past 10 years.

When investing in foreign stocks, however, there are a couple of things to keep in mind. First, because of the increasing globalization of the world's economies, there is greater correlation between movements in the U.S. market and movements in stock markets abroad, like in Europe and Asia. This would make sense. Consider the amount of business that U.S.-based multinationals engage in abroad these days: Procter & Gamble and Coca-Cola both generate more than half their sales abroad; Citigroup operates in more than 100 countries; and even Wal-Mart has around a third of its stores positioned outside the United States.

This means that if you're investing abroad purely for diversification, you should make sure that the foreign companies you invest in don't rely too heavily on the U.S. markets. If they did, you would essentially be sitting on a portfolio of companies that generally do business in the same markets.

The good news is, any time you invest abroad, you're exposing yourself to another form of diversification: currency diversification. As an American, whenever you invest overseas—whether on your own or through a fund—you go

Year	U.S. Market	All Foreign Markets	Developed Markets	Emerging Markets
2003	31.58%	39.22%	37.61%	55.27%
2002	−20.51%	−12.75%	−13.48%	−5.58%
2001	−9.52%	−15.55%	−16.89%	−2.94%
2000	1.73%	−14.45%	−12.92%	−28.76%
1999	27.35%	48.70%	46.35%	72.02%
1998	15.31%	7.18%	10.82%	−25.70%
1997	23.81%	4.53%	5.13%	−1.54%
1996	19.13%	15.15%	15.20%	14.52%
1995	31.19%	11.20%	12.32%	−2.25%
1994	−1.36%	−2.63%	−2.43%	−6.53%

FIGURE 5-11 · Annual Performance: U.S. versus Foreign Stocks.

Source: Morningstar

through the process of converting dollars into a foreign currency in order to buy those international shares. Similarly, whenever you sell a foreign investment, you'll eventually have to sell the foreign currency in which those shares are denominated to repatriate that money into U.S. dollars to capture the gain.

As it turns out, foreign currency fluctuation can either add to or subtract from your portfolio's performance. That's because if the dollar is falling in value against foreign currencies, it serves as a tailwind for American investors abroad. You could actually make money on the currency exchange even if the underlying foreign shares you buy don't budge. This took place throughout the 2000s, as the dollar gradually weakened, especially against the euro, making overseas bets even more rewarding.

Conversely, if the dollar gains in value between the time you buy a foreign stock and sell, that's a headwind for your portfolio. You could actually take a loss on the currency exchange even if the stock in question breaks even. This phenomenon took place throughout much of the 1990s, when the dollar strengthened as the U.S. economy improved relative to its peers. Not surprisingly, foreign investing back then was extremely unpopular, as most Americans put more than 90 cents of every dollar in their stock portfolios into U.S. equities.

While you may be similarly inclined to pull back on foreign stocks in times of dollar strength, you should think twice. Because it is next to impossible to predict which currencies will be in vogue, for how long, and when, it often makes sense to invest in foreign stocks to diversify the currency through which you invest.

The universe of foreign stocks can be broken out into two categories: **developed market** and **emerging market stocks**.

Developed Market Stocks

Developed market stocks tend to be companies domiciled in leading industrial nations, such as Germany, the United Kingdom, Japan, France, or Italy. As a result, these companies—which can range in size from small-cap to mid-cap to large-cap—fall under the auspices of major stock indexes in these developed nations. This means they are better regulated and more closely followed by professional investors than other foreign stocks. This is particularly true for large-cap foreign stocks in developed countries. Developed market stocks also tend to be more efficiently priced than their emerging markets counterparts, as a result of their coverage.

Even though developed market stocks are often assumed to be safer bets than their counterparts in the emerging markets, don't always assume that that's the case. There are plenty of established, large companies based in developing economies like South Korea or Brazil that are far more stable investments than small companies based in developed markets like Italy and Spain.

And just because the developed economies are older and more mature, it doesn't mean that they are inherently safer markets in which to invest. Consider the fiscal budget and debt crises that plagued Western European nations such as Greece, Portugal, and Spain, in early 2010 and that sent stock prices in those nations reeling.

Emerging Market Stocks

Emerging market stocks, on the other hand, are companies—both large and small—headquartered in countries whose economies are relatively young and therefore are undeveloped, erratic, but growing. Examples of emerging markets countries include Brazil, Malaysia, Mexico, Singapore, South Africa, and Taiwan. But emerging markets also can include what many would regard to be relatively powerful economies, such as China and South Korea. And within those countries, there are some companies that are technically classified as emerging markets stocks that are just as influential as companies in the developed markets. They include Samsung and Hyundai of South Korea, and PetroChina and China Mobile, which are based in mainland China and Hong Kong.

Obviously, there are additional risks one takes by investing in emerging markets stocks. One is the potential **political risk** of instability, or even, in some cases, revolution, in the countries where these companies are based. Such events can have a dramatic impact on how companies are regulated and whether firms are allowed to continue with their growth strategies. A sudden change in leadership can not only impact mundane matters—such as the tax structure the country imposes on its corporations—it can also affect larger questions, such as the degree to which private enterprise is allowed to operate unfettered.

Political risk often also leads to a bevy of economic risks in un- or underdeveloped nations. For instance, in the event of political instability, how will the local stock and bond markets react? Another big question, stemming from political instability, is whether the currency market will be dramatically impacted. Even a modest change in the value of local currency can have huge impacts on a locally based company's ability to import raw materials and export their goods.

Investors will recall that in the late 1990s, currency troubles in several Asian countries led to stock market declines throughout the emerging markets in the Pacific Rim. This was dubbed the "Asian currency crisis" or the "Asian flu." Currency instability also threatened the Russian markets in the late 1990s and in fact forced the Russian government to default on some of its debt.

Still Confused?

The term **emerging market** has nothing to do with the size or age of a company. Rather, this term refers to the stage of development of the nation in which a company is based. Similarly, a "developed market" stock could represent an investment in a start-up company or a mature firm—the term **developed** refers to the maturity of the economy in which that company is domiciled.

Access to Foreign Markets

Obviously, it will be difficult for individual investors—particularly investors with small account balances—to go abroad and invest directly in these shares on foreign exchanges. This is particularly true for investors interested in dabbling in the emerging markets. (And by the way, you should probably only dabble in these stocks—financial planners will often suggest limiting your emerging markets exposure to 10 percent or less of your overall equity allocation, due to their higher risks.)

But you can gain exposure to foreign stocks through an international stock mutual fund or ETF, which is a professionally managed portfolio that will give you access to hundreds of different stocks from dozens of different countries. There are also emerging markets stock funds that allow investors to gain access to companies in undeveloped countries in a relative safe way. (By investing in a diversified emerging markets portfolio, you can spread out stock-specific and political risks over a collection of hundreds of different investments, rather than putting all of your eggs in one or two risky baskets.)

Investors can also invest directly in foreign companies, particularly stocks in developed markets, through what's known as an **American Depositary Receipt**, or **ADR**. An ADR is a proxy of sorts that represents shares of a foreign company. The actual shares of that foreign stock are held by a bank in the United States, while the ADR itself, or the receipt of those shares, trades on the major U.S. stock exchanges, like the NYSE or the Nasdaq. Shares of the ADR, then, can be bought or sold by the investing public through basic brokerage accounts here in the United States as if the investment was normal common stock. Like common stock, these ADRs give the investor the requisite rights to the investment's dividends and capital appreciation for a full total return.

What You Need to Know Before Getting Started

Returns are Tied to Earnings

At the end of the day, as a stock investor, you are a part owner of the company whose shares you purchase. And like any owner of any small or large business, your reward comes in the form of profits.

As a stock investor, you won't receive all of your share of the company's profits. You may receive some in the form of dividend income. But often, companies reinvest a good portion of their profits back into the business, to expand. Even though you may not enjoy this money, corporate earnings are a proxy that other investors will use to value the price of your shares.

So it's not surprising, then, that long-term equity returns tend to mirror long-term corporate earnings growth. Over long, long stretches of time, companies in the S&P 500 have grown their earnings around 7 percent a year, on average. That happens to be in line with historic price appreciation for stocks. Throw in the long-term dividend yield of the S&P 500 of around 3 percent, and that brings a total return of 10 percent a year.

In the late 1990s, during the Internet bubble, many investors lost sight of the relationship between equity returns and corporate profits. Many stocks with absolutely no profits to speak of were being bid up to astronomical levels. Yet investors who stayed the course by concentrating only on profitable companies with consistent earnings growth rates wound up doing quite well in the long run, the bear market notwithstanding.

The Riskier the Investment, the Bigger the Reward

This is perhaps the most fundamental rule in all of investing. The less risk you expose your money to, the less incentive there is to compensate you for being an investor. The more risk you face, the bigger the carrot has to be to get you in the risky end of the investing pool.

Historic stock market returns would seem to bear this out. Over the past century, stocks, which are riskier than bonds, have outperformed fixed-income securities, which promise to return your principal to you at a certain date. And within the realm of equities, riskier ones have produced far better returns than less risky ones.

According to Ibbotson Associates, **small-capitalization stocks**—shares of small or young companies that are often more volatile than blue-chip firms—have returned 11.9 percent, on average, between 1926 and 2009. Compare that to the 9.8 percent returns of large-capitalization stocks.

The Riskier the Investment, the Riskier the Investment

Now, just because more risk delivers the promise of potentially greater returns does not mean that more risk *guarantees* bigger returns. This is a huge point.

Before the Lost Decade, many investors incorrectly assumed that the more risk they took, the greater their rewards would have to be. This drove investors to make big bets on technology stocks in the late 1990s, and on emerging market shares in 2008. While it's true that over extremely long periods of time—say, 20 or 30 or 40 years—more risk will deliver greater returns on average, it's never guaranteed that the timing will work out for every investor.

For example, say you invested successfully for 30 years and were preparing to retire in 2008, just before the global financial crisis struck. And let's assume that you were heavily invested in risky assets, including emerging market stocks, as you headed into that year. While such a strategy may have served you well for decades, your emerging market shares lost more than 54 percent of their value in 2008, just when you needed to preserve your capital. That's the nature of risk. While investors in the aggregate can try to reduce risk on average by investing over long periods of time, an individual investor can never be assured that he or she has entirely wrung out the risk of losing money at the worst possible time.

The Different Ways to Buy Stock

Most investors will buy and sell stocks through traditional brokerage accounts such as those found at places like Merrill Lynch, Morgan Stanley, Edward Jones, Charles Schwab, E*TRADE, etc. But there are other ways in which investors can transact stock investments.

For starters, there are new-fangled brokerages that allow investors—in particular, those with small balances—to buy **fractional shares** of a stock. So, for instance, if you're trying to build a portfolio of 100 different stocks but don't have the resources to purchase 100 shares of 100 different companies, some brokerages will allow you to buy a fraction of a share of each stock, to instantly diversify your holdings. These brokerages will also make it easier for individual investors to manage a basket of stocks altogether. Examples of such new-fangled services are Sharebuilder (www.sharebuilder.com) and FolioFn (www.foliofn.com).

There is a way for individuals to invest in stocks *without* having a brokerage account. That's by enrolling in so-called **dividend reinvestment plans**, or **DRIPs**, as they are known. A DRIP allows an investor to purchase stock *directly* from the publicly traded company itself. Corporations offer these programs in an effort to build loyalty among existing shareholders. All you need is to own one share of a company's stock to get started.

The idea of a DRIP is to allow investors to reinvest their dividend income in more shares of the company stock on a routine and automated basis, so shareholders who receive dividends can take advantage of this service. But the good news is, once in a DRIP, many companies will allow you to purchase additional shares of the stock—over and above what you reinvest through dividend income—directly from the company. And the best news of all is, many DRIP programs allow investors to do this with little or no fees.

The Different Types of Orders

When placing an order to purchase or sell stock, most investors rely on **market orders**. This is a type of order that asks your broker to execute the transaction as soon as possible, at the best possible price. For sellers, that means the highest market available price. For buyers, it means the lowest. This is by far the most convenient type of order to place, since you can be assured that your buy or sell order will be transacted immediately, so long as it is for a relatively liquid stock.

But there are other types of orders to consider, as well. For example, there is a **limit order**, where you can set the price—sort of the way you can buy airplane tickets and hotel rooms on Internet services like Priceline.com. For example, if you wanted to buy shares of Company X at $25 a share but the stock was currently trading at $30, you could put a limit order on the stock that would direct your broker to purchase shares once they fell to $25. This allows the investor to be disciplined about the prices they pay for stocks, while also allowing them to place the order in advance without having to babysit the stock for days.

Now, the one problem with these types of orders is that the stock may not fall to $25. In some cases the stock will just keep going higher, and the order won't be executed. In other situations the stock may fall so fast that it skips the $25 price mark and goes straight from $30 to $20. In this situation, you have to be sure that your limit order requests the transaction to be executed at $25 *or cheaper* for the buy order to go through. Another thing to be aware of: Many brokers will charge a slightly higher commission for limit orders versus market orders.

Within the realm of limit orders, there are special types that set a timetable for order executions to take place. A **day order** tells your broker to buy or sell a stock at a specific price. But if, for whatever reason, the stock in question does not hit that price on that trading day, then the order is automatically canceled. There are **good-this month orders**, which function similar to day orders, except they don't expire until the end of the last trading day of the month. There are also **good through orders**, which allow the investor to assign a specific date at which the limit order will expire. And finally, there are **good-till-canceled orders**, which allow the investor to keep open the limit order for an unlimited amount of time until the stock hits the price in question and the transaction is executed.

There is also another type of order for shareholders to consider, which comes in handy when trying to minimize losses: **stop-loss orders**. In a stop loss order, an investor can literally set a floor for his or her stocks. For example, say you own shares of Company A, which you bought for $15 a piece. But since that time, the stock has fallen to $10 a share. You're willing to hang on at this price, but you determine that if the stock should fall to $5, you want out. You can set a stop-loss order that directs your broker to sell at $5, even if you're on vacation.

Stop-loss orders aren't just good for minimizing losses. You can use them to preserve gains as well. Say you bought shares of Company XYZ for $50 a share, and since that time they've risen to $75. If you want to continue to own this stock but to lock in gains should the stock start to fall back, you can set a stop-loss at, say, $55. This will direct your broker to execute a sell at that price to preserve your gains. If the stock doesn't fall that far, you will keep owning it at ever-higher prices.

Different Prices for Stocks

Before you begin trading, it's important to understand a few things about a stock's price. While we typically refer to a stock as having a single price—which is quoted in stock tables published in newspapers and Web sites throughout the country—there are actually a couple of different prices associated with a stock. At any given moment there is a bid price and an ask price for the same shares.

The **bid price** is the price that a *buyer* states that he or she is willing to pay an existing shareholder for their stock. The **ask price**, on the other hand, is the price that current shareholders state that they are willing to sell their shares for. So, for instance, when you go to a financial Web site and look up a company's stock price, you might see something like the variations in Figure 5-12.

You'll notice that the last transaction for this hypothetical stock was made at a price of $30.03. But the current bid price for the stock is $30.15 a share. This means that investors are offering $30.15 to buy shares of the computer maker's stock. Meanwhile, there are existing shareholders out there willing to sell their shares for $30.04, the ask price.

Now to some, this doesn't seem to make sense: Why would an investor be willing to buy a stock for $30.15 when someone out there is willing to sell shares for a much cheaper price? The answer requires some basic knowledge of the way stock trading works.

In the stock market, buyers must match up with sellers. But often there's a middleman known as a **market maker** who stands in between the two of you, in order to facilitate trading and liquidity. These market makers are institutions whose job it is, when there is an imbalance of buyers and sellers in the marketplace, to step in and buy the shares no one wants or sell the shares

Computer Co.: X		
LAST PRICE	$30.03	CHANGE–$0.11
OPEN	$ 3.27	
HIGH	$30.50	
LOW	$30.03	
BID	$30.15	
ASK	$30.04	

FIGURE 5-12 · Stock Quote.

everyone wants. Without these players, the stock market could not operate efficiently, since people might not be able to enter or exit the equity markets with ease (this explains why the stock market is far more liquid than the real estate market, where a buyer might have to wait months for a seller to be located).

The term "market maker" typically refers to those institutions that play this role on the Nasdaq national market, which is run by the **National Association of Securities Dealers**, or **NASD**. On the New York Stock Exchange, this market-making function is carried out by people referred to as **specialists**. Different companies stake out roles as market makers or specialists in different stocks or industries.

In the example in Figure 5-12, the ask price is $30.04. This means someone out there wants to sell his or her shares for that price. It also means that market makers could step in and buy that stock for $30.04. Since the bid price is $30.15, that same market maker can turn around and sell the stock just purchased for $30.04 to a new buyer for $30.15. The difference between the bid and the ask price is known as the **bid-ask spread**, which the market maker gets to pocket. When you make a stock transaction, this spread is considered a hidden cost, which you pay in addition to the stock commission you are assessed.

Other prices to note include the **closing price**, which was the last price the stock traded for in the prior day's session; the **open price**, which is the price the stock started trading at during the current trading session; the **high price**, which simply refers to the highest trading price of the day; and the **low price**, or the lowest price at which a transaction was made during that day's session. Finally, another key price to consider is the **52-week range** of prices, which should give investors some context for the confidence—or lack of confidence—that investors have shown a stock in recent months.

Final Thoughts

As you can see, the equity markets present investors with enormous opportunities. But the greater the opportunities, the larger the risks. We've outlined several of those concerns in this chapter, ranging from market risks to stock-specific risks to inflation risk.

It's important to recognize all of these challenges that face you as an equity investor. At the same time, the stock market offers investors an enormous number of choices. Should you go with large stocks or small stocks? Value-oriented stocks or growth stocks? Foreign stocks or domestic stocks? The answer is: You probably want a mix of these types of equities. We'll get into greater detail on selecting stocks later, in Part Three.

QUIZ

1. Since 1926, stocks have returned nearly twice as much a year as government bonds. This means that over long periods of time, you will earn nearly twice as much in stocks as in bonds.
   A. True
   B. False

2. Which of the following is not a way to reduce market risks in owning stocks?
   A. Invest in a multitude of stocks.
   B. Invest in a multitude of assets.
   C. Invest with a multitude of different brokers.
   D. Invest in a multitude of different times.

3. The simplest way to reduce stock-specific risk is to . . .
   A. Own at least a dozen stocks.
   B. Invest in a diversified fund that owns hundreds of different stocks.
   C. Hold onto a stock for more than 30 years.
   D. Avoid investing in stocks.

4. In order, which assets have the best track record of outpacing inflation?
   A. Stocks, bonds, and cash
   B. Stocks, cash, and bonds
   C. Bonds, stocks, and cash
   D. Bonds, cash, and stocks
   E. Cash, bonds, and stocks

5. Over long periods of time, small stocks tend to outpace large stocks.
   A. True
   B. False

6. In general, small stocks tend to be riskier than large stocks.
   A. True
   B. False

7. A growth investor is one who seeks out . . .
   A. Companies that have the potential to grow faster than the market.
   B. Companies that are already growing faster than the market.
   C. Companies that may not be growing as fast as the market but that are priced attractively.

8. Growth stocks are considered a safer bet than value because . . .
   A. They offer greater dividend payouts.
   B. They throw off less dividend income.

C. They enjoy higher P/E ratios than value stocks.

D. Growth stocks aren't considered a safer bet than value stocks.

9. **The added benefit of investing in foreign stocks is that . . .**

A. They offer currency diversification.

B. They trade at lower P/E ratios than domestic stocks.

C. They throw off greater dividends than U.S. stocks.

D. There is no added benefit of investing in foreign stocks.

10. **The best way to control the exact price you want to buy a stock at is to . . .**

A. Place a market order.

B. Place a limit order.

C. Rely on the bid-ask spread.

chapter 6

Demystifying Bonds

CHAPTER OBJECTIVES

In this chapter, you will learn the following:

- Why bonds are a core part of a long-term portfolio
- The nature of bond market returns
- The nature of bond market risks
- How to minimize those risks
- Different fixed-income securities to consider

Why Invest in Bonds?

We just spent the previous chapter outlining why stocks, over the span of decades, tend to be the best asset class for long-term investors seeking to maximize their returns despite the Lost Decade. At the very least, equities are one of the few assets that can consistently and significantly outpace the long-term ravages of inflation. So why does a long-term investor—especially a young one with a time horizon of potentially two decades or more—even need to consider fixed-income securities for his or her portfolio?

The answer is simple. As the last decade has taught investors, even though equities are expected to perform better than bonds over time, there will be years and yes, even decades, when bonds will outperform equities on a total return basis. Moreover, it's important to remember that long-term gains are not the only measure of investing success. If the last decade demonstrated anything, it's that decades of success in the markets can unravel rather quickly based on as little as one bear market, especially if such downturns take place just when you need to rely on your investments to live on.

What's more, even though we all consider ourselves long-term investors—because a big reason why many of us invest in the first place is to secure our retirements—that doesn't preclude us from having other goals that may be shorter term in nature.

Consider the 60-something who is not only investing for retirement income a decade from now but also saving for a dream vacation in two years. Think about the 40-something who isn't just preparing for his or her own retirement in 20 years but also the kid's college bills seven years from now. Or the 30-something who can't even fathom retirement since it's so far down the road but is thinking of saving to get married and to buy a first home five years into the future.

Even 20-somethings, who just entered the workforce, may need to put some of their money in a more reliable and stable asset class like bonds, if only to safeguard a portion of their overall assets—the portion they'll need to fund immediate goals. Who knows—that 20-something may be thinking of going back to school to earn a master's or law degree in two or three years. If that's the case, putting 100 percent of one's money in equities would seem to be risky, since money might well be needed to fully fund short- and intermediate-term needs. You'll recall that over one-year periods of time, the odds of losing money in stocks is greater than one in four. Over three-year periods, it's about one in seven. You have to ask yourself: Am I willing to bet my college money or my house money on those odds?

For these situations—and many others—the certainties and assurances that bonds can provide make them attractive alternatives to riskier stocks.

Let's remember what a **bond** is: a loan that you provide to a government entity or corporation. This IOU, like any loan you've secured as a borrower, comes with contractual obligations that are clearly outlined for both parties. That contract—which is the bond itself—specifically states what annual interest rate you are to expect as compensation for the loan, how long the loan will last, and the exact date upon which you will receive your original loan principal back in full.

Unlike stocks, where the investor is part owner of the business, the relationship you enter into as a bond investor is at arm's length. Often, a bond investor couldn't care less if the corporation whose debt he or she purchases winds up being the next Microsoft or just some other successful medium-sized company. As a lender, what you care most about is if the company is strong enough to fulfill the terms of the loan contract. Will it be able to pay you the interest rate it promised? Will it be successful enough over the life of the loan to return your principal investment when the bond matures?

To the extent that a bond investor wants to be assured of both of these facts, he or she will want to do some homework, just like a stock investor.

Like equity investors, bond investors have to consider the financial strengths and weaknesses of the underlying debtor, and, if dealing with corporate bonds, the industry the firm is in. And depending on the maturity of the bond, a prospective investor will probably also want to investigate the long-term business strategy of that firm. After all, if you're thinking about buying a long-term loan that matures in 15 years, it would be prudent to analyze the odds that the company will survive for all 15 years.

Having said that, the threshold for success for a bond investor is generally much lower than the bar set for equity investors. This is because for most bond investors, the biggest concern is: Will my loan contract be honored? (To be fair, sophisticated and professional bond traders will also care about the business prospects for the underlying company, which we will get into at greater length shortly.) Stock investors, because they are owners and because they are interested in the long-term profitability of the company—not just its survival—have to be worried about a lot more than that.

The good news for bond investors is, once they undertake this basic research, the odds are substantially greater of finding some degree of capital preservation in the fixed-income market than in equities.

Bonds for Ballast

Many investors, in particular retirement investors, tend to fixate on the interest rates that bonds are paying out. This is understandable. For many retirees, these payouts determine the lifestyle they can lead in retirement. But bonds are so much more than income generators.

Indeed, one of the biggest reasons for all investors to consider having at least some portion of their money in bonds is the ballast they provide for an overall portfolio. During periods of market volatility and out-and-out downturns, bonds are often useful as a safety net to keep an overall diversified portfolio from falling too far. This was particularly evident in the bear market of 2000, when many portfolios that were heavily weighted toward equities, and growth-oriented equities in particular, were battered. Meanwhile, well-diversified portfolios that had core weightings toward bonds—which means anywhere from 20 to 50 percent—held up surprisingly well. Consider the

| Asset Allocation | Performance between March 31, 2000, and Sept. 30, 2002 | |
	Total Return	Growth of $100,000
100% Nasdaq stocks	−74.4%	$ 25,600
100% S&P 500 stocks	−43.8%	$ 56,240
60% stocks / 30% bonds / 10% cash	−20.8%	$ 79,165
47% stocks / 37% bonds / 16% cash	−12.9%	$ 87,136
25% stocks / 40% bonds / 35% cash	+ 2.8%	$102,838

FIGURE 6-1 · Performance of Various Portfolios in 2000 Bear Market.

Source: T. Rowe Price

performance of several hypothetical portfolios during that downturn, as shown in Figure 6-1.

As you can see, those who put all of their assets in stocks lost more than 40 percent of their wealth during this bear market stretch. And those who invested in the riskiest types of stocks—technology shares that make up a big portion of the Nasdaq composite index—lost even more: three-quarters of their money. A $100,000 portfolio in Nasdaq stocks shrank to a little more than $25,000 in about two and half years.

But investors who socked away at least 30 percent of their money in bonds during this stretch—while holding the majority or the remainder in equities— ended up losing only around a fifth of their money during the worst bear market since the Great Depression. And those who put 40 percent of their money in bonds and only 25 percent in stocks—with the remainder socked away in cash—actually ended up making money during this bloody period in the equity markets.

This brings up a good point: Bonds can be an opportunistic play for investors when stocks are being beaten down by the markets.

Bonds for Diversification

One reason why bonds provide ballast to a portfolio is that bonds and stocks are constantly in competition for investors' dollars.

For instance, when bond yields tend to be low by historic standards, investors will often look to shift money into equities in hopes of earning better relative returns. In times when Treasuries are yielding, say, 3 percent, while high-quality blue-chip stocks are paying out dividend yields of about 3 percent, some might decide to take a chance on the equity markets, given the competitive payouts.

Conversely, when equities look wobbly, investors are going to look for a place to hide from stock market volatility. And the classic place to seek shelter from stock losses is often in the bond market.

This dynamic means that bond returns tend to zig when stock returns zag—and vice versa (Figure 6-2). So from a diversification standpoint, bonds are a great way to pick up some gains when stocks are languishing. While many investors think that the only way bonds help a stock portfolio during a bear market is that they lose less money than equities, the fact is, when stocks fall, bonds often provide healthy positive returns as cash flows into the fixed-income market.

Years	Stock Returns*	Bond Returns[†]
1929	− 8.4%	+ 3.4%
1930	−24.9%	+ 4.7%
1931	−43.3%	− 5.3%
1932	− 8.2%	+16.8%
1933	+54.0%	− 0.1%
1934	− 1.4%	+10.0%
1935	+47.7%	+ 5.0%
1936	+33.9%	+ 7.5%
1939	− 0.4%	+ 5.9%
1940	− 9.8%	+ 6.1%
1941	−11.6%	+ 0.9%
1942	+20.3%	+ 3.2%
1943	+25.9%	+ 2.1%
1944	+19.8%	+ 2.8%
1945	+36.4%	+10.7%
1995	+37.5%	+30.1%
1996	+22.9%	− 1.3%
1997	+33.2%	+13.9%
1998	+28.6%	+13.1%
1999	+21.1%	− 8.7%
2000	− 9.1%	+19.7%
2001	−12.0%	+ 4.3%
2002	−22.2%	+16.7%

FIGURE 6-2 · Stocks and Bonds: Taking Turns.

*Stock returns prior to 1995 reflect performance of S&P 500. After 1995, they reflect the total returns of the Vanguard 500 fund that tracks the S&P 500.

[†]Bond returns prior to 1995 reflect performance of long-term Treasury bonds. After 1995, they reflect the total returns of the Vanguard Long-Term Treasury Bond fund.

Source: Edward Jones, Morningstar

As you can see in the above comparison, there have been periods when bonds produced stocklike returns. The classic illustration is the three consecutive years, starting in 2000, when bonds were going gangbusters while stocks lost a tremendous amount of money. In 2000, long-term Treasuries posted total returns of nearly 20 percent—nearly four times their long-term historic average annual gain. In 2001, when stocks were down in the double digits, government bonds were up more than 4 percent. And in 2002, when stocks lost more than a fifth of their value, Treasuries advanced nearly 17 percent. In any given year, you'd be lucky to earn 17 percent in any asset class.

But this raises a question: How can you tell if stocks or bonds are going to lead the market? One way investors can judge the relative attractiveness of bonds vis-a-vis stocks is to consider the **earnings yield** of the equity market. This term refers to the amount of corporate earnings an investor is purchasing for every $1 he or she is buying in equities. The theory is, if investors believe that $1 will buy them more in earnings in stocks than in yield from bonds, then stocks look more attractive. But if bonds are yielding more income per $1 of investment than stocks are generating in profits, fixed-income securities start to look appealing.

It's very simple to calculate the stock market's earnings yield. You simply take the *inverse* of a stock market's price-to-earnings ratio. So, for example, if the companies in the S&P 500 are earning $50 per share and the index is trading at 1,000, its P/E would be 20. Let's go back to the formula to calculate P/E ratios to see how we came up with that:

$$P/E = \text{Price of security/Earnings per share}$$

$$P = 1{,}000$$

$$EPS = \$50$$

$$1{,}000/\$50 = 20$$

So, if the earnings yield is the inverse of the P/E formula, its formula would be:

Earnings yield = Earnings per share/Price of security

Now, in our example, we know that the earnings per share is $50. And the price of the security—in this case the S&P 500—is 1,000. So:

$$\text{Earnings per share (\$50)/Price(1,000)} = 5\%$$

$$\text{Earnings yield} = 5\%$$

What do we do with this information once we've calculated it? Well, many investors compare the earnings yield for stocks against bond yields—specifically, the yield on 10-year Treasury notes. In fact, this analysis is informally referred to as the **Fed Model** of securities analysis, since it is believed that former Federal

Reserve Board chairman Alan Greenspan relied on such a comparison to determine whether stocks were over- or undervalued at any given point.

If 10-year Treasury notes are yielding 5 percent while the S&P 500's earnings yield is also 5 percent, both markets are considered fairly valued and compete head-to-head. But if Treasuries are yielding *more* than the earnings yield of the stock market, then bonds would appear more attractive than stocks at the moment, since an investor could earn more per yield through bonds than he or she could in corporate profits in stocks. Conversely, when bond yields are lower—if 10-year Treasuries are yielding 4 percent, for instance, while the earnings yield for stocks is 5 percent—then equities may be a better bet. The higher the yield, the more attractive the investment would be.

Still Confused?

The easiest way to tell if bonds are cheap or expensive is to take their yield and compare it to the earnings yield of the stock market. To figure out the market's earnings yield, just divide its P/E ratio by 1. In early 2010, 10-year Treasuries were yielding 3.5 percent while the earnings yield for the S&P 500 was 5 percent. That meant stocks were actually a better bargain than bonds.

Bonds for Income

Obviously, not all investors care about the relative attractiveness of bonds when it comes to producing total returns. Some are more interested in the income that bonds can generate relative to other asset classes. And when it comes to income, there really isn't an alternative to bonds.

There are two concerns for all fixed-income investors: How do I make the numbers work, and how do I deal with inflation? (We'll get to inflation in a second.)

Making the numbers work refers to the fact that for investors to generate any reasonable amount of income to live off of, they would need to amass huge sums of money. For example, if bank certificates of deposit (CDs) are yielding 3 percent and you as an investor want to structure a portfolio of CDs that would provide you with an adequate stream of income to live off of in retirement, how much money do you think you would need: $100,000, $250,000, what about $500,000?

Well, 3 percent of $100,000 is $3,000. For most people, that's hardly enough to pay a month's worth of expenses—factoring in food, shelter, and other routine costs—let alone a year's worth. To achieve $30,000 annual income, which is still a modest sum, you'd have to bring $1 million to the table at that interest rate. (Figure 6-3 charts annual income based on various rates of interest.)

Assets	2%	3%	4%	5%	6%	7%	8%
$ 100,000	$ 2,000	$ 3,000	$ 4,000	$ 5,000	$ 6,000	$ 7,000	$ 8,000
$ 150,000	$ 3,000	$ 4,500	$ 6,000	$ 7,500	$ 9,000	$10,500	$12,000
$ 200,000	$ 4,000	$ 6,000	$ 8,000	$10,000	$12,000	$14,000	$16,000
$ 250,000	$ 5,000	$ 7,500	$10,000	$12,500	$15,000	$17,500	$20,000
$ 300,000	$ 6,000	$ 9,000	$12,000	$15,000	$18,000	$21,000	$24,000
$ 400,000	$ 8,000	$12,000	$16,000	$20,000	$24,000	$28,000	$32,000
$ 500,000	$10,000	$15,000	$20,000	$25,000	$30,000	$35,000	$40,000
$ 800,000	$16,000	$24,000	$32,000	$40,000	$48,000	$56,000	$64,000
$1,000,000	$20,000	$30,000	$40,000	$50,000	$60,000	$70,000	$80,000

FIGURE 6-3 · Annual Income Based on Various Rates of Interest.

Shy of coming up with $1 million in assets, this means you have to find higher yielding instruments. Historically, short-term T-bills, which are a proxy for cash, have generated yields of around 3 percent. Depending on market interest rates, bank savings, and checking accounts might yield anywhere from 1 to 3 percent. Bank CDs, depending on their maturity, may yield slightly more. Yet to achieve a reasonable amount of income—let's define that as $25,000 to $50,000 a year—you'd have to do better.

That's where bonds come in. Because bonds tend to yield more than cash instruments and pay out more than the average dividend yield of stocks, investors naturally look to the fixed-income market for a solution to their income needs.

Different types of bonds will yield more or less, based on the amount of interest-rate risk and credit risk they expose an investor to. Generally speaking, *the longer the maturity of a bond, the higher the interest rate it will pay out.* This is because longer-term bonds tie up an investor's money for lengthy periods of time, and there are always additional risks associated with locking down your assets for long periods of time. Companies with poor credit quality must also pay out higher yields on their bonds, since investors who buy their debt are taking a risk by doing business with such a company. Moreover, corporate bonds tend to have to pay out more than government bonds, since they aren't backed by the full faith and credit of Uncle Sam.

What You Need to Know About Bonds

There are certain terms and concepts that are critical for all bond investors to understand. This is particularly true because bonds, unlike stocks, are contractual relationships. And it's helpful to know all the terms of a contract before signing on the dotted line. Yet the problem is, the language associated with fixed-income instruments isn't as intuitive as the jargon of equity investing.

For example, we can all appreciate concepts such as price and earnings and market value when it comes to stocks. But bond terms can be downright confusing. To learn more about the basics of bonds you can go to the Web site of the **Bond Market Association, www.investinginbonds.com**. There, you will not only find tutorials on what bonds are and how they work, there is also an extensive glossary of bond-related terms. The www.investopedia.com can also come in handy if you're confused about what a certain fixed-income-related term means. We'll tackle a few of them below.

Par Value

Par value simply refers to the face value of each bond. Since bonds are typically sold in $1,000 increments, chances are the par value of your individual bond is going to be $1,000. One exception might be with municipal bonds, where par might be set at $5,000 per bond.

When you seek your principal back at maturity, this is the amount you will likely get back, per individual bond, at redemption. Par value is not to be confused, though, with your principal investment, though the two could be the same amount. If you purchased a **newly issued bond**—one that a corporation or government just auctioned off to raise money—you may very well have bought it for par value, in which case your principal investment and par value would be the same: $1,000 per bond.

But remember that bonds can also be bought and sold in the **secondary market**, just like stocks, where older bonds can get passed around to new investors. (The same thing happens with other loans; for instance, even though you as a consumer may initiate a loan with your local bank for a home mortgage or even student loans, there is a good chance that your bank may resell that debt to another lending institution if it thinks it can get better terms by selling the paper than by hanging on to it.) If you purchased an older bond at a premium to par value—say you bought it for $1,100—then your principal would be $1,100 but par would still be $1,000.

Maturity

Maturity refers to the date at which the bond issuer agrees to redeem the bondholder. This is also the date at which the loan contract itself—the bond—expires, so interest payments and other benefits would also end at this time. It's important to note, however, that some bonds may be *called* prior to maturity. Within the bond universe, some bonds are **callable** and others are **noncallable**. A **callable bond** simply gives the bond issuer the right, under certain circumstances, to end the life of the contract sooner than expected.

Typically, the period before a callable bond can be called back by the issuer is referred to as the **deferment period**, during which time the bondholder enjoys **call protection**. But after the deferment period ends, all bets are off. Some callable bonds come with **call premium**, which means in the event that a bond is redeemed prematurely, the bond issuer agrees to pay the bondholder a slight premium above par to compensate him or her for the trouble.

Price

Like stocks, bonds come with a price. And that price can fluctuate throughout the trading day, depending on the level of demand for the fixed-income security. But there are major differences in the way bond and stock prices are listed. Indeed, while stock prices are fairly self-explanatory—a share listed for $20.50 sells for twenty dollars and fifty cents—it's not so simple to figure out the price of a bond.

For example, all new bonds auctioned off by the issuer are sold at a preset price—**par value**. So if you were to purchase a new Treasury bond at auction, you would pay $1,000 per bond. If the price of that bond falls below $1,000 in the secondary market, it is said to be trading at a **discount**. If it fetches a price that is above par value due to strong demand for the debt, than it trades at a **premium**.

There is a quirk, however, in the way bond prices are listed in newspaper tables and Web sites. Instead of listing the price of a bond trading at par value as $1,000, its price will be quoted as "100." Bonds trading at a discount would be listed below 100—for instance, 99.75. Bonds trading at a premium would have prices above 100—for example, 101.25.

More important, bond prices, unlike stocks, are not in decimals, even though the prices as shown look as if they are. *Treasury bonds, for instance, are quoted not as fractions of 100ths, but rather as fractions of 32nds.* In other words, the price of a Treasury does not move in increments of pennies, but in increments of 1/32nds of a $1, or 2/32nds of a $1, etc.

So let's say you're considering investing in a two-year Treasury note whose price is listed as 105.11 (sometimes, you will see that same price listed with a colon, as in, 105:11). This does *not* mean that the bond is trading for $1,051.10, even though that would be the logical conclusion. Instead, it means the bond is trading for $1,053.44. How do we figure that? *We arrive at this by first dividing 11—the figure after the decimal or colon—by 32.* Eleven divided by 32 is 0.34375. This is interpreted in bond prices to mean $3.4375, which we can round up to $3.44. Now, we add that to $1,050 (which is how we interpret the 105 price before the decimal or colon) and get $1,053.44.

To confuse matters even further, *many corporate issues trade not in 32nds, but in increments of eighths.* This means prices can tick up or down in as small as 1/8th fractions. So if a corporate bond is listed at a price of 90⅝, it is trading for $906.25. How did we figure that? We arrived at this figure by first dividing 5 by 8, which is 0.625. Because bond par values are in $1000s instead of $100s, we move the decimal and interpret it as $6.25. We add that to $900 (which is how we read the 90 price listed before the 5/8), and we get $906.25.

As if that weren't confusing enough, like stocks, *bonds have two prices*: the bid and the ask. The **bid price**, again, is the price at which a bond buyer is willing to purchase a bond, while the **ask price** is the price at which an existing bondholder is willing to unload his or her fixed-income security.

The Coupon Rate

When a bond is issued, it comes with a *fixed rate of interest*, which is known as your **coupon interest rate**. They call it that because bonds literally used to come with certificates or coupons attached to them. When it was time to receive an interest payment on the bond, the bondholder would cut out this coupon and deliver it to the bond issuer in an effort to redeem the interest payment due. In today's electronic world, the coupon has gone away, but the term has stuck around.

The **coupon rate** represents your interest rate if you purchased the bond at par. If you bought a Treasury bond with a 5 percent coupon for par value, for instance, you would earn $50 a year in interest on that $1,000 bond, so your real interest rate and coupon rate would be 5 percent.

It's important to note that some bonds, by design, do not pay any interest along the way to compensate investors for the IOU. Instead, these **zero-coupon bonds**, which are priced at discounts to their face value, in effect pay the investor all of the money that would have accrued as interest over the life of the loan in a lump sum at maturity—in addition to the principal investment that the investor is due back. From the standpoint of the bond issuer, these are great vehicles, since they don't require periodic payments and therefore don't tie up much needed capital. So a cash-strapped corporation may prefer to issue zero-coupon bonds.

Who would want to buy a bond that pays no interest along the way? Some investors put money in bonds not because they want to earn annual income, but to preserve and grow a pot of money for a specific use at a specific date in the future. So, for example, parents who know that college bills are due for a child in eight years and are investing for that purpose may not need their bonds to throw off annual income. Instead, they may simply be interested in knowing that eight years from now they will get their principal returned to them plus a known amount of accrued interest.

Investors in zero-coupon bonds, however, should be warned of a couple of important things: First, even though zero-coupon bonds don't pay out annual income, the federal government will still make you pay taxes on the **imputed interest**—or what you would have earned every year in bond income if your zero-coupon bond was like a traditional bond and threw off annual payouts. Obviously, many investors do not like having to pay taxes today for a benefit that they won't enjoy until several years down the road, so be careful when purchasing zero-coupon bonds.

Moreover, another drawback with zero-coupon bonds is that their prices tend to be more volatile than traditional fixed-income securities. So if you buy a zero-coupon bond and do not plan to hold it to maturity, be forewarned of the price risk that you face in these issues.

Yield

The simple definition of **yield** is the interest you collect on an investment. But there are many different yields associated with every bond, depending on the purchase price and the number of years until maturity. For example, we just described a bond's **coupon yield**. That would be the amount of annual income you would earn on the bond, expressed in percentage terms, if you purchased it new at par value. But this does not mean the coupon rate is the interest rate that all investors would collect on that bond. This is because your yield—in real terms—will also depend on other factors.

For example, because bonds can be bought and sold after initial issue, there is also the **current yield** *to* consider. A bond's current yield can be determined with the following formula:

Annual interest generated by the bond/Current price = Current yield

The current yield of a bond will differ from its coupon yield if the bond is purchased at a discount or premium to par. Let's go back to our previous example of a newly issued Treasury bond with a coupon rate of 5 percent purchased at $1,000 and assume that after some time has passed, it gets sold to another investor at a premium of $1,100. While the coupon yield for this bond is 5 percent, its current yield—which is the real rate of interest that a new buyer would enjoy based on the purchase price—would be 4.5 percent:

Annual interest ($50)/Current price ($1,100) = 4.5 percent

Now let's assume that instead of buying this bond in the secondary market at a premium, you purchase it at a discount. Say you pay $850. Going back to our example, this bond still pays $50 a year in real interest per $1,000. But since you're buying it a steep discount, the formula works like this:

Annual interest ($50)/$850 (price) = 5.9 percent

As you can see, the real rate of interest you will enjoy from a bond is dependent not just on the stated coupon, but what price you pay for the underlying security.

There is another yield calculation that is often used among fixed-income investors: the **yield-to-maturity**, or **YTM**. The calculation of this yield is complicated. You're going to be better off simply asking your broker to supply this figure for you—which he or she will. The yield-to-maturity factors in not only the real payout rate of a bond based on its interest and price, but also its par value and the number of years left until the bond matures. Yield-to-maturity calculation can come in handy when assessing the true payout of a bond investment versus other investments that throw off income.

Bond Risks

Inflation Risk

There are three things that bond investors hate with a vengeance. One of them, as we discussed earlier, is inflation.

To reiterate, **inflation** is a naturally occurring economic phenomenon where, over time, prices on goods and services rise as an economy expands. But as prices rise, the purchasing power of your money falls. This means that even as you appear to be nearing the achievement of a financial goal, inflation is actually pushing in the opposite direction. This is particularly worrisome for bond investors, because *bond total returns historically have barely outpaced the rate of inflation*. Moreover, bond investors often have to tie up their money for lengthy periods of time. What good would it be to earn, say, 4 percent on a bond and to receive your principal back in full 10 years later only to realize that inflation has eaten away at more than 4 percent of your original investment?

Going back to the Ibbotson data we discussed in Chapter 6, we know that government bonds have returned around 5.4 percent a year for much of the past century. But inflation has run at around 3 percent a year during that same time. This means that on an after-inflation basis, bonds have only returned around 2.4 percent a year. At that rate of growth, it would take 30 years for your money to double in real value through fixed-income investments. In contrast, equity investments would only require about a decade to double your money, based on their historic rate of growth as well as the historic inflation rate. (The chart in Figure 6-4 compares the annual returns of stocks and bonds to inflation since 1926.)

This is why during times of high inflationary pressure, when investors, fearing rising prices, pull their money out of the fixed-income sector and head to the more attractive alternative, bonds tend to underperform stocks. This is

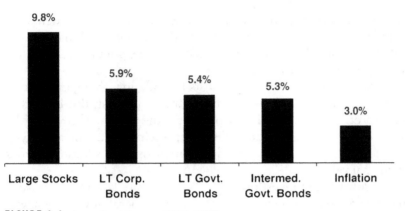

FIGURE 6-4 · Annualized Returns (1926–2009).

As this graph indicates, historically, stocks have done a far better job than bonds in outpacing the ravages of inflation.

Source: Ibbotson Associates

particularly true when inflation is running in the high single digits, or even the double digits—as they did in the early 1980s—since during those periods, bond investments could end up losing money in real terms even if they post positive total returns.

Managing Inflation Risk

There are a couple of ways bond investors can deal with inflation risk head-on. The first, obviously, is to search for higher-yielding bonds, since on an inflation-adjusted basis, higher yielding debt might produce greater returns in your portfolio. But the downside of this strategy is that you often have to expose yourself to greater credit risk to get those fatter payouts.

A simpler solution—which exposes you to no credit risk—has recently been supplied by the federal government: **Treasury Inflation Protected securities**, also known as **TIPs bonds**. TIPs are the first fixed-income product whose returns won't be eaten away at by inflation. In fact, these bonds are likely to do better in high-inflationary periods because not only is your investment safeguarded from rising prices, but demand for TIPs bonds should rise when inflation does (which means the price should go up too).

TIPs have a unique structure. Every year, the government adjusts the par value of these bonds to reflect the rate of inflation, as measured by the Consumer Price Index. So if inflation rises 4 percent a year, so too will the underlying value of these bonds for investors who hold them to maturity. Moreover, at maturity, you are guaranteed to get back either the **original par value** of the bond or the **inflation-adjusted par**—whichever is higher. This means that you cannot lose your original investment in these securities, even if deflation, rather than inflation, becomes the real threat to the economy. (**Deflation** is an economic phenomenon where, for short periods of time, prices fall, increasing the purchasing power of your money.)

The income thrown off by TIPs also adjusts for inflation, though indirectly. TIPs, like other Treasuries, come with a fixed rate of interest. But instead of being calculated on the bond's original par value, the income thrown off by these bonds is based on the **inflation-adjusted principal value**, meaning you are likely to receive higher payouts should inflation rise—in addition to your increased principal value.

There is one downside to investing in TIPs, which is similar to the downside of investing in zero-coupon bonds. Every year, the federal government will tax you on the **imputed interest** you receive on the inflation-adjusted principal value of your bond. The problem is, you don't get to enjoy the inflation-adjusted principal until the bond matures. Unfortunately, Uncle Sam will ding you with taxes along the way. So these investments may be better suited for a tax-deferred account.

If you don't want the hassle of buying TIPs bonds directly, you can invest in mutual funds that specialize in these inflation-adjusted bonds. Among some of the most popular are: Vanguard Inflation-Protected Securities fund (800-662-7447; www.vanguard.com), Fidelity Inflation-Protected Bond fund (800-343-3548; www.fidelity.com), and American Century Inflation-Adjusted Bond fund (800-345-2021; www.americancentury.com).

Since these bonds are issued by the U.S. Treasury, they are backed by the full faith and credit of Uncle Sam, and therefore expose you to no credit risk.

If you want inflation protection but don't have the finances to buy TIPs in $1,000 increments, you can also consider **inflation-adjusted savings bonds** that Uncle Sam now issues. The interest rate on these so-called **I-bonds** is determined by two factors: one is a fixed rate established by the government, and the other is a floating rate that fluctuates based on the rate of inflation as measured by the Consumer Price Index. This means that the interest paid by these savings bonds will always adjust and keep pace with inflationary trends. Best of all, I-bonds can be bought in increments of as small as $50.

Credit Risk

Just as a bank is always worried whether its borrowers will repay their loans in full and on time, bond investors must always be mindful of **credit risk**—the financial health of the companies whose debt they purchase.

While the vast majority of companies make good on their loans (if they didn't, it would be that much harder for them to seek financing in the bond market the next time around), there is always the chance that a company will

default, by failing either to pay the interest owed or to pay back the original principal. The most common occurrence of defaults takes place when a company's health deteriorates to the point where it must seek bankruptcy protection.

From the standpoint of the company, **bankruptcy** shelters it from its obligation to make good on its responsibilities. Unfortunately, this means that bond investors, alongside equity owners, are left holding the bag. This is why credit risk becomes an increasing concern for bond investors during periods of economic uncertainties or outright recessions, when bankruptcy filings tend to spike. This phenomenon took place most recently amid the credit crisis of 2008, when investors fled just about any type of asset that exposed them to credit risk. In that downturn, almost every type of bond that exposed investors to a possible default—especially in the corporate fixed-income world—lost value.

As an aside, there are different classifications of **corporate debt**, with varying degrees of bankruptcy safeguards. **Senior bonds**, for example, are placed higher up in the pecking order of claims in the event of a corporate bankruptcy. As a result of those greater assurances, senior corporate debt does not necessarily have to offer as high an interest rate to pique investors' attention. On the other hand, **subordinated bonds** force investors to wait until other lenders are made whole before making claims against the financially troubled firm. Having to take on more credit risk, owners of subordinated debt are often compensated with a slightly higher interest rate.

Managing Credit Risk

There are three basic strategies for addressing credit risk in your overall portfolio.

The first is simple: ***Stick with debt issued by Uncle Sam***. Federal government debt exposes investors to zero credit risk since the Treasury issues these bonds and can always print money to make investors whole even if the government runs into financial difficulties. This strategy worked to perfection in the recent financial crisis, when long-term U.S. Treasury bonds soared more than 25 percent at a time when the vast majority of corporate and municipal debt lost value.

A second strategy is: ***Diversify your holdings and spread out that credit risk over a portfolio of dozens, if not hundreds, of bonds***. By investing in, say, 100 bonds, your portfolio would be protected from losses even if one or two defaulted. Obviously, since bonds are issued in increments of $1,000—and are often sold in large lots—it's going to be hard for a small investor to achieve adequate diversification on his or her own. But a simple solution is to consider a bond mutual fund, since the average bond fund invests in nearly 400 individual securities.

The final way to manage credit risk is: ***Stick with high quality, investment-grade bonds***. Within the corporate bond universe, **investment-grade bonds** are those issued by corporations with healthy balance sheets and a strong degree of financial stability. Technically, they are bonds with credit ratings of BBB or higher. If you want to maximize protection from credit risk, you probably want to stay at the upper end of the investment grade universe, which means bonds rated AA or better.

Bond issuers, like consumers, are rated based on their credit-worthiness, ranging from **junk status** to investment-grade. The three major **bond rating agencies** that assess the quality of debt issuance are **Moody's, Standard & Poor's**, and **Fitch**. While they each have a slightly different rating system (Figure 6-5), their ratings are similar enough for investors to use as general guidelines for assessing the overall credit quality of the bonds they purchase.

Anything rated BBB or higher (or in Moody's system, Baa or higher) is considered investment-grade, while BB (or Ba) and lower is regarded as junk bonds. While the system of bond rating is by no means perfect—for example, debt issued by Enron was classified as investment-grade debt only days before the energy giant filed for what was then the biggest bankruptcy in corporate history—the rating system generally helps. Historically, only around one-tenth of 1 percent of bonds rated Aaa have ever defaulted. Meanwhile, less than 2 percent of bonds rated Baa have failed to meet their obligations. About 12 percent of bonds rated Ba have defaulted, and about 30 percent of bonds rated B have failed.

Interest-Rate Risk

The third major category of risks associated with bonds is interest-rate risk. There are two types of interest rate worries that plague fixed-income investors. The first has to do with *the prospect of rising rates.*

Credit Rating	Moody's	S&P	Fitch
Highest quality	Aaa	AAA	AAA
High quality, but small degree of risk	Aa	AA	AA
Good quality, but susceptible to risk	A	A	A
Medium quality	Baa	BBB	BBB
Start of "junk" status	Ba	BB	BB
Speculative grade; major uncertainties	B	B	B
Poor quality; vulnerable to nonpayment	Caa	CCC	CCC
Highly vulnerable, likely to default	Ca	CC	CC
Lowest quality	C	C	C
In default		D	D-DDD

FIGURE 6-5 · Bond Ratings.

As we've already discussed, bond prices move in the *opposite* direction of market interest rates. While this may seem counterintuitive—after all, don't we want our bonds to pay out ever higher interest rates?—it's actually quite logical, given that bonds have fixed rates. If you purchase a bond with a coupon yield of 5 percent and then market interest rates rise to say, 6 percent, why would anyone want to buy your older, lower-yielding bond when newer ones are paying out a full percentage point more? Obviously, many don't.

This means that as rates rise, the price of older bonds in your portfolio is likely to fall. So, for an investor who is in the bond market for total returns, rising rates threaten the market value of his or her fixed-income holdings. In years when rates rise dramatically, the value of one's underlying bonds may fall more than the bonds are yielding. On a total return basis, investors can actually end up losing money, though surveys show that many investors are not aware of this.

In 1994, for example, when the Federal Reserve hiked short-term rates quickly and aggressively, the fallout in the bond market was widespread. The chart in Figure 6-6, shows how bond funds in various categories performed in that year. You'll note that more than 88 percent of taxable bond funds lost money that year, with an average loss of what in fact was 3.41 percent. Long-term government bond funds did far worse, since longer-maturity and longer-duration bonds tend to be more vulnerable to interest-rate risks. Around 96 percent of all long-term government bond funds lost money in 1994, with an average loss of nearly 9 percent.

There's a second type of interest-rate risk that income investors face. Ironically, it's the opposite risk of the one we just described: that *interest rates will*

Bond Type	Percent of Funds That Lost Money	Average Loss in 1994
Long-term government	96%	−8.6%
Long-term corporate	100%	−6.4%
Intermediate-term government	99%	−3.8%
Intermediate-term corporate	99%	−4.1%
Short-term government	72%	−1.2%
Short-term corporate	65%	−1.0%
Ultra-short-term corporate	3%	+2.0%
High-yield bond	91%	−3.2%
Multisector bond	100%	−4.9%
All taxable bonds	88%	−3.4%

FIGURE 6-6 · Bond Performance in 1994.

Source: Morningstar

fall over time. Income-oriented investors—retirees, for instance—care about this type of interest-rate risk.

When rates fall, it certainly helps the fortunes of bond fund investors, since the price of older bonds in these portfolios rise. But for income investors who buy individual securities, falling rates mean that as their old bonds mature, they will have to reinvest that money at ever lower yields. For a retiree, this could be a dangerous development, since their incomes are often limited and any reduction in interest income could cut into their ability to fund their lifestyles. This was a particularly pronounced risk for income investors at the start of this century, as both long- and short-term interest fell to 40-year lows.

Managing Interest-Rate Risk

The good news is, there are ways to combat interest-rate risk, just as there are strategies to deal with the other concerns we've raised. Let's start with the first type of interest-rate risk we discussed: rising rates.

The simplest way for an investor to combat rising interest-rate risk is to buy individual bonds—not bond funds—and hold them to maturity. This is the equivalent of being a buy-and-hold bond investor. While fluctuations in bond prices matter to bond traders and to bond funds—because they flip into and out of bonds constantly—individual bondholders who simply buy bonds with the thought of collecting the interest and recouping their principal later on don't have to worry. To them, bond price fluctuations are all noise, because at the end of the day, they're not going to trade their debt.

Unfortunately, **bond fund investors** cannot use this strategy because bond funds have no fixed maturities. Instead, **bond funds** are diversified portfolios of fixed-income securities with varying maturity dates. Moreover, because investors can flow into and out of a bond fund at will, bond fund managers often are forced to sell securities before they mature simply to manage the cash flow of their portfolios. The upshot is, there is no way for a bond fund to completely avoid interest-rate risk.

Having said that, another strategy to address rising-rate risk is to stick with bonds with short maturities (or by extension, bond funds that focus on short-term debt). Why?

Let's define what a **short-term bond** is: a fixed-income security that typically matures in around two years or less. An **intermediate-term bond**, in contrast, matures in two to 10 years. And a **long-term bond** typically matures in more than 10 years. There are a couple of reasons why short maturities help in a rising market.

When rates rise, short-term bonds will come due much faster than long-term debt. This means you can then turn around and reinvest the money you get back from your old bonds quickly into higher-yielding new bonds. While this does not do away with the fact that older bond prices will still fall in a rising rate environment, hopefully, the higher yields you can earn on the new bonds will offset some of your losses. Shorter-term bonds also come with lower durations. And as we discussed, the lower the duration of your investment, the less vulnerable it is to interest-rate risk.

But what about investors who are worried about falling interest-rate risk? They too can manage this risk with a basic—and popular—fixed-income strategy. It's called **laddering your bonds**. The term refers to a common strategy of diversifying *when* an investor buys new bonds. It is the equivalent of dollar-cost-averaging for bond investors, whereby one would take their bond assets, divide it relatively evenly, and purchase equal amounts of bonds that come due in routine intervals.

So instead of putting all or most of your money in bonds maturing in, say, seven years, you would split it up and buy bonds of different maturities, thereby averaging out your portfolio's overall maturity and duration. In Figure 6-7 we see what a **typical** ladder might look like.

The way this works is, at the end of the first year, your one-year bond will come due. In addition, all of your bonds will be one year closer to maturity. You would then take the proceeds of the redemption of the one-year bond— $10,000—and reinvest it at the long end of the curve, in a new 10-year bond. Remember, by this time, your existing 10-year bond only has nine years left until maturity. This means you reset your ladder every year—and you are buying incrementally every year. This way, you never have to buy a whole new slate of bonds just when interest rates have fallen to historically low levels.

Total Amount to Invest: $100,000	
$10,000	Treasuries maturing in 1 year
$10,000	Treasuries maturing in 2 years
$10,000	Treasuries maturing in 3 years
$10,000	Treasuries maturing in 4 years
$10,000	Treasuries maturing in 5 years
$10,000	Treasuries maturing in 6 years
$10,000	Treasuries maturing in 7 years
$10,000	Treasuries maturing in 8 years
$10,000	Treasuries maturing in 9 years
$10,000	Treasuries maturing in 10 years
$100,000	*Average maturity: 5.5 Yrs.*

FIGURE 6-7 · Bond Ladder.

Types of Bonds

Long Term versus Short Term

To reiterate, **long-term bonds** are those that mature in 10 years or more, while intermediate-term bonds mature in two to 10 years, and **short-term bonds** come due in around two years or less. Though you could be investing in the exact same type of issue—for instance Treasury bonds—the length of maturity of the bond you choose changes the very nature of the investment.

In general, long-term bonds are regarded as more aggressive—and risky—investments, while short-term bonds are considered more conservative. (The fluctuations in the table in Figure 6-8 reflect this.) The reason for this is that in the bond market, anything that forces you to tie up your money for a sustained period of time adds risk to your profile. While you may be certain that a company whose bond you purchase will be around for another two or three years, who knows, for instance, if the bond issuer will survive 10 to 15 additional years after that? Who knows where interest rates will be that far down the road? And who knows what the stock market will be like a decade from now?

In a short-term bond, investors at least have the luxury of being able to extricate themselves from a bad situation more quickly—and to redeploy their money into better assets for a changing situation. But long-term bond investors don't have that luxury. To compensate investors for this added risk, bond issuers will provide fatter yields for long-term debt.

There are other reasons why an investor might choose a long-term bond over short-term debt. As we stated earlier, it's important for investors to match up their financial investments with their goals. This is why we discussed the

Year	Long-Term Corp. Bonds	Short-Term Corp. Bonds
2003	7.96%	2.42%
2002	9.03%	5.29%
2001	7.89%	7.17%
2000	9.71%	7.83%
1999	−3.12%	2.23%
1998	6.71%	6.10%
1997	11.59%	6.47%
1996	3.82%	4.40%
1995	22.89%	11.40%
1994	−6.37%	−0.95%

FIGURE 6-8 · Bond Performance: Long-Term versus Short.

Source: Morningstar

need to outline all of your goals—and their time horizons—before you start investing.

For some investors, financial goals may not come up for years. If you're investing for retirement, for example, you may not need the money for 20 years. If you're the parent of a newborn, you may not need to pay for college for another 18 years. That said, long-term bonds, with their higher yields and higher risks, may be appropriate for an investor who wants to park money for the long term with the intention of holding the bond until maturity.

Government versus Corporate

Investors seek out government bonds and corporate debt for two entirely different reasons.

Investing in government debt is a way to eliminate credit risk while still participating in the fixed-income market. In this sense, buying Treasuries is a defensive play. In comparison, corporate bond buyers are looking for opportunities. And they are willing to take on credit risk in exchange for higher interest rates and the potential for higher total returns.

It should be noted that it's fairly simple for investors to purchase individual Treasury bonds either through their brokerage accounts or directly from the federal government. For as little as $1,000, you can purchase Treasury bills (securities maturing in one year or less) or notes (those maturing in two to 10 years) directly from the government at auction at www.treasurydirect.gov.

The same cannot be said for corporate bonds. In addition to sizable commissions, it is very difficult for small investors to get good pricing on small lots of corporate debt. In fact, it may take at least $100,000—if not more— to adequately assemble a diversified mix of corporate debt for your personal portfolio. As a result of the difficulties and fees, most individual investors gain exposure to corporate bonds through funds.

But again, there is a distinction in investing in individual bonds and investing in a fund. A fund is more convenient and will be more cost-effective in creating a total bond portfolio. A fund will also reduce your exposure to credit risk, since it will spread out small amounts of money over hundreds of different bonds. But at the same time, a fund, because it has no fixed maturity, takes away one of the tools investors have to reduce interest-rate risk: the ability to simply hold the security to maturity.

As for performance, Figure 6-9 compares government and corporate bonds over the past 10 years.

Investment Grade versus High Yield

Just as there is a distinction between growth and value stocks, there is a division in the fixed-income universe between investment-grade and high-yield, or junk, bonds.

Year	Corp. Bond Funds	Corp. Bond Funds
2003	2.02%	4.51%
2002	9.11%	7.44%
2001	6.77%	7.49%
2000	10.85%	9.21%
1999	−1.00%	−0.52%
1998	7.44%	6.94%
1997	8.54%	8.45%
1996	2.84%	3.71%
1995	16.24%	16.27%
1994	−3.41%	−3.40%

FIGURE 6-9 · Bond Performance: Government versus Corporate.

Source: Morningstar

As we discussed, investment-grade bonds are a way to invest in individual corporate issues without exposing oneself to excess credit risk. In this sense, investment-grade debt is kind of like a growth stock, since the investor is assured that the underlying company is healthy and firing on all cylinders. If one does his or her homework, there should be few surprises when it comes to investing in high-quality debt. In fact, investment-grade bonds are designed to make up the core holdings in a fixed-income portfolio.

High-yield debt, in contrast, is a bigger gamble, and therefore should only make up a sliver of one's overall bond portfolio—perhaps 10 or 20 percent, but probably no more.

Like a value investor who is willing to buy a broken-down company for a cheap price in hopes that it will soon be able to turn things around, a junk bond investor is willing to take a flier from time to time on the debt of low-quality companies. Sometimes, when speculation is in favor in the markets, this type of bet can pay off handsomely. In 2009, for example, when investors were beginning to emerge from the shadows of the global credit crunch, junk bond funds generated total returns of around 47 percent. Compare that to the 4.7 percent gains for Treasury bonds.

This is why many people regard junk bonds as a proxy of sorts for the equity markets. While junk bonds are still bonds, the relative uncertainty of the bond issuer's credit profile means an investor is making a bet on the turnaround of that company, not necessarily on the debt itself. If the company fixes its financial problems, the underlying value of these bonds often soars. If it doesn't, investors still receive compensation in the form of the higher yield. But it's important to note that the underlying price of junk bonds can fall more than even the high yields, and these investments lose money more frequently than investment-grade debt (Figure 6-10).

Year	High Quality	High Yield
2003	3.90%	23.95%
2002	7.49%	−1.63%
2001	7.45%	2.34%
2000	9.44%	−7.11%
1999	−0.31%	4.88%
1998	6.99%	0.10%
1997	8.18%	12.97%
1996	3.66%	13.19%
1995	15.71%	17.21%
1994	−3.13%	−3.23%

FIGURE 6-10 · Bond Performance: Investment-Grade versus High-Yield.

Source: Morningstar

Not only do junk bonds pay out significantly higher yields than investment-grade debt—because the issuers have to in order to attract investors—this debt typically trades at steep discounts to par value. This is especially true for junk bonds issued by companies that are teetering on bankruptcy.

While many associate junk bonds with low-quality companies, the fact is, bonds issued by brand-name firms have fallen to junk status at one time or another. These companies include giant companies like Georgia-Pacific, El Paso Corp., and Qwest Communications.

Because of the credit quality concerns of these bonds, and questions concerning access to these markets, high-yield debt should be held by investors through funds—and not individually. Whereas only around 1 percent of investment-grade bonds default over time, there are years in which the default rate of the junk bond universe rises above 10 percent. With 1 in 10 odds of failing, it's important to invest in a fund with more than 100 funds, to prevent such losses from taking down an entire portfolio. The good news is that the average high-yield bond fund holds nearly 300 different issues.

QUIZ

1. **The best reason to invest in bonds is that they . . .**
   A. Provide income and ballast to your portfolio.
   B. Are guaranteed to outpace the rate of inflation.
   C. Are often the best-performing asset class around.
   D. Make money more dependably than stocks.

2. **The best way to measure a bond's performance is by considering its . . .**
   A. Coupon rate.
   B. Current yield.
   C. Total return.
   D. Price appreciation.

3. **The major risks that you face as a bond investor include . . .**
   A. Interest-rate risk.
   B. Credit risk.
   C. Currency risk.
   D. A and B.
   E. B and C.

4. **If you're a bond fund investor, the ideal time to invest in a bond fund is . . .**
   A. When interest rates are rising.
   B. When interest rates are falling.
   C. When the economy is deteriorating.
   D. When stocks are doing poorly.

5. **If you invest in individual bonds and plan to hold the debt to maturity, the biggest threat to your strategy is . . .**
   A. Rising interest rates.
   B. Falling interest rates.
   C. An improving stock market.
   D. Needing to spend the money before the bond matures.

6. **Bonds will always protect your portfolio in a market downturn.**
   A. True
   B. False

7. **If 10-year Treasury bonds are yielding 4 percent and the broad stock market has a P/E ratio of 25, bonds should be considered . . .**
   A. Cheap alternatives to stocks.
   B. Expensive alternatives to bonds.

C. Good buys.
D. Terrible buys.
E. None of the above.

8. **The easiest way to reduce the level of credit risk in a bond portfolio is to . . .**
A. Buy investment-grade bonds.
B. Buy Treasury securities.
C. Buy many different bonds.
D. All of the above.
E. None of the above.

9. **If a Treasury bond's price is shown at 100.15, it is selling for how much?**
A. $1,001.50
B. $100.15
C. $1,001.05
D. $1,004.68
E. $1,040.68

10. **What makes bonds so attractive is that all bonds pay you interest income as you go.**
A. True
B. False

chapter **7**

Demystifying Cash

In this chapter, you will learn the following:

- Why cash is different from stocks and bonds
- The various uses for cash
- The advantages and disadvantages of various cash vehicles
- The role cash plays in your investing strategy

We all know why we need cash in our lives and why we need to raise more of it to fund our financial futures. But why does an investor, as opposed to a saver, expressly need cash in his or her portfolio?

While many people regard cash and bonds as interchangeable assets—perhaps because both offer a degree of ballast for an equity portfolio—they are actually quite different instruments. Bonds are an income and diversification tool that investors use to stabilize their growth-oriented portfolios while simultaneously generating income that exceeds the rate of inflation. This is a fancy way of saying that bonds are designed to grow your pot of money. Even conservative shorter-term bonds, ultra-short-term issues, which purchase debt that matures in a year or less, have different characteristics than bank certificates of deposit or savings accounts. That's because, even on the margins, short-term bonds put some of your money at risk in order to eke out slightly higher yields than traditional savings instruments can offer.

Consider what transpired in 2008. When the credit crisis sent investors into a panic that year, the average short-term bond lost more than 4 percent of its value while the average ultra-short-term bond sank nearly 8 percent. Part of the reason: Even though these funds owned short-term bonds, they also invested in securities that exposed investors to credit risk, including short-term mortgage-backed securities. And anything with mortgage exposure got hammered in that meltdown.

Saving versus Investing

Perhaps the biggest distinction between bonds and cash is that you *invest in bonds* but *save in cash*. This is a critical point. Cash is designed first and foremost to protect your money. Cash accounts, for instance, are not designed to beat inflation over the long term. And they won't. Going back to the Ibbotson numbers, the average long-term rate of return for cash is about 3 percent, which is precisely what the long-term rate of inflation is. So on a net basis, you are not likely to advance one iota in a cash account in real terms.

To be sure, this doesn't mean that the interest you earn in a savings account is irrelevant. Far from it. But the point of maximizing your interest in a cash account is to keep up with inflation in order to protect your principal, not to leave inflation in the dust. To do that, you'll need longer-term and riskier instruments, such as stocks and bonds.

Moreover, though cash represents one of the three pillars of a portfolio, along with stocks and bonds, the purpose of holding cash is not to beat those other two asset classes in the short term—though in fact in some years you may. Investors who moved money into cash in 2000, 2001, or 2002 probably felt victorious because their accounts, which were yielding perhaps 1 or 2 percent, still wound up doing better than stocks. They experienced a similar sense of victory in 2008. But that's not the reason one goes to cash.

How Investors Use Cash

In theory, cash should be the final asset that investors shift their money into as they near a financial goal. It all works as part of a continuum.

For example, if you are 20 years from retirement, you've probably put most of your money in stocks, for reasons of capital appreciation. But to avoid suffering major losses in a bear market as you get within five to 10 years of that goal (it can often take around five years to fully recover from such downturns) you will want to shift into bonds, to keep the money growing but with much more stability. You wouldn't want to shift all of your money into bonds at this point, only the portion you will absolutely need to spend in around five years.

Then, as you get within one or two years of needing to spend that pot of money, you'd probably want to shift at least portions of it into cash (again, only that chunk that you will absolutely need to tap in two years or less) to preserve it for immediate spending purposes.

If you own what's called a **target date retirement fund**, you will notice that this is how a professional adviser will manage your money for you. A target date fund is designed to be an all-in-one fund that gives investors exposure to the proper mix of stocks, bonds, and cash across time. For younger investors, target date funds are mostly in equities. For instance, the T. Rowe Price Target Retirement 2050 fund (designed for those who plan on investing in the year 2050) has nearly 90 percent of its assets held in stocks and almost nothing in cash. But the 2020 fund, for those who plan to retire in around a decade, has only around two-thirds of its assets in stocks and nearly 4 percent in cash. Meanwhile, the 2005 retirement fund, designed for those already in retirement, has less than half its holdings in stocks and nearly 10 percent in cash.

Capital Preservation

The allure of cash is that it's designed to offer de facto or de jure principal protection. Cash accounts offer a floor for people who want to make absolutely certain that a particular pot of money will remain fully intact and available for other purposes.

You'll recall that in any given year the odds are about 1 in 4 of losing money in the stock market. And while many investors might assume that bonds can protect one's portfolio in the short run, remember that in certain years bonds have lost value. The risk you run by putting your savings into those assets is that you will need to spend the money in the same year that they suffer losses.

Cash, on the other hand, is designed principally to protect your money. This is why your emergency stash or rainy day fund belongs in cash. Some types of cash accounts explicitly guarantee 100 percent principal protection. And while others don't contractually guarantee that much, they deliver those assurances in practice.

Short-Term Parking

In addition to preserving your gains, cash is also a convenient place for investors to move money temporarily when they can't find decent opportunities in other markets, such as stocks, bonds, or even real estate.

Mutual fund managers, for example, often sit on anywhere from 5 to 10 percent—or even more—in cash when they run out of good ideas (Figure 7-1). When times look especially lean in the stock and bond markets, some managers will put as much as one-quarter or even a third of their assets in cash while they investigate their options.

While putting money into cash might slow a stock fund down in the long run—because stocks tend to generate higher returns than cash instruments—in the short run, the low single-digit returns that cash provides are better than making a foolhardy decision in equities and losing money. So instead of forcing the issue by putting money into second-tier ideas, professionals would rather put some money in cash—or as they say, "move it to the sidelines"—until better ideas surface. This explains a phrase on Wall Street during times of market instability: "Cash is King!"

Type	Percentage of Assets in Cash
All taxable bonds	7.9%
All domestic stock funds	3.7%
All international stock funds	4.6%
Intermediate-term bond funds	8.0%
Municipal bond funds	2.8%
Large-cap growth funds	2.4%
Large-cap value funds	2.8%
Small-cap growth funds	2.7%
Small-cap value funds	4.2%
Technology funds	2.8%
Financial services funds	2.0%
Health-care funds	2.3%
Emerging market funds	2.8%
High-yield bond funds	6.4%

FIGURE 7-1 · Average Cash Positions of Mutual Funds.*

This table shows what percentage of an average mutual fund's assets are held in cash. Virtually all funds hold a portion of their assets in cash to facilitate stock purchases and redemptions.

*Data as of December 2009.

Source: Morningstar

Why not go into bonds instead? For starters, cash is an ultimately liquid investment, where you can go into and out of these accounts with little or no restraint, penalty, or commissions. Every time you buy or sell a bond, on the other hand, you're likely to pay transaction costs, taxes, and commissions. For these reasons, investors regard cash accounts as ideal short-term parking places for their money.

Funding Source for New Ideas

In addition to being a good defensive parking place, cash can also help investors take advantage of opportunities in other assets.

If you were to invest 100 percent of your money in stocks and bonds, it would be difficult to jump on new, better ideas as they make themselves known. After all, you as a fully invested person would have to sell stocks and bonds currently in your portfolio—which could take time if you wanted to obtain the best prices—to fund those new investment ideas. Moreover, if you were forced to sell other stocks or bonds that have appreciated in value to fund new ideas, you would have to take the time to make tax-related decisions as you sell.

But if you left a small portion of your assets in cash—say, 5 or 10 percent— you would always have access to a funding source for new investments, which would allow you to jump on them in a moment's notice. As a result, cash could be an ideal place to leave a fraction of your money to deploy elsewhere in the near future.

Types of Cash Accounts

Savings Accounts

A traditional savings account at a bank is perhaps the first place where many of us look to park our cash. There are two basic types of savings accounts: the old-fashioned **passbook savings accounts** and the more modern **statement savings accounts**. From the standpoint of minimum balance requirements and liquidity, both accounts work pretty much the same. The only major difference, other than the fact that statement savings accounts tend to pay out higher yields, is that traditional passbook accounts literally record all of your transactions inside a booklet that you maintain. Statement savings accounts, on the other hand, do not rely on booklets, but rather, mail out monthly and quarterly statements to customers showing them their account activity.

Not only are savings accounts convenient—you probably chose your bank because it was located around the corner from where you live or work—they typically come with low minimum balance requirements. In many cases you can open a savings account for as little as few hundred dollars, though there may be a slightly higher balance requirement to avoid monthly account maintenance fees.

Another benefit: We all know how to withdraw from and deposit money into these accounts—and we can do both as many times as we want. Indeed, pretty much all statement savings accounts give customers ATM access, which comes in handy not just for managing your investments, but also your day-to-day or week-to-week cash flow situation.

Savings accounts at a regulated bank will come with **FDIC (Federal Deposit Insurance Corporation) insurance**. This means that in the rare chance that your bank goes under, up to $250,000 of your deposits are guaranteed by the federal government. FDIC insurance applies to virtually all state and federally chartered banks, as well as credit unions. However, if your bank is not state or federally chartered, your account may not be covered. Banks chartered in foreign countries, for example, or even some Internet banks, may fall into this latter category, so make sure you know if your savings account is insured.

Keep in mind, however, that in the event of a bank failure, just because your money is insured does not mean it will be easy or convenient for you to recover such losses. Though you are assured of recovering your principal savings, there are no guarantees that you will recoup every last dime of potential interest income you could have generated on that savings account.

The actual interest you will earn from a savings account is likely to be among the lowest rates of return around. In 2009, traditional passbook and statement savings accounts were paying less then 1 percent interest, which was considerably less than what they've traditionally paid.

The other thing to watch out for in a savings account are the basic fees that add up, including ATM fees, account servicing fees, and low balance fees. Many savings accounts will come with a minimum balance threshold. If your account falls below that level, the bank may begin charging an added layer of monthly fees that could eat up your already paltry interest income.

Certificates of Deposit

Bank certificates of deposit, or **CDs**, are another popular savings vehicle. Like traditional savings accounts, CDs are FDIC insured. But unlike regular bank accounts, a CD will make you commit a certain amount of money for a specified length of time. Like a bond, CDs come with maturity dates, typically ranging anywhere from one month to five years. As a result of this relative inflexibility, CDs often pay a notch more in interest than savings accounts or even money market accounts.

As further compensation for tying up your money, CDs offer savers a level of certainty that other traditional savings vehicles don't. When you commit money to a CD, you know exactly how much interest you will earn on that sum for a specified length of time. In a savings account, on the other hand, your interest rate will fluctuate based on market interest rates.

This ability to lock in an interest rate obviously helps when rates are falling, as they had throughout much of the 1980s and 1990s. The downside of this assurance, of course, is that if rates should rise, your existing CD will keep paying the same amount of interest while more flexible savings vehicles will start to adjust their rates higher.

In this sense, saving money in a CD comes with some of the same types of risk that bonds pose. Should interest rates rise, money already in a CD won't be able to benefit from the higher yields.

One way to manage this risk is to ladder your CDs as you would your bonds. So, if you wanted to park $50,000 in cash, you could spread the money out evenly over a ladder stretching out for five years. You could accomplish this by putting $10,000 into a CD maturing in one year, $10,000 into a CD maturing in two years, $10,000 into a three-year CD, $10,000 into a four-year CD, and the final $10,000 into a CD maturing in five years. This way, if interest rates are rising, you can take the proceeds of the one-year CD when it comes due and reinvest the money in a new five-year CD whose interest rate will reflect the higher market yields. If rates should fall, your CD ladder would ensure that at no time will you have to reinvest all of your cash at the worst possible moment—when rates have fallen to historical lows.

A typical CD may require $500 or $1,000 to open, though many banks will pay higher interest rates for savers willing to commit $10,000 or $25,000 at a time. The terms of a CD can run anywhere from one month to five years, though six-month, one-year, and two-year CDs tend to be among the most popular. Just as with bonds, the longer you agree to commit your money, the bigger the interest rate is likely to be. Figure 7-2 shows the average national CD rates at the start of 2010 for various lengths of time.

Maturity	Average Rate*
1-month CD	0.29%
3-month CD	0.28%
6-month CD	0.41%
1-year CD	0.70%
2-year CD	1.12%
5-year CD	2.06%

FIGURE 7-2 · Average CD Rates.*

*As of May 2010.

Source: Bankrate.com

To find out the current average rates for CDs across the country, you can go to www.bankrate.com. The figures are updated daily on this banking Web site.

Though CDs are very popular with many savers—in part because they pay out slightly higher yields while also enjoying FDIC insurance—they are not necessarily a great vehicle for investors who simply want to park their cash for offensive or defensive reasons.

CDs are also not necessarily the most appropriate place to stash emergency funds, since you are discouraged from removing your assets from a CD until the certificate matures. If you do extricate your money before maturity, you will likely face stiff penalties. It differs from bank to bank, but you should expect to lose around three months of interest income if you withdraw money prematurely from a one-year CD and up to six months of income for early withdrawal from a two-year CD.

Money Market Accounts

Money market accounts are a type of bank account that puts restrictions on the number of transactions you can make. But in exchange, these accounts will often pay out noticeably higher yields than savings accounts, while still offering FDIC insurance for worried savers. (Money market accounts are not to be confused with **money market mutual funds**, which we will get to in a moment.)

Money market accounts are attractive because they can be opened for as little as $1,000 or $2,000. But investors should be aware that money market accounts with small balances typically pay only slightly higher rates than statement savings accounts. You will start to see a noticeable bump up in rates if you commit at least $10,000 or, better still, $25,000 to these accounts.

For investors, there's an advantage to relying on money market accounts over savings accounts as you downshift your portfolio. Assume you shift money out of stocks and bonds as you get within two years of needing to spend it. In 2009 you could have found a money market account yielding 1.2 percent; at the same time, savings accounts were yielding just 0.5 percent. Had you stuffed $50,000 into a money market account yielding 1.2 percent, your money would have grown to $51,207 in two years' time. That same amount in a savings account earning 0.5 percent would have grown to $50,500—a difference of more than $705.

In addition to yielding more than savings accounts, money market accounts are more flexible than CDs, while still offering competitive interest rates. You can put money into these accounts any time you want, and typically withdraw funds from your account three to six times a month without penalty. Moreover, some money market accounts come with check writing privileges.

Having said that, if you make more than three to six withdrawals a month—or write more than three to six checks a month—many banks will ding you with a penalty fee of some sort. Those who abuse their withdrawal privileges by making numerous transactions in a short period of time may be asked to take their assets elsewhere.

Money Market Funds

Money market funds are mutual funds that invest in extremely short-term debt—much shorter than even ultra-short-term bond funds. By law, the average maturity of investments held in a money fund cannot be longer than 90 days—so money funds are considered much safer than short-term bond funds.

There are different classifications of money funds. Those that invest in extremely short-term government debt are called **government money funds**. Those that invest primarily in private-sector debt are referred to as **corporate money funds**. And those portfolios that invest in short-term municipal paper are known as **tax-free money funds**.

Because they invest in debt and are not FDIC insured, these funds do expose savers to greater risks than **money market accounts** do. Typically, money funds will compensate investors for this risk with slightly higher yields than money market accounts offer, but this is not guaranteed. For example, at the start of this decade, when interest rates fell to 40-year lows, money funds were actually returning considerably less, on average, than money market accounts were yielding.

Part of the reason is that money funds, like all mutual funds, deduct fees and other expenses from their returns. Investors who seek out money funds must be cognizant of this and should also focus only on the cheapest money funds around. Those tend to be run by large, low-cost leaders within the mutual fund industry, including Vanguard, T. Rowe Price, and TIAA-CREF.

In addition to investing in debt and not being FDIC insured, there's another risk money fund investors should be aware of: *These funds are designed to ensure that every share trades for $1 each.* The idea is that investors are never supposed to lose money in these accounts. But in fact there are no guarantees that the underlying investments in a money fund will maintain their value. If a money fund manager bets incorrectly, the portfolio's shares could indeed fall below $1 a share, meaning that investors could, in theory, lose money. And in fact, during the financial crisis, a handful of money funds did threaten to lose their investor's money, which further rattled the investment markets.

It should be noted, however, that throughout history there have been only a handful of instances where money funds either "broke the buck"—which is Wall Street's way of saying they lost value—or threatened to. In most cases, financial firms that run money funds will step in and promise to make any investor whole should the portfolio lose value.

It would be a huge scandal if a major mutual fund company broke the buck and failed to return at least $1 for every $1 investors put into the fund. So these firms will do anything in their power to avoid such bad publicity. This is why investors should stick with money funds managed by large, reputable—and low-cost—firms.

Despite these concerns, money funds are among the most popular cash vehicles for investors. Unlike money market accounts, money funds will let you buy or sell shares of your fund daily with few limitations—so they are particularly useful if you want to park cash from time to time as you scope out stock or bond opportunities. Moreover, a money fund can be held in the same brokerage account in which you invest in stocks and bonds—so there is an added convenience factor.

Treasury Bills

Another common cash vehicle for investors is a **Treasury bill**. A **T-bill** is a short-term Treasury security that functions somewhat like a CD. Every week, the Treasury Department auctions off new T-bills of varying maturities, ranging from one month to one year, with three-month and six-month T-bills in between.

T-bills are backed by the full faith and credit of Uncle Sam, so there are never any concerns about not being paid. But the way you're paid by the federal government is a bit different than other interest-bearing vehicles. Unlike Treasury notes or bonds, for example, where you are paid interest along the way, T-bills pay no direct interest. Instead, investors purchase these bills at auction at a price below par value. And when it comes time to redeem your money, you get the full par value of the bill. So, for instance, you might buy a three-month T-bill for $980 and redeem it for par at $1,000 three months later. The difference between par ($1,000) and what you paid for the bond ($980) represents your interest. In this case, it works out to slightly more than 2 percent (we arrived at this by subtracting $980 from $1,000 and dividing the answer by $980).

Like CDs, T-bills are a good place to park money if you know exactly when you will need to spend it. But if you're looking for a place to stash your emergency cash or simply to move money to the sidelines, then T-bills might not be the best place to be, given the time commitment they require. While T-bills can be sold prior to maturity, the transaction will cost you $34 per bill if you make the sale through the Treasury department Web site. That could easily eat away at most or all of your interest. Moreover, you are not assured of getting close to par value back. It all depends on what other buyers and brokers are willing to pay for your existing bill.

T-bills can be purchased directly from the federal government at www .treasurydirect.gov in $1,000 increments, or they can be purchased through your bank or broker. Beware of the fees and commissions when buying through a broker.

QUIZ

1. There are times when cash will beat bonds and even stocks in terms of total returns.
   A. True
   B. False

2. Which of these cash investments is not guaranteed by the federal government?
   A. Money market accounts
   B. Money market funds
   C. CDs
   D. Passbook savings accounts

3. One of the purposes of having cash in your portfolio is to . . .
   A. Provide income.
   B. Give you the flexibility to invest in new ideas.
   C. Keep pace with inflation.
   D. Outperform the market.

4. As with bonds, you can ladder which type of cash investment?
   A. CDs
   B. Money market accounts
   C. Money market funds
   D. Passbook savings accounts

5. For investment purposes, the most liquid form of cash is the following:
   A. CDs
   B. Money market accounts
   C. Money market funds
   D. Passbook savings accounts

6. The highest-yielding form of cash is the following:
   A. CDs
   B. Money market accounts
   C. Money market funds
   D. None of the above
   E. It depends on market circumstances.

7. The interest rates you will earn on money market accounts and money market funds will typically be the same.
   A. True
   B. False

8. **Over long periods of time, cash has historically managed to beat inflation.**
   A. True
   B. False

9. **Cash will expose you to which of the following types of risks?**
   A. Market risks
   B. Interest-rate risks
   C. Inflation risks

10. **Treasury bills differ from CDs in that . . .**
   A. T-bills are sold by Uncle Sam.
   B. T-bills are guaranteed by the federal government and CDs are not.
   C. T-bills are more liquid.

chapter 8

Demystifying Mutual Funds I

CHAPTER OBJECTIVES

In this chapter, you will learn the following:

• Different types of funds based on management style
• Different types of stock funds
• Different types of bond funds

The modern mutual fund was born in 1924, when the Massachusetts Investors Trust opened its doors for business. Remarkably, the fund, which today goes by the name MFS Massachusetts Investors Trust, is still open to new shareholders. Even more remarkable, since the turn of the century, mutual funds have become so popular that they have attracted more than $11 trillion in total assets (Figure 8-1), making them the favorite way for Americans—particularly middle-class households—to invest.

Mutual funds began to get popular in the 1980s and 1990s, when the booming stock market gave rise to an entirely new generation of investors who grew to like investing, but also were forced to invest for their own retirement through 401(k) and similarly defined contribution plans. During the

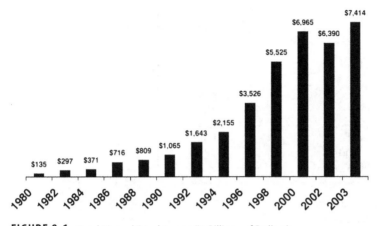

FIGURE 8-1 · Total Mutual Fund Assets (in Billions of Dollars).

Today, the mutual fund industry controls more than $7 trillion in assets.

Source: Investment Company Institute

bull market of the 1980s and 1990s, funds helped democratize Wall Street, and now a majority of households are investors (Figure 8-2). This is especially true with retirement accounts, where individuals have the choice of investing in an array of funds.

Back in the 1990s, the most popular type of fund invested primarily in U.S. stocks because, not surprisingly, domestic equities were the best-performing

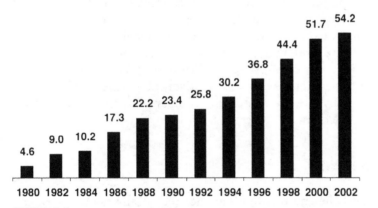
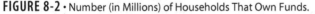

FIGURE 8-2 · Number (in Millions) of Households That Own Funds.

As this graph illustrates, the number of American households that invest in mutual funds skyrocketed in the 1990s. That decade was also the period in which 401(k) retirement plans, which utilize funds as investment options, rose into prominence.

Source: Investment Company Institute

Type of Fund	No. Funds
Domestic stock fund	14,518
International stock fund	4,016
Balanced funds	3,779
Taxable bond fund	4,005
Municipal bond fund	2,293
Large growth stock fund	1,917
Large value stock fund	1,358
Small growth stock fund	821
Small value stock fund	400

FIGURE 8-3 · Mutual Funds Gone Wild.*

*Data as of December 2009.

Source: Morningstar

assets back then. But when the U.S. stock market began to slow in the 2000s, investors didn't necessarily turn their backs on funds. Instead, they shifted the types of funds they owned. Rather than favoring funds that invested in U.S. equities, investors gravitated to funds that invested in better-performing foreign equities as well as bonds.

But while mutual funds make life simpler for investors—since many of us don't have the time or the interest to research more than 10,000 stocks to decide which ones to invest in—the irony is, choosing a fund today can be just as daunting as selecting the individual securities they invest in. Why? Because there are more mutual funds to choose from today than individual stocks listed on the New York Stock Exchange and the Nasdaq national market combined. At last count, there were more than 26,000 mutual funds in existence, according to the fund-tracking service Morningstar (Figure 8-3). This is not including so-called exchange-traded funds, which are relatively new types of fund investments that you don't buy directly from a fund company but rather buy and sell through a brokerage account.

What a Mutual Fund Is Not

Contrary to popular belief, mutual funds are not technically assets like stocks, bonds, or even cash. Rather, they are vehicles that allow investors to put money to work into stocks, bonds, and/or cash. Think of them as envelopes in which you hold individual securities, though actually they're a lot more than that.

When you buy a fund, you are in essence handing money over to a professional manager who pools your dollars along with the assets of thousands of other investors to build a single portfolio of securities. The fund itself is considered an investment company whose sole mission is to invest in financial securities to maximize your gains (and hopefully minimize your risks).

The mutual fund industry itself is governed under the **Investment Company Act of 1940**, which launched a series of regulations that require funds to be diversified, open, and considerate of the best interests of its shareholders. The existence of these regulations make mutual funds far safer entities than, say, hedge funds, which can invest in all sorts of different ways but face far fewer regulatory safeguards.

When you put money into a fund, you own a portion of the portfolio, alongside thousands of other shareholders. Hence the name: It is mutually owned by you and your peers. In this sense, the difference between investing in stocks on your own and buying a stock fund is like that between buying your own house and buying a professionally managed condo. And, as with all things that are jointly owned, there are pros and cons, which we will discuss in a moment.

Still Confused?

When you invest in a stock fund, you are not buying shares of a company directly. Instead, you are handing your money to an investment company whose job it is, in turn, to buy shares of other companies on your behalf (as well as on the behalf of fellow shareholders).

Fund Investors

The typical fund investor is pretty much everyman, as can be seen in Figure 8-4. The average fund investor, according to industry research, is in his or her 40s and 50s. The vast majority—81 percent—are married. Nearly half, have attended college. And the vast majority work. The typical household that invests in the stock and bond markets through funds tends to be middle class, though on average the household income may be slightly higher than the overall population's. Then again, most investors in general earn more than the average U.S. household.

Types of Funds

Actively Managed Funds

As mentioned before, most stock funds are **actively managed**. This means that stock pickers oversee these portfolios, making qualitative decisions as to which securities should be purchased, which should be sold—and in what amount and

Median	
Age	50 Years
Annual household income	$80,000
Total financial assets	$150,000
Total mutual fund holdings	$80,000
Percentage of Households Where Fund Investor . . .	
Is married	81%
Has four-year college degree or higher	48%
Is employed	82%
Owns an equity fund	81%
Owns a bond fund	54%
Owns a hybrid or balanced fund	45%
Owns a money market fund	65%

FIGURE 8-4 · The Typical U.S. Mutual Fund Shareholder.*

*Data as of December 2009.

Source: Investment Company Institute

at what time. This is the prototypical structure for funds, since one of the biggest reasons why investors turn to mutual funds is to benefit from professional money management.

More than 9 out of 10 domestic stock funds are actively managed. An even greater percentage of international stock funds are actively managed. And the vast majority of fixed-income funds—more than 95 percent—are run by active money managers.

While active fund management may seem the most logical way to go for many investors, there are some additional considerations.

First, an investor must choose which *style* of active management he or she prefers. This goes back to the different approaches to investing we discussed earlier in the book.

For example, there are active managers who are buy and holders, hanging onto stocks for decades at a time, in the belief that sound investing takes patience. And there are aggressive pick and rollers, who like to flip into and out of stocks in rapid-fire fashion. In fact, many active managers hang onto their stocks for less than one year.

A second decision investors of actively managed stock funds must make is to choose between growth- or value-oriented fund managers. **Growth managers** tend to favor stocks with the absolute best prospects for earnings and sale growth. **Value managers**, on the other hand, shop on the basis of price.

There is a subset of managers who fall in between, referring to themselves as **GARP managers**, which stands for "growth at a reasonable price." This school of investing says it is absolutely important to concentrate on shares of companies with the brightest growth prospects. But within that universe, GARP managers prefer to focus on those shares trading at relatively cheap prices, since they understand that lower valuations often equal lower risk.

Annual Fees

There's one more aspect of active management that investors need to know. The process of researching and selecting stocks can be expensive, especially if you're following obscure or foreign investments, which may require additional due diligence, if not travel.

Remember that you're not just paying for a fund manager to do all of this work. At most large mutual fund companies, there will be teams of analysts—sometimes numbering in the dozens, other times numbering in the hundreds—whose job it is to keep close tabs on investment securities in various areas of various markets around the world. These analysts, in turn, advise the fund manager not only about which stocks or bonds to buy but also about which to avoid and which to sell. Moreover, once a stock or bond is purchased, the analysts must help the manager keep track of its progress—and determine whether the security deserves to be kept in the portfolio or if it should eventually be sold. There's also the administrative costs that cover the costs of managing the back office functions of a fund.

This explains why actively managed funds are often more expensive to operate than basic index funds. The average actively managed stock portfolio charges annual fees of 1.43 percent of assets, which works out to a bill of $143 a year for every $10,000 you invest. In contrast, the average index stock fund, which is passively managed, costs only 0.75 percent of assets to run, which works out to $75 per $10,000 each year.

The same goes for bond funds. The average actively managed bond portfolio charges fees of 1.04 percent of assets each year, versus 0.34 percent for bond index funds.

Index Funds

While the major stock market indexes have been around for decades—the Dow Jones Industrial Average was concocted in 1896—index funds, which are designed simply to buy and hold all of the funds that make up indexes like the Dow or the S&P 500, weren't made available to retail investors until the 1970s. This is partly because mimicking an index as large as the S&P 500 (which has 500 stocks in it) or the Wilshire 5000 (which, despite its name, contains more than 5,000 stocks) can be a daunting task that requires some technological innovation.

The Vanguard 500 fund, which was the very first index fund made available to retail investors, wasn't born until 1976. At the time, the concept of indexing was ridiculed, since index funds do not allow their managers to use their skills to add value to their portfolios. All index managers do is mirror and track all the stocks that make up a market index.

Some referred to the Vanguard 500 fund as "Bogle's Folly," referring to Jack Bogle, the founder of Vanguard and a major proponent of indexing. It was more like Bogle's Last Laugh. Today, the Vanguard 500 is one of the largest mutual funds in the world, with nearly $100 billion in assets.

Why has this fund become so popular? Performance has a lot to do with it. While it is mathematically impossible for an index fund to be the best-performing fund in any period—since, by owning all stocks in an index, it achieves the *average* results of those holdings by definition—history has shown that index funds like the Vanguard 500 outperform a surprising number of actively managed portfolios. Over the past 15 years, through June 2010, the Vanguard 500 finished in the top thirty-first percentile of its peer group. This means that it beat 69 percent of other similar funds. And this took place during a stretch in which the broad stock market was stuck in neutral for several years following the bursting of the technology stock bubble in 2000. Think about that for a moment. In a period in which the broad stock market indexes languished, a passively managed fund that simply mirrored the modest returns of the S&P 500 ended up beating more than two-thirds of its actively managed peers. And those active managers aren't forced to own the entire market—good stocks and bad—as the Vanguard 500 fund is, but rather they are allowed to bet on only their best ideas.

How is it possible for a fund on autopilot to beat so many funds piloted by professional stock pickers? A lot of it has to do with the low cost of running an index fund. The Vanguard 500, for example, charges annual expenses of just 0.18 percent of assets, since there is no real need for stock research in such a fund.

While the Vanguard 500 is the best-known index fund, there are index portfolios that manage small-cap stocks too. There are also index funds that allow you just to invest in growth stocks and those that only invest in value stocks. Bonds and foreign stocks can also be indexed.

Still Confused?

By investing in an index fund, you are choosing to own all the stocks that make up a market. That means you are electing to be an *average* investor, since the performance of all the stocks in an index make up the average gains or losses of that index. By comparison, an investor in an actively managed fund is choosing to roll the dice and bet on only certain segments of the market. The risk is that you will bet wrong and perform worse than average. The potential reward is that you will be correct and do better than average.

Stock Funds

The universe of 26,000 long-term mutual funds is broken down into three major parts: stock funds, bond funds, and hybrid or balanced funds. The pie chart in Figure 8-5 shows the proportions of each of these, along with money market funds, which round out the fund offerings. As you can see, equity funds are the most common vehicle for individual investors. They control nearly half of the $11 trillion invested in the mutual fund industry.

Within the subset of stock funds, there are myriad different classifications. The first major subdivision of stock funds is between those that specialize in domestic stocks and those that invest internationally. According to Morningstar, there are more than 14,000 domestic stock funds and more than 4,000 internationally oriented stock portfolios.

Funds that invest overseas are sometimes called **foreign** or **international funds**, depending on which mutual fund tracking organization—Lipper or Morningstar—you follow. There is also a smaller subset of stock funds that invest primarily overseas but can also invest in the United States and North America, if the manager sees opportunities there. These are known as **world** or **global funds**. These types of portfolios often give the fund manager the latitude to determine what percentage of the fund's asset should be in domestic stocks

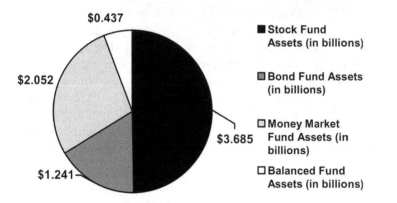

FIGURE 8-5 · Types of Mutual Fund Assets.*

As this graphic illustrates, stock funds dominate the mutual fund landscape, controlling roughly half of all fund assets.

*Data as of December 2003.

Source: Investment Company Institute

versus overseas shares. And that mix can change from time to time, depending on where the best opportunities are in the market at a particular moment in time, according to the manager. That said, most managers operate under a general set of rules or guidelines that restrict them (for diversification purposes) from tilting the portfolio too heavily toward any single asset class.

It should be noted that many funds will allow their managers to invest a sliver of their money outside of the style indicated in the **prospectus**, the official document letting shareholders know how the fund and fund company plan to operate. For instance, a European stock fund may require that the fund manager invest at least two-thirds or three-quarters of the portfolio's assets in that region. But the remainder may be allowed to be invested elsewhere, not just outside of Europe, but in some cases even outside of equities altogether. The same leeway exists for many fund managers in other fund categories. This is why it is important for investors to read their fund's prospectus.

Fund companies will gladly mail shareholders a copy of that prospectus upon request. These documents can also be found, for free, on fund company Web sites, alongside a fund's **annual and semiannual reports**, which outline the fund's performance and holdings during the year.

General Domestic Funds

Another distinction in the stock fund universe is between **general equity funds**—those that invest in a cross section of different industries and sectors that make up the stock market—and those that by design only invest in stocks within a single sector. These are referred to as **sector** or **specialty funds**.

Within the subset of general funds, there are funds that specialize in **large, mid-cap**, and **small-cap stocks**. In addition, there are funds that specialize in **growth stocks, value stocks**, and a combination of the two, which are referred to as **blend** or **core stocks**. These categories are actually broken into a grid of nine different types of general equity funds that is referred to in the mutual fund business as a **style box** (Figure 8-6).

You'll see that running along the left side of this grid are the **value-oriented funds**, ranging from small value funds to mid-cap value to large-cap value. As

Large value	Large blend	**Large growth**
Mid value	Mid blend	Mid growth
Small value	Small blend	**Small growth**

FIGURE 8-6 · Morningstar-Style Box.

your eyes move toward the right, you'll see the funds gradually grow more aggressive. In the middle are the so-called **blend funds**, which invest in a mix of growth and value stocks. And then on the far right side of the style box grid are the **growth funds**, which invest in growth-oriented companies, the most aggressive among general domestic equity portfolios.

Moreover, as your eyes move from the top of the grid to the bottom, you'll also see the aggressiveness of funds rise. Large-cap funds, because they invest in blue-chip stocks that are industry leaders, tend to be the most stable. Mid-cap stock funds invest in medium-size companies, while small-cap funds invest in young, sometimes untested companies, which therefore are the most volatile. The most aggressive type of general domestic equity funds are small-cap growth funds, found at the bottom right-hand side of the grid. The most conservative funds are at the top and to the left are large value funds.

Still Confused?

To determine the overall aggressiveness of a general stock fund, look at where it falls in the style box grid. The most conservative funds are generally found on the top left side of the grid—large-cap value portfolios. And the most aggressive, relatively speaking, are located on the bottom right side—small-cap growth funds.

Sector Funds

Let's turn our attention to sector funds. According to the fund tracker Lipper, there are around 1,500 sector funds in existence, divided into seven major industry groupings:

- *Health/biotechnology* sector funds, which can invest in companies ranging from hospitals to health insurers to medical device manufacturers
- *Natural resources* funds, which invest in energy stocks of all sorts
- *Science and technology* funds, which invest in tech companies
- *Telecommunications* funds, which invest in telecom and cable stocks
- *Utility* funds, which invest in utility companies
- *Financial services* funds, which invest in all types of financial firms, ranging from banks to brokers to insurers
- *Real estate* funds, which invest in real estate investment trusts

Figure 8-7 lists the number of funds in each of these sectors, as of June 2010, and their total assets.

Sector funds, by their very nature, can be much riskier than a diversified equity fund, since they invest in only one portion of the total stock market. If

Type of Fund	No. of Funds	Total Assets
Health/biotechnology	103	$19.3 billion
Natural resources	78	$19.0 billion
Science and technology	140	$25.5 billion
Telecommunications	43	$ 3.6 billion
Utility	90	$15.9 billion
Financial services	91	$18.3 billion
Real estate	242	$51.1 billion
Specialty/miscellaneous	88	$ 5.0 billion

FIGURE 8-7 · Sector Funds.*

*Data as of June 2010.

Source: Lipper

those industries are struggling as a result of the economy, then investors in these portfolios can suffer some damage.

Consider what took place in the most recent bear market, which was triggered by the financial crisis on Wall Street and the mortgage meltdown on Main Street. The typical financial services sector fund, which invested in shares of the banks and brokerages that owned toxic mortgage-related securities, wound up losing around 44 percent of their value in 2008. That was a much steeper loss than the average general domestic equity fund suffered that year. Some financial sector funds plummeted more than 70 percent due to the crash in bank shares that year.

General stock funds, because they are allowed to invest in a greater diversity of stocks—representing multiple sectors and industries—often are shielded from losses that steep.

Sector funds didn't just suffer in this most recent bear market, though. When the tech bubble burst in 2000, technology sector funds bore the brunt of the pain. The typical technology sector fund lost more than 30 percent of its value each year for three straight years on average between 2000 and 2002, as the Internet bubble burst and shattered that sector. Telecommunications sector funds, which were tied into the development of the Internet, also tumbled: The average portfolio fell more than 28 percent a year for three straight years. In contrast, the average general domestic stock fund was actually up in 2000, lost around 9 percent in 2001, and fell 20 percent in 2002.

On the flip side, because of their risks, sector funds offer investors the ability to make much more than a general domestic equity fund in years in which those industries are thriving. Again, turning to the performance of tech sector funds, earlier this decade they were up more than 128 percent, on average, in 1999, which was about 100 percentage points higher than the average returns for general domestic equity portfolios.

Bond Funds

Bond funds invest in a diversified portfolio of fixed-income securities. For many investors, this is the easiest way to gain access to fixed-income exposure, since individual bonds—in particular, corporate debt—can be difficult for small investors to purchase.

But to reiterate from a prior chapter, bond funds expose investors to a form of risk that they otherwise would not face if they held individual bonds to maturity. That, of course, is interest-rate risk.

While individual bonds have a **fixed maturity**—a date at which the bond issuer promises to pay back one's principal investment in full—bond funds have no such feature. This means a bond fund investor is never guaranteed any principal back by the fund company. This is something all bond fund investors need to be aware of before entering into this investment.

Just as there are different types of bonds, there are a variety of different bond funds. The first distinction is between **taxable bond funds**—which invest in either corporate bonds, government debt, or a combination of the two—and **tax-free municipal debt funds**.

Tax-Free Bond Funds

Typically, higher-income fund investors will focus on tax-free bond funds. Muni bond funds are particularly attractive to investors who are not only in high federal tax brackets, but live in high-tax states. As you'll recall, muni bonds have the advantage of not only being federal tax free, but in many cases, state and municipal tax free for residents who purchase muni debt issued by their home state.

If you're investing in a muni fund and are seeking state and local tax exemption, it's important to invest in a **single-state muni bond fund** that invests in debt issued only by your state of residence. In addition to the hundreds of national muni bond funds in existence, there are a number of single-state funds that focus on debt issued by states like California, New York, New Jersey, Pennsylvania, and Ohio. There are now single-state muni bond funds available for smaller states too, like Tennessee, Hawaii, Alabama, and Oregon. Figure 8-8 lists states with a choice of muni bonds.

The one caveat concerning single-state muni funds is that they don't provide the level of diversification that a national muni fund does. After all, if some bonds in a California muni debt fund are losing value because of problems with the state's finances, then many other Golden State muni bonds could also suffer.

States	
Alabama	Minnesota
Arizona	Missouri
California	New Jersey
Colorado	New York
Florida	North Carolina
Georgia	Ohio
Hawaii	Oregon
Kansas	Pennsylvania
Kentucky Muni Debt	South Carolina
Louisiana Muni Debt	Tennessee
Maryland Muni Debt	Texas
Massachusetts	Virginia
Michigan	

FIGURE 8-8 · Single-State Muni Fund Availability.

As the muni bond fund universe expands, there are now specialized funds, such as **high-yield muni bond portfolios**, that focus on higher-yielding debt issued by municipalities with lower credit qualities.

Because of their tax benefits, it would be a waste to invest in these tax-free bond funds within a tax-advantaged account, like a 401(k) or IRA. That's because you don't need tax advantages in an account that already shelters your gains from the reach of the federal government. These investments are far better suited for use in regular brokerage accounts by investors in high-income-tax brackets.

There's one more thing you need to know about muni bond funds. In the previous chapter we discussed ways for individual investors to gauge the relative attractiveness of muni bonds vis-à-vis Treasuries by calculating their taxable-equivalent yields. This is useful for investors of individual munis, but less so for investors of muni bond funds.

Remember, while an individual muni bond has a fixed yield, a muni bond fund—because it invests in hundreds of different issues (the average owns more than 220)—does not. Depending on which muni bonds get bought and sold by the fund manager, the average yield of that bond fund will fluctuate. So while it is mathematically possible to calculate a taxable-equivalent yield for a bond fund, it would be a useless number.

Ultra-Short and Short-Term Bond Funds

Within the corporate bond fund universe, portfolios are segmented based on the average maturities of their holdings. For example, an **ultra-short-term bond** fund will typically invest in bonds maturing in about a year or two or sometimes even less. According to Morningstar, the average maturity of the typical ultra-short bond fund is roughly two and a half years. And the average duration of such funds is about one year, meaning it's fairly conservative when it comes to exposing you to interest-rate risk.

Ultra-short-term bond funds are typically going to lose the least, among all types of bond portfolios, in periods of rising interest rates. That's because as ultra-short-term bonds come due faster, the money can be quickly reinvested by the fund in newer, higher rate bonds, which gives these portfolios some degree of interest rate protection.

Investors who are seeking slightly higher yields than those offered by money market funds will often use ultra-short-term bond funds as quasicash accounts. However, it is important to note that unlike a money market fund, which is virtually guaranteed not to lose money, ultra-short-term debt can lose money in certain periods.

In fact, during the 2008 market meltdown, several ultra-short-term bond funds actually posted double-digit percentage losses because they were invested in extremely short term mortgage-related securities. And when the mortgage meltdown imploded, the value of those bonds fell. So it's important to remember that an ultra-short-term bond fund is an investment that comes with risk; it is not a risk-free cash instrument.

As for **short-term bond funds**, they typically invest in securities maturing in about two to five years, with an average maturity of close to three years. There is a greater chance of principal losses in a short-term fund than in ultra-short-term funds when rates rise. In 1994, for example, when interest rates rose quickly, the average short-term bond fund lost money, whereas ultra-shorts, on average, held their ground. On the other hand, their slightly longer maturities have allowed short-term funds to average total returns of 4.8 percent over the past 15 years through December 2009. That compares with the 4.1 percent average annual returns produced by ultra-shorts during this period.

Intermediate-Term Bond Funds

Intermediate-term bond funds invest in a mix of corporate and government debt with maturities of around five to seven years, with an average maturity of close to seven years. As a result, these bond funds are likely to constitute the "core" fixed-income holdings of many bond investors. This is particularly true for bond investors who rely primarily on 401(k) accounts.

The country's largest bond fund, for example, is an intermediate-term bond fund that happens to be one of the most popular funds among 401(k) retirement plans: PIMCO Total Return. In fact, more often than not, if you are offered the choice of a bond fund within your company-sponsored retirement

Category	Average Maturity	Average Duration
Long-term general	14.9 years	9.2 years
Intermediate-term general	7.3 years	4.4 years
Short-term general	3.0 years	2.1 years
Ultra-short-term general	3.0 years	0.9 years
Long-term government	21.7 years	13.9 years
Intermediate-term government	6.8 years	3.6 years
Short-term government	3.2 years	2.0 years

FIGURE 8-9 · Average Durations of Various Types of Bond Funds.*

*Data through December 2009.

Source: Morningstar

plan, it is likely to be an intermediate-term bond fund rather than a short- or long-term fund.

As can be seen in Figure 8-9, according to Morningstar, the average duration of an intermediate-term bond fund is roughly four years, which means that if interest rates rise 1 percent, these portfolios are likely to lose around 4 percent in value. (You'll recall that **duration** is a statistical measure of interest-rate sensitivity; a bond fund with a duration of 1 is likely to fall 1 percent when market interest rates rise 1 percent. That same bond fund is likely to rise 1 percent should rates fall 1 percent.)

Despite its heightened interest-rate sensitivity, over long periods of time a well-managed intermediate-term bond fund can serve as a great source of ballast for your overall portfolio. And over time, it can produce sizable total returns. Over the past 15 years through December 31, 2009, the average intermediate-term bond fund generated average annual returns of around 6.0 percent, which is greater than the long-term historic average returns for bonds in general. To be sure, this is due in large part to the historic period of falling interest rates that took place in the 1980s, 1990s, and 2000s. Still, the numbers show that bond fund investors need to consider not just the yield of fixed-income securities, but the total returns.

Increasingly, investors are beginning to question whether they need exposure to a long-term bond fund, or if an intermediate-term bond fund is sufficient.

Long-Term Bond Funds

Long-term bond funds invest in securities that typically mature in around 10 years or more, making these the riskiest of all categories of investment-grade bond funds in periods of rising interest rates.

Typical long-term bond funds have an average maturity of nearly 15 years (Figure 8-9). Their average duration is more than 9 years, meaning a 1 percent rise in rates could lead to 9 percent losses for these portfolios. Of course, this also means that in periods of *falling* interest rates, these portfolios stand to perform the best among all categories of bond funds. Indeed, that has been the case in the past. This explains why the typical long-term bond fund lost more than 6 percent of its value in 1994, when rates rose dramatically, but surged nearly 23 percent in 1995, when rates subsequently fell.

Though long-term funds offer investors the fattest yields among bond portfolios, investors need to be cognizant of the added principal risks associated with these funds. Though most investors associate the phrase "long term" with a conservative approach to investing, within the bond fund universe long term bonds are the riskiest.

Government Bond Funds

In addition to general bond funds, there is a separate category of funds that invests primarily in federal government debt. These funds are also segmented based on their average maturities.

Funds that invest in Treasuries and other forms of government debt maturing in two to three years are classified as **short-term government bond funds**. Those that invest in government debt maturing in five to seven years are **intermediate government bond funds**. And those that hold government debt maturing in more than 10 years are **long-term government bond funds**.

As we noted and discussed in Chapter 6, there is also a new form of government bond fund that invests in bonds whose principal value is adjusted to reflect the impact of inflation over time. These portfolios, known as **TIPs funds**, invest in **Treasury inflation-protected securities**.

Balanced Funds

Balanced funds, or **hybrid funds** as they are sometimes called these days, are allowed to invest in a mix of both stocks and bonds. Typically, the mix is set at around 60 percent equities/40 percent bonds. But depending on the circumstances—for example, if the equity markets look appealing—the manager has the authority to change that allocation strategy to take advantage of opportunities.

During the bull market years of the late 1990s, many balanced funds shifted to a 70 percent stock/30 percent bond allocation. Others were even more aggressive, socking as much as three-quarters of the fund's assets into equities. But as the bear market took over in 2000, many of these portfolio managers downshifted their funds by going back to the usual 60-40 split.

There used to be only one distinction among hybrid or balanced funds: between **domestic hybrids**, which only invested in the United States, and **international**

hybrid funds, which could invest abroad. But today this class of funds has grown to the point where there are now further distinctions made within the realm of domestic balanced portfolios: **conservative allocation domestic hybrid funds** and **moderate allocation domestic hybrids**.

As the name would indicate, conservative allocation domestic hybrids tend not to shift too much into equities, for fear of the added risk that brings to an overall portfolio. In 2009, for example, the average conservative allocation fund held more than 50 percent of its assets in bonds, slightly less in stocks, and the remainder in cash. In comparison, the moderate allocation domestic hybrids are a bit more willing to overweight stocks. The typical moderate allocation fund has about two-thirds of its money in stocks and the remainder in bonds and cash.

Because balanced funds can shift their stock-bond weightings on a dime, it is important for investors who care about their overall asset allocation strategy to keep close tabs on these funds, to ensure that a shift by a balanced fund manager—either into or out of equities—does not throw an overall financial plan out of whack.

Final Thoughts

Mutual funds were designed to make our lives simpler, by allowing us to build a diversified portfolio of stocks and bonds with one or two simple decisions. But the fact of the matter is that deciding which mutual fund to buy has become as complicated—if not more—than choosing individual stocks or bonds. In part, that's because of the proliferation of tens of thousands of funds in the modern mutual fund industry. But it also has to do with the sophisticated nature of fund investing today. In addition to basic stock and bond funds, there are actively managed funds and index funds to choose from. There are large-cap, mid-cap, and small-cap portfolios to consider. There are general equity funds and specialty funds to choose between. And the bond fund universe has become just as specialized.

Because of the complex nature of the modern mutual fund—and the enormous popularity of these vehicles among all types of investors, ranging from 401(k) account owners to high-net-worth investors—we have broken our discussion on funds into two chapters. In the next chapter we will discuss some key mutual fund terms and concepts that will hopefully help you figure out how funds work.

QUIZ

1. **Which of the following does not belong on this list of asset classes?**
   A. Stocks
   B. Bonds
   C. Funds
   D. Cash

2. **A mutual fund is owned by . . .**
   A. Its shareholders.
   B. The companies whose shares it owns.
   C. The company that runs the fund.
   D. None of the above.

3. **The following types of investors use mutual funds in their investment portfolios:**
   A. The wealthy
   B. The middle class
   C. Both
   D. Neither

4. **Index funds always beat actively managed portfolios.**
   A. True
   B. False

5. **Actively managed funds are always riskier than index funds.**
   A. True
   B. False

6. **A small-cap growth fund is an example of what type of equity portfolio?**
   A. General stock fund
   B. Sector fund
   C. Actively managed fund
   D. Index fund

7. **Sector funds concentrate their bets on . . .**
   A. Stocks of a particular size.
   B. Stocks of a particular industry focus.
   C. Stocks of a particular style.
   D. Actively managed sectors.

8. **In a period of rising interest rates, the safest types of bond funds to own in general are . . .**
   A. Government bond funds.
   B. Municipal bond funds.

C. Short-term bond funds.
D. Long-term bond funds.

9. **A bond fund with a "duration" of 7 is likely to lose this much if interest rates rise by 1 percent:**
   A. 0.07 percent
   B. 0.70 percent
   C. 7 percent
   D. 70 percent

10. **A balanced fund typically splits its holdings between . . .**
   A. Actively managed stocks and indexes.
   B. U.S. and foreign stocks.
   C. Stocks and cash.
   D. Bonds and cash.
   E. Stocks and bonds.

chapter 9

Demystifying Mutual Funds II

CHAPTER OBJECTIVES

In this chapter, you will learn the following:

- How fund commissions work
- How fund fees work
- Different types of hidden fees you will encounter
- The case for mutual funds
- The case against investing through a mutual fund

Although mutual funds were designed to make our lives simpler, they aren't as simple to figure out as some would have us believe. For example, while mutual funds are sort of like stocks in the sense that investors own shares of them, stocks and mutual funds are structured entirely differently. Given that fact, it is important for all fund investors—and would-be investors—not only to familiarize themselves with different types of funds, but also to understand how these portfolios work. This includes obtaining a general knowledge of how funds are bought and sold as well as the fees and commissions they charge.

Let's start with some key mutual fund terms and concepts.

Net Asset Value or NAV

NAV stands for **net asset value**. Your fund's NAV is in essence the total **market value** of all the securities in the portfolio at a given moment, minus expenses and liabilities. If you were to then divide the NAV by the total number of shares that are outstanding, you would arrive at the fund's **NAV per share**, which represents the current price of your fund shares.

A mutual fund, like a stock, issues shares whose prices fluctuate. In a stock, the price of shares fluctuates depending on what investors are willing to pay for each unit of ownership of that company at that moment. Shares of mutual funds are also set by the market, but in a slightly different way. At the close of each trading day, a mutual fund will assess the total value of its portfolio based on the prices of the individual securities in that fund to determine its NAV per share. Here's the formula that funds use to calculate their NAV:

Total market value of portfolio − Liabilities/Total shares outstanding

= NAV per share

So, for instance, if the fund owns $10 million worth of stocks as of today's close, has $100,000 in liabilities, and has 1 million shares outstanding, its NAV would be $9.90.

$10 million = Total value of portfolio

$100,000 = Liabilities

1 million = Total shares outstanding

$10 million − $100,000/1 million = $9.90

Notice that the fund's NAV has nothing to do with the book value or intrinsic value of the securities in the portfolio. It only involves the market prices and values of its holdings. But this makes sense. The only way to gauge the fluctuations of an investment on a daily basis is to rely on market prices. After all, it is impossible to do minute-by-minute book value calculations for a stock since companies don't report changes in their book value daily.

To determine what your fund holdings are worth, then, you would simply take the total number of shares you own and multiply that by the current NAV per share.

Here are a couple of basic formulas to remember:

Total number of shares in the fund × NAV per share = Total assets of the fund

Your investment/NAV per share = Number of shares you receive

Total number of shares you own × NAV per share = Your total investment

Going back to our example, let's say you want to invest $10,000 in this fund with a current NAV per share of $9.90. Your investment = $10,000 and NAV per share = $9.90. Let's plug that into one of our formulas:

Your investment ($10,000)/NAV ($9.90)= 1,010.1 shares

Now, let's assume that the fund's NAV, over the course of the next year, jumps to $10.75 per share. We know the number of shares you own and we know the NAV per share. So we can calculate how much your current total investment is. Turning to another formula:

Total number of shares you own (1,010.1) × NAV ($10.75) = $10,858.58

Going back to our earlier formula for calculating returns, we take our new value, subtract out the old value, and divide by the old value. Here, the new value = $10,858.59. The old value = $10,000.

New value ($10,858.58) − Old value ($10,000) = $858.58

$858.58/Old value ($10,000) = 8.6 percent

Still Confused?

The NAV of a fund helps you understand what each share of that fund is worth. This figure is not a best guess or someone's subjective opinion of what the fund should be worth based on its holdings. Instead, it's based on the actual market value of all the securities that a fund owns at a particular moment in time.

No-Load Funds

No-load funds are also referred to as **direct-sold funds**, since investors do not require brokerage accounts to purchase these shares. No-load funds are purchased and sold directly through fund companies and do not come with any commission charges. In this sense, by purchasing a no-load fund directly from a fund company, you avoid two commissions—the first to your brokerage account for the basic transaction cost, and the second involving the load that goes to the advisor or third party who recommended the fund to you.

As such, no-load funds are often considered more cost-effective vehicles for individual investors who are comfortable selecting funds and making asset-allocation decisions on their own. Examples of classic no-load fund operations include those run by the Vanguard Group, T. Rowe Price, and Fidelity. While no-load funds tend to get the most publicity in the financial media—in part due to their favorable cost structure—they represent a minority of all the mutual funds sold in the country.

Typically, no-load funds will advertise their no-load status, since this is their selling point—that they're cheap. In addition to being cheap on a commission basis, no-load funds also tend to be cheaper on annual fees, which we will discuss in a moment. The average expense ratio for all domestic stock funds is 1.35 percent of assets each year. The typical annual expense for a pure no-load U.S. stock fund, on the other hand, is just 1.09 percent of assets.

Loads

A **load** is the commission you pay for purchasing shares of funds sold by financial advisors, brokers, or other intermediaries. Load funds come in basically three different forms: **A share class load funds** (front-end load), **B share class funds** (back-end or deferred load), and **C share class funds** (level load). An advisor-sold fund will often be made available in all three share classes.

For instance, the Growth Fund of America, one of the country's biggest stock funds in the country, with about $150 billion in total assets, is available to investors in A, B, and C share classes. While the underlying fund is the same, the way you pay the commission differs. And the important thing to remember is that you get to pick.

For the characteristics of these three classes of funds, which we will now discuss more fully, see Figure 9-1.

Front-End Loads

In an A share fund, the load is typically levied up front, before an investor puts money into the market. This is why A shares are sometimes referred to as **front-end load funds**.

	Total No. Funds	Average Front Load	Average Back Load	Average 12b-1	Average Expense
A share	3,261	4.66%	n/a	0.23%	1.27%
B share	2,818	n/a	4.59%	0.91%	2.00%
C share	2,591	0.15%	0.93%	0.92%	2.00%

FIGURE 9-1 · Characteristics of Different Share Class Funds.*

*Data as of March 31, 2004.

Source: Morningstar

Here's how it works: Say the A share fund charges a load of 5 percent. And say you are about to invest $10,000 into the market. With an A share fund, not all $10,000 will see its way into the market. Because the advisor, broker, or other intermediary is taking a commission for advising you to purchase the fund; 5 percent of your $10,000 will be deducted before being invested. This means in an A share fund, you would start out investing $9,500, not the original $10,000 you had planned. According to industry reports, approximately one-quarter of all domestic stock funds impose a front-end load, with a typical commission running between 3.25 and 5.75 percent.

Back-End Loads

In a B share class, the load is not taken up front, but rather, at the end, when you sell your shares. This is why these investments are sometimes called **back-end** or **deferred load funds**. These back-end loads typically run from about 1 to 6 percent. And a common feature of these loads is that they diminish gradually over time. So the longer you hold the fund without selling, the more time delay to pay the commission, and often, the lower the commission.

But don't think this necessarily makes B share class funds less expensive than A share class funds. That's because, to compensate for the delay in receiving commissions, B share class funds often charge more in annual expenses than A share class funds.

This is a critical point when it comes to investing in deferred load funds. After all, given the choice between paying a full commission now or paying a potentially smaller one in the future, many investors would jump at the chance to delay their commission. But the fact is, these investors end up paying as much—or in many cases more—since they end up losing more to annual fees in an attempt to avoid a onetime commission.

Level Loads

There are also C share class funds, which are sometimes referred to as **level-load funds**. These funds sometimes have a combination of a front- and back-end load. While the commissions themselves may be somewhat lower than what one might be charged in an A share or B share fund, C share class funds also tend to charge higher annual fees to compensate for the lower upfront commissions.

The average C share class fund charges annual expenses of 2 percent of assets, well in excess of the overall fund average. Some C share class funds will drastically reduce their front-end load, but may charge in excess of 3 percent of annual fees to compensate. In many cases, C share class funds charge the maximum allowable 12b-1 fee, a type of marketing fee we will discuss later in the chapter.

Still Confused?

The difference between an A, B, and C share class of a fund is not what the fund owns but how much the fund charges in commissions—and when you must pay that commission. A share class funds charge commissions up front, B share class funds defer those commissions, while C share class funds spread commissions out evenly over time.

Expense Ratios

It costs money to run a mutual fund, and the **expense ratio** represents the annual fees that fund investors must pay every year to fund those costs. These fees can generally be broken into three major categories: **management expenses, distribution fees**, and **shareholder servicing costs**.

The management fee is typically the largest of these fees. In addition to the salaries of fund managers, fund companies must also pay for a staff of analysts to research various investments. Plus, there is the cost of obtaining the research itself, be it through travel or other related expenses. Many fund companies, in addition to compiling their own analytical data, will purchase institutional stock and bond research from Wall Street brokerage firms to supplement their data. Others will rely on expensive software systems that help them track the financial strengths and weaknesses of an entire universe of tens of thousands of stocks.

These fees tend to run from about 0.25 percent to 1 percent of assets a year. This means that if you invest $10,000 in a fund charging 1 percent management fees, the company will deduct $100 from your account each year. If you invest $100,000, it will deduct $1,000 a year.

Distribution fees, which are also known as **12b-1 fees**, are marketing expenses, which we will discuss in a second.

As for **shareholder servicing costs**, they refer to the expenses that arise from having to provide customers with basic service. This includes everything ranging from record keeping, printing and mailing documents, and operating phone banks. While **shareholder record fees** are typically the smallest of the three basic fees, they can sometimes run as much as 0.25 or 0.33 percent of assets.

Unlike management and 12b-1 fees, which are broken out and listed as separate line items on fund reports provided by fund tracking organizations, shareholder servicing fees often aren't listed. To determine how much you're being assessed every year, go to your fund's prospectus and turn to the page that lists annual operating expenses. Shareholder servicing fees might be called "other fees" in the prospectus, near the section where the document discusses the fund's 12b-1 charges and management expenses.

Combined, these three basic fees represent your **total expense ratio**, which is deducted from your fund's returns. The average total expense ratio for all mutual funds—including stock and bond funds—is about 1.30 percent, while the average total expense ratio for domestic stock funds is about 1.35 percent. This figure should be highlighted in your fund's prospectus, but it should also be easily found when looking up a fund through various Web sites like www.morningstar.com, www.cnnmoney.com, and finance.yahoo.com.

Hidden Expenses

It is important for all investors to understand two things about the total expense ratio.

First, despite its name, it does *not* represent the totality of all fees. For example, every time your fund manager places a buy or sell order on a stock or bond, he or she incurs the same type of brokerage commissions that individual investors must pay when they make an investment transaction. Yet the costs of these **transaction fees** do not appear in the total expense ratio, even though it can sometimes be as big an expense as overall management fees.

Industry studies have shown that these transactional fees cost investors another 0.25 percent of assets. And the fact of the matter is, fund investors still end up footing the bill. Even though this expense isn't included in the calculation of the expense ratio, it is still deducted from a fund's net asset value, which means that you end up paying for it anyway. On a $50,000 fund account, you may be paying an additional $125 a year that you might not be aware of. Over time, this could work out to be a substantial sum, given the effects of compound interest.

Fees are Deducted from Returns

The second thing you need to know about a fund's expense ratio is that it comes straight out of your fund's total returns. In other words, instead of presenting you with a bill, your fund will deduct that sum from its performance. Indeed, the total return figures you see published in newspapers tables and on Web sites are calculated *after* the fees have already been deducted. Here's how it works:

- Say you invest in a fund that gains 10 percent in gross market performance but charges 1.5 percent in total expenses. Its total return would be 8.5 percent. While fees of 1.5 percent don't sound like a lot, it can actually turn into a huge sum over long periods of time. Consider this: A fund that grows 8.5 percent a year over 25 years will turn $100,000 into $768,700 during this time. On the other hand, a fund that returns a full annualized

10 percent over this time will turn that same $100,000 into nearly $1.1 million. That's a difference of more than $300,000.

- Now, say you're comparing two funds, one that charges 0.25 percent total annual expenses and another that charges 3 percent. And assume that both funds deliver the same gross market return of 12 percent. The fund that charges 0.25 percent will report a total return of 11.75 percent; the fund that charges 3 percent will show a total return of only 9 percent. A $100,000 investment that grows 9 percent a year for a quarter century becomes around $860,000. A $100,000 investment growing 11.75 percent for 25 years becomes nearly twice that: $1.6 million.

- Fees are particularly damaging to lower-returning investments, since they eat up a greater percentage of gross returns. So say you're investing in a bond fund, which typically returns far less than an equity portfolio. Assuming your fund earns 5 percent in gross returns and you lose 2 percent of that to fees, you'd have only 3 percent left over. That's hardly enough to outpace inflation.

12b-1 Fees

The **12b-1** is sometimes called a **hidden load** because its function, like that of a traditional front-end load, is to compensate brokers or advisors for driving client assets into a portfolio.

The 12b-1, which is among the most controversial fees in the fund business, was devised in the early 1980s, at a time when the mutual fund industry was having difficulty attracting assets. The original purpose of the fee was to jump-start fund sales by assessing a fee on existing shareholders that could then be used to turn around and pay brokers and other third-party advisors to sell the fund to new shareholders.

To many, this seems unfair, since it penalizes the very clients who've agreed to invest money, so that the fund company can go out and attract new clients. It's akin to Home Depot adding 10 cents to every purchase that customers make in order to get more new customers in the door. Would Chrysler be allowed to get away with adding a $250 surcharge to all cars so that customers could subsidize television commercials?

For their part, mutual funds argue that these fees can actually be beneficial to existing shareholders. After all, if a fund grows as a result of additional marketing efforts, its larger asset base will allow existing shareholders to pay lower fees in the future, since costs will spread out over a larger base. This may or may not be the case, but the fact is, many funds that are closed to new investors—and therefore do not require marketing at all—still charge 12b-1 fees.

Obviously, it makes sense to avoid as many fees as possible. And this one in particular is worth avoiding. At the very least, make sure to weigh these costs against other expenses and the general performance and service that your fund delivers.

More than 17,000 out of the country's 26,000-plus funds levy 12b-1 fees, and the average 12b-fee among these funds is 0.51 percent of assets each year. The maximum 12b-1 fee that funds can levy is 1 percent of assets, according to current regulations.

Fund Turnover

A fund's **turnover rate** refers to the speed with which its manager replaces stocks in his or her portfolio. A turnover rate of 100 percent, for example, would indicate that the manager sells virtually all of his stocks in a given year. A turnover rate of 50 percent would indicate that he replaces about half of his holdings in any given year. (Figure 9-2 shows the annual turnover rate for equity funds in recent history.)

Higher turnover rates may be an indication that a fund manager is jumping on opportunities. But they also can have negative implications. Higher turnover leads to higher trading costs. And as we just discussed, every time your manager buys and sells stocks, he or she incurs regular brokerage and transactional expenses. These costs aren't borne by the investment management companies that run your funds, but rather, by the shareholders who invest in them.

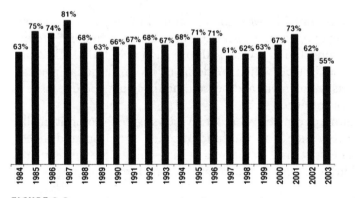

FIGURE 9-2 • Annual Turnover Rate for All Equity Funds (as a Percentage of Assets).

The annual turnover rate of stock funds fluctuates. But over time, it tends to hover just below 100 percent.

Source: Investment Company Institute

The fees are deducted from your total returns just like your expense ratio. So if a fund manager turns over his portfolio to the extent that brokerage expenses are, say, 0.25 percent of total assets, his stock picks would have to improve the fund's net returns by at least 0.25 percent to justify the expenses. If his trading leads to fees in excess of 0.33 percent of assets, then he needs to beat the market and his peers by 0.33 percent to justify that activity.

Frequent trading can also lead to higher tax bills, which are paid by fund investors too. By law, most funds must distribute to their shareholders at least once a year (typically in the fall) the capital gains realized by the fund in that tax year.

Funds realize those gains, of course, by selling stocks at a profit. While it may seem like a good idea for a fund manager to realize profits frequently, the fact is, such behavior leads to higher tax bills quickly. And the investor is responsible for paying taxes on the capital gains distribution. Now, if the manager can achieve market-beating performance as a result of such activity, that's great. But the question that the investor should ask is: Is my manager beating his peers and benchmarks at least by the same amount he's costing me in higher fees and taxes?

A low turnover fund, by contrast, is considered more tax-efficient because it delays realizing capital gains. There's also a new breed of **tax-efficient stock funds** that combine relatively low turnover with other tactics to keep tax bills low. Many of these funds will sell stocks at a profit only if they can also sell another holding at a loss. By being mindful to realize capital gains and losses at the same time, the fund can offset its gains for tax purposes and minimize capital gains distributions.

Minimum Initial Investment

All funds set a **minimum initial investment**, amount of money that a prospective investor must bring to open a new account. In most cases, fund minimums for retail share classes run from as low as $50 to as high as $10,000. There are institutional share classes as well, which are designed for professional investors and institutions such as endowment and pension funds. Those could require as much as $1 million for entrance.

In many cases, minimums can be lowered if investors agree to commit smaller amounts of money every month to the fund, through an automated investment plan. The good news is, once inside a fund, shareholders are subsequently allowed to invest additional sums in much smaller amounts.

Manager Tenure

Manager tenure does not speak to the overall experience of a fund manager, but rather, the number of years that the current fund manager has been in charge of that specific portfolio. The average mutual fund manager has a tenure of around

Type of Fund	Average Tenure (Years)*
Domestic stock fund	4.6
International stock fund	3.9
Taxable bond fund	5.3
Municipal bond fund	6.7
Balanced funds	3.4

FIGURE 9-3 • Experience Levels of Fund Managers.

*Data as of December 31, 2009.

Source: Morningstar

five years (Figure 9-3), but many have been at their funds less than that, since the fund industry perpetually rotates its managers.

Mutual Fund Advantages

Instant Diversification

The typical stock fund owns more than 200 different individual stocks, on average, at one time, according to industry reports. As for bond funds, they may own more than 400—in many cases, more than 500—individual fixed-income securities to achieve a diversified mix.

Obviously, choosing to invest through mutual funds has one big advantage: **instant diversification**. Given the choice of investing in five or six different funds or 100 or 200 individual securities to establish a diversified portfolio, the answer is easy: Go with a fund if you want to take the easy approach (Figure 9-4).

Type of Fund	Average Number of Securities Held*
Domestic stock fund	207
International stock fund	210
Taxable bond fund	500
Municipal bond fund	224
Balanced funds	314

FIGURE 9-4 • Instant Diversification.*

*Data as of December 31, 2009.

Source: Morningstar

Academic research indicates that due to increasing volatility in the stock market, investors may need 50 or more stocks in their portfolio to compensate for the **stock-specific risk** that exists in the market (you'll recall we discussed this term in Chapter 5), whereas, in the past, 20 or 25 stocks may have been sufficient. Investors can often gain exposure to more than 50 stocks with just one fund (though, for reasons we'll discuss later, you probably should diversify *among* your funds too).

Low Minimums

Not only can fund investors gain instant diversification, they don't need that much money to achieve that diversification. The typical fund will require initial minimum investments of $1,000 to $3,000 (Figure 9-5). After that, you will be able to invest additional sums of as little as $50. Many funds don't even require that big an upfront commitment. So long as an investor is willing to automatically deduct $50 or $100 a month from their checking accounts into these plans, many funds will waive the lump sum minimum initial investment.

Compare that to investing directly in the equity market and having to assemble a portfolio consisting of 200 stocks. Do you know how much it would

Fund Name	Minimum Initial Investment*	Minimum Investment for IRA	Automated Plan
Vanguard 500	$ 3,000	$ 3,000	$ 3,000
Investment Co. of America	$ 250	$ 250	$ 0
Growth Fund of America	$ 250	$ 250	$ 0
Fidelity Contrafund	$ 2,500	$ 500	$ 2,500
American Cent. Ultra	$ 2,500	$ 2,500	$ 2,500
Janus	$ 2,500	$ 500	$ 500
Templeton Growth	$ 1,000	$ 250	$ 50
Dodge & Cox Balanced	$ 2,500	$ 1,000	$ 2,500
Putnam Fund for G&I	$ 500	$ 500	$ 500
T. Rowe Price Equity-Inc.	$ 2,500	$ 1,000	$ 0
Franklin Income	$ 1,000	$ 250	$ 50
Legg Mason Value	$ 1,000	$ 250	$ 50
Longleaf Partners	$10,000	$10,000	$10,000
Clipper	$ 2,500	$ 2,500	$ 2,500

FIGURE 9-5 · Cost of Opening Accounts at Some of the Biggest Funds.

*Data as of June 2010.

Source: Morningstar

cost an individual investor to assemble a portfolio of 200 individual stocks? Probably more than $5,000—and that's just in commission costs. This doesn't reflect the actual money you're putting to work in the market.

If you invest in individual stocks through a discount brokerage, for example, you're probably looking at commission costs of around $9.95 per trade. Multiplied by 200, that works out to $1,990. But you may need to adjust your holdings over the course of the next few years, and eventually you'd have to sell. So assuming three transactions per stock—a buy, an adjustment, and a sell—that works out to close to $5,970 just in commission costs (again, not factoring in the actual principal amount of the underlying investment):

$$200 \text{ stocks} \times 3 \text{ trades per stock} = 600$$

$$600 \times \$9.95 = \$5,970$$

In a stock fund, you have the option of selecting a **no-load fund**, which, as we discussed, is a portfolio that does not levy a commission of any kind simply for buying shares.

Investors can purchase shares of no-load funds through a traditional brokerage account or also through what's known as a **mutual fund supermarket**. You're probably familiar with these supermarkets—they're run by outfits like Charles Schwab, E*TRADE, and Fidelity. These are brokerage accounts through which an investor can gain access to thousands of different funds run by hundreds of different fund companies. Like food vendors dealing with grocery stores, the mutual fund companies themselves may pay the fund supermarket for "shelf space" to sell their wares.

Though brokerages tend to charge investors a commission every time fund shares are bought and sold, there is often an exception made for fund transactions through mutual fund supermarkets. Within these fund platforms, investors can choose from what's known as the **no transaction fee menu**. This is a list of funds, often numbering in the thousands, in which a brokerage customer can purchase or sell shares of select funds without having to pay a commission to the brokerage or the mutual fund company.

The pie chart in Figure 9-6 gives the percentage of mutual funds sold via fund supermarkets and through other distribution channels.

Professional Money Management

In addition to instant diversification, a mutual fund will often buy you access to **professional money management**. The exception, of course, is with index funds, which have money managers that oversee them, but whose stock-picking decisions are left entirely up to the composition of an existing index.

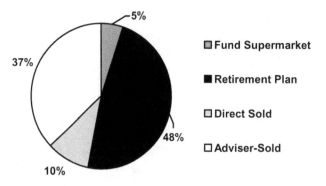

5%
37%
48%
10%

☐ Fund Supermarket

■ Retirement Plan

☐ Direct Sold

☐ Adviser-Sold

FIGURE 9-6 · How Mutual Funds Are Sold.*

This chart indicates the percentage of funds sold through so-called fund supermarkets as compared with other distribution channels.

*Data as of May 2004.

Source: Investment Company Institute

Most actively managed funds not only have a professional fund manager, they often have comanagers or even an entire team that oversees security selection. And in accordance with security regulations, these fund managers must act in the shareholders' best interest. Moreover, there are scores of analysts who work for those managers, researching individual companies, poring over financial statements and in many cases visiting the managements of those firms the fund is considering investing in. These analysts and fund managers literally kick the tires before purchasing shares of a company on your behalf.

A direct investor would have to continue to monitor his or her stocks or bonds after purchase, but a fund investor can leave all of those chores up to the professionals. For instance, if a company begins to blow up within a portfolio, your fund manager—not you—will have to deal with the decision of leaving it in the fund or exiting from it. And the fund manager is responsible for all rebalancing decisions that come up routinely over the course of a year.

Before the advent and popularity of retail mutual funds, this type of service was only available to wealthy investors who had the capital to hire their own professional money managers. Today it's available to investors with as little as $1,000, and in some cases even less.

Open-Ended Access

Though we are often advised to invest money in funds for the long term, one of the advantages of fund investing is the ability to transfer money in and out of these accounts routinely. This is sometimes called **liquidity**. The term, in the context of funds, refers to the ease—and speed—with which an investment can be purchased or sold without hassle.

Fund shares can be purchased on a daily basis with few restrictions, and fund investors can decide to pull money out of a fund on any given day. There are some circumstances, though, where funds will impose some restrictions on putting new money in—or may even block new investors from starting an account—as when a fund has become too popular or too big in a short period of time. An instant flood of cash may make it hard for the fund manager to put all of that money to work immediately in the market. And any delays in putting new money to work might hurt the short-term performance of a fund. Many index funds, for example, in an effort to keep short-term market timers from jumping into and out of a fund, may impose other restrictions as to how often an investor can jump in and out.

Mutual Fund Disadvantages

As with any entity that's jointly owned, mutual funds have a downside too. We will discuss the most prevalent ones.

Mutual Ownership

Like sharing a house with a friend, mutual fund shareholders' interests are often in conflict. This concern can be regarded as **other shareholder risks**.

For example, a longtime shareholder of an undiscovered mutual fund may find his or her returns negatively impacted by the growing popularity of the fund. Here's one possible scenario: Say you're in a modest-sized fund with $100 million in total assets under management. And let's say that over the past decade, this fund has delivered average annual returns of 15 percent. Now, assume that due to its good performance numbers or a successful marketing campaign, this fund of yours doubles in size, as more and more investors clamor to put their money in it. While momentum can often drive individual stock prices up, as demand for a finite number of shares rises, momentum can actually hurt your fund performance.

Here's why: All of a sudden, your fund manager has to manage not $100 million, but $200 million. This challenge can be daunting, for he has to find a way, virtually overnight, to invest another $100 million in stocks. If he can't find enough good stocks to put that new money into, he may be forced to leave the money in cash while he continues his search. But as we discussed before, the performance of cash accounts badly trails the average returns for stocks. If it takes weeks or months for the manager to deploy this new money, the fund will have what's known as a **cash drag**. If stocks on average return close to

11 percent annually while cash returns only 2 or 3 percent, having a portion of your assets in cash can drag your fund's short-term returns down.

Another possibility is that, in an attempt to sweep all of that new money into the market, your fund manager selects his second-choice stocks—shares of companies he likes, but not quite as much as his top picks. This too, in theory, can have a deleterious impact on your portfolio's performance.

Your fellow shareholders can also negatively impact your performance when they sell their shares of the fund. Say you're satisfied with the stock fund you're in, despite recent problems in its performance. But assume that a number of your fellow shareholders decide to exit. Think about what would happen if a quarter or a third of the shareholders in a fund decide to pull their money out at once. This is akin to a run on a bank. Remember, a fund, by law, must **redeem** shareholders who want out on a daily basis. In other words, funds have to be willing to cash out shareholders who want to exit the investment. And if a fund has to meet an inordinate number of redemptions, a couple of negative things can happen.

In one scenario, the fund manager is forced to sell some of his or her holdings in order to raise cash to meet redemptions. This may force the manager to sell at inopportune moments—when share prices are temporarily down, for instance. In addition to poor pricing, selling stocks to meet redemptions also means fund managers may have to realize capital gains sooner rather than later. And this means you, as the remaining shareholder, may be presented with a tax bill for something a former shareholder caused.

Fellow shareholders who are quick to sell their fund shares can also impact a fund's long-term performance. This happens when a manager, forced with on-going problems with redemptions, has to keep more cash on hand at all times, than he or she is comfortable with. So, instead of employing that cash in the stock or bond market, the money has to sit on the sidelines, where it creates another cash drag on the portfolio.

Once-a-Day Restrictions

As we discussed a moment ago, mutual funds are generally regarded as **liquid assets**, meaning you can access your investments and cash them out daily. But the downside of investing in funds is that you can only buy or sell shares once a day, at the day's closing price, or net asset value (NAV).

This puts funds at a disadvantage compared with individual stocks. If you own individual securities directly through a brokerage account, you can buy and sell those shares as many times as you wish throughout the day, during trading hours. Generally, that means 9:30 A.M. EST to 4:00 P.M. EST (though in the modern era, investors can virtually trade shares overnight, in after-hours markets).

While this isn't too big an inconvenience (since, with the exception of day traders, most investors don't need to make transactions more than once a day), the issue does come into play during volatile periods of the market.

Let's say that the stock market were to lose 20 percent of its value in a single day. While such moves are extremely rare, the markets did lose more than a quarter of their value in the crash of October 1987. In theory, on days where the markets are experiencing steep losses, a stock investor may be able to liquidate his or her holdings during the middle of the day, though it's unclear what type of prices a would-be buyer would be willing to pay. A fund investor, however, is stuck for the remainder of the day. Even if a fund investor places a sell order at, say, 2:00 P.M., the fund company will not redeem those shares until the trading day's close at 4:00 P.M.

This same inconvenience exists during days in which the markets are moving significantly higher. If, for instance, your fund holdings are up 5 percent or more intraday, and you decide to sell in order to book the profits, you'll have to wait until the end of the day to redeem your shares. And who knows, by then the markets might have given back some of those early gains.

This inconvenience is one reason why a new type of fund, exchange-traded funds, has started to grow in popularity. An **exchange-traded fund**, or **ETF**, is very similar to a traditional mutual fund. The only difference is, the shares of an ETF trade on an exchange like a stock. As a result, ETFs can be bought and sold throughout the day multiple times. The downside, though, is that each of those ETF trades triggers a brokerage commission. And virtually all ETFs are index funds. So if you're looking for an actively managed portfolio, a traditional mutual fund is still likely to be your simplest option.

Fund Manager Risk

We've just discussed other-shareholder risk. A second risk of investing in professionally managed mutual funds is the possibility that a poor fund manager will oversee your investment. We'll call this **fund manager risk**.

While there is some comfort in knowing that your money is being managed by a professional stock picker, there are no guarantees that the stock picker will be able to outperform his or her peers, or the markets in general. In fact, there is some evidence to suggest that over the long term, the average professional money manager can't even beat the basic indexes that he or she gets paid to best. In other words, you may be better off putting your money into basic index funds that simply hold all of the stocks in the S&P 500 index, for instance, or the Wilshire 5000 total stock market index.

A study by Standard & Poor's, the financial research firm, seems to confirm this (Figure 9-7). It found that only 39 percent of large-cap stock fund managers beat the S&P 500 index over the five-year period ending on December 31, 2009;

Type of Fund	Index	% That Beat Index Over 3 Years*	% That Beat Index Over 5 Years*
All large caps	S&P 500	50.6	39.2
All mid caps	S&P 400	26.3	22.8
All small caps	S&P 600	36.8	33.4
Large-cap growth	S&P 500/growth	31.0	23.1
Large-cap blend	S&P 500	50.4	34.9
Large-cap value	S&P 500/value	73.6	61.2
Mid-cap growth	S&P 400/growth	18.5	19.9
Mid-cap blend	S&P 400	23.8	24.3
Mid-cap value	S&P 400/value	25.6	29.8
Small-cap growth	S&P 600/growth	24.6	22.2
Small-cap blend	S&P 600	34.7	34.5
Small-cap value	S&P 600/value	51.6	51.2

FIGURE 9-7 · Active Fund Managers versus Indexes.

*Data as of December 31, 2009.

Source: Standard & Poor's

only 23 percent of mid-cap stock fund managers outperformed the S&P 400 mid-cap index; and barely 33 percent of small-cap stock fund managers outgained the S&P 600 index of small-cap stocks.

So, one way to minimize fund manager risk is to avoid fund managers altogether and stick with passively managed index funds. With index funds available today that mirror both the stock and bond markets, along with just about any foreign market you can think of, an investor can literally index his or her total portfolio.

The other option to minimize some of the damage a poor stock picker can do to your overall portfolio is to invest in more than one fund—and possibly more than one fund per asset class. For instance, instead of putting all your eggs in one basket, invest in at least two different large-cap stock funds, small-cap stock funds, foreign funds, and bond funds.

Costs

One reason why mutual fund performance generally lags the indexes is that funds must charge investors for the services they render. Indexes, because they aren't an investment, but rather a benchmark, do not. Meanwhile, index funds, because they are not actively managed, charge considerably lower management fees than actively managed funds.

Load	$100,000 Initial Investment	Year 5*	Year 10*	Year 25*
No load	$100,000	$140,255	$196,715	$542,743
1% load	$ 99,000	$138,853	$194,748	$537,316
3.25% load	$ 96,700	$135,697	$190,322	$525,104
5.75% load	$ 94,250	$132,191	$185,404	$511,536
No load vs. 5.75%		$ 8,064	$ 11,311	$ 31,207

FIGURE 9-8 · The Impact of Loads on Investor Returns.

*Assumes an average annual return of 7 percent.

Stocks				
Stock Fund	**Market Return**	**Expense Ratio**	**Net Return**	**Growth of $100,000 in 25 years**
Low cost	6.0%	0.50%	5.5%	$381,000
Average cost	6.0%	1.50%	4.5%	$300,500
High cost	6.0%	2.00%	4.0%	$266,500
Difference between high-cost fund and low-cost fund				*$114,500*
Low cost	10.0%	0.50%	9.5%	$967,000
Average cost	10.0%	1.50%	8.5%	$768,500
High cost	10.0%	2.00%	8.0%	$685,000
Difference between high-cost fund and low-cost fund				*$282,000*
Bonds				
Bond Fund	**Market Return**	**Expense Ratio**	**Net Return**	**Growth of $100,000 in 25 years**
Low cost	4.0%	0.50%	3.5%	$236,000
Average cost	4.0%	1.50%	2.5%	$185,500
High cost	4.0%	2.00%	2.0%	$164,000
Difference between high-cost fund and low-cost fund				*$ 72,000*
Low cost	7.0%	0.50%	6.5%	$483,000
Average cost	7.0%	1.50%	5.5%	$381,000
High cost	7.0%	2.00%	5.0%	$338,500
Difference between high-cost fund and low-cost fund				*$144,500*

FIGURE 9-9 · The Impact of Annual Expenses on Investor Returns.

Fund fees, as we mentioned earlier in this chapter, come in two forms: sales commissions, or loads, and annual expenses. Both types of fees are deducted from a mutual fund investor's account, and therefore hurt overall performance.

Figure 9-8 details how the impact of a no-load and various load possibilities will impact an investment of $100,000 over three periods of time.

Don't forget that in addition to the onetime commission, there are the day-to-day annual fees to consider. The stock and bond tables in Figure 9-9 show how various expense ratios will impact your total returns.

Final Thoughts

Despite a number of the shortcomings that we rattled off in this chapter concerning mutual funds—including some hidden fees and some flaws in the "mutual" ownership structure—the fact remains that funds are a convenient vehicle for all sorts of investors. Yes, their commission structure is sometimes difficult to understand. And fund companies should do a better job delineating all of the fees they charge and how those fees affect our bottom lines. But funds have several key advantages that should not be ignored. Among them: instant diversification, professional management, low thresholds for entry, and open-ended access to your money. As a result of these and other attributes, funds are likely to remain the most popular vehicle for middle-class investors for years to come.

QUIZ

1. **The net asset value of a fund represents . . .**

   A. The fund's market value.
   B. The market value of the securities that the fund owns.
   C. The intrinsic value of the securities that the fund owns.
   D. The fund's intrinsic value.

2. **No-load funds are portfolios that do not charge . . .**

   A. Expense ratios.
   B. Commissions.
   C. Hidden fees.
   D. 12b-1 fees.

3. **No-load funds are best suited for . . .**

   A. Investors who want to choose funds on their own.
   B. Investors who want to choose funds with the help of an adviser.
   C. Investors who don't mind paying fees.

4. **A front-end load will always be cheaper in the long run than other types of loads.**

   A. True
   B. False

5. **Which of the following funds is likely to perform better over time?**

   A. A fund that charges 0.5 percent in annual expenses but earns 9 percent in gross returns
   B. A fund that charges 1 percent in annual expenses but earns 10 percent in gross returns
   C. A fund that charges 2 percent in annual expenses but earns 11 percent in gross returns
   D. A fund that charges 2.5 percent in annual expenses but earns 11.5 percent in gross returns

6. **A fund's total returns includes which types of fees?**

   A. Front-end loads
   B. Back-end loads
   C. Annual expenses
   D. Transactional costs

7. **If a fund makes 7.5 percent in market returns but charges 1.5 percent in annual expenses, its actual total returns are . . .**

   A. 7.5 percent.
   B. 11.25 percent.
   C. 6.0 percent.
   D. 9.0 percent.

8. **In a mutual fund, your fellow shareholders can influence the portfolio's performance by . . .**
   A. Selling too much too quickly.
   B. Buying too much too quickly.
   C. Both.
   D. Neither.

9. **The fact that a majority of actively managed stock funds fail to beat their benchmarks is an example of . . .**
   A. Fellow shareholder risk.
   B. Market risk.
   C. Fund manager risk.
   D. Index fund risk.

10. **A fund's total expense ratio includes the following:**
    A. Shareholder servicing fees, management fees, and transactional costs
    B. Management fees, 12b-1 fees, and shareholder servicing fees
    C. Management fees, 12b-1 fees, and transactional costs

chapter 10

Demystifying Other Assets

In this chapter, you will learn the following:

- The role of real estate among your investments
- The role of commodities in your portfolio
- How ETFs work
- How closed-end funds work

Real Estate

Our Homes

Stocks and bonds get the lion's share of attention in the investing world. But the one asset that most of us are probably more familiar with, and more comfortable with, is real estate—namely, our homes. We all have to live somewhere, as the saying goes. So the idea of buying a home seems second nature to us.

In fact, while around half of all households own stocks, nearly 70 percent of Americans own their homes, which is a record number. Just as mutual funds and 401(k)s democratized the stock market for retail investors, cheap, affordable, and easy-to-obtain home mortgages have opened the door to real estate investing for tens of millions of us.

Yet ironically, many of us don't regard our homes as investments, per se. We distinguish buying a house from buying stocks or bonds. Many of us consider the former as a requisite step in adulthood, while we regard the latter as an integral part of our investment portfolios. The irony is, buying a house is probably the single biggest and most consequential investment decision you're ever going make in your financial life. Think about it: How often do most stock investors commit $300,000 or more of their money in a single transaction? What about $500,000? What about more? And how often are we willing to make a financial commitment that can last 30 years in the stock market? But in the housing market, transactions like these happen every day, among the working middle class as well as the wealthy.

A home is an investment. In fact, it is the ultimate buy-and-hold investment. Families are constantly building wealth in their properties—be they single family homes, condominiums, or rental property—simply by making their monthly mortgage payments. A home is something we put our money into, not only to feel better about where we live but in the hope of receiving a financial gain down the road. And though it does not literally pay dividends like a stock, a home offers other benefits, which we'll get to in a moment.

Of course, buying a home isn't just *a financial* decision. At the end of the day, it's still a personal choice. But you have to weigh the financial considerations too. Because if the numbers don't work in your favor, you can always rent for a few more months or years—until the numbers do work. There's no shame in that.

What Home Ownership Isn't

The way most of us go about the decision to buy a home is to ask ourselves: "Can I do better buying a home outright rather than renting?" If the answer is yes—based on the interest rate you might receive on a mortgage, what rents are going for in your neighborhood, and local and federal tax considerations—then many Americans feel utterly comfortable buying property.

It's true that for many of us paying off a mortgage is only slightly more costly than footing for rent, especially in a low interest rate environment, when mortgages are charging 6 or 7 percent annual interest, rather than 10 or 11 percent. But it's not that simple. The decision to make an investment in a home does not boil down simply to owning versus renting. The real consideration is between buying a home or renting one and doing something else with the money left over.

In other words, ask yourself, "Would it make more sense, financially speaking, to rent while simultaneously using the money that would have gone toward buying a house—the down payment, additional monthly payments that would have gone to the mortgage, money earmarked for insurance, property taxes, broker fees, etc.—toward investing in another asset?"

What Home Ownership Is

Before you invest in real estate, make sure you understand the following:

- *An investment in real estate is a bet on the economy.* To be sure, most investments implicitly count on the health of the overall economy to succeed. But when dealing with a stock or corporate bond, you are also making a wager that the underlying company you are investing in can find a way to thrive in both good times and bad. In other words, you are considering the microeconomic circumstances of the firm in addition to the macroeconomic conditions that surround it.

  When it comes to residential real estate, however, it's all about the macroeconomy. Your land and home are what they are—not a business, but a piece of property. While you can make improvements to the house itself—by updating the kitchen, renovating the bathroom, or building a swimming pool in the backyard—you can't single-handedly create a market for your house. If the job market is bad—or if interest rates are high— you might not be able to get the price you want for your home. Or you might not get any buyers, period. The bottom line: You can't force people to take the property off your hands. While stock market investors can at least count on market makers ultimately to take unwanted shares off their hands, there are no such guarantees in the housing market.

- *An investment in real estate is a bet on your local economy,* since real estate, like politics, is local. At the end of the day, the economy could be booming nationally. But if you happen to live in a town where the main employer picks up and leaves, your investment may lose value nonetheless. So in addition to the national economic scene, you also have to worry about the local economy.

  Unlike stocks, which are traded among investors around the globe, the real estate market is generally limited to the buyers who live within a certain radius of the property. (The exception are cases where people are shopping for vacation homes and their primary residences aren't in the immediate vicinity of the homes in question.) This adds an additional layer of risk to real estate investing versus stock investing: In real estate, you not only have to know when to buy or what to buy, but *where* to buy. The worst case scenario is to be forced by personal circumstance to buy high and sell low.

- *An investment in real estate is a bet on your personal economy.* A stock or bond portfolio is mobile. No matter where you live, you can maintain the same basket of securities you choose at the brokerage you choose. The same isn't true for a home. Since most of us actually have to live in the home we purchase, we require a certain level of confidence that our jobs are secure for the foreseeable future. If you lose your job or if you're forced to relocate, then your ability to succeed as a home investor may dramatically decline. To be sure, a wealthy investor can own multiple homes and sell the one he or she wants at will. But typical home investors will have to sell their existing property to buy new ones. This means you may be forced to sell your house at an inopportune time if your job situation changes. So before you enter into such an investment, be sure you're relatively confident about your own economic outlook.

- *An investment in real estate is a bet on the personal economy of your peers.* If the housing market crash of the 2000s taught us anything, it's that it takes a village to prop up a housing market. But when your neighbors run into financial troubles—for instance, if they start losing their jobs, if interest rates rise and they can no longer afford the homes they are in—it can often lead to an increase in selling in the housing market. And as more sellers come into the market, the value of your home is likely to sink with that of your neighbors'. This is why individual homeowners must pay attention not only to their own financial health but also to the well-being of their neighbors if they want to enjoy a stable housing market.

Having said that, let's talk about the pros and cons of investing in the real estate market.

Advantages to Real Estate

One of the reasons we regard home ownership differently than stock ownership is that homes are the one asset that have a dual purpose: You can put your money into them in the hope that over time someone will be willing to pay more for your property than you did. But until that happens, you can also live in the property itself, using the money that would have gone toward paying rent to building equity in your home in your name. You can't do that with a stock certificate.

This brings us to the first advantage of investing in a home: You don't have to count on quick returns. If the housing market is stalled, for example, you can always just live in the home and enjoy it for what it is—even if it takes years, if not decades, for prices to rise sufficiently to interest you in selling. Whereas the concept of "dead money" arises frequently in the stock market—that is, if a stock is languishing, an investor may want to explore alternatives that represent better short-term opportunities—there isn't the same concern in home ownership. After all, while you're living in the home, it is still serving a purpose—shelter—no matter what price other would-be buyers are currently placing on your property.

But there are a number of other reasons why buying a home or other real estate is attractive.

Broad Access to Financing

To be sure, credit is by no means as easy to obtain and widespread as it was at the height of the housing boom in the early 2000s. Back then, would-be homeowners didn't have to put more than 5 percent down to legitimately qualify for a mortgage. Or in many cases, they weren't required to put anything down. And as for one's credit health, some lenders didn't even check borrower's credit scores during the boom. And that's certainly no longer the case.

Still, after the financial crunch of 2008, credit has slowly begun to resurface. True, you may have to put 20 percent down toward the purchase of a home. But certain FHA-qualified loans may allow you to put as little as 3.5 percent down.

The fact is, as long as you have a decent track record of paying back your debts, and as long as you can show proof of income, you are likely to be able to obtain a 15- or 30-year loan whose value is about three or four times your annual income. Assuming you earn $100,000, that might work out to a home purchase of about $300,000.

Homes Are a Hard Asset

The problem with stocks is that equities are an abstract investment: Though you own a piece of a company, there is little tangible evidence of your endeavor. And unless you are a major investor in the company, you have little control over what the company does or what strategy it undertakes.

Residential real estate, on the other hand, is a **hard asset**. You can see it, touch it, and step into it. If you have the money and wherewithal, you can physically improve the asset by repairing it, fixing it, adding to it, and beautifying it. These are all decisions that you, as the homeowner, control. Best of all, as we stated before, while you're waiting for the asset to appreciate, you can live in it.

Real Estate Diversifies Your Portfolio

If anything, real estate serves a key asset allocation purpose: *Home prices tend not to correlate with movements in the stock market.* We know this anecdotally. For example, during the 2000 bear market, houses experienced one of their greatest bull markets in history, as investors pulled money out of equities and used it to buy homes, to buy bigger houses, or to renovate their existing homes in an attempt to invest in a more tangible asset. Similarly, in 2006 and 2007, when stocks and bonds were enjoying relatively strong years, home prices fell. While people never want to see losses in their investments, the point is that home values zigged when stocks and bond values zagged.

But we also know that real estate is a good diversifier based on statistical measures. One way investing professionals weigh the similarities or dissimilarities between two assets is to consider a statistical measure called **R-squared**. The term refers to a mathematical estimation of how much of an investment's behavior can be explained by the movements of a benchmark.

For example, the R-squared of a typical large-cap growth stock fund might be around 90, meaning 90 percent of the ups and downs of that fund can be explained by the ups and downs of the S&P 500. This makes sense, since large-cap growth stock funds tend to invest in stocks found in the S&P 500 index.

But the R-squared of a typical fund that invests in real estate is only around 68 (Figure 10-1), meaning that far less of its behavior can be attributed to the volatility of the S&P 500. From a diversification standpoint, this is a meaningful distinction. So investing in real estate allows some of your money to zig when the stock market zags.

Investing in What You Know

Investing in what you know is one of the most popular concepts in the stock market. Simply stated, it calls for putting money into businesses that we're most familiar with, on the theory that familiarity builds expertise. This may

Investment	R-squared*
Technology stocks	79
Telecommunications stocks	73
Financial stocks	74
Utilities	64
Health-care stocks	64
Natural resources stocks	58
Real estate	68

FIGURE 10-1 · Correlations to the S&P 500.

*Data as of December 2009.

Source: Morningstar

mean buying the stock of McDonald's if you're a soccer mom who takes the kids to the Golden Arches after soccer practices. It may mean considering the stock of Pep Boys if you're a Nascar dad who likes to work on the family car every weekend.

How does this translate into home ownership? Presumably, if you've done some research prior to buying a home—or if you already live in the neighborhood that you're thinking of buying in—then you're familiar with the basics: the school district, proximity to the highway, proximity to the grocery store and local mall, traffic patterns in the neighborhood, crime patterns, and the quality of other homes on the block. And as you move into the home and become even more familiar with the town, you, above all others, should know whether your community has a future or not.

Indeed, who knows more about a neighborhood than the people who live in it? All of this would seem to give homeowners an edge as investors, since they know more about the health of the local economy than pretty much anyone.

Prices Generally Appreciate—Really

Despite the losses homeowners suffered in the 2000s, in general, over the past 30 years, investments in real estate have delivered roughly modestly positive gains. And with the exception of this most recent bout of volatility in residential real estate prices, average home prices have rarely declined in this country in any calendar year, since economists began studying home prices on a national scale in the late 1960s.

This should be a comforting thought to investors who fear the volatility of equity markets. But keep in mind what we discussed earlier: While the national housing market has consistently appreciated, home prices are still set locally. And even if average home prices nationwide have rarely dipped, it does not mean that local markets don't suffer routine losses. Just ask anyone who lived in New Orleans after Hurricane Katrina or in Pennsylvania after the Three Mile Island accident.

Home Mortgages Offer Leverage

The term **leverage** refers to the act of borrowing money to invest it. The idea is, if you can borrow money, you can use the proceeds to bolster or leverage your investment to even greater gains than you could otherwise afford on your own. This is particularly true if you can borrow at a far lower interest rate than the investment itself is yielding.

In the stock market, a simple way to leverage your bets is to **buy on margin**. Your broker may offer you a margin loan at, say, 6 or 7 percent interest (depending on the prevailing market interest rates, including the prime lending rates charged by banks), to allow you to buy more stock than you can currently afford. If you borrow at 6 percent and invest in a stock that rises 12 percent, you would reap the rewards of those shares bought with borrowed money, despite the fact that you couldn't afford to buy those shares without the loan, and despite the negative interest you're being charged on the loan.

It works somewhat the same way in the housing market. When we seek out a 15- or 30-year mortgage, we're betting that the house we are purchasing will appreciate more, over the life of the loan, than the interest rate we're being assessed. So if you're planning on taking out a 5-percent 30-year fixed rate mortgage, you are betting that the house will appreciate more than 5 percent a year for the next 30 years. Over the past 30 years, through the end of 2003, this has proven to be a good bet in general, as the real estate market has delivered more than double those gains.

Homes are the one asset investors can purchase with 90 percent or even 100 percent or more leverage. In other words, you can reap the financial rewards of home ownership even though you are taking out a loan that represents virtually the entire purchase price. By comparison, many brokerages will require that stock investors who seek out margin loans have, in their accounts, holdings representing roughly half the value of the debt they're seeking.

Real Estate Can Pay Off in Two Ways

Like stocks, a good deal of the gains in real estate investments comes in the form of capital appreciation. As home prices rise and as new home buyers are willing to pay ever higher prices for your property, opportunities present themselves to book a profit. But don't forget the income-generating opportunities through real estate.

For starters, you can invest in **real estate investment trusts (REITs)**, companies that invest in commercial and residential real estate properties. These investments, which we'll discuss at greater length in a moment, tend to throw off decent amounts of income and represent an alternative to some types of bonds or bond funds.

There is also the income that real estate investors can enjoy if they purchase rental property. This property can be anything from renting out a room in your existing single family home to buying an entire apartment building. Obviously, becoming a landlord requires an investment of both time and money. The checklist in Figure 10-2 includes the things landlords must research before purchasing rental property.

But if the numbers work and if you have both the time and interest in being a landlord, the additional income that renters provide cannot only help pay your own mortgage, it may permit you to seek out a higher-than-normal mortgage limit. This is because projected rental income can count toward your total household income when qualifying for a loan.

- Neighborhood vacancy rates
- Neighborhood rental rates
- Renovation and repair costs for building
- State and/or local building requirements for apartment owners
- State and/or local fire code requirements
- State and/or local eviction and collection laws
- Property and liability insurance requirements
- Insurance costs
- Maintenance costs
- Costs for professional building management and/or maintenance service
- Utilities
- Parking restrictions and/or requirements
- Property taxes
- Legal consultation
- Tax and accounting consultation

FIGURE 10-2 · Checklist for Would-Be Landlords.

There's a third way in which real estate can provide income for investors, particularly seniors. As long as you've built up equity in your home, your house can serve as a financial resource for you in numerous forms. Homeowners, for example, are familiar with home equity loans and home equity lines of credit, which can be used to pull money out of a real estate investment for emergency or strategic purposes, such as funding home repair or renovation or even consolidating credit card bills.

There's a difference between a **home equity loan** and line of credit. The former is actually a loan, for a set amount of money at a set amount of interest (which is often favorable to other interest rates, since the home itself backs the loan amount). A **home equity line of credit**, however, is simply an agreement that in the event you need the cash, you can tap it from the home. In this sense, a home equity line of credit is the equivalent of establishing a credit card account—no one is cutting you a check, but in the event you need some spending money, you can have it. The advantage of establishing a home equity line of credit is that it can serve as an emergency source of cash. Moreover, you need only take out the amount you want when you want it—and no more.

But there is a third, lesser known source of cash that a house can provide. It's called a **reverse mortgage**. Like a traditional one, a reverse mortgage represents a loan. The proceeds of the loan can be paid to you in a lump sum, in monthly payments, or in some other form of routine installments. But unlike a traditional mortgage, a reverse mortgage does not require you to pay back the loan as long as you continue to live in the house against which the mortgage is applied.

Obviously, the loan must be paid back in full. But that requirement does not kick in until and unless you sell the house, move out for good, or die, at which point the house itself will serve as repayment for the reverse mortgage. The way these loans are structured, you (or your estate, upon your death) cannot owe more than the value of the home at the time of sale.

Now, there are certain limitations to reverse mortgages. Given their usefulness in supplementing income for seniors, reverse mortgages are restricted to homeowners 62 or older. Moreover, the house on which you are applying for this type of loan must be your principal residence. And not all properties are eligible for reverse mortgages. For example, mobile homes are ineligible. And while most single family homes qualify, there may be some question as to whether certain condominium arrangements and multifamily structures qualify.

In general, there are two types of reverse mortgages you can seek. One is called a **public sector reverse mortgage**, and it is sponsored by states and municipalities. These loans are only good for certain uses, like home repair and renovation. Then there are **private-sector reverse mortgages**, which tend to pay out more and whose proceeds can be used for general purposes.

Because reverse mortgage amounts are tied to the equity you have in the home, the value of the home itself, your age, and your residence, they are best suited for homeowners who have built considerable equity in their properties. Moreover, because the house you live in will be used to pay off the loan, this is probably not appropriate for homeowners who are considering bequeathing their properties to their children.

Home Ownership Has Tax Benefits

Capital gains earned on home sales, like stock sales, are subject to taxes. But there are huge advantages for homeowners when it comes to taxes. For example, though the value of your home may appreciate consistently over time, homeowners don't have to pay taxes on the appreciation until the property is sold and the gain is actually realized. In theory, this could delay paying taxes for 20 years or more. So, unlike investing in, say, zero-coupon bonds, where you will have to pay taxes on phantom income, you can control taxes in a home.

Moreover, if you're selling your primary residence, you are allowed to exclude from capital gains up to $250,000 if you're single and $500,000 for married couples filing jointly. That's the amount of **appreciation** you can exclude from capital gains taxes—not the sale price of the home. So in theory, if you and your spouse purchase a home for $500,000 and sell it for $1 million, the entire profit—$500,000—can escape capital gains taxes. What's more, you can take advantage of this capital gains exemption once every two years, which means you can be a serial homeowner who flips properties for quick profits and still avoid paying taxes on the gains. But again, this is only good for your principal place of residence.

If the property in question is rental property, you can also avoid paying capital gains taxes upon sale in certain circumstances. If you sell your primary residence and then move into a property you had been renting out for a while, for instance, you could convert the status of the rental property back to a primary residence—and after a couple of years you could then turn around and sell the property as a principal home, rather than as a rental unit. Here again, married couples could shield as much as $500,000 in gains from taxes. Or, if you immediately convert the proceeds of the sale of an existing rental property into another rental property, you can avoid capital gains taxes on the profits.

Another benefit of home ownership is that home mortgage interest is one of the few forms of debt that's deductible. Home mortgage interest on acquisition loans of up to $1 million, for instance, is fully deductible. And interest on home equity loans of up to $100,000 is also tax deductible.

Disadvantages to Real Estate

As with all things in life, there are also drawbacks to consider when investing in real estate, as homeowners are no doubt now aware of. Though many investors used to assume that real estate was a steady, stable, and conservative holding, home prices have proven to be just as volatile, if not more volatile, than the stock market. It all depends on where you live and what transpires in your neighborhood.

Aside from widespread panics, the perceived value of your home could fall quickly if negative factors surface, such as city plans to build a dump nearby, or if environmental hazards are discovered in your neighborhood. Similarly, home prices could rise dramatically if positive factors develop. Among them: the arrival of new luxury retailers and restaurants down the street, or the development of new city parks and recreational areas nearby.

The old myth that home prices shift gradually, unlike stock prices arose from the fact that we price our homes only periodically. The only time we truly get a sense of what our homes are worth is when we buy them, when our next door neighbors sell (and we get a sense of comparable values), or when we put our properties on the market. Stocks, on the other hand, are priced in real time, five days a week, 52 weeks a year, and constantly throughout each working day.

Think about it: If you were to keep your home on the market perpetually, and constantly received bids on your property, every minute of every day, you'd get a pretty divergent range of offers. Only then would you truly see how volatile home prices can be.

What are some of the other disadvantages to investing in real estate? We'll enumerate them.

There's a Long Time Horizon

While stocks can literally move 10 percent or even 20 percent in a single trading day, the economic circumstances surrounding home prices typically take a bit longer to engineer such gains. In fact, you may need to be in the home for years, if not decades, to see this type of appreciation.

To be sure, you may be lucky and a positive surprise may develop that increases property values in your neighborhood. But keep in mind that when property values rise, you probably won't be the only homeowner selling. Your neighbors, also sensing rising values, may decide to put their homes on the market at the same time. And when supply floods the market, it might not just meet demand, but in fact may exceed demand for new homes in your neighborhood. And we all know that rising supply has the effect of eventually lowering prices.

It's Less Rational Than Stocks

In the highly competitive world of the equity market, there are literally thousands of would-be buyers at any given moment for blue-chip stocks. And many of those investors—the professionals in particular—are armed with spreadsheets of financial data that guide them in pricing each share. A good number of retail investors are also being assisted by professional brokers in setting prices for their stocks. As the bids and offers are averaged out, equity market pricing becomes homogenized and the market becomes more efficient and rational.

But when it comes to buying or selling a home, there may be only a handful of buyers. And most of them are individuals who are likely to base their offers on gut feelings or on what similar homes in the area recently went for—even if the similarities are limited to basic considerations like the number of rooms in the home and square footage. This is an inexact process, which means you as a buyer run the risk of seriously overbidding for the home. Or as the seller, you run the risk of accepting a bid that does not fully account for the true value of the property and everything inside of it.

Homes Are Often Illiquid

Stock investors can easily raise cash for emergency purposes. Or they can bail out of their portfolios for strategic purposes with ease. In fact, in this day and age of online brokerages, you can liquidate any number of your stock holdings at the touch of a button.

The same is not true for home ownership. For starters, there are no guarantees that you will be able to find a buyer in a short window of time. Depending on your neighborhood and home, it may take weeks, if not months—or in some rare instances, years—to attract an appropriate bid. And this could spell trouble if your local housing market is crumbling or if you simply need to relocate for work or personal reasons. And even if you find a buyer and accept his or her bid, it could easily take another two months before the house is thoroughly inspected, the financing is worked out, and the closing is finalized. So, if you desperately need to move, an investment in a home can be problematic.

Getting Financing May Be Too Easy

While the widespread availability of home mortgages is a good thing, there is a danger in it. For starters, home investors may be tempted to take full advantage of loans that cover 100 percent or even 105 percent of the value of the property. While such loans may seem attractive at first, you run the risk of stretching yourself too thin.

This means one runs an added risk in investing in real estate: In addition to buying an overvalued property, the loan you take out could be too much for you to handle. If you fall behind on your mortgage, two things are likely to happen. First, your mortgage lender may charge steep penalty fees. And higher costs mean your property values have to increase that much more to justify the original investment. The worst case scenario is that the bank will foreclose on the property, at which point you lose ownership of the home. If this happens, not only do you lose the investment, you lose all the interest and penalty fees you had to pay to the lender.

There is yet another risk that arises with easy home loans. With the widespread availability of home equity loans in the 2000's, more and more homeowners had been dipping into their real estate investments to pay other expenses, such as vacations or home renovations or even credit card bills. In fact, while home ownership rates are at or near record highs, Americans in general own less of their homes—thanks to home equity loans and other factors—than they did a generation ago.

What's the danger? While it's true that home equity loans are relatively cheap and that interest on them is tax deductible, the risk you run is tapping most of your equity, thereby diluting your investment. The problem arises when it comes time to sell your property. If you've already tapped most of the equity from your home, most of the sales price—if not all of it—may go to your lender, not to you.

Mortgage Rates Work Against You

In an earlier chapter, we discussed how **total return** is defined as an investment's yield *plus* any changes to its price. But when it comes to buying a home, your total return is actually the change in the home's value *minus* the interest rate you're being charged on the mortgage.

Remember, as an investor, you have a choice. You can buy a home or you can rent and put the extra money into the stock or bond markets. By choosing to invest in a home, you are making an affirmative election to take on a mortgage. To be sure, some of you may have built enough equity in your prior real estate holdings to roll those profits into your new home. In that case, you may not need a mortgage, or you may not need a big one. But many of us do require mortgages to purchase real estate. And if that's the case, we need to enter into those arrangements with the full knowledge that the *mortgage interest works against us*.

For example, if you were to pay off a mortgage that charged you 8 percent, and your home appreciated 8 percent, your net returns would in essence be flat. If you took on that same 8 percent mortgage and your property did not appreciate at all during the time you owned it, your real total return would be closer to negative 8 percent.

Interest Costs May Offset Gains

While it's true that low interest rates in the 1990s and early 2000s fueled an unprecedented boom in home buying, the fact is, not all investors are eligible for such beneficial rates. Mortgage interest rates, like most consumer rates, are in part established by one's **FICO score**, or **credit score**.

FICO stands for **Fair, Isaac Co.** This is a somewhat obscure California-based company that assesses consumer credit worthiness based on information found in credit reports maintained by the **major credit bureaus: TransUnion, Equifax**, and **Experian**. Your score will range from 300 to 850. The higher your FICO score, the better your credit rating.

The good news is the majority of Americans score above 700, which is considered the threshold for good credit and therefore favorable interest rates. Even better, 40 percent of Americans score 750 or better, which is regarded by some as the threshold between good and excellent credit (Figure 10-3).

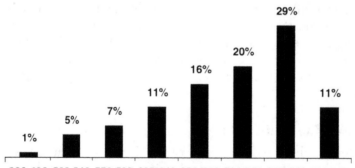

FIGURE 10-3 · FICO Score Distribution.

As this table shows, the vast majority—80 percent—of American consumers have credit scores above 700, which is considered a strong score.

Source: Fair, Isaac Co.

FICO Score	Average Mortgage Rate*	Average Monthly Payment on $300,000, 30-Yr. Loan
760–850	4.48%	$1,516
700–759	4.70%	$1,556
680–699	4.88%	$1,558
660–679	5.09%	$1,627
640–659	5.52%	$1,707
620–639	6.07%	$1,811

FIGURE 10-4 · Mortgage Rates and FICO Scores.

*Data as of June 2010.

Source: Fair, Isaac Co.

In the summer of 2010, for example, an investor with a FICO score above 760 could easily expect to obtain a 30-year fixed rate home mortgage for under 4.5 percent annual interest, which is attractive by historic standards.

Figure 10-4 depicts the consequences of a poor FICO score—and the benefits of a good score—on mortgage interest rates. In the summer of 2010, a score of 620 to 639 earned an average mortgage interest rate of more than 6 percent, about 1.5 percentage points more in interest every year than a person with a FICO score of 800.

The difference in monthly mortgage payments between a person scoring 800 and 620 worked out to $295 a month in 2010. Over the course of 30 years, if you were to save $295 each month and invested that money in the stock market at an annual rate of 7 percent, you'd amass $335,000 at the end of this period.

This is a major consideration that anyone with a poor credit rating has to consider before investing in a home. A poor credit score will mean your cost of capital will grow dramatically, which may negate the potential positive appreciation of the underlying home. Moreover, it can mean that renting, while investing in the stock market—an arena of investing that doesn't penalize you for poor credit—may be a better bet.

You Need to Commit a Lot of Money

Obviously, investing in a home is no small undertaking. Even a small starter home, or a condo, could cost you well over $150,000, if not $200,000, in today's economy. If you live in an urban setting, it could cost you significantly more.

The downside of investing in a home is that you have to commit a large chunk of your financial portfolio, potentially for years. To be sure, most of that money is borrowed or leveraged. But mortgages commit you to making payments of $1,000, $2,000, or even more, a month, every month, for potentially 30 years. And every dollar in mortgage payments you make over and above what rent would have cost you is a dollar of lost potential equity earnings. Bear in mind, shares of a stock fund can be purchased for as little as $100 or $500.

Real Estate Investment Trusts

There is an alternative way to invest in real estate, however, that does not require the commitment of hundreds of thousands of dollars. It's called a **real estate investment trust**, or **REIT**, for short. In essence, this is a company devoted to investing in real estate in some form or fashion.

There are three basic types of REITs. **Equity REITs** own and manage residential and/or commercial properties. **Mortgage REITs** extend and purchase mortgages used by others to invest in real estate. And **Hybrid REITs** are a combination of both of these strategies.

By far, equity REITs dominate the market. Some of them specialize in certain types of real estate holdings, such as office buildings, retail real estate, or residential properties. So, depending on your assessment of the economy, you can pick the type of real estate you invest in by selecting the REIT that suits you.

Though few REITs are household names, some of these firms are among the biggest financial companies in this country (Figure 10-5).

Name	Ticker	Exchange
Simon Property Group	SPG	NYSE
Equity Residential	EQR	NYSE
General Growth Properties	GGP	NYSE
Vornado Realty Trust	VNO	NYSE
Pro Logis Trust	PLD	NYSE
Public Storage	PSA	NYSE
Kimco Realty	KIM	NYSE
Boston Properties	BXP	NYSE
Duke Realty	DRE	NYSE
Avalon Bay Communities	AVB	NYSE
Liberty Property Trust	LRY	NYSE

FIGURE 10-5 · Largest Publicly Traded REITs in the United States.

Because a REIT is a publicly traded real estate company, its shares trade on stock exchanges, just like any other company. Most are listed on the New York Stock Exchange. And just like other equities, you can purchase shares directly, through a brokerage account, or you can go a safer route and buy a REIT mutual fund, which invests in a diversified collection of REITs and other real estate holdings. According to Morningstar, there are around 300 REIT funds.

The advantage of investing in REITs is clear. They are accessible like other stocks. They have a low barrier to entry, like equities and equity funds. And they are liquid. In other words, you can buy and sell shares of your REIT at will, unlike a home, which takes time to sell.

But though a REIT is traded like a stock, it is actually a different asset class entirely. In fact, some regard REITs as an alternative to bonds rather than to equities. Why? By law, three-quarters of a REIT's income must be generated through real estate holdings, and about 90 percent of its profits must be distributed to shareholders every year in the form of dividends.

This means REITs, which generate their income through property rents or mortgage interest, throw off income every year just like bonds or bond funds. In fact, the historic dividend yield of a REIT is somewhat similar to the yield on 10-year Treasury notes.

But beware: REITs are much more *volatile* than bonds. A REIT, like a stock, offers no guarantees for principal protection. So while REITs throw off income like bonds, they have the upside potential and downside risk of equities.

In fact, over the past decade through the December 2009, the average REIT generated annualized total returns of nearly 10 percent. By comparison, the S&P 500 during this stretch lost nearly 1 percent during the Lost Decade. Yet in the two-year period between 2007 and 2008, REIT funds fell by more than double digits annually, which was considerably worse than stocks.

It should be noted, however, that the dividends thrown off by REITs are not considered qualified dividend income and therefore are taxed as normal income. In other words, they do not receive the preferential 15-percent tax rate that **qualified stock dividends** do. Part of the reason is that REITs themselves do not pay taxes on the profits they distribute to their shareholders. Therefore, if you decide to purchase a REIT or REIT fund, you should give strong consideration to doing so through a tax-advantaged account, such as an IRA.

Because the behavior of REITs is not closely correlated to movements in the equity markets, a small investment in REITs can help reduce risk in an overall portfolio. For example, the financial research firm Ibbotson Associates studied the performance of portfolios with and without REIT holdings between 1972 and 2003. It found that a portfolio without REITs consisting of 50 percent stocks, 40 percent bonds, and 10 percent cash generated average annual total returns of 10.9 percent during this stretch. But if just 20 percent of that portfolio were held in REITs, that portfolio would have returned slightly more during this period—11.5 percent a year during this stretch—and with lower volatility.

Commodities

In addition to companies and real estate, you may also want to consider investing in **commodities**. What are commodities? They are pretty much any unfinished or unprocessed good that can be traded in bulk. Commodities can range from agricultural products (which are sometimes referred to as **soft commodities**)— these include pork bellies, orange juice, coffee, soybeans, cotton, wheat, and corn—to basic materials necessary for the manufacturing process, including mined metals like copper, silver, and even gold (we'll discuss this below).

When you invest in a commodity, you are doing one of two things: You either are betting on the economy or betting against it by hedging some of the risks that the economy poses. Typically, you bet on the economy with commodities tied to manufacturing, like copper, nickel, or other basic materials. Because these raw materials represent the building blocks of factory output, their prices rise as economic activity improves and demand ramps up. On the other hand, their prices are likely to fall when the economy sours and factories stop ordering these raw materials.

Meanwhile, you can bet against the economy with some precious metals commodities like gold or silver. The third category of commodities, the soft commodities, are affected less by the broad national economy as they are by specific external factors, such as the weather or some short-term trends. For instance, something as silly as the Atkins diet, which calls for eating low carbohydrate and high protein meals, can affect the price of things like livestock or wheat.

Investing in commodities is quite different than investing in stocks or real estate. After all, when you invest in shares of a company, there is always the possibility that the company can distinguish itself and add shareholder value through superior management. If you are investing in a home, you can always add value to it by repairing it, renovating it, or expanding it.

But a commodity is a raw material whose units are indistinguishable from one another. It is what it is. There is no value you can add to the commodity itself. A bushel of corn is a bushel of corn no matter who you buy it from and what you paid for it. A metric ton of scrap iron is a metric ton of scrap iron no matter what company or country it's headed for. This is why commodity investing is all about forecasting.

That being said, individual investors will be hard-pressed to invest in commodities directly. This market is primarily geared for institutional investors who can bring tens of millions of dollars to the table. And while retail investors can dabble in **commodity futures**—financial contracts tied to the delivery of metals or agricultural products at some point in the future—this can be a dangerous game. Investing in futures contracts can be especially risky if it involves high amounts of leverage. Among agricultural commodities, a surprise change in the weather can drastically alter future prices for items ranging from soybeans to coffee.

Instead, individual investors are likely to gain exposure to various commodities through mutual funds that invest in them either directly or indirectly. Like REITs, commodities—in small doses—have been shown to help diversify a portfolio of stocks and bonds over the long term.

Precious Metals

Among all the commodities, investors are probably most aware of precious metals—in particular **gold**. While gold is used in some manufacturing settings (in the making of car air bags, for one), it is primarily considered a financial asset. The Chinese, for example, started using gold coins as a form of money going back to around 1000 B.C.

Gold's historic relationship with currency—the value of a U.S. dollar used to be pegged to gold—has made it a benchmark financial asset. To this day, investors bet on gold during times of volatility in the stock market and instability in the U.S. currency market. This makes this precious metal a **hedge**, or bet, against the economy.

Gold is particularly in demand during periods of high inflation. The thinking is that if the value of the U.S. dollar is diminished by spiraling inflation, investors will seek an alternative asset that won't lose as much value because of rising prices. This explains why gold prices soared to record levels in the so-called "stagflationary" period of the 1970s, but steadily sank in the late 1980s and 1990s, when inflation was wrung out of the U.S. economy.

Investors have several options when it comes to investing in gold. They can buy it directly—through the purchase of gold coins, or even jewelry—and also invest in **gold stocks**. These are companies whose core business is tied to the mining, processing, or distribution of gold. Among some of the better known gold mining companies are Barrick Gold, Newmont Mining, and Freeport-McMoRan Copper & Gold. While shares of these publicly traded companies move with the price of gold, at the end of the day these are still shares of a company, not the underlying commodity. So an investor in a gold stock is not only making a bet on the commodity, but a bet that the management of a specific business knows how to exploit fluctuations in gold prices to generate solid long-term profits.

Name	Ticker	Net Assets*
SPDR Gold Shares	GLD	$51.1 billion
Fidelity Select Gold	FSAGX	$ 3.5 billion
American Century Global Gold	BGEIX	$ 1.1 billion
Vanguard Precious Metals & Mining	VGPMX	$ 3.8 billion
Tocqueville Gold	TGLDX	$ 1.5 billion
First Eagle Gold	SGGDX	$ 2.4 billion
Franklin Gold & Precious Metals	FKRCX	$ 2.7 billion
USAA Precious Metals & Mining	USAGX	$ 1.8 billion
U.S. Global Inv. World Precious Min.	UNWPX	$635 million
Van Eck International Inv. Gold	INIVX	$ 1.2 billion

FIGURE 10-6 · Largest Precious Metal Funds.

*As of June 2010.

Source: Morningstar

The easiest way to invest in gold stocks is to invest in a professionally managed fund that specializes in them. This is easy to do since an entire category of
mutual funds is devoted to investing in these companies. According to Morningstar, there are about 50 precious metal sector mutual funds. The biggest
funds are listed in Figure 10-6.

Basic Materials

If precious metals allow investors to bet *against* the economy, basic materials are
a direct bet on it. So are **basic materials stocks**. These are shares of companies
that are tied to the mining or production of commodities or to the production of basic components that go into the manufacturing process. Though they
aren't pure commodity plays, they are often a safer way to gain exposure to the
asset class.

Basic materials stocks can operate in a wide array of traditional smokestack
industries ranging from chemical companies to mining stocks to steel. This includes companies like Dow Chemical, DuPont, and Monsanto. It also includes
aluminum manufacturers like Alcoa, paper companies like International Paper,
and timber firms like Weyerhaeuser.

Here again, the simplest way to gain exposure to basic materials stocks is
through a fund. But unlike precious metal funds, there is no separate category
of basic materials sector stock funds. If you invest in a large-cap or mid-cap
value fund, however, there's a decent likelihood that you will gain exposure to

basic materials stocks, since their shares are often overlooked or undervalued by growth investors. You can also gain exposure to basic materials through **natural resources funds**. While these portfolios tend to focus on energy stocks, the typical natural resources fund also has decent exposure to traditional industrial concerns.

Unmutual Funds

For years, mutual funds were pretty much the only way for individual investors with small account balances to gain exposure to a diversified portfolio of stocks and bonds with relative ease and relatively few dollars. While wealthier investors had access to so-called **separate accounts**, which are private funds that cater to the specific needs and sensibilities of high-net-worth investors, middle class investors were stuck with traditional retail portfolios.

But as we discussed earlier, there are concerns stemming from the "mutual" aspect of a mutual fund. Think of a mutual fund as a community swimming pool. Because it is collectively owned, it costs little to enjoy. But whenever too many people jump into or out of the pool too quickly, it's bound to make a few waves.

Today, however, there are other options. Let's call them "unmutual funds." What are **unmutual funds**? They are investment vehicles that give folks exposure to a basket of diversified securities—in one shot—without exposing those same investors to the other fund shareholder risks we spoke of in prior chapters.

Exchange-Traded Funds

Perhaps the best-known of the unmutual funds are **exchange traded funds**, or **ETFs**. Introduced to U.S. investors in the mid-1990s, these products have grown in popularity in recent years, as can be seen in Figures 10-7 and 10-8.

ETFs are index-fund-like vehicles that track **market benchmarks**. This includes broad indexes like the S&P 500, the Wilshire 5000, or even the Russell 2000 index of small stocks. But it can also include specific sector indexes, such as the Dow Jones U.S. Technology or the S&P Global Healthcare sectors. You can also find ETFs that track a particular style of investing, like large-cap value stocks or small-cap growth. Today, there are even bond ETFs.

While they are passively managed products with low fees, there are major differences between an ETF and a regular index fund. For starters, ETFs trade on a stock exchange like the New York Stock Exchange. This means they can be bought and sold like a stock any number of times throughout the day. Regular mutual funds, on the other hand, can only be bought once a day, at the day's closing price.

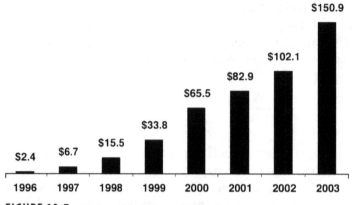

FIGURE 10-7 · ETF Assets (in Billions of Dollars).

While assets in exchange-traded funds have grown over the years, they still represent a tiny fraction of the $7 trillion mutual fund industry.

Source: Investment Company Institute

This feature can come in handy from both an offensive and defensive stand-point. If the market is tumbling, an investor in an ETF can simply trade out when the trouble occurs, at least in theory. A regular mutual fund investor, on the other hand, would have to wait until the end of the trading day. Similarly, if there are opportunities in, say, the health-care sector on a particular day, in theory an ETF investor could buy an S&P Global Healthcare ETF or a Dow Jones U.S. Healthcare sector ETF to take advantage of it— without taking on too much individual stock risk (remember, these are diversified baskets of stocks). But again the regular mutual fund investor would have to wait until the close of trading to get in.

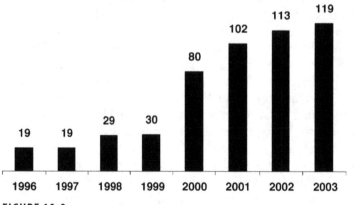

FIGURE 10-8 · Number of ETFs.

Source: Investment Company Institute

The appeal of ETFs is the way they're structured. Think of it as buying a self-contained investment that represents a cross section of ownership of dozens—in some cases hundreds—of stocks within a market benchmark or sector. Your fellow ETF shareholders also own a self-contained basket of stocks—and the good news is, their purchases or sales don't affect you. Why? It has to do with the way ETFs are put together.

ETFs are created by financial firms like BlackRock, Vanguard, and State Street. These companies can create or unbundle ETF shares at will. If you wanted to buy an S&P 500 ETF, for example, an ETF sponsor would go out and get shares of all 500 stocks, in proportion, and bundle them for you to create your own ETF. But when you go to sell that ETF, your exit won't affect your fellow shareholders. This is because instead of being forced to sell the stocks in the ETF to meet your redemption—as happens in a regular mutual fund—the ETF sponsor can simply unbundle the package and release back the individual holdings. Those individual stocks can then be used to create other ETFs for other people. This ability to bundle ETFs when necessary or unbundle them when not is what takes the "mutual" out of mutual funds.

One of the biggest advantages of ETFs is their cost. You can invest in an iShares S&P 500 ETF—an exchange-traded fund run by BlackRock that tracks the S&P 500—for 0.09 percent in annual fees. (Figure 10-9 lists other iShares ETFs.) In comparison, Vanguard 500, among the lowest cost index mutual funds around, charges 0.18 percent in annual fees. The average regular mutual fund charges 1.35 percent in annual fees. Virtually all ETFs sport annual

Name	Expense Ratio*
iShares S&P 500	0.09%
iShares S&P 500/Growth	0.18%
iShares S&P 500/Value	0.18%
iShares S&P 400	0.21%
iShares S&P 400/Growth	0.25%
iShares S&P 400/Value	0.25%
iShares S&P 600	0.20%
iShares S&P 600/Growth	0.25%
iShares S&P 600/Value	0.25%
iShares Barclays Aggregate Bond	0.24%
iShares Cohen & Steers Realty	0.35%
Average Domestic Stock Mutual Fund	1.35%

FIGURE 10-9 · Low-Cost Advantage of ETFs.

*Data as of June 2010.

Source: BlackRock, Morningstar

expense ratios of less than 1 percent, and most ETF expenses are under 0.6 percent a year.

There is one major drawback to ETFs. Because they trade like stocks, investors have to pay brokerage commissions *every time* they buy or sell. This makes them a costly option for an investor who is dollar-cost averaging. If you were on an automated program where you purchased shares incrementally every quarter, and owned 15 different ETFs, you could be looking at nearly $600 in commissions just for routine investments, based on an average commission of $9.95 per trade and 60 transactions a year. In contrast, there are no commissions with a regular, no-load index fund. Thus, ETFs are best suited for investors who make infrequent, lump-sum purchases and sales, rather than frequent, incremental trades.

To get more information about ETFs, you can go to www.morningstar.com. Another good source of information is www.ishares.com, an ETF Web site run by BlackRock, the world's leading purveyor of exchange-traded funds. Finally, www.tdameritrade.com (the Web site of the online broker TD Ameritrade, which caters to ETF investors) also offers, great educational materials on these investments.

Closed-End Mutual Funds

Like an ETF, a **closed-end mutual fund** is a portfolio of securities that trades like a single stock on a stock exchange. But closed-end funds, which have actually been around for decades, are a lot different than exchange-traded funds.

Unlike an ETF, for example, a closed-end fund is professionally managed. In other words, these aren't index products. And unlike an ETF, which can be created or unbundled at will, a closed-end fund has only a fixed number of shares to offer. In this sense, it is closer to a stock than an ETF.

So, for instance, if you are interested in buying shares of a closed-end fund, you have to find an existing shareholder from whom to purchase them. Similarly, to sell shares of a closed-end fund, you don't go to the fund company to redeem your investment—you go into the open market to trade the security. The fact that sellers have to find buyers and buyers have to find sellers regulates the flow of money into these investments. And this feature takes away a major concern that regular fund investors have: the arrival or departure of too many fund shareholders at once.

However, the flip side of having a fixed number of shares is that the price of a closed-end mutual fund is directly tied to the supply and demand of those shares—not the value of the investments in the fund. For example, while a regular mutual fund is valued by its net asset value, or NAV, the value of a closed-end mutual fund is determined by its share price. When the supply of shares exceeds demand, a closed-end mutual fund may trade at a discount to the actual underlying value of the holdings in its portfolio (this never happens in a regular fund, and in fact doesn't really take place in an ETF either, because of its unique bundling/unbundling mechanism).

So even though the fund itself is worth, say, $10 a share based on its portfolio, the market could price it at $9 a share. Similarly, there will be times when closed-end funds trade at a premium to their underlying value. During the China stock boom of 2003, to cite one instance, many closed-end China stock funds were trading 10 or even 20 percent above the actual net asset value of those portfolios.

This dynamic presents both a challenge and an opportunity for closed-end fund investors. Though the ability to buy a closed-end fund at a discount to what it's intrinsically worth makes these investments attractive to value hunters, at the same time some investors are frustrated because their closed-end fund may not fetch as much on the open market as it's truly worth.

Because closed-end funds can trade at a premium or discount to net asset value, closed-end fund investors must not only wager that they know how a particular basket of stocks or bonds will perform, but also that they are right in guessing the behavior of other closed-end fund shareholders in the open market.

There are nearly 600 closed-end funds (see Figure 10-10 for the number of closed-end funds and Figure 10-11 for the amount of their assets in recent years), and they invest in a variety of asset classes both foreign and domestic. However, because of their unique structure, closed-end funds are often considered niche investments. In fact, a vast majority of closed-end fund investments are domestic bond funds. And many others invest in niche equity and bond markets overseas.

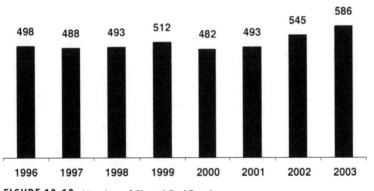

FIGURE 10-10 · Number of Closed-End Funds.

Source: Investment Company Institute

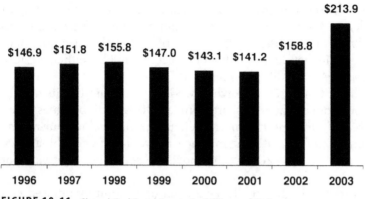

FIGURE 10-11 · Closed-End Fund Assets (in Millions of Dollars).

Although closed-end funds have been around for years, they control less than half a billion dollars in total assets.

Source: Investment Company Institute

For more information on closed-end funds, you can go to www.ici.org, the site of the Investment Company Institute, the trade organization that oversees both open- and closed-end funds.

QUIZ

1. **History shows that residential real estate is a better long-term investment than stocks.**
    A. True
    B. False

2. **Homes are considered a safe investment vehicle because ...**
    A. You can use leverage to invest in real estate.
    B. Homeowners are buy-and-hold investors.
    C. They throw off income.
    D. They are not necessarily considered a safe investment.

3. **You can tap the equity in your home through which of the following vehicles?**
    A. Home equity loan
    B. Home equity line of credit
    C. Reverse mortgage
    D. All of the above
    E. None of the above

4. **Home ownership is an inherently longer term investment than stocks or bonds.**
    A. True
    B. False

5. **Which of the following investments is considered highly liquid?**
    A. ETFs
    B. Homes
    C. Both
    D. Neither

6. **A real estate investment trust should be considered an alternative to ...**
    A. Stocks.
    B. Bonds.
    C. Cash.

7. **Commodities throw off more dividend income than REITs and stocks.**
    A. True
    B. False

8. **For fast intraday trades, the best vehicle to invest in is a ...**
    A. Mutual fund.
    B. Closed-end fund.
    C. ETF.

9. **ETFs expose you to which of these risks?**
    A. Fund manager risk
    B. Other shareholder risk
    C. Market risk
    D. None of the above

10. **A big advantage for exchange-traded funds is their . . .**
    A. Low fees.
    B. Low turnover.
    C. Professional management.
    D. Overall size.

Part III

Selecting Your Assets

chapter 11

Demystifying Stock Selection

In this chapter, you will learn the following:

- Where to research stocks
- The key elements of a company's financial statements
- How to determine a company's growth prospects
- How to judge the valuation of a stock

There is a big caveat when it comes to investing in equities. While the broad stock market is likely to be your best-performing asset over time, as we discussed in an earlier chapter, there are no guarantees that the individual stocks you select will similarly outperform competing assets like bonds or even cash. In other words, while stocks *in general* may be good bets, *your* stocks may not be.

The overall stock market reflects the *average* performance and experiences of all the shares that are available to the investing public. To arrive at that average, some stocks will outperform the average while others will under-perform it. The risk you face as an investor is: Will the stocks you choose be among those underperformers?

This means that stock investors who pick and choose their own portfolios, instead of putting their money, say, into a broad-based mutual fund, must be that much more vigilant when it comes to safeguarding their equity holdings against **company-specific risk**. While an index fund investor with a long time horizon may feel comfortable with exposure to equities regardless of what's going on in the real economy, investors in individual securities must care about trends that are taking place within their specific firms.

Truth be told, individual investors are at a distinct disadvantage in this endeavor versus professional mutual fund managers, since fund managers are backed by legions of analysts who help ferret out good companies from a sea of mediocrity. Moreover, because fund managers bring with them the backing of hundreds of millions—if not billions—of dollars in assets, they often have personal access to the companies they invest in. In other words, they can literally "kick the tires" of a company by visiting the headquarters, talking to management, and walking the factory floors to get a visceral sense of how busy and efficient the business actually is. This access allows fund managers to gauge firsthand the health and vulnerabilities of the stocks they invest in.

In contrast, individual investors, who may only be investing thousands of dollars, rarely get to meet with management. Perhaps the only setting where retail investors can associate with the company's executives is at the annual meeting, which typically takes place at or near the company's headquarters. So unless you also happen to live near the offices of the companies you invest in, you probably won't ever get to speak with their officials.

But this doesn't mean that individuals don't have access to basic tools that can help them conduct fundamental research on their stocks. In fact, in the Internet age, there are plenty of free sources of financial data, screening tools, and stock selectors to help you determine the level of company risk you're exposing yourself to by investing in a particular stock.

Stock Research Resources

Before we get into the specifics of stock selection, it's important to consider what type of information we're looking to glean. Every stock investor has to worry about two basic sets of considerations:

1. *Is the company deteriorating or likely to deteriorate?* To help you determine that, you will need information from the company's own financial documents. In addition, there's also the possibility that a company may not be deteriorating from a financial standpoint, but that other investors have simply bid up its shares so much that its price has now actually overshot the true market value of the business. In this regard, you aren't looking for

problems with the company so much as problems with the expectations that other investors are imposing on it. To determine this type of risk, you'll have to pay attention to various valuation measures.

2. *What is the upside potential of the stock?* To reiterate, stock performance correlates to profit growth. This means that as an investor one thing you'll absolutely need to know is a firm's *recent earnings performance* and the *consistency of its earnings growth over time*. This information can be obtained from various financial Web sites that we will discuss in a second. In addition, it's important to appreciate the fact that the stock market is a forward-looking indicator. This means it's also critical to weigh the *future earnings growth potential* of the business. To this end, you can turn to a whole host of financial Web sites that gather and analyze information on Wall Street analysts' projections on a stock.

Let's start by taking a look at some of the basic—and free—resources all of us can turn to. While some of you may have access to professional Wall Street research—if you have brokerage accounts established at full-service firms that assemble proprietary equity research, like Morgan Stanley, Merrill Lynch, Goldman Sachs, UBS, and Citigroup—most of us aren't privy to this type of information. These free sites, then, can come in handy for quick analysis of company risk.

Morningstar

In Chapter 13, concerning mutual fund selection, we will discuss at length the screening tools that the fund-tracking company **Morningstar** offers to fund investors. The good news for equity investors is that Morningstar has recently added similar screening capabilities and tools for stocks. Through Morningstar's free Web site **(www.morningstar.com)**, you can now screen for stocks based on the following factors:

- *Stock sectors*. If you're only interested in finding stocks in a particular industry, you can screen for technology, telecom, health care, financial services, utilities, energy, natural resources, industrial materials, or consumer-related firms.

- *Stock types*. This is based on Morningstar's own proprietary determinations concerning stock attributes. Morningstar divides the equity universe into aggressive growth, growth, slow growth, or speculative growth classifications. Moreover, you can screen for high-dividend-yielding stocks, distressed stocks, and **cyclically oriented stocks**, which are those that tend to do well when the economy is firing on all cylinders but tend to do poorly in times of recession. Typically, companies in technology, retail, telecom, consumer discretionary, and some parts of financial services are considered cyclically oriented, while many firms in health care, utilities, consumer staples, and, to some extent, energy will be classified as **noncyclical**, meaning they could do well even if the economy sours.

- *Morningstar-style boxes.* You'll recall that Morningstar breaks the general equity fund universe into nine categories: large growth, large value, and large blend; mid-cap growth, mid-cap value, and mid-cap blend; and small growth, small value, and small blend. Similarly, Morningstar will put stocks into those same classifications for direct equity investors who want to be mindful of their overall asset allocation decisions. So if you're only searching for stocks that are classified as small value, for instance, to round out a portfolio that may be large-cap and growth-oriented, you can screen for only that type stock.

- *Market caps.* With Morningstar, you can screen for stocks based on their **market values**, which again is calculated by multiplying a stock's price by the total number of shares the company has outstanding. This is particularly useful for equity investors who seek stocks with certain risk-return characteristics. If you're looking for speculative investments with high risk but high growth potential, it's likely you'll search among the **small-cap** companies (market values under $1 billion). If you're looking for large, steady eddies, you'll probably focus on the blue-chip companies found among **large-cap** companies (market values of $10 billion or more). And if you're looking to split the difference, you can always search among mid-cap companies (those stocks with market capitalization between around $1 and $10 billion). You can also screen for **micro-caps** (shares of companies with total market values of $250 million or less).

- *Morningstar grades.* As an equity research firm, Morningstar has its own proprietary grading systems for stocks based on their overall growth, their earnings outlook, and their financial stability. These grades, like report cards, range from A through F, with A being the best grade.

- *Revenues.* In addition to profits, you can screen for stocks based on sales, the importance of which we'll discuss in a moment.

- *Earnings.* Morningstar's stock screener lets you screen for stocks based on various measures of profitability.

- *Past returns.* You can screen for stocks based on their share price performance over the past one and three months, as well as the past one and five years. Investors can use Morningstar to look for stocks that are on a roll or are in distress—growth investors will be interested in the former; value investors in the latter.

- *Valuations.* Since valuations are a major consideration of a stock's relative risk, Morningstar allows investors to screen based on trailing price-to-earnings (P/E) ratios.
- *Dividend yield.* Though many investors overlook stock dividends, a stock's payout percentage is also terribly important for an investor's long-term performance. Morningstar will let you screen for stocks based on the actual percentage that stocks are currently yielding.

Zacks Investment Research

On Wall Street, there are thousands of analysts whose job it is to research companies in a variety of industries. In addition to making buy, sell, and hold recommendations on a given stock, analysts are also responsible for forecasting the earnings growth and earnings growth rates for the companies they follow.

These forecasts, while not always accurate, do shed light on expectations that Wall Street is placing on a firm's earnings, sales, and stock price performance. Unless you have a full-service brokerage account, though, chances are you're not going to have access to those forecasts—unless you're willing to pay.

This is where **Zacks Investment Research (www.zacks.com)** comes in. This financial research Web site gathers data on analysts' recommendations on a stock, their earnings estimates for that stock, and calculates a consensus of those earnings estimates. When you hear news reports, for example, indicating that Yahoo! "beat the Street's consensus forecast" for quarterly earnings, that consensus is often calculated by Zacks and represents the Street's latest thoughts on a particular stock.

Zacks provides a host of other information as well. The site will show you how many analysts follow a stock; how many have buy, sell, or hold recommendations on that stock; and what the consensus recommendation is—along with information on how that consensus has changed in the recent past. Zacks also provides industry comparisons for key financial data points, which can be enormously helpful to investors.

Context is the key. For instance, it might do you little good to know that Microsoft's five-year earnings growth forecast, based on consensus analysts' forecasts, is, say, 11 percent a year. But if you knew that its industry peers are expected to grow, say, 15 percent annually, you might be able to do something with that information. This Web site will provide both data points.

Knowing a stock's earnings growth rate vis-à-vis that of its industry peers may not in and of itself be a reason to sell the stock. But it may be a sign that an investor should demand lower P/E ratios or higher dividend yields for investing in a particular company.

Other points of data that Zacks provides is a stock's:

- Beta
- 52-week high and low prices
- Net margins
- Return on equity
- Debt load

Zacks also provides the average daily volume of shares that trade in a stock. This is particularly useful for followers of technical analysis, who may be interested in knowing what level of conviction there is in the market for a particular investment.

In addition, investors can retrieve annual reports, balance sheets, income statements, and other financial data for thousands of different companies from this Web site.

And finally, Zacks will allow you to screen for stocks too, and offers preset screens so investors can find stocks based on popular criteria. Thus, you can find information on which stocks have had the biggest recent upgrades in analysts' recommendations, if that's what you want to know, or the biggest recent adjustment in earnings forecasts.

Yahoo! Finance

When researching stocks, it's important to be able to compare apples to apples. The **Web site Yahoo! Finance (finance.yahoo.com)** helps you do just that when it comes to assessing the recent and historic performance of a particular stock's price movements. For instance, if you want to see how, say, shares of Microsoft have historically done relative to its peers, you can chart its performance against that of, say, Apple, Cisco Systems, or even a technology stock index of the broader market.

Yahoo! Finance is particularly useful in helping investors who don't have access to more sophisticated systems like Bloomberg terminals, which professional money managers and traders rely on. Through the free site, you cannot only look up a stock's basic performance but you can also study its fundamentals. The chart will link you to a company's financial statements, its government filings, analyst research, and key news that might affect the company's shares.

Standard & Poor's

Standard & Poor's is known for a lot of things, including the S&P 500 index, which has become as ubiquitous as the Dow Jones Industrial Average as a yardstick to measure the performance of the overall markets. But **Standard &**

Poor's Web site (www.standardandpoors.com), is particularly good at producing industry and index data that will give investors the proper context to gauge a stock's financial performance.

For example, say you're thinking of investing in Healthcare Company X, and you discover that its earnings are growing 12 percent annually and the stock is trading at a P/E ratio of 18. Without proper context, it's impossible to determine if those are good numbers. If you go to the Standard & Poor's Web site, click on the section titled *Indices*, and then click on the tab titled *S&P U.S. Indices*, you will find all of the various S&P indexes we discussed before: the S&P 500, the S&P 400 index of mid-cap stocks, and the S&P 600 index of small stocks. You can find out the earnings and P/E trends in each index. Moreover, you can find similar data for each sector within those indexes.

So, if Healthcare Company X is a small-cap stock, you would look up the S&P 600, search for how individual sectors in that index are doing, and look up the small-cap health-care sector. There, you might find that the average small-cap health-care stock is growing earnings, say, at 9 percent annually and trades at a 19 P/E. This would indicate that the company you are considering is at least attractive on both those counts.

Annual Reports

All investors need to become familiar with the major financial documents that companies are required to file and make available to shareholders. The biggest of these is the annual report, which is available on a company's Web site or through third-party Web sites.

While many shareholders who receive annual reports in the mail never read through these documents, there is actually a wealth of information found in these reports. Every **annual report** reflects the performance and activities of the firm in the prior year. Some companies, for accounting purposes, report on their activities in the prior **calendar years**, while others use **fiscal years** ending in June, October, or some other month to measure their performance. Still others rely on a customary fiscal year, based on when the company was established.

Every annual report includes a **Letter to Shareholders** from the chief executive and/or chairman of the corporation. This brief note tends to highlight important accomplishments, challenges, and setbacks of the company in the prior year. In addition, the annual report will often include financial highlights and a review of operations, which should provide more detail on important recent developments, including new product launches, acquisitions, mergers, or sales of units.

Perhaps the most important element of the annual report is the firm's major financial statements, including its **balance sheet, income statement**, and **statement of cash flows**.

Balance Sheet

The **balance sheet** is a measure of a company's overall health at a particular point in time. It will list all of the company's **assets**, including its current assets, which are those things that can be converted into cash within about a year, such as inventories, accounts receivable, and cash on hand (Figure 11-1). The balance sheet will also reflect all of the firm's **property, plant, and equipment**, or **PP&E**, in addition to intangible assets like patents and copyrights. Similarly, the balance sheet will detail all of a company's **liabilities**, including its long-term debt.

By subtracting a firm's liabilities from its assets, you can figure out what's known as its *shareholders' equity*, a term that simply refers to the **total net worth** of the company. This is a fundamental formula to remember:

$$\text{Assets} - \text{Liabilities} = \text{Shareholders' equity (net worth)}$$

Or:

$$\text{Assets} = \text{Shareholders' equity} + \text{Liabilities}$$

This is a simple but critical measure. While the sign of a healthy company is one of *growing* assets, it's more important to see *increasing* shareholder equity, since that reflects a company's health factoring in its liabilities.

Income Statement

If the balance sheet offers a snapshot of a firm's overall health, an **income statement** measures something a bit more specific: the profitability of that firm over a given period of time, typically on a quarterly or annual basis (Figure 11-2).

The income statement goes by other names, including **profit and loss statement**, the **P&L**, and also the **statement of earnings**. Regardless of what it's called, a whole host of relevant information about a company's business progress can be found in this financial statement, among them:

- *Total sales or revenues.* The income statement will show the current quarterly and/or annual sales figures for the firm and compare that with prior periods. **Revenues** are often the first line item listed in an income statement, which is why we refer to sales growth as **top line growth**.

- *The cost of goods sold.* This reflects the total costs it took to manufacture and distribute those goods and services that were sold in that period, including from labor, raw materials, shipping, insuring, and warehousing.

	6/30/10	6/30/09
Assets		
Cash	$49,048	$38,652
Receivables	5,196	5,129
Notes receivable	0	0
Inventories	640	673
Other current assets	4,089	4,122
Total current assets	58,973	48,576
Net property and equipment	2,223	2,268
Investments	13,692	14,191
Other noncurrent charges	0	0
Deferred charges	0	0
Intangibles	3,512	1,669
Deposits and other assets	1,171	942
TOTAL ASSETS	79,571	67,646
Liabilities and Shareholder Equity		
Notes payable	0	0
Accounts payable	1,573	1,208
Current portion L/T debt	0	0
Current portion capital leases	0	0
Accrued expenses	1,416	1,145
Income taxes payable	2,044	2,022
Other current liabilities	8,941	8,369
Total current liabilities	13,974	12,744
Mortgages	0	0
Deferred taxes/income	1,731	398
Convertible debt	0	0
Long-term debt	0	0
Noncurrent capital leases	0	0
Other noncurrent liabilities	2,846	2,324
Minority interest (liabilities)	0	0
TOTAL LIABILITIES	18,551	15,466
Shareholder Equity		
Preferred stock	0	0
Common stock	35,344	31,647
Capital surplus	0	0
Retained earnings	25,676	20,533
Other equity	0	0
Treasury stock	0	0
Total shareholder's equity	61,020	52,180
TOTAL SHAREHOLDER EQUITY + LIABILITIES	79,571	67,646

FIGURE 11-1 · Sample Balance Sheet: Company X.*

*All figures in millions.

	6/30/10	6/30/09
Sales	$32,187	$28,365
Cost of goods sold	5,686	5,191
Gross profit	26,501	23,174
Selling, admin., depreciation, and amortization	13,284	11,264
Income after depreciation and amortization	13,217	11,910
Nonoperating income	1,509	−397
Interest expense	0	0
Pretax income	14,726	11,513
Income taxes	4,733	3,684
Minority interest	0	0
Investment gains	0	0
Other income	0	0
Income from continuing operations	9,993	7,829
Discontinued operations	0	0
Net income	9,993	7,829

FIGURE 11-2 · Sample Income Statement: Company X.*

*All figures in millions.

- **Indirect costs.** These expenses include long-term research and development costs, general administrative expenses, and other costs such as consulting fees.

- **Interest income and expenses.** Companies, like individuals, may invest the cash they have on hand in an effort to maximize the use of their capital. This is particularly true for financial services firms. Income statements not only account for the success a company has had in generating interest income, but simultaneously account for the interest expenses the firm incurs to finance projects or simply to deal with day-to-day matters.

- **Taxes.** Obviously, companies, like individuals, have to manage their tax expenses. And for companies with locations in multiple cities, states, and countries, this could be a complicated task. The income statement will show a firm's income before and after taxes.

- **Net income.** It is the most common measure of a company's profitability, since it takes all of the revenues and interest income enjoyed by the firm in a reporting period and subtracts all of the costs required to engineer those sales.

Earnings Per Share

If you divide a firm's net income by the total number of shares it has outstanding, you get its **earnings per share**, or **EPS**:

Net income/Total shares outstanding = Earnings per share

So, if a company earns $1 billion and it has 100 million shares floating in the public, its EPS would be $10 per share:

Net income ($1 billion)/Total shares (100 million) = $10

This explains why companies often choose to buy back their own shares in the open market. Through share buy-back programs, a company can improve its earnings per share (since there are fewer shares outstanding) without actually improving net income. In the example above, if the company still reported $1 billion in net income but only had 90 million shares outstanding, its EPS would be $11.11.

As an aside, **net income** is often referred to as the **bottom line**, because it literally is the last line in an income statement.

Cash Flow

While most investors who peruse a company's financials will look at its income statement and balance sheet, many overlook the third major financial statement: the statement of cash flows (see Figure 11-3). A company's cash flow statement, which is also available in the annual report, does not speak to profitability, but to something more tangible. It answers the question: Is the company a net user or collector of cash in its day-to-day activities?

To gauge this, the **cash flow statement** will add up all of the cash that comes in a company's front door through its profits, its accounts receivable, and its inventories. Then, cash that routinely leaves the company in the form of obligations (like accounts payable), debt financing, and depreciation of plant, property, and equipment, are subtracted. What's left—if it's a positive figure—is considered a company's cash and cash equivalents for the end of a particular period.

The bigger the number, the better. But just as important is the growth of this figure over time. So a company with dramatically rising cash flows but modest cash reserves could be seen as just as attractive—if not more so—than another firm with huge cash reserves which are only modestly growing.

Why is cash flow important to begin with? While a balance sheet analysis will speak to the financial underpinnings of a firm, a company with a strong balance sheet (in other words, a firm that has far more assets than liabilities) could nevertheless land in financial trouble if, for even a brief moment in time,

Cash Flow from Operations, Investments, and Financial Activities		
	6/30/10	**6/30/09**
Net income	$9,993	$7,829
Depreciation/amortization	1,439	1,084
Net change from Assets/ Liabilities	1,046	1,084
Net cash from discontinued operations	0	0
Other operating activities	3,319	5,827
Net cash from operations	15,797	14,509
Property and equipment	−891	−770
Acquisitions/subsidiaries	−1,063	0
Investments	−5,259	−10,075
Other investing activities	0	0
Net cash from investing	−7,213	−10,845
Issuance/repurchase of stock	−4,366	−4,572
Issuance/repurchase of debt	0	0
Increase in short-term debt	0	0
Dividend payments	−857	0
Other financing activities	0	0
Net cash from financing	−5,223	−4,572
Change of exchange rates	61	2
Net change in cash	3,422	−906
Cash at beginning of period	3,016	3,922
Cash at end of period	6,438	3,016

FIGURE 11-3 · Sample Cash Flow Statement: Company X.*

This statement includes cash flow from operations, investments, and financial activities.

*All figures in millions.

it experiences negative cash flow. This will be particularly problematic if more money is flowing out of the business than coming in when major short-term obligations and bills must be met.

It's sort of the way consumers operate in the real world. You can have mountains of credit card debt, but as long as you have enough cash flowing into your coffers each month to meet your basic obligations, you may be just fine—at least for the moment. On the other hand, a person who owns substantial assets that are illiquid—say, hundreds of thousands of dollars' worth of property in

Florida that can't be flipped for months—may be seemingly healthy based on a balance sheet analysis, but could run into huge financial troubles if he or she is bleeding cash every month and can't pay taxes on that property.

At the end of the day, cash is king for a company, because cash gives it short-term flexibility to do certain things. For example, even if a company is profitable, it might not be able to pay out substantial dividends if its cash flow is weak. The firm may need to retain that cash to pay creditors, rather than reward shareholders.

This is why investors will often focus on a company's **free cash flow**. This is defined as the money left over once you take a firm's operating cash flow (the cash flow generated from its basic operations), subtract dividend payments and also capital expenditures, which are investments in upgrading or adding to plant, property, and equipment. Free cash flow represents the true financial flexibility a company has to do new things. It could use that money to invest in new projects, acquire competitors, acquire new types of businesses, buy back some of its shares in the open market, or pay out even bigger dividends.

10-K and 10-Q

In addition to a firm's annual report, all publicly traded companies must file periodic financial statements and updates with the **Securities and Exchange Commission (SEC)**. These documents, while available on most corporate Web sites, can also be found at the SEC's Web site, www.sec.gov.

But these days, investors can just as easily link to current and historic SEC 10-K and 10-Q filings by researching stocks at Web sites like Morningstar.com and Finance.Yahoo.com. Once you type in a ticker symbol of a specific stock, those sites will link you to historic government filings for the underlying firm—for free.

Once every quarter, firms must file a public document called a **10-Q report**, which details the financial activities of the company within the prior quarter. This document also updates a firm's major financial statements and highlights any major changes that may have taken place during the quarter in terms of the company's management team or business ventures. By SEC regulation, companies must file their 10-Qs within 35 days of the end of their fiscal quarters.

In addition, within two months of the end of their fiscal years, corporations have to file an annual **10-K report**, which is somewhat like an annual report, but offers considerably more detail. In addition to the financial documents in an annual report, the 10-K will also list compensation considerations for management and the board, as well as the ownership stake that management has in the form of company stock. Moreover, 10-Ks list detailed information on the business activities and risks faced by the firm's major subsidiaries, which provides investors more data through which to gauge the company-specific risk of a stock.

Profitability Measures

Historic Earnings Growth

When assessing a stock, you are also assessing the performance of the management team that has run the underlying company. At the end of the day, the only real, tangible evidence of success is **profitability**. And the most basic measure of profitability is **actual net income**, or **net income (earnings) per share**. Sure, you can also look to market share gains as a sign of success. But gaining market share in a dying industry, for example—or gaining market share at the expense of earnings—is hardly proof of financial success.

Fortunately, the equity market tends to reward companies with good earnings histories. If you're using the Zacks free screening tool, for instance, you can search for stocks with a particular five-year historic earnings growth rate. To do this, go to www.zacks.com, click on the "screening" tab, and then go to "custom screener." There, you can go the "select category" drop-down box and select various screening variables. In this case, you would select "EPS Growth" and set parameters for five-year historic earnings growth rates.

Future Earnings Growth

While earnings over the long run are a great indicator of the health of a company, they are not necessarily a great predictor of short-term stock performance. This is because, as we discussed earlier, the stock market is a forward-looking mechanism. It reflects the investors' expectations for the economy and corporate profits six to nine months into the future.

Indeed, one study of stock market performance found that when corporate profits are growing more than 20 percent a year, stock prices have risen only around 2 percent. Ironically, the best stock performance comes during periods when corporate earnings are modest or even in the red. This is because investors tend to move into those stocks in anticipation of improvements, and once those improvements materialize, they often sell and move on to the next opportunity. This is an example of that old Wall Street saying: "Buy on the rumor and sell on the news."

The good news for individual investors is that it's fairly simple to gauge Wall Street's expectations for a stock's future earnings performance. At Zacks.com you can punch in the ticker symbol of the stock you're interested in and call up a full-page report on that firm. It will tell you not only how fast a company's earnings have grown in the last five years, but how quickly they're expected to expand in the next three to five years. You can then compare these growth rates against those of industry peers.

If you're interested in finding out how fast a sector or industry in the broad market is expected to grow relative to the stock in that sector or industry, you can again go to the Morningstar.com site. At Morningstar.com, type in the name or ticker symbol of any stock you're interested in studying. Then, when information about that stock is pulled up, scroll down to the part of the page where it says "Key Stats." There, you can look up how, say, Microsoft is growing relative to its technology industry peers.

If you're screening for companies based on future earnings growth rates, you can go to either www.zacks.com or www.morningstar.com. Both stock screeners allow you to screen for stocks based on rates of projected long-term earnings growth.

Return on Equity

In addition to basic earnings growth, there's another, slightly more sophisticated measure of earnings performance that many professional money managers rely on. It's called **return on equity (ROE),** and it is a measure of a company's earnings relative to its shareholder equity. The formula looks like this:

Net income/Shareholder equity = Return on equity (ROE)

You'll recall that "net income" can be found as the last line on a company's income statement, while "shareholder equity" is one of the last lines on its balance sheet. If a company earns $1 billion and has total shareholder equity on its balance sheet of $10 billion, its return on equity would be 10 percent.

Net income ($1 billion)/Shareholder equity ($10 billion) = 10 percent

Let's go back to the examples we provided for financial statements earlier in the chapter. In our hypothetical examples of Company X's balance sheet and income statement, the company reported net income in June 2010 of $9.993 billion. At the same time, its shareholder equity was $61.02 billion. So in our example, Company X's ROE, based on June 2010 earnings, would have been 16.4 percent:

$9.993 billion/$61.02 billion = 16.4 percent

Why is it necessary to calculate return on equity instead of simply relying on net income? Because ROE doesn't consider earnings in a vacuum. Instead, it measures net income in the context of how much money shareholders have invested in the firm (which is another way of saying a company's net worth). In other words, ROE lets investors know how much profit the company is generating for every $1 investors are sinking into the business.

Think about it: While it's useful to know that a company earned $10 million in a given period, wouldn't be even more helpful to know how much money was invested in the firm to generate those profits? If two companies earned $1 million each—one with shareholder equity of $1 billion and another with $10 billion—wouldn't you consider the smaller company more profitable? After all, it found a way to squeeze out $1 million in profits on less invested capital.

By measuring profitability this way, investors can gauge whether they are getting more bang for their buck in one investment over another. As a result, ROE can be a useful comparative tool for investors who face the daunting challenge of knowing where, in a universe of thousands of different stocks, to put their money.

This is one reason why so many mutual fund managers swear by this measure. It casts a spotlight on the most efficiently run companies in the market. The managers of the Jensen Fund, for instance—a $2.7 billion stock fund with one of the best track records in recent years—only consider stocks that have reported returns on equity of 15 percent or higher for at least 10 consecutive years. If a company fails to meet that threshold, it won't be considered for purchase. And if the ROE of a stock already in the portfolio falls below 15 percent in any single year, the managers of the Jensen Fund will sell and won't reconsider the investment for at least another decade—that is, if the company can pull together another string of 10 consecutive years of 15-percent-plus returns on equity.

Historically, an ROE of 20 percent or higher was considered the gold standard. But if you're screening for stocks, you may want to start off by focusing on firms with ROEs of 15 or better, simply to cast a wider net.

Morningstar's stock screener will allow you to screen for stocks with ROEs greater than or equal to 5, 10, 15, or 20 percent.

Sales Measures

While profits are the true measure of a firm's efficiency, sales are a sign that its products and services are in demand. And that too can be useful for investors to know (Figure 11-4).

One of the problems with only relying on profitability measures is that a company can generate rising profits without generating more business. A firm that simply does a good job cutting costs can maintain high profits even as its products and services become increasingly irrelevant.

But that can only last for so long. At some point you're cutting so much that you're losing manufacturing, marketing, and distribution capabilities, which at the end of the day will threaten the ability of your firm to continue to do business. This is why investors often consider the *top line growth* of the firm as well as the *bottom line growth* when selecting stocks.

Top line growth, again, represents the firm's total sales. Using Morningstar's stock screener, you can search for stocks with three-year average annual

Period	Revenue Growth*
1st quarter 2009	10.6%
4th quarter 2008	9.5%
3rd quarter 2008	8.1%
2nd quarter 2008	10.1%
1st quarter 2008	7.6%
4th quarter 2007	6.9%
3rd quarter 2007	6.2%
2nd quarter 2007	6.9%

FIGURE 11-4 • S&P 500 Sales Growth by Quarter.

*Data as of December 2009.

Source: Thomson Renters

revenue growth of greater than zero percent, 10 percent, 20 percent, 40 percent, or 80 percent.

Profit Margins

Yet another measure of efficiency, in addition to ROE, is how much profit a company can squeeze out of a certain amount of sales. While it's important to know whether a company is building its core business by selling more goods and services, generating ever-higher revenues, it's equally important that companies you invest in have the ability to convert sales into earnings. A company accomplishes this through cost efficiencies, rising productivity, and sound business investments.

To find out the **profit margin** of a business, plug in the following formula:

Net income/Sales = Profit margin

Let's go back again to our sample financial statements for Company X. We know, based on the P&L, that the company's net income was $9.993 billion in 2010. And overall revenues for the period ending June 2010 were $32.187 billion. This means Company X's basic profit margin was 31.05 percent:

Net income ($9.993 billion)/Sales ($32.187 billion) = 31.047 percent

One thing all investors should be aware of is that *certain industries have higher profit margins than others.* Newspaper publishing companies, for example, because of high labor and paper costs, are likely to have far lower profit margins than, say, an Internet company with far less overhead.

This is why, unlike ROE, profit margins are best suited only to compare stocks within a particular industry. If you don't want to do the math, there is an easy way to find out what a company's profit margin is. Go to Zacks.com and obtain a company report on the stock. In it, you'll see not only your company's profit margin, but the relative industry margin rate as well.

Stock Valuation Measures

Price-to-Earnings Ratio

While it's important to know the quality of the company you're investing in, it is impossible to judge whether that particular stock is attractive without knowing how much it costs. It's like shopping for a Rolls-Royce. We can all appreciate the beauty, quality, and craftsmanship of the car, but if its price tag is $350,000, you're likely to reconsider whether it's automatically a "good buy."

The same goes for investing in stocks. But determining how much a stock costs is more complicated than simply looking up its price tag. If you just focus on the share price, you won't know what percentage of the firm you're buying at that price or the level of profits your holdings will entitle you to.

This is why it's important to consider a stock's **price-to-earnings ratio (P/E ratio)**, which is the most widely relied upon valuation measure among investors. To reiterate, a stock's P/E ratio is determined by taking its price and dividing that by its earnings per share:

$$\text{Price per share/Earnings per share (EPS)} = \text{P/E ratio}$$

The long-term average P/E ratio for stocks in the S&P 500 has been around 16 times earnings. But from time to time investors have been willing to pay more or less for stocks, depending on the state of the economy, corporate profits, and momentum in the market. In general, the lower the P/E, the better. In fact, historically, the broad stock market has performed better in periods of low P/E multiples. Why? Low P/E ratios are like a "Clearance Sale" sign: They tell investors that there are good buys to be found. Consider the chart in Figure 11-5. It shows the annualized performance of the S&P 500, going back to 1940, based on various P/E ratios for the market.

Typically, investors are willing to pay higher P/Es for stocks when alternative investments, like bonds, are not yielding as much. This goes back to what we discussed earlier: stocks, bonds, and other assets are in constant competition with one another for investors' dollars. In Figure 11-6 you can see the average P/E ratio that investors tend to place on the S&P 500 based on prevailing bond yields. Generally speaking, the lower the payout of bonds, the higher the price

P/E Range	Average Annual Return
P/E <8	16.5 %
P/E >8< 10	10.9 %
P/E > 10< 12	9.1 %
P/E > 12< 14	7.5 %
P/E >14<16	17.0 %
P/E >16<18	5.6 %
P/E >18<20	7.0 %
P/E >20	−1.6 %

FIGURE 11-5 · S&P 500 Performance.

As this table indicates, stocks tend to produce the best total returns in periods when P/E ratios are low. When P/E ratios soar above 20, stocks have historically lost money.

Source: Citigroup Smith Barney

that investors are willing to pay for stocks, since equities will be that much more attractive during such periods.

There are numerous Web sites through which you can check on a stock's P/E, both based on past earnings and future projected profits. Morningstar and Zacks will also let you see how your stock's P/E measures up against the valuation of its peers.

Different sectors, based on their historic growth rates, tend to trade at different average P/Es. For example, investors are typically willing to pay higher prices for technology stocks, because their earnings growth rate is considered

10-Year Treasury Note Yield	Average P/E Ratio for S&P 500
3–4%	29.3
4–5%	22.8
5–6%	24.4
6–7%	19.8
7–8%	14.7
8–9%	13.4
9% plus	10.3

FIGURE 11-6 · S&P 500 P/E Ratios Based on Bond Yields.

As this table indicates, stocks tend to produce the best total returns in periods when bond yields are low. This makes sense. When bond yields are low, fixed-income securities pose little competition to stocks for investor assets.

Source: Ned Davis Research

relatively high. On the other hand, slow-growth sectors like utilities tend to be assigned much lower multiples, since the profit payout is lower.

Again, it's critical to compare apples with apples. The only way to know whether or not your stock is truly cheap is to measure its valuation against that of similarly sized industry peers. Figure 11-7 shows the average P/Es of industry sectors within the S&P 500, S&P 600, and S&P 400 indexes—comparing apple to apples and oranges to oranges. This information can be assessed at Standard & Poor's Web site, www.standardandpoors.com.

PEG Ratio

While value investors pay particularly close attention to P/Es, since they care most about prices, growth investors are often willing to overlook a stock's P/E ratio if its growth rate is impressive.

This is not to say that all growth investors ignore P/Es entirely. In fact, a sub-set of growth investors—the **GARP** ("growth at a reasonable price") **investors** we described earlier—will split the difference and rely on a different valuation measure that reflects both a company's P/E ratio and its long-term earnings growth rate.

This measure is referred to as the **PEG ratio**, which is short for P/E divided by Growth. The formula is:

P/E ratio/Annual earnings growth rate = PEG ratio

Assume a stock trades at a P/E multiple of 30, which by historic standards is considered high. Now let's say the underlying company's annual earnings growth rate is expected to be 25 percent. This stock's PEG ratio would be 1.2. Compare this to a company with a relatively low P/E, another company you're considering, which trades at a multiple of 15 times earnings but is only growing 7 percent a year. That would make its PEG 2.1.

While a strict value investor might gravitate to the 15 P/E stock, the GARP investor will likely prefer the 30 P/E stock since the underlying company's earnings growth rate is close to the P/E.

The lower the PEG, the more attractive a stock is said to be. Companies with PEG ratios of 1 or less—meaning companies whose earnings growth rates meet or exceed their P/Es—are considered very attractive by some investors. Indeed, many growth investors will forgive a high P/E stock so long as it trades a multiple that is close to its long-term growth rate.

PEGY Ratio

There's a slight variation on the PEG ratio that says you should add a stock's dividend yield to its growth rate, and then divide that into the stock's P/E multiple. This is called the **PEGY ratio**.

S&P 500 Large-Cap Sectors	Average P/E[†]
Consumer discretionary	15.4
Consumer staples	14.1
Energy	11.9
Financials	27.0
Health care	11.3
Industrials	15.3
Technology	14.1
Materials	14.9
Telecommunications	13.3
Utilities	11.5
S&P 500 Total	13.4

S&P 400 Mid-Cap Sectors	Average P/E[†]
Consumer discretionary	17.3
Consumer staples	8.4
Energy	14.5
Financials	21.8
Health care	19.2
Industrials	16.2
Technology	17.3
Materials	16.0
Telecommunications	19.9
Utilities	13.2
S&P 400 Total	17.3

S&P 600 Small-Cap Sectors	Average P/E[†]
Consumer discretionary	18.8
Consumer staples	6.2
Energy	19.6
Financials	31.8
Health care	19.1
Industrials	18.2
Technology	17.1
Materials	17.2
Telecommunications	15.9
Utilities	13.6
S&P 600 Total	19.5

FIGURE 11-7 · P/E Averages Based on Industry Groups.*

*Data as of June 2010.

[†]P/E ratios based on estimated 2010 corporate earnings.

Source: Standard & Poor's

If the whole point of the PEG ratio is to determine how much of a good thing (in this case earnings) you are getting for the price you're paying (the P/E ratio), then dividend payouts are certainly another good thing. Or so the argument goes. In this case, the formula would look like this:

P/E ratio/Annual earnings growth rate + Dividend yield = PEGY ratio

So assume the stock you are looking at has a P/E multiple of 25, which again is a bit high by historic standards. And assume that the underlying company's annual growth rate is 15 percent. Its PEG ratio would be 1.67. That would make it a borderline stock, according to many investors.

But let's say that this stock has a dividend yield of 4.7 percent. All of a sudden, the denominator in the equation becomes 19.7, not just 15. And the PEGY ratio would be 1.27, much more attractive than a straight PEG ratio of 1.67. Here again, the lower the PEGY, the better. And the closer to 1 the PEGY is, the better.

Price-to-Book

While most investors rely on P/E ratios, there are other basic valuation measures, as we explained. Another traditional one is the **price/book value ratio (P/B ratio)**, which measures the priceyness of a stock not against its earnings, but against its book value, which again reflects a company's assets after liabilities have been deducted. Here's how it's calculated:

Price per share/Book value per share = P/B ratio

Why is it necessary to consider a stock's P/B ratio in addition to its P/E? To a certain extent, it represents a sort of belt-and-suspenders approach to investing. Why not consider two valuation measures instead of just one? The good news is: It's just as easy to look up a stock's P/B ratio through the Web sites we've talked about, Morningstar and Zacks.

But there is something additionally useful about the price/book value ratio. Sometimes, a company's earnings are high not because of its operational success, but due to onetime events. A classic example is a company that sells a major division—and all of the assets that go with that unit. This onetime sale, which cannot be repeated in the future, is likely to boost earnings in the short run but may not speak to the long-term health of the company's earnings.

Now, if you were to only look at a stock's P/E ratio, the denominator in the ratio, the *E*, will be momentarily bigger in such an event, driving down the overall ratio. While this may make the stock look more attractive from a valuation standpoint, the P/E in this particular instance might not offer a true picture of the firm.

This is where the P/B ratio comes in handy. If a company lowered its P/E by boosting its earnings in a onetime sale of assets, that sale will simultaneously lower the book value of the firm. So the lower book value in this scenario will make the stock seem more expensive, not less, from a P/B standpoint.

Hopefully, if you screen for stocks based both on their P/E and P/B ratios, you'll pick up on these discrepancies, and it may cause you to do some extra due diligence.

Again, like P/E ratios, P/Bs have to be compared not against the broad stock market, but against similar ratios of industry peers. You have to consider that some industries—like the industrials or utilities—have more assets on their books than other sectors—financial services, for instance. Web sites like Zacks and Morningstar will help you determine how a stock's P/B stands up against those of its industry peers.

Dividend Yield

In the 1990s, many of us began to overlook dividends, because many companies stopped issuing them. At the peak, in 1980, about 469 out of the 500 companies in the S&P 500 paid out dividends to their shareholders. That figure fell to as low as 350 in 2002, though it's back on the way up.

In the 1990s it became fashionable for companies to retain their earnings instead of paying shareholders, so the firm could reinvest the money back into the business. Moreover, in the late 1990s many stocks were enjoying capital appreciation gains of 20 percent or more a year. In that environment, a dividend yield of, say, 2 percent hardly seemed a sufficient carrot to drive investors to dividend-paying stocks.

But it's important to remember that going back to 1926, dividend payouts have accounted for more than 41 percent of the total returns that equity investors have enjoyed. That's a lot of money to turn your back on. Moreover, dividends—and rising dividend payouts in particular—are a great indicator of the financial health of a company.

Even if the payout itself is paltry, the fact that a company is increasing its dividends is a sign that (1) it has more cash coming into the business than flowing out, and (2) it is financially strong enough to return the money to shareholders and does not need to retain the cash to meet basic obligations. Conversely, if a company were to cut or eliminate its dividend, it would be an ominous sign indeed about the health of that firm. It would tell investors that the firm has such cash flow problems that it needs its cash to meet basic short-term obligations.

What investors also overlook is the fact that a stock's dividend yield—not to be confused with its actual payout—can be an effective valuation tool. While a stock's dividend is measured in dollars and cents, a stock's **dividend yield** reflects that payout in the context of the current price of the stock. Again, the formula looks like this:

Annual dividends per share/Current price of stock = Dividend yield

So if a company paid out $1 a share in dividends and those shares went for $20 a piece, its dividend yield would be 5 percent:

Annual dividends per share ($1)/Current price of stock ($20) = 5 percent

There are a couple of ways that the dividend yield will move higher. The first is simple: If the company pays out higher dividends and the price of the stock stays put, its dividend yield will rise. Going back to our example, if this company doubled its dividends and started paying out $2 per share, but if the stock price remained at $20, its new dividend yield would be 10 percent:

Annual dividends per share ($2)/Current price of stock ($20) = 10 percent

The higher dividend yield, in this case, would be a sign of increasing value. After all, in this situation the market is paying the same price for a stock even though it now issues $2 in dividends instead of just $1. That's considered value.

But what if instead of raising its dividends, the company simply sees its share price fall to, say, $5? Then its new dividend yield would be 20 percent:

Annual dividends per share ($1)/Current price of stock ($5) = 20 percent

In this case, the company didn't pay out more, but investors paid less for the stock even though it is still offering $1 per share in dividends.

The bottom line: When dividend yields rise, the shares of the company are considered to be trading at a discount to their former price.

This is why many value investors focus on dividend yields to ferret out low-priced stocks. In fact, there's a whole strategy of investing called the "Dogs of the Dow," in which investors buy the 10 stocks in the Dow Jones Industrial Average (which is made up of 30 total stocks) with the highest dividend yields.

While there are many variations of the "Dogs of the Dow" strategy, the simplest calls for holding the 10 highest yielding Dow stocks for one year. (Figure 11-8, for example, lists the "Dogs" as of December 31, 2009.) After a year passes, you would go back to the index and find the new 10 highest yielding Dow components. You would then readjust your portfolio accordingly and hang onto those stocks for another year.

Dow Component	Price	Dividend Yield
AT&T	$28.03	5.85%
Verizon	$33.13	5.73%
DuPont	$33.67	4.87%
Kraft	$27.18	4.27%
Merck	$36.54	4.16%
Chevron's	$76.99	3.53%
McDonald's	$62.44	3.52%
Pfizer	$18.19	3.52%
Home Depot	$28.93	3.11%
Boeing	$54.13	3.10%

FIGURE 11-8 · Dogs of the Dow.*

*As of December 2009.

Source: DogsoftheDow.com

Investors can screen for stocks based on their dividend yields at www. morningstar.com. Moreover, you can look up most stocks' dividend yields in newspaper stock listings. As for the "Dogs of the Dow" strategy, there are several newsletters that help investors follow this approach, as well as a Web site, www.dogsofthedow.com.

Once again, it's important to consider a stock's dividend yield in the context of its industry. While many industrial firms like DuPont or General Motors are known for paying handsome dividends, newer, technology-oriented companies still don't pay much. As a result, tech stock dividend yields are likely to be much smaller than the yields of companies in the smokestack industries. So compare apples with apples.

QUIZ

1. **_Shareholder equity_ refers to . . .**
   A. A company's net worth.
   B. The total returns that shareholders earn in a given stock.
   C. The total assets that shareholders own in a given company.

2. **By looking at a company's income statement, investors will get a better sense of that firm's . . .**
   A. Overall financial health.
   B. Profitability at a specific moment in time.
   C. Profitability in the long run.
   D. Chances of generating profits in the future.

3. **A company with strong free cash flow is likely to . . .**
   A. Be able to invest in its own future profit growth.
   B. Buy other business to grow more rapidly.
   C. Be attractive to would-be suitors.
   D. All of the above.
   E. None of the above.

4. **The shares of companies whose earnings are growing faster than the market as a whole will always perform better than the market as a whole.**
   A. True
   B. False

5. **The best way to compare a company's profitability is against . . .**
   A. The market's historic earnings growth rate.
   B. The market's current earnings growth rate.
   C. The earnings growth rate of its industry peers.
   D. None of the above.

6. **Return on equity helps investors judge the profitability of a company . . .**
   A. Across the broad market.
   B. Within its industry.
   C. Within its investment style.
   D. Within an asset class.

7. **Investors tend to favor a stock whose price-to-earnings ratio is lower than . . .**
   A. Its historic average.
   B. Its peers' P/E ratios.
   C. The market's historic average.

D. The market's current P/E ratio.

E. All of the above.

8. **The price-to-book ratio of a company can help determine how cheap a stock is relative to ...**

A. What the company owns.

B. What the company earns.

C. What the company generates in revenues.

D. None of the above.

9. **Based on so-called PEG ratios, which of the following stocks would be most attractive?**

A. Shares of a company with a P/E of 10 and a growth rate of 10

B. Shares of a company with a P/E of 20 and a growth rate of 20

C. Shares of a company with a P/E of 10 and a growth rate of 20

D. Shares of a company with a P/E of 20 and a growth rate of 10

10. **Companies that consistently raise their dividends are signaling to investors that ...**

A. They are financially stable enough to pay out dividends.

B. They are financially desperate and need to attract new investors.

C. They aren't growing fast.

D. They are growing fast.

chapter 12

Demystifying
Bond Selection

When it comes to putting together a fixed-income portfolio, the first question you have to ask yourself is: Should I go with individual bonds or bond *mutual funds*? The answer is important. While there is little difference between how a stock and a stock fund work—other than the fact that stock funds are baskets of different equities—there's a world of distinctions between bonds and bond funds.

For starters, the structure of a **bond mutual fund** gives them an entirely different risk profile than individual fixed-income securities. You'll recall that in Chapter 6 we talked about the two major types of risks that all bond investors face: interest-rate risk and credit risk. We said that one of the simplest ways for an investor to combat **interest-rate risk**—that is, the possibility of losing money in your fixed-income portfolio when interest rates rise and prices on older bonds fall—is to buy individual bonds and hold them to maturity.

Investors who plan to hold a bond to maturity don't need to concern themselves with short-term fluctuations in bond prices caused by interest rate movements. As long as the issuer of the debt does not default, the investor could care less whether the bond's price may have changed in the course of its life on the secondary market. The only thing buy-and-hold bond investors care about is that they'll still get their original principal value returned to them at redemption—in addition to the interest payments along the way.

But bond fund investors are not guaranteed of being made whole at maturity. That's because bond funds have no fixed maturities. As we discussed earlier, no single maturity date can be assigned to a bond fund. This is in part because bond funds invest in a collection of different fixed-income securities with various maturities. Moreover, cash constantly flows into and out of bond funds, as old investors leave the fund and new investors arrive. This forces bond fund managers to buy and sell debt intermittently to meet redemptions, which means the fund managers can't hold all of their securities to maturity even if they wanted to.

The upshot of all of this is that without a single fixed maturity date, a bond fund simply cannot guarantee its investors that they will not suffer losses if they were to redeem their shares on a particular date (as we discussed earlier, there have been several years when certain types of bond funds have lost value). In other words, bond funds expose investors to a great deal of interest-rate risk that can otherwise be avoided through individual bonds.

On the other hand, bond funds, because they are baskets of numerous debt securities, are considerably safer than individual bonds when it comes to dealing with **credit risk**. After all, if you own one bond and the issuer of that debt defaults, 100 percent of your fixed-income portfolio would have blown up. However, if you own 10 bonds, that one bond, should it default, would only affect 10 percent of your total bond portfolio. And if you own 100 bonds, it would only affect 1 percent of your portfolio. And if you own 392 different securities, as the typical taxable bond mutual fund does, then less than half of 1 percent of your portfolio would be at risk.

So therein lies the dilemma for bond investors: which option to go with, and which type of risk to minimize?

Bond Funds

Though bond funds expose you to interest-rate risk, there are a number of reasons for investors—particularly those just starting out or those with small account balances—to consider going with a bond mutual fund. A major reason is the low minimum initial investments that bond funds require.

As a rule of thumb, an investor in individual bonds can achieve sufficient diversification by owning securities issued by around 10 different corporations (if one is dealing with corporate bonds) or municipalities (if one is dealing with tax-free munis). That's what researchers at the brokerage firm Charles Schwab recently discovered after studying bond risks.

But the fact is, even purchasing 10 bonds can be costly. The bond market is largely controlled by institutional investors—pension funds, hedge funds, mutual funds, private foundations, and the like—not individuals. And to get any type of competitive pricing for a lot of bonds you might be interested in, you have to bring at least $10,000—preferably more—to the table. Otherwise, the lot of bonds you purchase may be marked up in price considerably, since such orders are tiny from the standpoint of bond brokers, who facilitate trading in fixed-income securities, and at brokerage houses that keep inventories of bonds.

What does this mean? If you want to construct a portfolio of individual corporate or muni bonds, you'd ideally need at least $100,000 in assets. We arrive at this figure by multiplying $10,000 by the 10 bonds we'd need to own to diversify our fixed-income portfolios. By itself, $100,000 is a lot of money— far more than the typical retail investor has at his or her disposal.

And the fact of the matter is, most of us put only a minority of our assets in bonds. As we will discuss at greater length in Chapter 14, a typical asset allocation for a diversified investor may be 60 percent stocks and 40 percent bonds. With that allocation, your account would need to be at least $250,000 in assets or larger—so that $100,000 could be earmarked to fixed-income securities— for individual bonds to make sense.

In comparison, many bond funds allow investors to gain exposure to a diversified mix of fixed-income securities for as little as $1,000 to $2,000. Some funds require even less—perhaps as little as $100.

To be sure, if you're only interested in investing in credit-risk-free Treasury bonds, then the threshold of assets required to put together a portfolio of individual bonds would be far lower than in our prior example. After all, a retail investor can purchase Treasuries directly from the government. In fact, you can buy Treasury notes and bills directly from the Treasury Department, online, at www.treasurydirect.gov. There, the minimum initial investment is only around $1,000.

But while Treasuries don't come with credit risk, they are still vulnerable to interest-rate risk. And as we discussed in Chapter 6, one way to reduce interest risk is to **ladder** your bonds. Again, this means purchasing bonds of various maturities so that as one comes due, another is bought. This has the effect of averaging out your maturities so that you minimize interest-rate risk.

Well, a common bond ladder may require an investor to purchase Treasuries maturing in one, two, three years, and so on, up to 10 years. In this example, 10 different Treasuries would achieve a diversification of maturities. And that may require you to have more than $10,000 to invest. Again, if you were to go with a mutual fund, you could easily find Treasury bond funds with minimum initial investment requirements as low as $250 to $1,000.

There is another reason to seriously consider investing in bond funds, especially if you're interested in gaining corporate fixed-income exposure. In the investing world, stocks get most of the attention, while bonds get short shrift. To some degree this is because stocks are thought to be sexier than bonds. But it's also because fixed-income investments are a lot harder to understand. While the equity market is largely transparent, the same cannot be said for fixed-income securities.

Part of the problem is that there are so many more individual bonds that trade on the open market than stocks. Think about it: The bond market is comprised of both government and corporate securities. The stock market only constitutes the private sector. Moreover, while each publicly traded company represents just one stock, that company may, over the course of decades, issue dozens of different series of bonds, depending on its financing needs. Some of those bonds may be short-term in nature, others long. Some may be callable—others not. So even if you get to know the issuer of the bond and feel comfortable with its financial health, that doesn't mean the bond itself may be appropriate for you.

The fact of the matter is, many individual investors don't understand how bonds work. For example, a basic principal of fixed-income investing—perhaps the most important—is that *bond prices move in the opposite direction of market interest rates*. So, if market interest rates rise, bond prices will fall. Conversely, if interest rates fall, bond prices are likely to rise. It looks like this:

Interest rates ▲ Bond prices ▼
Interest rates ▼ Bond prices ▲

Yet many of us still don't understand this crucial relationship. Starting in the 1990s, the mutual fund company American Century began routinely quizzing investors on their "Bond IQ." It has consistently found that "investors still are in the dark on some basic fixed-income principles." Indeed, in a recent survey, only 38 percent of investors understood this basic relationship between interest rates and bond prices. About a quarter thought the opposite was true—that bond prices rise when market interest rates rise. Nearly a fifth thought that interest rates weren't affected by rising rates. And the rest said they simply did not know what happens when rates rise.

Among some of the other findings in these surveys:

- Nearly half of us think that the longer a bond's maturity, the *less* sensitive its price is to changing interest rates—when in fact the opposite is true: *The longer a bond's maturity, the more sensitive it is to interest-rate risk.*

- Only one in five understand that high-yield bonds are low in credit quality and high in credit risk.
- Some investors incorrectly believe that credit ratings are a function of a bond's maturity, not the credit profile of the issuer.
- Some of us even think that bonds with lower credit ratings are actually a safer investment than a high-credit-quality bond.

There are two basic dangers that could arise from this confusion. The first is that we still go ahead and invest in individual bonds, but do so incorrectly. The second is that we avoid this asset class altogether, fearing the unknown. And there is some evidence that the latter is occurring. About one in five investors indicate in polls that they avoid bonds and bond funds because they are too difficult to understand.

But going with a bond fund is an easy way around this—since you will get the help of professional management to guide you through some of these decisions.

What to Look for in a Bond Fund

In Chapter 6 we discussed the different categories of bonds in the marketplace. After figuring out which types of bond funds are best suited for you based on your time horizon, tax bracket, and tolerance for risk, the next big question is: How do you find bond funds to fill those needs? Since interest-rate risk is the biggest risk bond funds expose us to, why not start there—with an assessment of a fund's interest rate profile.

Consider Duration

Clearly, long-term bonds in general, because they tie up our money for greater lengths of time, expose us to more interest-rate risk than short-term bonds do. After all, should rates rise and the price of our short-term bonds fall, we'd only have to wait a brief amount of time before those short-term bonds come due, at which point we could reinvest the money at higher yields. A long-term bond fund investor would have to wait substantially longer, meaning exposure to greater risks. You could downplay this risk by sticking with shorter-term bonds.

But what if a long- or intermediate-term bond fund is appropriate for you, based on your long-term goals? Moreover, within each category, how would one determine which funds expose investors to greater or less interest-rate risk? For example, what if, instead of choosing between a long- or short-term bond fund, you want to know which long-term bond fund to choose? Here, as we discussed earlier, investors can make good use of a bond fund's average duration.

To reiterate, **duration** is a mathematical measure of a bond fund's interest-rate sensitivity. The higher the duration, the more a bond fund is likely to lose should interest rates rise. Let's assume you're investing in a bond fund with a duration of three years. Roughly translated, this means that should interest rates rise 1 percent, the bond fund is likely to lose about 3 percent of its value. A bond fund with a higher duration, say five years, would lose even more under these circumstances: 5 percent.

We will get into the topic of fund screening techniques at greater length in the following chapter, where we discuss mutual fund selection. But it may be useful to go over fund screening here briefly as well.

One resource for bond fund investors is the quick and free fund screening tool at www.morningstar.com. Click on the tab labeled "Funds," and then from that page, click on the tab labeled "Mutual Fund Screener." There, a series of drop-down boxes list the various categories of stock and bond funds.

In our case, say you wanted to find intermediate-term corporate bond funds with relatively favorable interest-rate characteristics. Screen for the following:

Morningstar category = Intermediate term bond

That narrows the list to the proper category. Once there, screen for funds based on their average durations. Morningstar's free fund screen will search for bond funds with durations of less than 3 years, 5 years, 10 years, or greater than 10 years. In our case, we want the lowest interest-rate sensitivity. So we would punch in:

Duration = Lower than 3 years

This will call up a list of funds that meet your criteria. From there you can select funds based on other preferences you have, including loads and past performance. Remember, when weighing investments, it's important to compare apples with apples. So you can search www.morningstar.com for basic information concerning the average duration of funds based on their categories, or you can consult a Morningstar table like the one depicted in Figure 12-1.

Still Confused?

Think of duration as a bet. The higher the duration of your bond fund, the greater your bond fund is likely to return if interest rates fall. So by going with a fund with a duration of, say, 15 years instead of 3, you are swinging for the fences. The risk in this strategy is that if rates rise by 1 percent, your supposedly safe bond fund could end up posting double-digit losses.

Bond Fund Category	Average Duration*
Emerging markets bonds	5.8 years
High-yield bonds	3.8 years
Intermediate government bonds	3.6 years
Intermediate-term bonds	4.4 years
World bonds	5.2 years
Long government bonds	13.9 years
Long-term bonds	9.2 years
Short government bonds	2.0 years
Short-term bonds	2.1 years
Ultra-short-term bonds	0.9 years

FIGURE 12-1 · Durations by Bond Fund Categories.

*Data as of December 2009.

Source: Morningstar

Consider Risk and Reward Characteristics

While investors tend to associate "style boxes" with equity investing, there are style boxes that can help bond fund investors too.

You'll recall that with equity funds, the mutual fund tracker Morningstar puts general stock funds into one of nine basic categories, based on the size of stocks the funds invest in (large-cap, mid-cap, small-cap) as well as the style of equities (growth versus value) they prefer. And those style boxes help investors visually understand the risk and reward characteristics of stock funds. That style of box diagram is repeated in Figure 12-2.

The higher up on the grid you go, the more conservative you grow. Similarly, the farther left you head, the more conservative you get. This means that large-cap-value funds, referred to merely as "Large Value" in the upper left-hand corner of the chart, are considered the most conservative of all general stock funds, while small-cap growth funds, called "Small Growth" and found on the lower right-hand corner, are the most aggressive.

Large value	Large blend	Large growth
Mid value	Mid blend	Mid growth
Small value	Small blend	Small growth

FIGURE 12-2 · Morningstar Equity-Style Boxes: Stock Funds.

Short term High quality	Intermediate term High quality	Long term High quality
Short term Medium quality	Intermediate term Medium quality	Long term Medium quality
Short Term Low Quality	Intermediate term Low quality	Long term Low quality

FIGURE 12-3 · Morningstar Equity-Style Boxes: Bond Funds.

When it comes to bond funds, the style box works the same. But instead of market capitalization and investment styles, the bond style boxes consider **credit quality** and **maturities** (Figure 12-3).

Just as with equities, there are nine fixed income style boxes to consider. But in this case the farther up you go in the diagram, the higher the credit quality of the bond fund (from low quality, to medium quality, to high). Similarly, as you go from right to left, you move from long-term bond funds to intermediate-term bond funds to short-term bond funds. So the horizontal axis measures interest-rate risk.

To figure out the absolute most conservative category of bond funds based on credit and interest-rate risk, go to the upper left corner. There, you'll find short-term high-quality bonds. To figure out what the most aggressive types of general bond funds are, go to the lower right-hand corner. There, you'll find long-term low quality—in other words, high-yield—junk-bond funds. The conservative investor who prefers short-term and high-quality debt is probably looking at only modest yields. Still, he or she is likely to enjoy capital preservation. On the other hand, a bond fund investor who goes to the most aggressive corner of the style box can expect higher than average yields—but at some point credit quality will become a concern.

To look up which style box a bond fund falls under, go to www.morningstar.com. If you punch in any bond fund, Morningstar will kick out a fund report that shows the fund's risk-reward characteristics. For example, according to Morningstar, Pimco Total Return fund, the world's biggest bond fund, falls under the intermediate-term, high-quality box. That would make this fund an ideal core holding.

Still Confused?

If you want the safest bond funds when it comes to guarding against both interest-rate risk and credit risk, stick with funds that are short term, high quality. But if you want to roll the dice on both counts, perhaps to search for the potentially highest returning bond fund, then your search will focus on long-term, low-quality bond funds. But beware that long-term, low-quality junk bond funds can lose as much as stocks in some years.

Consider Costs

As we outlined in Chapter 7, fund fees come straight out of your total returns. So it's always important to consider a portfolio's total expense ratio. This is particularly true for bond funds.

Why? A stock fund may, over long periods of time, return 8 percent on average, or even in some instances 10 percent a year. In that case, fund fees amounting to, say, 2 percent would represent around a fifth of total returns. But bond funds, on average, may only return 5 or 6 percent a year, given the asset class they invest in. In that case, 2 percent in fees, on a base of just 5 percent, represents a huge portion of the fund's total returns. And to reiterate, funds have to overcome those fees to post positive net returns.

This is why, as we noted earlier, and Financial Research Corp. determined in a study that fees are one of the few consistent predictors of mutual fund outperformance. FRC found that this is especially true when it comes to government bond funds, as shown in Figure 12-4.

So how should we screen for fees? Let's go back to Morningstar's Web site. Find your way back to the fund screener tool. Say you want to screen for funds in the intermediate-term government bond category. You would punch in:

Morningstar category = Intermediate term bond

Then, under the "expenses" category, you could punch in: *Expense ratio less than or equal to: category average.*

This is the easiest way to screen for costs, since it's important to look for funds with below-average costs. Another way to screen for funds, though, is to

Type of Fund	1-Year Returns	3-Year Returns	5-Year Returns
Government bond funds	89%	100%	100%
Corporate bond funds	67%	81%	64%
Municipal bond funds	78%	88%	100%

FIGURE 12-4 · Percentage of Lowest-Fee Funds That Generated Better-Than-Average Returns.*

*The study divided each fund category into 10 segments, based on their total expense ratios. In most cases, funds in each of these five categories that ranked in the lowest decile in fees produced better-than-average returns.

Source: Financial Research Corp.

look for those with particular expense ratios. In this case, Morningstar's screening tool lets investors search for funds with expense ratios below or equal to 2 percent, 1.5 percent, 1 percent, and 0.5 percent.

Individual Bonds

Despite the advantages of going with a bond fund, there are still investors who prefer the control that a portfolio of individual bonds can provide. Moreover, there is the comfort that individual bond investors have in being able to manage interest-rate risk. But as we discussed, there's the issue of credit risk that arises in assembling one's own portfolio of bonds. So what can investors of individual bonds do to reduce this risk?

Invest in Treasuries

The simplest solution to controlling credit risk, for those seeking to hold individual securities, is one that we have spoken about at length: Stick with debt issued by Uncle Sam. Because Treasury bonds are backed by the full faith and credit of the federal government, there is never any worry that Treasuries will default. This is why U.S. government debt is considered a safe haven for many investors—both here in the United States and among those abroad—during periods of instability in the political or economic landscape.

The good news is: Treasuries are the easiest form of debt to purchase, and they come in various maturities. For example, you can purchase Treasury notes maturing in two, three, five, and 10 years. You can also purchase Treasury bills of shorter maturities.

The only downside with investing solely in Treasuries is the income you may be giving up in exchange for credit risk protection. This is especially true during periods of economic or geopolitical risks. In the first years of the current decade, for example, yields on 10-year Treasury notes fell to 40-year lows of around 4 percent, far below the historic average returns for long-term Treasury and corporate bonds.

The only way for an investor to seek out higher yields in fixed-income instruments is to assume some level of risk. This is more than likely to come in the form of corporate debt. But within the realm of corporate bonds, there are ways for investors to keep credit risk in check.

Invest in High-Quality Debt

The easiest way to control—though not eliminate—credit risk among corporate bonds is to rely on the credit ratings that rating agencies like Standard & Poor's, Fitch, and Moody's assign to bond issuers. We discussed these earlier in the book.

Credit Rating	Moody's	S&P	Fitch
Highest quality	Aaa	AAA	AAA
High quality, but small degree of risk	Aa	AA	AA
Good quality, but susceptible to risk	A	A	A
Medium quality	Baa	BBB	BBB
Start of "junk" status	Ba	BB	BB
Speculative grade, major uncertainties	B	B	B
Poor quality, vulnerable to nonpayment	Caa	CCC	CCC
Highly vulnerable, likely to default	Ca	CC	CC
Lowest quality	C	C	C
In default		D	D–DDD

FIGURE 12-5 · Bond Ratings.

As you'll recall, bonds are rated with letter grades of sorts, with AAA being the best and D being the worst. The table in Figure 12-5, which was shown earlier, lists the credit ratings assigned to bonds by the three rating agencies.

As the chart indicates, any bond with a rating of BBB (or in the case of Moody's system, Baa) or higher is classified as "investment-grade" debt. Generally speaking, this is considered suitable for most fixed-income investors. Anything rated BB or Ba or lower is considered junk. Junk bonds yield more than investment-grade debt, but also carry with them the greater risk of default.

Obviously, investors focused on minimizing credit risk will want to stick with investment-grade debt. But keep in mind that within the realm of investment-grade or junk-bond status, there are several gradations. So even though a BBB-rated bond might still be considered high quality, it is considered much poorer in quality relative to AAA-rated bonds.

While this system of rating bonds is by no means perfect—remember, the major credit-rating agencies failed to downgrade many toxic mortgage-backed bonds before the financial crisis of 2008, and similarly failed to lower the ratings on Enron bonds to junk status until the energy giant was about to file for bankruptcy—it can still be useful.

Consider the chart in Figure 12-6. It shows that on average, bonds rated by S&P as AAA almost never default. Meanwhile, bonds rated AA default barely over 1 percent of the time. That is far less than bonds rated A, which in turn default less frequently than bonds rated BBB—and so on. This template gives bond investors a great visual guide as to what level of credit risk they can expect based on the type of corporate debt they purchase.

What does this mean? Investors most fearful of credit risk should stick with individual issues rated A or even AA or higher. While such bonds won't get you the highest yields in the corporate bond universe, it should protect

S&P Bond Rating	Default Rate*
Investment Grade	
AAA	0.67%
AA	1.30%
A	2.88%
BBB	9.77%
Junk Status	
BB, B	24.51%
CCC, CC, C	41.09%
D	60.70%

FIGURE 12-6 · Cumulative Default Rates Based on Bond Ratings.

*Figure represents cumulative default rate in 15-year period following initial rating.

Source: Charles Schwab, S&P

investors against the possibility of default risk. After all, if you own 10 bonds and buy only AA issues, only one of your bonds is likely to default over a 15-year stretch.

Needless to say, a person interested in opportunities presented by high-yield junk bonds probably should gain that exposure through a diversified mutual fund, which typically invests in nearly 300 different bonds. Consider the fact that there is a better than 1 in 4 chance, over a 15-year stretch, of junk bonds defaulting. Held in a portfolio of just 10 or 20 bonds, that could wreak havoc on your total returns. In a portfolio of 300 bonds, however, one bond defaulting may not be as big a problem.

Focus on Financial Health

Though bonds are ultimately safer than stocks, an investor who purchases corporate debt should go through the same due diligence that individual stock investors do. Whether you are buying the debt or stock of a corporation, you are buying into the promises made by an individual company.

As we noted in the last chapter, investigating stocks entails studying the underlying company's balance sheet, income statement, and statement of cash flows. But bond investors probably would want to go through an additional level of checks, given the nature of the security. After all, a stock investor who spots trouble after purchasing the security can sell out fairly quickly—and easily. A bond investor may not find that type of liquidity in the secondary market for fixed-income securities. Moreover, many bond investors go into the market with the idea of holding their securities to maturity. That entails a five, seven, or 10-year relationship, or even longer.

So what else should a bond investor consider? While stock investors are busy poring over a company's financial statements in search of signs of growth and prosperity, bond investors need to be more defensive. Because their concern is default, they need to go through the process of due diligence with worst-case scenarios in mind. This means a bond investor must look for signs that the company, at the very least, has enough financial strength to continue business as usual throughout the life of the bond.

Debt Measures

One simple thing to look for, then, is the amount of debt the company has outstanding. While bonds are a form of debt, bond investors tend not to want to buy fixed-income instruments of companies awash in debt. This makes sense. While the function of a lender is to loan out money, it never wants to extend debt to creditors who seek out too many new loans. In and of itself, too much debt is a sign of potential financial problems.

But how can you tell what an appropriate level of debt is? For example, a $100 million company with $1 million in debt outstanding is probably far better off than a $500,000 company with $100,000 in loans.

One way is to consider a company's **debt ratio**. This term refers to the amount of debt a company has outstanding, relative to its total assets. This way, one can fairly judge the debt of small and large companies alike. The formula for calculating a company's debt ratio is simple:

Total liabilities/Total assets = Debt ratio

To see how this works, let's go back to the sample Company X balance sheet we used in the last chapter while discussing financial statements (Figure 12-7).

As of June 30, 2010, Company X had $79.571 billion in total assets. It also had $18.551 billion in total liabilities. Let's plug those into our formula:

Total liabilities ($18.551 billion)/Total assets ($79.571 billion) = 23.3%

Debt ratio = 23.3%

Typically, you would not want to invest in a company with a debt ratio over 100 percent, since that would indicate that the firm owes more than it owns. Even a company with a ratio of 50 percent might require extra scrutiny. But in this case, the hypothetical Company X debt ratio would indicate some degree of safety when it comes to the firm being overexposed to debt. So a bond investor may feel some sense of comfort purchasing this company's debt—all other things being equal.

	6/30/10	6/30/09
Assets		
Cash	$49,048	$38,652
Receivables	5,196	5,129
Notes receivable	0	0
Inventories	640	673
Other current assets	4,089	4,122
Total Current Assets	58,973	48,576
Net property and equipment	2,223	2,268
Investments	13,692	14,191
Other noncurrent charges	0	0
Deferred charges	0	0
Intangibles	3,512	1,669
Deposits and other assets	1,171	942
TOTAL ASSETS	79,571	67,646
Liabilities and Shareholder Equity		
Notes payable	0	0
Accounts payable	1,573	1,208
Current portion L/T debt	0	0
Current portion capital leases	0	0
Accrued expenses	1,416	1,145
Income taxes payable	2,044	2,022
Other current liabilities	8,941	8,369
Total Current Liabilities	13,974	12,744
Mortgages	0	0
Deferred taxes/income	1,731	398
Convertible debt	0	0
Long-term debt	0	0
Noncurrent capital leases	0	0
Other noncurrent liabilities	2,846	2,324
Minority interest (liabilities)	0	0
TOTAL LIABILITIES	18,551	15,466
Shareholder Equity		
Preferred stock	0	0
Common stock	35,344	31,647
Capital surplus	0	0
Retained earnings	25,676	20,533
Other equity	0	0
Treasury stock	0	0
Total shareholder's equity	61,020	52,180
TOTAL SHAREHOLDER EQUITY + LIABILITIES	79,571	67,646

FIGURE 12-7 · Sample Balance Sheet: Company X.

*All figures in millions.

A second ratio to consider is something called the **debt-to-equity ratio**. Like the debt ratio, the debt-to-equity ratio attempts to measure the extent to which a company has borrowed too much money. But instead of weighing liabilities against assets, this ratio measures liabilities against total shareholder equity. The formula looks like this:

Total liabilities/Shareholder equity = Debt-to-equity ratio

This measure is an equally important way to judge the indebtedness of a firm, particularly for companies that may not have huge asset bases. For example, this may be a more useful—and fair—measure for judging the debt level of a service-oriented company versus an old industrial firm with huge allocations toward plant and equipment. Going back to our Company X example, we know that the firm had total liabilities of $18.551 billion. Its total shareholder equity was $61.020 billion. Let's plug those figures into our formula:

Total liabilities ($18.551 billion)/Shareholder equity ($61.020 billion) = 30.4%

Debt-to-equity ratio = 30.4%

Here again you should be wary of companies with debt-to-equity ratios above 100 percent and even above 50 percent, since risks increase when a company borrows more than its total net worth.

Liquidity Measures

There a couple of other financial ratios that may come in handy for bond investors as back-of-the-envelope gauges of a company's true financial health. Both involve the liquidity of a company, or its ability to convert assets to cash to pay immediate obligations.

The first measure is simple to calculate. Called the **current ratio**, it is a measure of a company's ability to meet its short-term obligations simply with its short-term assets. The formula is as follows:

Current assets/Current liabilities = Current ratio

Let's go back again to Company X's balance sheet (Figure 12-7). It indicates that the firm's current assets totaled $58.973 billion. Current assets refer to those assets that can be converted into cash within one year or less. They include cash, obviously. In addition, a company's inventories, accounts receivable, and investment securities, among other things, are part of current assets.

Meanwhile, in our hypothetical example, the company's current liabilities—liabilities that come due within a year, like short-term loans and accounts payable—totaled $13.974 billion. So going back to our formula, we know the following:

Current assets ($58.973 billion)/Current liabilities ($13.974 billion) = 4.22

Current ratio = 4.22

This is actually a great sign of health. Typically, investors will want to see that companies have *at least twice* as much cash and other current assets on hand as is required to meet short-term liabilities. In other words, a current ratio of 2 to 1 is considered good. In our example, the company's current ratio is 4.22 to 1.

Now, some would argue whether inventory should be thrown into this mix, since it's not altogether certain that a company, if in trouble, can actually convert its entire stockpile of goods into cash in less than one year's time. So some analysts strip out inventories from the current ratio to arrive at a more narrow analysis of a company's liquidity. This is called a company's quick ratio.

The **quick ratio**, which is also referred to as a company's "acid test," helps determine whether a company has enough short-term assets on hand—without having to resort to its inventory—to meet its basic obligations. The formula looks like this:

Current assets − Inventory/Current liabilities = Quick ratio

Let's go back to our prior example once again. We already know that based on Company X's balance sheet, the company had $58.973 billion in current assets as of this date. That balance sheet also indicates that inventories accounted for just $640 million. We subtract $640 million from $58.973 billion and arrive at $58.333 billion. We divide that by current liabilities of $13.974 billion and arrive at a quick ratio of 4.17. Generally speaking, a quick ratio of 1 to 1 is considered decent, since it means that not counting inventories, the company is equipped to meet its obligations. The higher the ratio, the safer the company would be regarded by a bond investor.

($58.973 billion − $640 million)/$13.974 billion = 4.17

Concentrate on Total Returns

Finally, no matter whether you go with bond funds or individual bonds, one thing all fixed-income investors need to remember is: *Consider a bond's potential total returns, not just its yield.* **Total returns**, again, refers to the income the bond throws off in addition to the price change in the underlying bond.

While a bond investor may fall in love with the interest income a bond promises, he or she must be cognizant of the fact that some bonds yield more because they have to attract risk-averse investors. Higher yields expose you to higher risks, and it serves no purpose to invest in bonds with high yields only to see their prices deflate due to concerns about the credit quality of the underlying firm.

So if you are investing in individual bonds, consider all the credit risks that your securities will expose you to. And the greater the credit risk that you are thinking of taking on, the more it may make sense to consider investing in a well-diversified bond fund rather than individual securities. Similarly, the more you fear interest-rate risk, the more reason there is to consider individual securities.

QUIZ

1. **A big reason why some investors favor bond funds over individual bonds is to safeguard their portfolios against . . .**
   A. Credit risk.
   B. Interest-rate risk.
   C. Inflation risk.

2. **It is easier to control interest-rate risk by investing in an individual bond than by investing in a bond mutual fund.**
   A. True
   B. False

3. **Bond prices move in which direction when interest rates move higher?**
   A. Higher.
   B. Lower.
   C. Neither. They don't move.

4. **By investing in a bond fund with a higher-than-average duration, you are making a bet that . . .**
   A. Interest rates will rise.
   B. Interest rates will fall.
   C. Credit quality will rise.
   D. Credit quality will fall.

5. **Longer-term bond funds tend to have lower durations.**
   A. True
   B. False

6. **Costs are just as important to consider with a bond fund than with a stock fund.**
   A. True
   B. False, because they are not as important
   C. False, because they are more important

7. **Bond fund fees are a good determinant of how the bond fund will perform relative to its peers.**
   A. True
   B. False

8. **If you are investing in individual bonds, one way to increase the potential yield you can earn on your bonds is to . . .**
   A. Go with lower-quality bonds.
   B. Go with longer-term securities.

C. Both.

D. Neither.

9. **An AAA-rated bond is just as safe as a U.S. Treasury bond.**

A. True

B. False

10. **A company's debt ratio measures its liabilities against what?**

A. Its earnings

B. Its shareholder equity

C. Its assets

D. Its current assets

chapter 13

Demystifying Mutual Fund Selection

CHAPTER OBJECTIVES

In this chapter, you will learn the following:

- How funds differentiate themselves
- What you get when you buy different types of funds
- How to fairly compare funds
- How to screen for funds

The real problem with mutual funds, as we outlined in Part Two, is not they're bad investments. They're actually quite good for most investors. The difficulty lies in being able to pick out good funds from a universe that now exceeds 26,000 portfolios. The funny thing is, the mutual fund's raison d'être is to simplify the lives of Americans who don't have the time or the interest to cobble together a diversified portfolio of stocks and bonds while working full-time and raising a family. But how do you assemble a portfolio of mutual funds given so many choices?

Stock Fund Categories

To classify the 26,000 funds, the major fund trackers, Morningstar and Lipper, have created systems that include more than 60 different fund groupings. They are listed in Figures 13-1 and 13-2.

You'll notice that the Morningstar and Lipper categories are essentially the same, except that what Morningstar describes as **blend**—which is a happy medium between growth and value stock funds—Lipper refers to as **core** funds (as in large-cap core funds, small-cap core funds, etc.). What's more, what Morningstar refers to as **foreign** stock funds, Lipper calls **international funds**. And what Morningstar calls **world stock** funds, Lipper labels **global stock** funds.

These last two distinctions can be confusing. To clarify, keep the following in mind: The terms "foreign" and "international" always refer to funds that invest *exclusively* overseas, be it in Europe, Asia, Latin America, or a combination. "World" or "global" stock funds, on the other hand, refer to a breed of fund that is allowed to invest not just overseas, but also in the United States and North America.

Fund Redundancy

Just because there are 60-plus fund categories does not mean that investors must have exposure to funds in every single one of these classifications. In fact, some of these categories, particularly among international stock funds and municipal bond portfolios, are quite obscure.

Moreover, many of these fund categories overlap. For example, if you invest in a diversified foreign fund, you will get exposure to all the foreign regions, so you don't need to invest separately in a Japan fund. Similarly, if you invest in a diversified emerging markets fund, you will get exposure to most of the developing markets like China, India, Russia, and Brazil. The only reason, in this case, to invest separately in a Latin American stock fund or an Asian Pacific fund would be to increase your bets in those regions.

The same goes for domestic stock funds. Assume you put money into a stock fund that generally invests in companies found in the S&P 500 index. Given the makeup of the S&P 500 (Figure 13-3), if you invest in a diversified domestic stock fund that tracks the index—or better still, if you invest in an S&P 500 index fund—you don't need to buy a separate sector fund, be it a technology, health care, financial services, or energy sector portfolio. By putting $1 into the S&P 500, in effect 18.8 cents goes into the tech sector, 11.8 cents goes into health care, 16.2 cents goes to financial services, and 11.0 cents is invested in energy, and so on.

Some investors may want to be in a separate sector fund, in addition to investing in a general domestic equity portfolio, because they believe that a sector

Domestic Stock Funds
Large Growth
Large Blend
Large Value
Mid-Cap Growth
Mid-Cap Blend
Mid-Cap Value
Small Growth
Small Blend
Small Value
Bear Market

Stock Sector Funds
Technology
Health Care
Financial
Utilities
Natural Resources
Communications
Real Estate

Hybrid Funds
(a.k.a. Balanced Funds)
Moderate Allocation
Conservative Allocation
World Allocation
Convertibles

International Stock Funds
World Stock
Foreign Large Growth
Foreign Large Blend
Foreign Large Value
Foreign Small/Mid Growth
Foreign Small/Mid Blend
Foreign Small/Mid Value
Europe Stock
Japan Stock
Diversified Asia/Pacific
Pacific/Asia except Japan
Latin America
Diversified Emerging Markets
Specialty Precious Metals (Gold)

Taxable Bond Funds
Long-Term Bond
Intermediate-Term Bond
Short-Term Bond
Ultra-Short-Term Bond
Multisector Bond
Long Government
Intermediate-Term Government
Short-Term Government
World Bond
Emerging Markets Bond
High Yield Bond
Stable Value
Bank Loan

Municipal Bond Funds
Muni National Long Term
Muni National Short Term
Muni Single State Long Intermediate Term
Muni Single State Intermediate Term
High Yield Muni Bond
Muni California Long
Muni California Intermediates/Short
Muni New York Long
Muni New York Intermediate/Short
Muni New Jersey
Muni Pennsylvania
Muni Minnesota
Muni Florida
Muni Ohio
Muni Massachusetts

FIGURE 13-1 · Morningstar Fund Categories.

Diversified Domestic Stock Funds	Mixed Equity Funds (a.k.a. Balanced Funds)	Municipal Bond Funds

Diversified Domestic Stock Funds
Large Growth
Large Core
Large Value
Multi-Cap Growth
Multi-Cap Core
Multi-Cap Value
Mid-Cap Growth
Mid-Cap Core
Mid-Cap Value
Small Growth
Small Core
Small Value
S&P 500 Index Objective
Equity Income
Specialty Diversified Equity

Sector Equity Funds
Science and Technology
Health/Biotechnology
Financial Services
Utility
Natural Resources
Telecommunications
Real Estate
Specialty/Miscellaneous

World Equity Funds
World Stock
Global Large Growth
Global Large Core
Global Large Value
Global Multi-Cap Growth
Global Multi-Cap Core
Global Multi-Cap Value
Global Small/Mid Growth
Global Small/Mid Core
Global Small/Mid Value
International Large Growth
International Large Core
International Large Value
International Multi-Cap Growth
International Multi-Cap Core
International Multi-Cap Value
International Small/Mid Growth
International Small/Mid Core
International Small/Mid Value
European Region
Pacific Region
Japanese Stock
Pacific Region
Pacific Except Japan
China Region
Latin American
Emerging Markets
Gold Oriented

Mixed Equity Funds
(a.k.a. Balanced Funds)
Flexible Portfolio
Global Flexible Portfolio
Balanced
Balanced Target Maturity
Convertible Securities
Income Funds

Taxable Bond Funds
General Bond Funds
Multisector Income Funds
High Yield
Flexible Income Funds
Loan Participation Funds
Target Maturity Funds
Short World Multimarket
Income Funds
Global Income Funds
International Income Funds
Emerging Market Debt
General U.S. Treasury Funds
U.S. Government Funds
Adjustable Rate Mortgage Funds
GNMA Funds
U.S. Mortgage Funds
Corporate Debt A-Rated Funds
Corporate Debt BBB-Rated Funds
Intermediate Term Investment
Grade Debt
Short/Intermediate Investment
Grade Debt
Short Investment Grade Debt
Intermediate U.S. Government
TIPs Funds
Short/Intermediate U.S. Government
Short U.S. Government
Short U.S. Treasuries

Municipal Bond Funds
Short Muni Debt
Short/Intermediate Muni Debt
Intermediate Muni Debt
General Muni Debt
Insured Muni Debt
High Yield Muni Debt
Alabama Muni Debt
Arizona Muni Debt
California Intermediate Muni Debt
California Insured Muni Debt
California Muni Debt
California Short Muni Debt
Colorado Muni Debt
Florida Muni Debt
Florida Intermediate Muni Debt
Florida Insured Muni Debt
Georgia Muni Debt
Hawaii Muni Debt
Kansas Muni Debt
Kentucky Muni Debt
Louisiana Muni Debt
Maryland Muni Debt
Massachusetts Intermediate
Muni Debt
Massachusetts Muni Debt
Michigan Muni Debt
Minnesota Muni Debt
Missouri Muni Debt
New Jersey Muni Debt
New York Intermediate Muni Debt
New York Insured Muni Debt
New York Muni Debt
North Carolina Muni Debt
Ohio Intermediate Muni Debt
Ohio Muni Debt
Oregon Muni Debt
Pennsylvania Intermediate Muni Debt
Pennsylvania Muni Debt
South Carolina Muni Debt
Tennessee Muni Debt
Texas Muni Debt
Virginia Muni Debt
Other State Intermediate Muni Debt
Other State Short/Intermediate
Muni Debt

FIGURE 13-2 · Lipper Fund Categories.

Sector	% of Index*
Consumer discretionary	10.5%
Consumer staples	11.3%
Energy	11.0%
Financials	16.2%
Health care	11.8%
Industrials	10.4%
Technology	18.8%
Materials	3.5%
Telecommunications	2.9%
Utilities	3.6%

FIGURE 13-3 · S&P 500 Industry Breakdown.

*Data as of June 2010.

Source: Standard & Poor's

manager has expertise in picking stocks in that industry that a general fund manager may not. But this isn't always the case. Keep in mind that just because a manager runs a sector portfolio does not mean that he or she has more experience in picking stocks in that sector than a generalist. In fact, the average tenure of a tech fund manager is roughly the same as the average tenure of a general fund manager: less than five years.

Measuring Fund Performance

Morningstar, Lipper, and other fund trackers did not create these categories to imply that you must invest in 60 different types of funds in order to be diversified. Rather, these categories were established to allow investors to benchmark the performance of their funds.

Without categories, investors would be forced to compare the performance of, say, a REIT fund, which reflects the ups and downs of the real estate market, against the returns of a technology fund, which invests in some of the most volatile stocks in the equity markets. While ideally you would want the absolute biggest returns you could get from all of your mutual funds, it is simply not fair to ask a REIT fund or a bond fund to compete against a technology sector fund. Similarly, it would be unfair to expect a tech fund, with all of its volatility, to hold up as well as a bond fund during a bear market.

The fact of the matter is, certain asset classes act differently than others. This is the very reason why investors diversify—so that some investments in their portfolio are rising as others may be falling. While we would all like all of our investments to rise at all times, history has shown that *different sectors and different types of stocks will do well at different times in the economic cycle.*

In the late 1990s Internet bubble, value funds, for example, were unfairly shunned by some investors because these conservative funds consistently lagged the performance of growth stock funds, which invested not only in Internet companies, but shares of large tech leaders like Microsoft and Intel, which were among the decade's best performers. In 1999 in particular, large growth stock funds gained around 40 percent on average, while large value stock funds returned only around 5 percent. But in 2000, which marked the start of the bear market, large value gained more than 9 percent while growth stock funds lost more than 13 percent. Had you turned your back on the best large value stock funds in 1999, based on their returns that year, you would have lost out on all those gains in the subsequent year.

In essence, there are two ways investors can judge whether their funds are performing adequately. One is to compare the fund against its **best fit index**. This term simply refers to the stock or bond market index that the fund's holdings correspond to. So, if you invest in a large-cap growth fund, you might choose to compare your results against those of the S&P 500 Growth index. This index covers only the growth stocks found in the S&P 500. If you invest in a small-cap value fund, you would probably compare your results against the Russell 2000 Value index, which only considers the value stocks in the Russell 2000 small-cap index. These two indexes are among the 16 types of specialty indexes listed in Figure 13-4.

Fund Category	Possible Best Fit Index
Large-cap growth	S&P 500 Growth, Russell 1000 Growth
Large-cap blend	S&P 500, Russell 1000
Large-cap value	S&P 500 Value, Russell 1000 Value
Mid-cap growth	S&P 400 Growth, Russell Mid-cap Growth
Mid-cap blend	S&P 400, Russell Mid-cap
Mid-cap value	S&P 400 Value, Russell Mid-cap Value
Small-cap growth	S&P 600 Growth, Russell 2000 Growth
Small-cap blend	S&P 600, Russell 2000
Small-cap value	S&P 600 Value, Russell 2000 Value
Technology	S&P Technology Index, Dow Jones U.S. Technology
Health care	S&P Healthcare Index, DJ U.S. Healthcare
Financial	S&P Financial Index, DJ U.S. Financial Svs
Utilities	S&P Utilities Index, DJ U.S. Utilities
Natural resources	S&P Nat. Res. Index, DJ U.S. Natural Resources
Communications	S&P Telecom Index, DJ U.S. Telecom
Real estate	S&P REIT Index, DJ U.S. Real Estate

FIGURE 13-4 · Breaking Down the Stock Universe.

If you go to www.morningstar.com, which is a mostly free site, you can punch in the name of your fund or its ticker symbol (like stocks, every fund has a ticker symbol that allows you to look up the fund more quickly). There, you can look up not only the fund's category, but its best fit index.

The other way to judge your fund's performance, of course, is to compare its returns against those of its category average. These averages are published by newspapers and Web sites throughout the country every quarter, for the most part, using either Morningstar or Lipper data. You can go directly to www. morningstar.com or www.lipperweb.com to see these performance tables as well.

First Core, Then Explore

Even if you wanted to invest in almost every single category of mutual funds, it would be cost-prohibitive—and redundant—to do so. One way to simplify this morass of fund categories is to start with the essentials and work your way out. As we discussed in Chapter 5, stock investors should, at the very least, always have some exposure to a mix of growth and value stocks, as well as large and small stocks. This means you should have exposure to the four corners of what the fund industry refers to as the **mutual fund style boxes**, which we've discussed and looked at before. As you might recall, this is a graphic way to illustrate the major categories of funds that are most necessary to an investors' portfolio. Take a look at the Morningstar and Lipper style boxes for domestic stock funds, shown in Figures 13-5 and 13-6.

As you're constructing your portfolio, consider starting with a large-cap growth fund, a large-cap value fund, a small-cap growth fund, and a small-cap value fund, as emphasized in both style box figures. Then, if you have additional money to work with—and determine that it's in your best interest to have some exposure to mid-cap funds—you can fill out the rest of the style boxes. And then, if you feel the need to go into a sector fund—to bet on a particular set of industries—you can do that as well.

Large Value	Large Blend	Large Growth
Mid Value	Mid Blend	Mid Growth
Small Value	Small Blend	Small Growth

FIGURE 13-5 · Morningstar-Style Box.

Large Value	Large Core	Large Growth
Multi Cap Value	Multi Cap Core	Multi Cap Growth
Mid Value	Mid Core	Mid Growth
Small Value	Small Core	Small Growth

FIGURE 13-6 · Lipper-Style Box.

By placing most of your money in these "core" style boxes, you not only anchor your portfolio with sound diversification, but make it safer to then dabble in riskier segments of the market. After all, if you bet a small amount of money in an emerging markets stock fund, for example, but have the bulk of your equity assets in large-cap growth and value and small-cap growth and value stocks, any losses in that emerging markets fund is likely to be masked by gains in your core investments.

Simplifying Your Fund Strategy

There is an even simpler approach to starting a portfolio of funds. If you think it's too much work to invest in four domestic stock fund categories—or that it costs too much money—one alternative is to invest in just two categories: **large-cap blend (or core)** and **small-cap blend (or core)**. Funds in the blend or core categories own a mix of both growth and value stocks, so they tend to fall smack dab in the middle of the growth-value continuum. By investing in a combination of large- and small-cap blend funds, you will ensure that some of your money is in growth and value and large and small stocks at all times.

If you invest in a broad market index fund, like one that mirrors the Wilshire 5000 or the Russell 3000 total stock market index, you pretty much have all your bases covered. After all, these two indexes represent the total U.S. equity market—large and small, growth and value. So this might well be the simplest approach to take. If you plan to get domestic stock fund exposure through one or two actively managed funds, you have to be certain that they invest in as broad a reach of stocks as a Wilshire 5000 stock fund. There are a number of index funds that track the total U.S. stock market, including those listed in Figure 13-7.

Name	URL	800 Number
Vanguard Total Stock Market Index	www.vanguard.com	1.800.662.7447
Wilshire 5000 Index Fund	www.wilfunds.com	1.888.200.6796
Fidelity Spartan Total Market Index	www.fidelity.com	1.800.343.3548
T. Rowe Price Total Equity Market	www.troweprice.com	1.800.638.5660
Schwab Total Stock Market Index	www.schwab.com	1.800.435.4000
iShares Russell 3000 Index	www.ishares.com	1.800.474.2737
iShares Dow Jones U.S. Index	www.ishares.com	1.800.474.2737

FIGURE 13-7 · Total Stock Market Index Funds.

Financial Service Providers

Not only are there different types of mutual funds available to retail investors these days, there are different types of companies that run funds in a variety of categories. This is because in the late 1990s many financial services firms realized that there was tremendous opportunity in managing a family's investments over time. With the growth of the 401(k) and IRA markets, the so-called **asset gathering industry**, which the mutual fund business is a part of, began to boom.

So in addition to selecting specific funds and types of funds, investors must also decide what type of financial services providers to work with. When you're shopping for a large-cap growth fund, are you better off going with a fund offered by a direct-sold mutual fund company, or does it make sense to go with a portfolio that's run by a financial services company that you already have a relationship with, like a bank or an insurance company? In general, questions like these are difficult to answer, since it's impossible to predict with absolute certainty which funds will end up doing better in the future.

The pie chart in Figure 13-8 shows the investors' preferences for various financial service providers.

The knee-jerk answer as to what kind of provider to choose is to go with a no-load fund company over a bank or brokerage, because bank- and brokerage-run funds often come with steep loads that cut into your returns. And as we discussed, a no-load fund allows you to put 100 percent of your investing capital to work in the market, whereas a load fund may only get 94 cents of every dollar into stocks and bonds. Moreover, a number of bank-run funds have had trouble gaining widespread notoriety, relative to competitors in the mutual fund universe, largely because of lackluster performance. And some of that might be explained by the high costs of some bank-run funds.

But it's important not to color all fund companies with too broad a stroke. Investors need to consider each fund on its own merits. Indeed, in picking

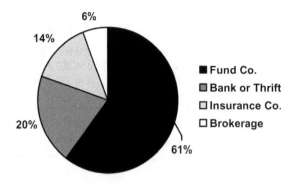

FIGURE 13-8 · Fund Industry Market Share.

As this chart shows, mutual fund companies aren't the only types of financial services firms that operate funds. Many funds are run and sold through banks or insurance companies as well as through brokerages.

Source: Investment Company Institute

funds it's important to concentrate on the specific fund itself, rather than the company that manages it. Often, there are hidden gems in otherwise lackluster fund complexes. Conversely, some of the best fund companies—even household brands like Vanguard, Fidelity, and T. Rowe Price—run some portfolios that have lagged the markets over substantial periods of time.

We'll cite some basic principles to keep in mind as you're trying to weed out the leaders from the laggards.

Consider Past Performance

Past performance matters, but not for the reason you might think. You will often hear the phrase: "Past performance is not an indicator of future returns." This is absolutely true. Consider the 10-year period between 1994 and 2003.

In 1994, the absolute best performing domestic stock fund was a technology fund. That was followed in 1995 by a large-cap growth fund. Then, in 1996, the top performer was a natural resources sector fund, which invests in energy stocks. In 1997, a small-cap growth fund led the field. That was followed by an Internet stock fund, Kinetics Internet, in 1998, which marked the start of the dot.com bubble. The bubble economy in 1999 propelled a small-cap growth fund to the top of the heap, but in 2000 a health-care fund, which doubled its investors' money that year despite the start of the bear market, was the best performer. In 2001, a small value fund led the way, and in 2002 a **bear market fund**—a new type of fund that appreciates when stocks fall and loses value when stocks rise—was the absolute top performer. And in 2003 it was a small-cap growth fund again. After that, bond funds and real estate funds took charge.

Year	Fund	Type	Returns That Year	Returns in Year Following
1994	Seligman Comm. & Info.	Tech	35.30%	43.38%
1995	Alger Capital Appreciation	Large growth	78.32%	13.90%
1996	State St. Global Resources	Natural resource	70.64%	5.85%
1997	Munder Micro-Cap Equity	Small growth	71.61%	−6.00%
1998	Kinetics Internet	Internet	196.14%	216.43%
1999	Van Wagoner Emerging Gr.	Small growth	291.14%	−20.90%
2000	Evergreen Health Care	Health care	119.49%	2.38%
2001	Ameristock Focused Value	Small value	60.42%	−18.63%
2002	Prudent Bear	Bear market	62.87%	−10.43%
2003	Apex Mid Cap Growth	Small growth	165.27%	−6.3%

FIGURE 13-9 · Top Performing Domestic Stock Fund.

Not only does this illustrate how different assets do well in different periods of the economy, it shows that mutual funds have a hard time repeating their performance. Indeed, if you study this 10-year period, you will see that not only did fund leadership change hands every year, but in the year following their top performances, many of these calendar-year champions floundered (Figure 13-9).

The trouble that many investors get into is what's known as "chasing fund performance." They pick up a newspaper and read that a particular fund has performed the best in a given year, then put their money into the fund, only to discover that it has gone cold. As we mentioned earlier, chasing fund performance can lead to terrible results in one's overall portfolio.

Having said that, there is one big reason why a fund investor needs to at least consider some aspect of past performance when selecting funds. When investing in an individual security, whether stocks, bonds, or real estate, an investor is making a bet on an asset and the economy. He or she is making a calculated guess that a business or piece of property will thrive at a given point in time. And there are numerous objective ways to try to gauge this.

When selecting an actively managed mutual fund, however, you aren't just betting on an asset class (like technology or small value stocks). You are betting on the ability and discipline of another human being—the fund manager—to properly and consistently find the best investments in that grouping. Shy of moving in next door to this fund manager and looking him in the eye to see what kind of person he is, the only thing that retail investors can do is consider how this manager has done in the past.

What you're looking for isn't necessarily the best performer in a given period of time, since, as we just discussed, it's almost impossible for a fund manager to repeat a championship-style run. It's more important to look for signs of solid performance throughout a career.

Why Don't Funds Repeat?

There are three possible explanations as to why fund managers can't seem to repeat as the top performers in the universe:

1. Reversion to the mean.
2. It's just plain hard to beat the stock market.
3. The Heisenberg principle of investing.

Reversion to the Mean

This is a fancy way of saying that over time, all assets that are performing better than or worse than average eventually will perform like the average. And sometimes, to revert to the mean, an asset will have to go through years of underperformance following years of outperformance.

This is exactly what transpired in the Internet bubble years of the late 1990s, when the stock market, after enjoying five consecutive years of 20-percent-plus returns (double its historic average annual return) suffered three consecutive years of double-digit or near-double-digit losses. Prior to the start of the bear market, many investors began to believe that somehow the rules of investing had changed. But the laws of mean reversion clearly did not, and the results were self-evident.

It's Hard to Beat the Stock Market

It's hard to beat the market, let alone 26,000 peers, year in and year out. With all due respect to managers like Bill Miller of Legg Mason Value—who outperformed the S&P for more than a decade before plummeting significantly more than the S&P in 2007 and 2008—there are only a few managers who have achieved such records. And even after posting stellar records, many of these managers often stumble, like Miller did. In the three years after his S&P-beating streak, Miller's fund trailed 99 percent of its peers.

The fact is, over the 15-year period ending December 2009, only about 40 percent of domestic stock fund managers consistently beat the S&P 500. And this was during a volatile period for the broad market that included a decade in which stocks went nowhere.

The Heisenberg Principle of Investing

In science, the Heisenberg principle states that one cannot truly observe anything in nature since the very act of observation tends to change the behavior of things.

Shine a light on a chemical reaction, for example, and you could end up affecting the reaction itself. The same type of problem occurs with mutual funds.

When a fund posts big numbers, it tends to attract a good deal of attention. Not only will newspapers write about its market-beating performance, but many newsletters and financial advisors will tout the fund to their client base. As this occurs, money will naturally flow into the top performing funds, while flowing out of poor performers. This is why there's a saying in the $11 trillion mutual fund industry: "Flows follow performance."

Indeed, academic studies have found that the vast majority of investors, rightly or wrongly—but mostly wrongly—put new money into funds that are ranked by Morningstar as four- or five-star-rated funds. Yet Morningstar fund ratings are based on *past performance*, which means that by the time a fund has received such high marks, it is probably unlikely to repeat as a top performer.

When too much money flows too fast into a hot stock fund, the portfolio naturally has a way of cooling down. This is because fund managers are only human. They may not be able to invest all the cash immediately in high-quality stocks, as we mentioned in Chapter 9. He or she may not have enough "good ideas" to invest this flood of money. So if too much cash pours in all at once, the manager may either have to stash some of it in a cash account (until new opportunities present themselves) or invest it in a second- or third-best idea. Both of these options have the affect of dragging down a fund's performance, which might explain why hot funds cool down so often.

This is why it's vital not to chase performance in the absolute best performing funds. Instead, you're probably better off focusing on stability and consistency of performance.

Where to Find Screening Tools

Many financial Web sites have mutual fund screening tools that allow investors to search for funds that meet certain specific criteria. While many charge investors a fee, there are plenty of free sites for fund screening. Some of these free sites allow investors to screen based on a variety of sophisticated variables.

For example, Yahoo! Finance, the financial page of this leading Internet portal, allows investors to search for funds based on their categories, fund families, fund rankings within their categories, past performance, expenses, loads, size, turnover, and even market capitalization.

If that's too complicated, you can go to MSN's Moneycentral site to screen for solid performing funds in more basic categories. There is even a site that allows investors who are into *socially responsible investing* to screen for funds that only invest in shares of companies that don't promote smoking, violence, gambling, environmental damage, etc.

Company	URL
Morningstar*	www.morningstar.com
Yahoo! Finance	finance.yahoo.com
Smart Money magazine	www.smartmoney.com/funds
Money magazine	cnnmoney.com
Forbes magazine	www.forbes.com
Kiplinger's Personal Finance	www.kiplinger.com
MSN Moneycentral	moneycentral.msn.com
Marketwatch	www.marketwatch.com
Fidelity Investments	www.fidelity.com
Charles Schwab	www.schwab.com
E*Trade Financial	www.etrade.com
Mutual Fund Education Alliance	www.mfea.com
Quicken	www.quicken.com

FIGURE 13-10 · Mutual Fund Screening Tools.

*The basic fund screening tool is free. To use Morningstar's premium fund screener, you will have to pay a fee.

Moreover, many of the mutual fund supermarkets, run by discount brokerages, allow customers and noncustomers alike to utilize screening tools to find good funds. Among them: Fidelity, Schwab, and E*TRADE. Figure 13-10 lists these, among others, along with their Web site URL.

And finally, another good source of free but comprehensive data is available on the Web sites of the major personal finance magazines, including *Money* magazine, *Smart Money*, and *Kiplinger's Personal Finance.*

But perhaps the best tool is available at www.morningstar.com, since Morningstar has become a leading data provider for the entire fund industry. Its basic, free screening tool allows investors to search for funds based on fund companies, categories, manager tenure, proprietary ratings and risk scores, relative returns, turnover, assets, loads, expenses, and minimum initial purchase requirements. It will also allow you to screen for bond funds based on credit quality and duration. Morningstar's premium service allows you to search far more sophisticated criteria, but that service comes with a fee.

What to Screen

Load or No-Load?

When screening for funds, perhaps the best place to start is with the little things. If you have a preference for load versus no-load funds, you might as well start by screening out funds you don't want based on their commission structure. On

Morningstar's site, that would mean going to the screening criteria section and starting with the line labeled *Cost and Purchase*. If you didn't want to consider load funds, you'd punch in:

Load Fund: No Load Funds Only

Then, let's assume you will only consider funds that allow investors to get in the front door with as little as $2,000. So once again, on Morningstar's basic screener, you would punch in:

Minimum Initial Purchase Less than or Equal to: $2,000

Past Performance

As we just discussed, past performance matters, but it has to be regarded in the right way. When screening for funds, it is not necessary to screen for the absolute best performance numbers. You should start by screening for good relative performance—both long term and short term—within a fund's category. Good relative performance would indicate that a manager has the ability to do well consistently, in good markets and in bad. Moreover, long-term performance would show that the manager has done well even when his or her asset class is out of favor.

Instead of concerning yourself with total return figures, focus instead on **category rank**. As a fund tracker, Morningstar maintains records on all 26,000-plus funds and ranks portfolios against their peers on a daily basis. If you go to Morningstar's Web site and try to look up a fund's performance, you will see a table like the one in Figure 13-11, for the Fidelity Magellan fund.

The first line shows the total returns for this fund in each calendar year. While the numbers appear to be informative, it does not do you much good to know how well Fidelity Magellan or any other fund is performing without some context. The second line in this performance chart provides that context.

The line labeled +/− *Category* indicates how well Magellan performed in each year *relative to* its fund category, as defined by Morningstar. Fidelity Magellan is a large-cap blend fund, and looking at its 2009 results, you'll see that it outperformed its category average by nearly 6 percentage points. In the previous year, 2008, the fund underperformed by nearly 9 percentage points.

	2004	2005	2006	2007	2008	2009
Total return	7.49	6.42	7.22	18.83	−49.40	41.13
+/− Category	−2.58	+0.53	+0.27	+5.62	−8.69	+5.86
+/− Index	−3.39	+1.51	−8.58	+13.33	−12.40	+14.67

FIGURE 13-11 · Fidelity Magellan Performance History.

Time Period	Total Return %	+/− S&P 500	% Rank in Category
1 day	0.74	+0.26	32%
1 week	2.83	+0.26	5%
4 weeks	−5.25	+0.07	69%
3 months	−5.13	−0.48	36%
Year to date	−2.22	−1.01	42%
1 year	14.82	−3.09	59%
3-year annualized	−9.02	−0.83	85%
5-year annualized	−1.00	−1.24	83%
10-year annualized	−2.50	−1.47	47%

FIGURE 13-12 · Fidelity Magellan Trailing Total Returns.*

*Data through June 12, 2010.

Source: Morningstar

This type of data is useful because it shows that even though a fund might generate sizable gains, it can still be a laggard. In 2006, for example, Fidelity Magellan returned 7.2 percent. Yet this chart shows that Magellan's peers returned slightly more in that year.

The third line in this chart, labeled +/− *Index*, is just as useful, since it indicates whether the fund outperformed or underperformed its best-fit index in recent years. We can see that Fidelity Magellan beat its index—in this case the S&P 500, since Magellan is a large blend fund—by 14.7 percent in 2009 and 13.3 percent in 2007, but lagged the S&P by more than 12 percentage points in 2008.

An even better way to consider past performance is not by calendar year, but by trailing total returns over particular, longer time periods. The chart in Figure 13-12 illustrates this. (Again, this information for all funds is available at www.morningstar.com.)

Here we see that Fidelity Magellan has averaged annual losses of −2.5 percent a year for the past decade, ending June 12, 2010. But over the past five years the fund has lost 1 percent on average annually. So does that make Magellan a good or bad investment? This can't be answered unless you know how it has performed relative to its specific peer group, which is indicated in the right-hand column, labeled *% Rank in Category*. Morningstar updates this number on a daily basis, so investors will always have the most recent information when they check their funds on this Web site.

The numbers in the far-right column show where, in the total universe of large blend funds, Magellan falls in any given time period. Over the past one-year period through June 12, 2010, for instance, it ranked in the 83rd percentile of all large blend funds. That means if there were 100 funds in the category, this one would rank number 83. Over the past 10-year period though, the fund ranked in the 47th percentile, which means it performed slightly above average. The higher the percentile figure, the worse the fund.

Morningstar's fund screener will allow you to search for funds based on the various time periods we can see in the Magellan analysis. Since consistency is what we want, and not sporadic gains, you can screen for the following:

1-YR return greater than or equal: Category Average
3-YR return greater than or equal: Category Average
5-YR return greater than or equal: Category Average
10-YR return greater than or equal: Category Average

If you have access to a more sophisticated fund screener, like Morningstar's premium service, you might try to be even more demanding. You might focus only on funds that ranked in the top third of their categories over the past one, three, and five years. In Morningstar's premium screener, you would punch in:

% Rank in Category 1 YR < 33
% Rank in Category 3 YR < 33
% Rank in Category 5 YR < 33
% Rank in Category 10 YR < 33

Obviously, many funds don't have a 10-year track record. So you don't necessarily have to go out 10 years when screening for funds. But you would probably want to stick with funds with at least a five-year track record. That way, you can determine how the fund has performed in bull markets, bear markets, and even trading range markets.

Stability

Given the choice between steady-as-she-goes performance in a fund and volatile swings, investors are often better off with stability. After all, you never know when you'll need to sell your shares. If it happens that you must redeem your investment at an inopportune moment, things could work out poorly in a volatile fund.

Here is an illustration of the benefits of stable performance. Take two funds with average annual returns of 10 percent. Fund X is consistent, with gains of 8 percent in the first year, 10 percent in the second, and 12 percent in the third. If you were to invest $10,000 in this fund, you'd have $13,300 by the end of Year One. The math works like this:

Year One

$$\$10,000 \times 0.08 = \$ \quad 800$$

$$\$800 + \text{original } \$10,000 = \$10,800$$

Year Two

$$\$10,800 \times 0.10 = \$ \ 1,080$$

$$\$1,080 + \text{original } \$10,800 = \$11,880$$

Year Three

$$\$11,880 \times 0.12 = \$ \ 1,425.60$$

$$\$1,425.60 + \text{original } \$11,880 = \$13,305.60$$

Now let's look at Fund Y, also with average annual returns of 10 percent. But Fund Y achieves that average by losing 20 percent in Year One, gaining 10 percent in Year Two, and gaining 40 percent in Year Three. If you invested the same $10,000 in Fund Y, you'd have only $12,320 by the end of Year Three. That's right—you'd earn less than in Fund X, even though both had the same average annual returns. Here's how the math works:

Year One

$$\$10,000 \times -0.20 = -\$2,000$$

$$-\$2,000 + \text{original } \$10,000 = \quad \$8,000$$

Year Two

$$\$8,000 \times 0.10 = \$ \quad 800$$

$$\$800 + \text{original } \$8,000 = \$ \ 8,800$$

Year Three

$$\$8,800 \times 0.40 = \$ \ 3,520$$

$$\$3,520 + \text{original } \$8,800 = \$ \ 12,320$$

What this shows is that by betting on steady, consistent growth, you can actually do better than by gambling on volatility. This is because one terrible year in the market could set your portfolio back for years.

Standard Deviation

One way investors can judge the steadiness of their funds is to look at the so-called standard deviation of those portfolios. As you'll recall, we mentioned this term in Chapter 3.

Standard deviation, in this setting, measures a fund's volatility relative to its average performance in a set period of time. The lower the standard deviation, the less volatile a fund is considered to be, since it deviates less from its average performance than does a high standard deviation fund. Every fund's standard deviation is listed by Morningstar. What an investor can do, then, after screening for other characteristics, is to check if their fund's standard deviation is in line with—or better still, lower than—its category peers (Figure 13-13).

Beta

Another way to gauge the relative volatility of a fund is to consider whether it fluctuates more or less than the broad stock market. As we discussed earlier in the book, a beta measure of 1 indicates that the fund will likely move in lockstep with the S&P 500. This explains why the Vanguard 500 fund, which mirrors the S&P, has a beta of exactly 1.

On the other hand, a fund with a beta of greater than 1 is likely to move higher than the market when the S&P is up, but lose more than the market when the S&P falls. Conversely, a fund with a beta of less than 1 is likely to lose less

Type of Fund	5-Year Standard Deviation*
Domestic stock funds	21.35
International stock funds	25.75
Large-cap growth funds	17.49
Large-cap value funds	16.78
Large-cap blend funds	16.64
Mid-cap growth funds	20.01
Mid-cap value funds	19.81
Mid-cap blend funds	19.92
Small-cap growth funds	21.21
Small-cap value funds	21.21
Small-cap blend funds	20.83
S&P 500	16.04

FIGURE 13-13 · Average Standard Deviation among Fund Categories.*

*Data as of December 2009.

Source: Morningstar

Type of Fund	Beta / S&P 500*
Domestic stock funds	1.07
International stock funds	1.05
Large-cap growth funds	1.00
Large-cap value funds	1.01
Large-cap blend funds	1.01
Mid-cap growth funds	1.09
Mid-cap value funds	1.15
Mid-cap blend funds	1.13
Small-cap growth funds	1.14
Small-cap value funds	1.17
Small-cap blend funds	1.17
S&P 500	1.00

FIGURE 13-14 · Average Standard Deviation among Fund Categories.*

*Data as of December 2009.

Source: Morningstar

than the market when the S&P is down, and gain less when the S&P rises. Ideally, it would be great to focus on funds with betas of less than 1. But because certain asset classes are just naturally more volatile than the S&P (particularly smaller stocks and growth stocks), it's important to weigh your fund's volatility relative to its peers. Figure 13-14 lists the average betas for various fund categories.

Like standard deviation, beta figures are also available through various financial Web sites, including Morningstar.

Still Confused?

Standard deviation and beta are both measures of how volatile a fund or investment is. The difference is, with standard deviation, you are measuring how volatile an investment is relative to how volatile it has historically been. On the other hand, beta measures how volatile an investment is relative to the broad market, like the S&P 500.

Fees

In most industries, you get what you pay for. The more expensive a car, for example, the better the performance often is. Yet study after study indicates that among mutual funds, low-fee funds tend to outperform high-fee portfolios. This is because of the reason we outlined in Chapter 9: Fees come straight out of your total returns.

Type of Fund	1-Year Returns	3-Year Returns	5-Year Returns
Domestic stock funds	83%	94%	100%
International stock funds	83%	94%	79%
Government bond funds	89%	100%	100%
Corporate bond funds	67%	81%	64%
Municipal bond funds	78%	88%	100%

FIGURE 13-15 · Percentage of Lowest-Fee Funds That Generated Better-Than-Average Returns.

This study divided each fund category into 10 segments, based on their total expense ratios. In most cases, funds in each of these five categories that ranked in the lowest decile in fees produced better-than-average returns.

Source: Financial Research Corp.

No matter how good the fund manager is, the higher the fees the fund charges, the better the fund must perform to be just average. As you'll recall, a fund that charges 0.2 percent fees need only beat the market by 0.2 percent. Compare this to a fund with a *total expense ratio* of 3 percent, which of course needs to outpace the market by 3 percentage points just to break even with the indexes. Again, this is why a 2002 study by Financial Research Corp., a financial services research firm in Boston, determined that fees are one of the few consistent predictors of mutual fund outperformance (Figure 13-15). The study concluded: "There is significant evidence that funds with [the lowest] total expense ratios do deliver above-average future performance across nearly all time periods."

Low expenses are a "good to significant predictor" of the future performance of U.S. stock funds, according to the study's findings. They are an "exceptional" predictor of government bond fund performance, and a "moderate or good" predictor of better-than-average corporate bond fund performance.

A separate study in 2004 conducted by Standard & Poor's agreed with many of these conclusions. It determined that funds charging lower-than-average fees outperformed more expensive funds in eight out of nine investment styles over one-, three-, five-, and 10-year time periods (Figure 13-16).

Standard & Poor's concluded: "It is important for both investors and financial advisors to keep fund expenses in the forefront of their analysis when assembling a portfolio." When doing so, however, it is necessary to compare apples with apples. Certain funds tend to be more expensive to run than others. Researching obscure stocks in faraway regions in the emerging markets, for example, is likely to be much more expensive for a mutual fund manager and his or her team of analysts than managing blue-chip U.S. equities.

Type of Fund	1-Year Returns	3-Year Returns	5-Year Returns	10-Year Returns
Large Growth				
Above average fees	14.75%	−6.97%	−5.04%	7.19%
Below average fees	16.07%	−5.32%	−3.37%	8.90%
Large Blend				
Above average fees	14.93%	−3.89%	−2.50%	7.93%
Below average fees	17.27%	−2.51%	−1.26%	10.01%
Large Value				
Above average fees	17.74%	−1.53%	0.84%	9.19%
Below average fees	18.79%	0.01%	1.81%	10.53%
Mid Growth				
Above average fees	21.03%	−4.45%	0.69%	6.56%
Below average fees	22.83%	−3.14%	2.39%	9.47%
Mid Blend				
Above average fees	23.35%	3.38%	8.37%	12.13%
Below average fees	25.47%	4.93%	7.99%	12.12%
Mid Value				
Above average fees	25.94%	6.89%	8.01%	11.01%
Below average fees	26.18%	7.29%	9.83%	12.21%
Small Growth				
Above average fees	26.04%	−2.58%	2.88%	6.47%
Below average fees	27.50%	−0.77%	5.65%	10.29%
Small Blend				
Above average fees	30.67%	5.60%	7.83%	10.72%
Below average fees	30.01%	7.33%	9.79%	11.51%
Small Value				
Above average fees	30.73%	9.39%	12.20%	11.36%
Below average fees	31.78%	11.22%	13.33%	13.40%

FIGURE 13-16 · The Low-Fee Fund Advantage.*

*Data as of May 2004.

Source: Standard & Poor's

The average expenses for mutual funds in various categories are listed in Figure 13-17.

Think of fees this way: There are myriad things we don't know as mutual fund investors, including which types of funds—and which particular funds

Type of Fund	Average Total Expense Ratio*
Domestic stock funds	1.35%
International stock funds	1.55%
Taxable bond funds	1.03%
Municipal bond funds	1.00%
Balanced funds	1.26%
Large-cap growth funds	1.38%
Large-cap value funds	1.29%
Large-cap blend funds	1.26%
Mid-cap growth funds	1.48%
Mid-cap value funds	1.39%
Mid-cap blend funds	1.40%
Small-cap growth funds	1.61%
Small-cap value funds	1.53%
Small-cap blend funds	1.45%
Emerging markets funds	1.78%
High-yield bond funds	1.21%
Technology stock funds	1.82%
Financial sector funds	1.78%

FIGURE 13-17 · Average Expense Ratios for Mutual Fund by Category.*

*Data as of December 2009.

Source: Morningstar

within those categories—are likely to do well in the coming years. Those questions are unanswerable without a crystal ball. In lieu of that crystal ball, it would seem prudent to start screening based on some variables that we do know with absolute clarity. Fees are one of those variables.

By law, a fund must disclose its annual fees to investors. So if you are comparing two funds, one with a total expense ratio of 0.5 percent and another with an expense ratio of 3 percent, you know with certainty that the *odds* are greater in finding success with the low-cost fund.

Turnover

It is impossible to tell with absolute certainty whether a fund that trades securities rapidly will beat a fund that buys and holds. There are years when high turnover funds are the absolute best performers and years when low turnover funds do the best. But over time, according to industry data, the *odds* of finding success in a low-turnover fund are better.

This might seem counterintuitive, since one of the reasons we invest in actively managed funds is to rely on the expertise of professional stock

Turnover Rate	3-Year Returns	5-Year Returns	10-Year Returns
Turnover < 50%	4.17%	4.49%	10.79%
Turnover 50%–100%	2.92%	3.32%	9.64%
Turnover 100%–200%	2.25%	2.87%	9.13%
Turnover > 200%	−0.55%	0.95%	8.72%

FIGURE 13-18 · Performance Based on Turnover Rates.*

*Data as of March 31, 2004.

Source: Morningstar

pickers. A fund manager who trades frequently would seem to be doing his or her job.

But whenever a fund trades a stock, two things are likely to occur: The fund will absolutely trigger brokerage commissions, and, as we mentioned, those costs (while not expressly included in the expense ratio) are paid out of a shareholder's returns. Moreover, trading often leads to tax bills, since funds are likely to realize gains when they step out of long-term holdings. Those capital gains are then distributed to existing shareholders in the year in which they are realized through stock sales. And that could drag down an investor's performance. Industry studies have shown that taxes can cost investors about 2 percentage points in returns annually over the long term, making it just as big an issue as expense for many fund investors.

Consider Morningstar's findings, in Figure 13-18, on turnover rates. They are based on long-term historic data.

Again, there are no guarantees that a fund with low turnover will always beat a high turnover fund. But because of the additional costs generated by trading stocks rapidly, a manager with high turnover makes it harder on him- or herself to beat the averages. You can look up a fund's turnover rate on any mutual fund Web site, including the fund's own home page.

QUIZ

1. **If you own a general domestic stock fund, you still need to invest in sector funds to gain exposure to specific industries in the economy.**
   A. True
   B. False

2. **The "best-fit" index for all domestic stock funds is the S&P 500.**
   A. True
   B. False

3. **Which of the following fund categories is not considered a "core" holding?**
   A. Large-cap growth funds
   B. Small-cap value funds
   C. Technology stock funds
   D. Mid-cap blend funds

4. **If you want to simplify your investment strategy, you really need to own only this many funds to cover your "core" equity holdings:**
   A. 1
   B. 2
   C. 3
   D. 10

5. **Past performance is a useful measure in determining . . .**
   A. The consistency of a fund over long periods of time.
   B. How well a fund is expected to perform in the near future.
   C. The odds that a fund will make money in the future.
   D. Past performance is not useful at all.

6. **When comparing the performance of a specific fund, you should weigh a fund's gains relative to . . .**
   A. The gains of the S&P 500.
   B. The gains of its best-fit index.
   C. The gains of its category peers.
   D. A and C.
   E. B and C.

7. **A fund that sports a high standard deviation is considered . . .**
   A. Stable.
   B. Volatile.
   C. Neither.

8. Historically, low-fee funds have outperformed competitors that charge higher fees.
   A. True
   B. False

9. Historically, high-turnover funds have outperformed competitors that don't trade as frequently.
   A. True
   B. False

10. When screening for potential funds to invest in, which variable should not matter to you?
    A. Its fees.
    B. Its beta.
    C. Its standard deviation.
    D. Its best-fit index.

Part IV

Organizing Your Assets

chapter 14

Demystifying Asset Allocation

CHAPTER OBJECTIVES

In this chapter, you will learn the following:

- Why your mix of assets matters
- How asset allocation strategies affect risks and returns
- How to determine your appropriate asset allocation
- Strategies to maintain your portfolio mix over time

Could it be Google? Or eBay? What about Dell? Or Amazon.com? Investors are constantly in search of the next big thing in the stock market—the next Microsoft, the next stock that will double in value and double once more, turning a small investment into a paper fortune. But this holy grail of trying to find the next Microsoft is often futile.

This is in part due to the fact that the odds of identifying the next hot stock—before the rest of the market does and bids up those shares to astronomical levels—are about the same as buying a winning lottery ticket. But it's also futile because the individual stocks we select will, at the end of the day, have far less impact on our long-term performance than the *types* of assets we choose. In other words, our *asset allocation* strategy is more important than our asset selection skills.

What Is Asset Allocation?

Asset allocation refers to the amount of money, in percentage terms, we invest in stocks versus bonds versus other assets, be they cash accounts or real estate.

For example, if you owned a $100,000 portfolio and $60,000 of that was held in stocks with the remaining $40,000 in bonds, your asset allocation would be 60-40, stocks to bonds. If you were to split the pot evenly between stocks and bonds, your asset allocation would be 50-50.

Asset allocation can also refer to how one invests within an asset class. For instance, a balanced investor might not only be 50 percent stocks and 50 percent bonds, but within his equity allocation, he may evenly split his stock holdings, with half of that equity stake going into growth stocks and the other half going to value-oriented shares. He may also choose to take a so-called market weighted approach between large stocks and small stocks.

Market weighting refers to allocating your assets in the same manner as the broad stock market indexes are divided. Thus, since the allocation between large stocks and small stocks in the Wilshire 5000 Total Stock Market index is roughly 80 percent to 20 percent, a balanced investor seeking to market weight his holdings would construct a portfolio that is 80 percent large stocks and 80 percent small stocks. This way, you're not taking any more risk than the broad market exposes you to. In weighting between growth and value stocks as well, a passive investor might follow broad market indexes like the Wilshire and the S&P 500, which are about 50-50 between growth and value.

Allocation Matters

Why is it important to measure a portfolio in this manner? Part of it has to do with diversification. For safety's sake, it's good not to have all your eggs in a single basket, but to spread your assets among a number of different types of baskets. By considering your portfolio's asset allocation, you will always be mindful of how diversified (or not) it is at any given moment in time. But in addition—and more important—the mix of stocks, bonds, and other assets we hold, and the types of stocks and bonds we own in our portfolio, will dictate the vast, vast majority of our success.

This may seem counterintuitive, since we've been trained to think in terms of individual stocks. The notion of being a good investor and a good stock picker are synonymous in popular culture, but they often require entirely different skills in the real world. After all, you may be smart enough to find the next Microsoft. But if you only allocate 2 percent of your equity portfolio to those shares, and invest the bulk of your money in bonds, your stellar pick may not have much impact on your overall performance.

In a study published in 2003, the mutual fund giant Vanguard looked at the performance of so-called balanced funds, which have the option of investing in a mix of stocks and bonds. Vanguard researchers examined 40 years worth of data and came to the conclusion that nearly 77 percent of the variability of a fund's monthly returns can be explained not by the individual stocks and bonds the manager selects, but by the percentage of money those funds hold in stocks versus bonds. In other words, less than a quarter of the average fund's month-to-month fluctuations can be attributed to its manager's stock-picking or market-timing acumen.

This seems to support the groundbreaking study, "Determinants of Portfolio Performance," which examined the performance of pension funds from the mid-1970s to the mid-1980s. Published in 1986, the study looked at the same basic question: How much of a fund's performance is dependent upon its allocation strategy? It concluded that 93.6 percent of those pension funds' quarterly returns could be explained by asset allocation decisions, not stock selection.

And in 2000, a study published by Yale finance professor Robert Ibbotson showed that over longer periods of time, nearly 100 percent—that's right, virtually all—of a portfolio's long-term returns can be explained by its mix of stocks and bonds, not its individual holdings.

To be sure, in a single year, the stock-picking skills of a specific manager can make a big difference. A professional stock picker, like any other human being, can have a good or bad year. A wrong—and big—bet on tech stocks or gold or bonds could easily blow up a single portfolio in a brief window of time. But among a universe of tens of thousands of stock pickers, it all averages out. And over long periods of time, averaged out over those tens of thousands of investors, stock selection becomes almost irrelevant when compared with asset allocation.

To some of you, this may still seem far-fetched. After all, if you held 100 percent of your money in a stock like Enron, and saw it go from around $80 a share at its peak all the way down to pennies on the dollar after the company filed for bankruptcy, then the individual stock you held—in this case, Enron—would explain 100 percent of your performance. But the fact is, most investors don't just own one or two stocks—they own a diversified mix of equities, to reduce risk in their portfolios.

And as your diversified mix of stocks grows and begins to mimic the overall market in terms of risk, then stock selection matters less and allocation strategies matter more. Think of it this way: If you own an S&P 500 fund, you are a part owner of 500 different companies. If one of those companies soars, that works to your advantage. But the fact remains that it is still only one of 500 different holdings. And the performance of each of those stocks tends to average out over time.

The Power of Asset Allocation

If you don't believe the power of asset allocation, consider the historic performance of different asset allocation strategies. First, let's examine the downside risk of being overly weighted toward equities.

Between 1926 and 2009, a 100-percent-equity portfolio invested in the S&P 500 lost as much as 43.1 percent of its value in its single worst 12-month period. This means a $100,000 investment would have turned to just $56,900 in only one year's time.

Now, had you put half of that money in bonds during this long-term stretch, the worst one-year loss you would have suffered would have been only half as painful. You would have lost 22.5 percent in the worst 12-month span under this asset allocation strategy. Had you put the majority of your money in bonds—80 percent—your single worst loss would have been just 10 percent (Figure 14-1).

Lowering Risk

The risks of an overly aggressive asset allocation strategy can also be measured in other ways. Portfolios weighted toward equities not only lose more in extreme downturns, they tend to lose money more frequently when the markets are wobbly.

Asset Mix	Worst 1-Year Performance
100% stocks, 0% bonds	43.1%
80% stocks, 20% bonds	−34.9%
60% stocks, 40% bonds	−26.6%
50% stocks, 50% bonds	−22.5%
40% stocks, 60% bonds	−18.4%
20% stocks, 80% bonds	−10.3%

FIGURE 14-1 · Asset Allocation: Worst-Case Scenarios.*

*Based on stock and bond market performance between 1926 and 2009.

Source: Ibbotson, Vanguard, *Straight Talk on Investing*

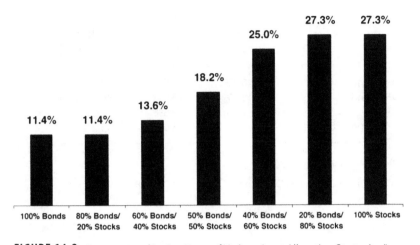

FIGURE 14-2 · Percentage of Losing Years of Various Asset Allocation Strategies.*

As this chart shows, the odds of losing money grow as you add equities to your portfolio.

*Based on stock and bond market performance between 1960 and 2003.

Source: Vanguard Group

Consider the fact that between 1960 and 2003, all-stock portfolios invested in the S&P 500 have suffered 12 losing years out of 44. In comparison, all-bond portfolios have lost money in only five out of the past 44 years (Figure 14-2). So in addition to degrees of losses, aggressive asset allocation strategies expose investors to greater frequency of risk. This is something that all investors should realize before constructing their portfolios of stocks and bonds.

There is yet more evidence that asset allocation can have a huge effect on your portfolio. Even a slight reduction of your holdings in equities can dramatically lower your risk profile.

Between the end of 1955 and the end of 2003, for instance, 100-percent-stock portfolios invested in the S&P 500 had an annualized standard deviation score of 17 percent, on average. Again, **standard deviation** is a measure of volatility that considers the variability of an investment's returns against its past performance. In other words, it measures an investment's volatility relative to its past behavior.

By reallocating just 20 percent of your assets into bonds, however, you could have reduced your standard deviation to 13.8 percent during this period of time. Had you gone even further, by allocating your money in a 60 percent stock/30 percent bond/10 percent cash mix, you could have come close to halving your volatility over this long-term stretch (Figure 14-3).

Asset Mix	Worst Year	Best Year	Standard Deviation
100% stocks	−26.5%	43.4%	17.0%
80% stocks, 20% bonds	−20.3%	33.7%	13.8%
60% stocks, 30% bonds, 10% cash	−13.7%	28.1%	10.6%
40% stocks, 40% bonds, 20% cash	−7.0%	22.8%	7.6%
20% stocks, 50% bonds, 30% cash	−1.1%	21.9%	5.2%

FIGURE 14-3 · Asset Allocation: Volatility.*

*Based on market performance between December 31, 1955, and December 31, 2003.

Source: T. Rowe Price

Remember, diversifying your portfolio by investing some money in stocks, some in bonds, and some in cash not only ensures that you will be able to participate in rising markets, it also protects you from downturns and bear markets. When one asset class zigs, typically one or two others zag. In our example, the worst loss that a 60 percent stock/30 percent bond/10 percent cash allocation has had since 1955 was 13.7 percent. In comparison, the worst one-year loss for a 100-percent-stock portfolio was 43.4 percent.

Increasing Returns

Of course, the flip side of reduced risk is lower returns. And history has shown that over long stretches of time, the aggressiveness of one's asset allocation strategy will dictate the average annual returns they enjoy. Researchers at Vanguard looked at the historic performance of various asset allocation mixes and discovered something we already know: *The greater the percentage of stocks in your portfolio, the greater the odds of enjoying bigger returns over the long run.*

Studying the performance of various allocation strategies from 1960 to 2003, Vanguard found that the while the odds of losing money in any given year were greatest with 100-percent-stock portfolios, the average return you would have earned with such a mix was more than 40 percent greater than with an all-bond portfolio during this stretch (Figure 14-4).

The average performance of a 100-percent-stock mix, for example, was 10.5 percent a year since 1960. Meanwhile, a 100-percent-bond allocation earned just 7.3 percent. While it may not seem like a big gap, there is a huge difference in being able to earn 10.5 percent returns versus 7.3 percent. A $10,000 investment in 1960 earning 10.5 percent a year would have grown

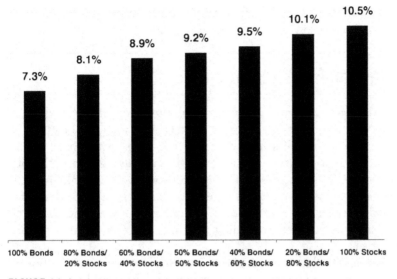

FIGURE 14-4 · Average Annual Returns Based on Asset Allocation Strategies.*

As this table illustrates, your average annual returns grow over time as you increase your stake in equities.

*Based on stock and bond market performance between 1960 and 2003.

Source: Vanguard Group

into $808,985 by the end of 2003. That same $10,000, invested at an interest rate of 7.3 percent, would have become just $222,020. That's a difference of nearly $600,000.

Now here's the good news: If you're starting out from an extremely conservative allocation, even a slight increase in exposure to equities can, over the long term, have a meaningful affect on your portfolio with *minimal* additional exposure to risk.

For example, since 1960, the average portfolio that consisted of 100 percent bonds generated annualized returns of 7.3 percent, as can be seen in the above figure. In fact, these portfolios lost money in just five of 44 years since the Kennedy administration. By reallocating just 20 percent of an all-bond portfolio into equities, you would have earned 8.1 percent a year between 1960 and 2003. And on a $10,000 investment, the difference between earning 8.1 and 7.3 percent a year for 44 years comes out to more than $85,000.

Meanwhile, you wouldn't have exposed yourself to that much more risk. Historically, 20 percent stock/80 percent bond portfolios have lost money on average in only five of the past 44 years—exactly the same number of years that all-bond portfolios posted negative returns. And like all-bond portfolios, an

80-20 bond/stock strategy would have lost only around 8 percent of its value in its single worst year, according to Vanguard's study.

Strategic versus Tactical Asset Allocation

Before we discuss ways to figure out your ideal allocation, it's important to distinguish the two types of asset allocation strategies: strategic and tactical.

The term **strategic asset allocation** refers to the long-term mix of stocks and bonds you feel is appropriate for a person in your age group with your level of risk tolerance. Think of strategic asset allocation as a basic blueprint. It represents the general path you plan to take, one that balances your desire for high returns and low risk. However, like all blueprints, you may find a need to adjust it or tweak it as you begin building your plan, as new realities surface and problems arise.

Since strategic asset allocation considerations are long-term—reflecting in part your age and when you plan to retire—in general they should not be overly affected by short-term market or economic developments. So, any short-term volatility in the market should not cause you to stray that much from your strategic mix of stocks and bonds. Similarly, any short-term opportunities you see in certain sectors—like technology or energy stocks— should not influence you to alter your long-term mix of stocks and bonds by more than a few degrees, financial planners argue. After all, whether the Dow Jones Industrial Average is soaring or collapsing does not change the fact that a 60-year-old worker who plans to retire in five years will need to tap his or her account in the near term. So your long-term preparations must go forward.

That being said, there are times when investors may feel the need—either for opportunistic or defensive purposes—to tweak their allocation strategies. These types of short-term moves are referred to as **tactical asset allocation decisions**.

If, for example, the market is favoring dividend-paying stocks over shares of pure growth companies at present, an investor may decide to move more money into dividend-paying stocks, to take advantage of the situation. If, on the other hand, an investor feels the economy is hitting a soft patch and thinks it may be worthwhile to reduce exposure to stocks tied to the cyclical recovery of the economy, then he or she may decide to shift out of economically sensitive sectors like retail and move into industries that don't require a healthy economy to shine—such as consumer staples or health care.

One way to tweak your tactical allocation strategy without upsetting your long-term strategic mix of assets is to adjust the *types* of stocks or bonds you plan to buy—not the percentage of those asset classes. For example, assume that you believe a 60 percent stock/40 percent bond allocation strategy is the most appropriate mix for your long-term needs. But say you think that small stocks have seen their best days. You can keep your 60-40 general allocation, but within the equity portion of your portfolio, you can overweight large stocks and underweight small ones.

Similarly, if you want to reduce risk in your portfolio without changing that 60-40 split, you can invest in short-term bond funds instead of long-term bond funds within your fixed income allocation. This reduces the risk profile in your overall portfolio without requiring you to shift more of your money out of stocks and into bonds.

Of course, there may be instances when an investor believes that short-term forces are so strong, they must adjust both their tactical and strategic allocations. A change in your family situation—a marriage or the birth of a child—could also require you to reexamine your investment mix, as new time horizons (like college funding or buying a new house) develop.

But it's important to be cautious whenever making any dramatic shifts in your allocation strategy. While it may feel safe, for instance, to flee stocks when the market is volatile, there comes a point in time when such moves add risk to your portfolio rather than reduce it. That's because if you shift too much out of one asset and into another, you could upset your diversification strategy. And a portfolio that is too concentrated even in fixed-income securities can expose an investor to greater market risks.

Moreover, stepping completely out of the stock market poses another risk we already addressed: of investing so conservatively that you miss out on much needed gains. Consider this interesting statistic: Had you invested your money in the S&P 500 between 1994 and 2003, you'd have earned 11.1 percent a year on average. Had you missed just the best 10 days within that decade, your equity returns would have fallen to 6 percent. Had you missed the best 20 days, you'd have earned just 2.1 percent (which is far less than even bonds were earning during the time). And had you missed the best 40 days in this decade stretch, you'd be sitting on average annual losses of more than 4 percent.

Still Confused?

The difference between strategic and tactical asset allocation strategies is simple. Your strategic allocation is the mix of stocks and bonds you think is appropriate for the long term. Your tactical allocation is the mix of stocks and bonds you think is right for the current market environment.

Determining Your Asset Allocation

There are an infinite number of ways to determine your strategic asset allocation. In fact, asset allocation is considered more of an art than a science, since so many nuances (like your age, your health, the size of your family) and subjective variables (your tolerance for risk, your sensibilities when it comes to investing, your confidence in your future income) can have a huge impact on the appropriateness of your mix of stocks and bonds.

The good news is, there are many sources for assistance. If you have a full-service broker or a financial planner, chances are that he or she would have helped you formulate an asset allocation plan already. If you're a direct investor, you also have access to help. Many online brokers such as Charles Schwab (www.schwab.com), and mutual fund companies like Fidelity (www.fidelity.com), Vanguard (www.vanguard.com), and T. Rowe Price (www.troweprice.com), offer investors free asset allocation tools that should help them get started. In fact, most fund companies and other financial Web sites—such as www.morningstar.com or www.mfea.com (the Mutual Fund Education Alliance)—will provide investors with templates that offer model portfolios, which in most cases, will suit your needs.

In general, there are some basic guidelines that investors often use to help them get started, which we'll go into below.

Your Age

Investing is a dynamic, long-term endeavor tied to a particular goal. As you move closer to your goals, it often makes sense to rein in risk. After all, the worst thing that could happen to an investing plan is to suffer losses a year or two before needing to tap those accounts. This means younger investors have more room for error. A 20-something may have a decade or two before his or her first real financial goal (perhaps buying a home) comes due. Therefore, that young investor may feel justified in putting 100 percent of his or her money in stocks, so long as it is properly diversified among a variety of styles, sectors, and sizes.

Earlier in the book we mentioned that over rolling 10-year periods of time, there is only about a 4 in 100 chance of losing money in the broad stock market. At the same time, there is about a 14 percent chance of losing money in equities in any three-year stretch. So an investor who is older—perhaps three years or less from needing the money—probably would want to reduce his or her exposure to equities substantially.

As you can see, the age of an investor, in broad strokes, can play a role in determining an asset allocation mix. That's why traditionally there has been a widely followed age-based approach to allocating your assets. It's referred to as the **100-minus rule**. It's simple: *Take your age and subtract it from 100. The answer tells you what percentage of your assets should be held in stocks. The remainder, then, can be put into bonds, or a combination of bonds and cash* (Figure 14-5).

Age	100 Minus Age	Asset Allocation
20	80	80% stocks, 20% bonds
25	75	75% stocks, 25% bonds
30	70	70% stocks, 30% bonds
35	65	65% stocks, 35% bonds
40	60	60% stocks, 40% bonds
45	55	55% stocks, 45% bonds
50	50	50% stocks, 50% bonds
55	45	45% stocks, 55% bonds
60	40	40% stocks, 60% bonds
65	35	35% stocks, 65% bonds
70	30	30% stocks, 70% bonds
75	25	25% stocks, 75% bonds

FIGURE 14-5 · Asset Allocation by Age: 100-Minus Rule.

So if you're 20 years old and just starting out, the 100-minus rule says you should have 80 percent of your money in stocks (100 − 20 = 80). The remainder can be invested in bonds. If you're 40, this rule says 60 percent of your money should be in equities. And if you're 65, only about a third of your assets should be held in the stock market.

Many financial planners believe this is an overly simplistic approach to strategic asset allocation, since it does not factor one's specific needs. At the very least, Americans are living longer today than they did a generation ago (as we mentioned in the opening chapter). And longer lives mean we need to outpace the ravages of inflation for that many more years. It also means we have to think of growing our portfolios even in our golden years, since we may live 30 or even 40 years beyond retirement. As we discussed, the only way to consistently beat inflation and generate growth is to include equities in one's plan.

As a result, there is a somewhat amended approach to the 100-minus rule. Let's call it the **110-minus rule** (Figure 14-6). Instead of taking your age and subtracting it from 100, subtract it from 110. This will lead you to a strategic asset allocation that's a bit more aggressive through the years than the traditional 100-minus rule. Under the amended rule, if you're 30 you should consider putting around 80 percent of your money in stocks. If you're 45, the 110-minus rule means putting 65 percent of your money in equities. And even at age 65, according to this rule of thumb, 45 percent of your holdings ought to be stocks. (Again, these are only guidelines to use as starting points—you may find your own circumstances require adjustments here and there.)

Age	110 Minus Age	Asset Allocation
20	90	90% stocks, 10% bonds
25	85	85% stocks, 15% bonds
30	80	80% stocks, 20% bonds
35	75	75% stocks, 25% bonds
40	70	70% stocks, 30% bonds
45	65	65% stocks, 35% bonds
50	60	60% stocks, 40% bonds
55	55	55% stocks, 45% bonds
60	50	50% stocks, 50% bonds
65	45	45% stocks, 55% bonds
70	40	40% stocks, 60% bonds
75	35	35% stocks, 65% bonds

FIGURE 14-6 · Asset Allocation by Age: 110-Minus Rule.

Your Risk Tolerance

At the end of the day, the right asset mix for you will depend not only on your age, but your sensibilities too. After all, even if you're told that as a 40-year-old you ought to have 60 or 70 percent of your money in equities, that may not be the right mix if you're so worried about losses that you can't sleep at night. Taking an overly aggressive stance—even if conventional wisdom says it's appropriate—can often lead investors to panic and sell, and at the worst possible time. So when deciding upon your asset allocation, it's also important to gauge your *tolerance for risk*.

Clearly, this is a subjective exercise. But investors who seek the help of financial planners will often be asked a series of questions that are meant to illicit a general sense of risk aversion. Typically, investors will then be categorized into one of three basic groups: *conservative* (or risk averse), *moderate*, and *aggressive investors*. Some financial Web sites may refer to these basic groups in another way: for instance, as *stability-minded*, *income-minded*, and *growth-oriented investors*.

Whatever you call them, there are some basic attributes for investors in each group.

Conservative Investors

Conservative or **stability-minded investors** tend to worry the most about risk. While other investors can psychologically handle a 30 or 40 percent short-term drop in their asset values, conservative investors can't. Often, this group is likely to panic even if their portfolios lose 20 percent of their value in the short term.

As a result, it's likely that conservative investors will be willing to give up some upside gains for downside protection. In addition, this group of investors favors conservative vehicles like fixed-income funds or even cash. Among stocks, this group of investors would probably gravitate toward old-fashioned blue-chip dividend-paying names, since these investors seek dependability and stability.

Investors in this group may decide to take the results of the 100-minus rule and dial the equity allocation down by around 10 or 20 percentage points. In other words, they may take what you would call an 80-minus approach or a 90-minus approach. For example, a 30-year-old conservative investor who would normally have 70 percent of his or her money in equities may choose a 50 or 60 percent allocation instead. Older investors who fall into this category, because they have lower risk tolerance and a shorter time horizon, may decide to put less than half of their holdings into stocks. So a 40-60 stock/bond allocation—or a 30 percent stock/50 percent bond/20 percent cash allocation— may be closer to their liking.

Moderate-Risk Investors

Moderate-risk or **income-minded investors**, on the other hand, are looking for a combination of capital appreciation and income stability in their portfolios. Often, they can withstand a 20 or even 30 percent short-term drop in their stock portfolios, because of their temperament, and since they might have a bit more time to work with. Moderate investors would probably feel comfortable owning a number of different types of stocks, so long as they are held in a diversified manner.

Often, these consumers are investing for two purposes: a shorter-term goal, like college savings, along with a long-term goal like retirement. These investors will probably accept the types of allocations typically called for under the 100-minus rule. At the very least, they may choose to fall back on the classic balanced allocation of 60 percent stocks and 40 percent bonds.

Aggressive Investors

And then there are the **aggressive** or **growth-oriented investors**. This group tends to be young, since time allows for investors to bear risk. And aggressive investors also tend to be more active when it comes to managing their money.

While conservative and moderate investors tend to favor a buy-and-hold approach, there are segments within the aggressive set that like to roll the dice. These investors not only favor stocks over bonds, but tend to favor growth stocks over value shares. And they may favor smaller, riskier stocks with more potential than bigger, stable stocks with a proven track record. The attitude of many aggressive investors is: Why hit a single when you can swing for the fences?

Typically, an aggressive investor will have at least 70 percent of his or her money in equities, with the remaining 30 percent—or less—in bonds. Some feel comfortable going to a 90-percent-equity allocation. And in some instances, based on tactical decision making, aggressive investors may choose to go 100 percent in equities.

Your Time Horizon

A criticism of using risk tolerance to gauge your asset allocation is that it's too subjective. Moreover, according to this criticism, investors may not know how tolerant they are of risk until they experience real losses in the market.

Meanwhile, age-based asset allocation strategies are sometimes criticized for being too simplistic. After all, you can have two people with the exact same age who have entirely different asset allocation needs.

For example, say you have two 60-year-olds. One is an executive earning six figures who has a good pension, a large investment portfolio, and the ability to work another 10 years in his field. The other 60-year-old makes a middle-class living but has little savings and is in poor health—and is therefore likely to be forced to retire within a year.

Obviously, the same asset allocation strategy cannot be right for both people. In the case of the 60-year-old executive, you've got a person who has the wherewithal—thanks to his or her pension (which should, for the sake of asset allocation, be considered fixed income since it provides a guaranteed income stream) and his or her career—to take on substantial risk. In fact, his or her time horizon until retirement, though 60, may actually be more than 10 years long. The other 60-year-old, in comparison, may have a time horizon of less than one or two years, even though the typical age of retirement is 65.

A simple way to deal with these concerns is to peg your asset allocation strategy not to your age, but to your retirement timetable. This makes for a slightly more sophisticated approach than the 100-minus rule. At the same time, it often reflects a truer sense of risk tolerance than simply asking someone to describe him- or herself as conservative, moderate, or aggressive.

One simple approach to pegging an allocation strategy to your retirement is to multiply the number of years that you're scheduled to retire by a factor of 2. Let's call this the **two times factor**. A 20-year-old worker 45 years away from retirement should therefore have 90 percent of his or her assets in stocks ($45 \times 2 = 90$). A 35-year-old 30 years from retirement may want to put 60 percent of his or her money in equities (Figure 14-7).

However, there are two adjustments you should probably make to this rule. Though it's good for getting going at a young age, the rule turns decidedly conservative when you get within 10 years of retirement. So you may want to tweak the guidelines as you get older and consider holding a greater percentage

Years from Retirement	Asset Allocation Strategy
45	90% stocks, 10% bonds
40	80% stocks, 20% bonds
35	70% stocks, 30% bonds
30	60% stocks, 40% bonds
25	50% stocks, 50% bonds
20	40% stocks, 60% bonds
15	30% stocks, 70% bonds
10	20% stocks, 80% bonds

FIGURE 14-7 · Time Horizon: Two-Times Factor Rule.

of your assets in equities than this strategy calls for as you get within 20 years or so of your goal. Moreover, it's important to customize your calculations based on your personal estimate of retirement—don't just use the age of 65 as the target. Many people retire well before or after that age.

Another approach is to combine risk tolerance with your general time horizon. For example, say you have a long time horizon—anything 10 years or more—before you need to tap your money. A reasonably aggressive person may decide that with more than 10 or 20 years, he or she can still afford to put 80 percent in equities. But a relatively conservative or moderate investor may believe that 60 percent is more like it.

With these sensibilities in mind, we can consider various model portfolios based on a combination of time horizon and risk tolerance. (Again, these are only starting templates, and investors should consider their own specific sensibilities and time horizons to arrive at a custom allocation.) Figures 14-8 through 14-13 depict various allocation approaches for the three types we discussed above, as well as hybrid types.

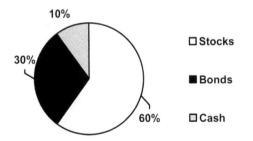

FIGURE 14-8 · Hypothetical Long-Term Conservative-Moderate Approach.

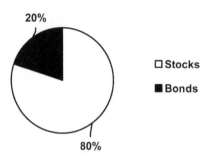

FIGURE 14-9 · Long-Term Moderate-Aggressive Approach.

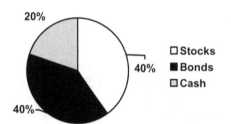

FIGURE 14-10 · Intermediate-Term Conservative-Moderate Mix.

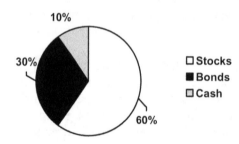

FIGURE 14-11 · Intermediate-Term Moderate-Aggressive Mix.

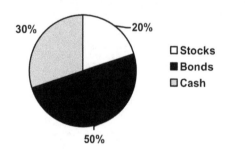

FIGURE 14-12 · Short-Term Conservative-Moderate Mix.

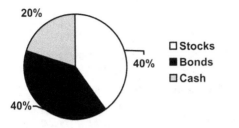

FIGURE 14-13 • Short-Term Moderate-Aggressive Mix.

A Mix and Match Approach

Perhaps the most customary approach you can take to asset allocation is to figure out exactly what you're investing for—and to match your approach with your goals, based on how far off each goal is.

What do we mean by this?

1. *Sit down and write down all your investment goals*. They may include your children's college fund, your retirement fund, your dream vacation fund, or new house fund.

2. *Then figure out exactly how much money you have in all your accounts, including your 401(k)s, IRAs, and taxable brokerage accounts*.

3. *See if you can put your money into the separate hypothetical buckets*. Since your 401(k) money is a retirement account that can't be tapped until age 59½, it should be counted in your **retirement bucket**. Your college fund money, be it in a 529 savings plan or a regular account, should be in the **college bucket**. And so on.

4. *Next, write down how many years you are from needing the money*. Retirement is probably a long-term goal that's more than 10 years off. But college may be only five years away. Your new house may be only three years away. Your daughter's wedding maybe only a year away.

All of the money that's **long term** (more than 10 years off) can be invested in stocks. Your **intermediate-term money** (for goals that come due in five to 10 years) can be invested in a mix of stocks and bonds, based on your risk tolerance. Your **short-term money** (for goals due in three to five years) can be invested in a mix of bonds and cash. And your **ultra-short-term money** (for goals less than two years away) should probably be invested mostly in cash.

By doing this, you can reverse-engineer the perfect asset allocation strategy for you.

Rebalancing

An asset allocation strategy is not complete without a rebalancing strategy. The term **rebalancing** simply means to reset, periodically, your mix of stocks, bonds, and cash. The reason to do this is because, over time, the market will change your allocation for you unless you monitor it. And often the market will take an appropriate allocation strategy and make it either too conservative or too aggressive within a few years.

For example, say you determine that a 50 percent stock/50 percent bond allocation is the best way to go. So you invest half your $100,000 in a stock fund and the other half in a bond fund. Now let's say that over the next five years, the stock fund gains 10 percent annually, while the bond fund goes up just 3 percent. Within five years the $50,000 you staked in the stock fund would grow to $80,525, based on its 10 percent annual returns. Meanwhile, the $50,000 you put into the bond fund would become around $58,000, based on a 3-percent annual return.

The upshot is, your $100,000 portfolio has grown to nearly $140,000 within five years. However, your asset allocation wouldn't be 50 percent stocks/50 percent bonds anymore. It would be closer to 58 percent stocks and 42 percent bonds. And that may be too risky for your situation.

You might ask: What's the harm in letting the market dictate your allocation? After all, the example above shows the gains you would have earned had you let your winners ride.

The problem arises when trends in the market turn around. Consider, for instance, that investors in the go-go 1990s did well by not rebalancing, as their stock portfolios grew ever larger. But once the bubble burst, those investors got hit the hardest, since they entered the bear market of 2000 with dangerously high allocations to stocks.

T. Rowe Price crunched some numbers and discovered that investors who had rebalanced periodically during the 1990s bull market and the bear market of 2000 would have done better than those who didn't rebalance—since they would have booked profits and reduced risk along the way.

Consider the numbers in Figure 14-14. While investors who did not rebalance shined in the 1990s, when stocks were going straight up, they saw their advantage evaporate in the bear market, because so much of their money had been allocated to stocks. The more disciplined investor who rebalanced surely lagged in the 1990s. But by taking profits incrementally along the way, these investors outperformed over the long run.

Conventional wisdom says that, at the very least, investors ought to rebalance their mix of stocks, bonds, and cash back to their original plan once a year. But you may want to revisit your plan once a quarter or perhaps twice a year,

Nonrebalanced Portfolio				
Date	Stocks	Bonds	Cash	Value
12/31/94	60%	30%	10%	$100,000
3/31/00	78%	17%	5%	$271,000
7/31/02	69%	25%	7%	$203,800
Rebalanced Portfolio				
Date	Stocks	Bonds	Cash	Value
12/31/94	60%	30%	10%	$100,000
3/31/00	58%	31%	11%	$255,300
7/31/02	56%	33%	11%	$215,200

FIG. 14-14. Power of Periodic Rebalancing.

Source: T. Rowe Price

just to see if things have changed. You probably want to do this at the end of the quarter, as opposed to when you're overly excited or fearful of market trends. This way, you take some of the emotions out of the situation.

Still Confused?

Rebalancing does not involve changing your asset allocation plan. It simply refers to the routine practice of bringing your portfolio strategy back in line with your original asset allocation strategy after market forces have tweaked your mix.

QUIZ

1. Asset allocation may explain almost all of the performance of one's investment portfolio over time.
    A. True
    B. False

2. The greater your exposure to equities, the greater the chances that . . .
    A. Your portfolio will generate decent-sized returns over the long run.
    B. Your portfolio could be hit with a short-term loss.
    C. Your portfolio could lose money in multiple years.
    D. All of the above.
    E. None of the above.

3. The greater a portfolio's exposure to equities, the greater the likelihood that . . .
    A. Its standard deviation will be high.
    B. Its total returns will be low.
    C. It won't lose money.
    D. Its beta will be low.

4. The odds of a 100-percent-bond portfolio losing money in any calendar year are . . .
    A. High.
    B. Moderate.
    C. Low.
    D. None of the above. Bonds never lose money.

5. Investors who make tactical asset allocation shifts in their portfolio always upset their strategic asset allocation strategy.
    A. True
    B. False

6. Say your long-term strategy is to be 60 percent in stocks and 40 percent in bonds. But because of market circumstances, you decide to boost the percentage of stocks that make up that 60-percent-equity allocation to dividend-paying shares. This is an example of . . .
    A. Income investing.
    B. Rebalancing.
    C. Tactical asset allocation.
    D. Strategic asset allocation.

7. The best way to determine your asset allocation is by considering . . .
    A. Your age.
    B. Your retirement target.

C. Your risk tolerance.

D. All of the above.

8. **Investors in their 20s who have 60 percent of their portfolios in stocks and 40 percent in bonds would be considered . . .**

A. Conservative.

B. Moderate.

C. Aggressive.

9. **Investors in their 70s who have 60 percent of their portfolios in stocks and 40 percent in bonds would be considered . . .**

A. Conservative.

B. Moderate.

C. Aggressive.

10. **If you never rebalance your portfolio back to its original mix of stocks and bonds, then . . .**

A. The markets will rejigger your portfolio for you.

B. Your portfolio will grow increasingly more aggressive over time.

C. You will lose control of your asset allocation strategy.

D. All of the above.

E. None of the above.

chapter 15

Demystifying Asset Location

CHAPTER OBJECTIVES

In this chapter, you will learn the following:

- Where you hold stocks and bonds matters
- How taxes impact your investments
- The various types of taxable accounts
- The various types of tax-deferred accounts

So far, we've discussed what assets to own, how much of each asset to own, and even when to rebalance that mix of assets. But what we haven't talked about is *where* to hold those assets. This is not an insignificant point. In this day and age of 401(k)s, IRAs, and taxable accounts, you have to consider not only the proper allocation of your assets, but the appropriate *location* of those holdings as well.

In fact, while it may seem hard to believe, deciding the types of accounts in which to hold your stocks and bonds can make a noticeable difference in your long-term total returns. Consider this basic example: Say you invested $10,000 in an average growth-oriented stock mutual fund in your regular, taxable brokerage account. And let's say you invested another $10,000 in an average bond mutual fund inside your tax-deferred 401(k). In this case, your asset allocation would be 50 percent stocks and 50 percent bonds. Based on the actual performance of average stock and bond funds between 1982 and 2002—and based on the current 15 percent tax on long-term capital gains and qualified dividend income—this asset allocation and location strategy would have turned your original $20,000 investment into $98,000 in 20 years' time, according to research conducted by T. Rowe Price.

But let's say you flipped it. Instead of putting your $10,000 stock investment in a taxable brokerage account and your $10,000 bond stake in a 401(k), let's assume that you used your tax-deferred retirement account to purchase the stock fund while you used your taxable brokerage account to invest in the bond fund. In that case, your original $20,000 investment would have grown to just $90,700, according to T. Rowe Price. That's around 7 percent less money—even though you invested in the exact same funds in the exact same proportion for the exact same length of time as in the previous example.

This simple illustration shows just how important one's asset location strategy is, and demonstrates that asset location ought to be an important consideration in putting together an overall investment plan. While it may not be as important as asset allocation, it is still a major decision, alongside asset selection, in creating a blueprint for your money.

Taxes

What accounts for the difference in returns in the previous examples? It's simple: taxes. Try as we might, we can't forget that Uncle Sam takes a cut of our investing success, be it in the form of capital gains, dividends, or ordinary income taxes. Sometimes the government's cut can be substantial. As we noted in an earlier chapter, taxes can often subtract as much as 2 percentage points from a typical mutual fund investor's annual average returns over time.

Having said that, it should be noted that the recent rounds of federal tax cuts have made investing in regular brokerage accounts more tax efficient than it used to be. Moreover, investing in equities has become far more tax efficient than investing in bonds, since the government has generally reduced capital gains and dividend taxes over the years. These changes mean investors need to think about what assets they hold in certain types of accounts.

But before we get too far ahead of ourselves, let's recap the tax situation that we find ourselves in today. By lowering most income tax brackets, in recent decades, Uncle Sam has reduced the ordinary income taxes that most households pay. That means the income taxes we pay on certain investments—like

Tax Rate	Single Filers	Married Couples Filing Jointly
10%	First $8,375	First $16,750
15%	$8,375–$34,000	$16,750–$68,000
25%	$34,000–$82,400	$68,000–$137,300
28%	$82,400–$171,850	$137,300–$209,250
33%	$171,850–$373,650	$209,250–$373,650
35%	$373,650 or higher	$373,650 or higher

FIGURE 15-1 · 2010 Federal Income Tax Brackets.

Source: Bankrate.com

withdrawals from traditional IRAs or bond income—have also come down generally speaking. Figure 15-1 shows the income tax brackets for 2010.

Prior to the recent tax cuts in the 2000s, the brackets ran from as low as 10 percent to as high as 38.6 percent. In 2010 the highest bracket was 35 percent. Moreover, middle-income investors who used to pay 27, 30, or 35 percent now pay 25, 28, or 33 percent, respectively.

But income taxes are only one part of the picture. For investors, taxes on capital gains and dividend income are equally important. And the good news again is that taxes on those forms of investment profits have also come down in recent years. Prior to the 2003 tax cuts, the maximum tax rate on **long-term capital gains**—gains on assets held for a year or longer—had been 20 percent. As of this printing, long-term capital gains were being taxed at a maximum of 15 percent. In comparison, **short-term capital gains**—gains on assets held for less than a year—are still taxed as ordinary income.

Note that this is under **current law**—these things can change in any given year, depending on what Congress does.

As for dividend income thrown off by stocks, it used to be taxed as ordinary income, which had been as high as 38.6 percent. But again, as of this printing, **qualified dividend income** was being taxed at 15 percent. For those investors in the 15 percent income-tax bracket or lower, dividend income is treated the same as long-term capital gains for those in the lowest two tax brackets—they will be taxed at just 5 percent until 2008. (Certain types of dividends, such as those thrown off by REITs, are not eligible for favored treatment. To find out if your dividend income qualifies for the 15 percent rate, go to www.irs.gov. Or you can ask your brokerage and/or mutual fund companies to determine which of your dividends qualify for the beneficial tax treatment.)

But as with all things that are tax-related, it's impossible to plan perfectly for what may or may not change in the future. As an investor, the only thing you can do is act on what you know to be true today while recognizing that things could change in any number of ways.

Tax-Deferred Beats Tax-Efficient

Now, even though taxes are lower across the board than they have been in past generations, the fact of the matter is, no taxes or deferred taxes are still almost always better than low taxes. T. Rowe Price confirmed this in a study that looked at the performance of investing in taxable versus tax-deferred investment plans. Consider these hypothetical comparisons:

Say you invested $5,000 on a pretax basis in a 401(k) every year for five years. Assume that your investment earns 8 percent a year and that you withdraw your money at the five-year mark, at which point you'll have to pay ordinary income taxes on the withdrawal. The after-tax value of that 401(k) would be $21,555, according to T. Rowe Price.

But let's say you took that same $5,000, paid taxes on it, and invested the remaining sum in a traditional brokerage account for five years—this is the fairest way to compare the two, since 401(k) accounts are funded with pretax dollars, and traditional accounts are funded with after-tax money. Assuming that you're in the 27-percent-federal-tax bracket and pay an additional 5 percent in state income taxes—and assuming current rates on long-term capital gains and dividend income are maintained throughout this entire period—you would have $22,572 in five years. So you're still better off funding your 401(k).

Over longer periods of time, the gap widens. Over 25 years, for example, a $5,000 annual pretax investment in a 401(k) earning 8 percent a year would grow to $281,275. That's accounting for the fact that you would tap the account at the 25-year mark and have to pay taxes on it. That same amount, contributed into a taxable account, would grow to just $225,135 (Figure 15-2).

So remember the importance of contributing to tax-deferred investment plans in addition to traditional brokerage accounts. Not only are 401(k)s and

Time Horizon	Taxable Account	401(k)
5 years	$ 21,555	$ 22,572
10 years	$ 51,090	$ 55,737
15 years	$ 91,709	$104,468
20 years	$147,726	$176,069
25 years	$225,135	$281,275

FIGURE 15-2 · Taxable versus Tax-Deferred Investing.*

The table illustrates the growth of $5,000 invested every year in a 401 (k) versus a taxable brokerage account. This example assumes the following: that the investor is in the 27-percent-federal-tax bracket and pays an additional 5 percent in state income taxes; that current tax rates and rules on long-term capital gains and qualified dividend income remain constant; and that the money is invested in a typical growth stock fund earning 8 percent a year.

Source: T. Rowe Price

IRAs advantageous from a tax standpoint, they offer investors the diversification of locations through which to purchase a diversified mix of assets.

401(k) Retirement Accounts

What They Are

Though they were created in 1981, these employer-sponsored retirement plans didn't really take off until the 1990s (Figure 15-3). It was during that decade when these so-called *self-directed investment plans* helped democratize Wall Street and made investors out of the majority of American households. **Company-sponsored 401(k)s** are classified as self-directed plans because workers who enroll in these plans, not employers, make all the investment decisions and bear all the investment risk. In other words, should workers fail to meet their investment goals 20 or 30 years down the line, they themselves would be responsible for finding a way to pay for retirement.

This makes 401(k)s the polar opposite of traditional pensions, where the company that offers the pension oversees the account and bears the risk of making up any shortfalls should the portfolio not do as well as expected. On the flip side, 401(k) participants who invest well could earn more in their accounts than they need to retire on. That "extra money" would be theirs to keep. In a traditional pension, if the company earns more on its pension fund than it needs to generate, the company keeps the extra assets—it does not trickle down to the worker.

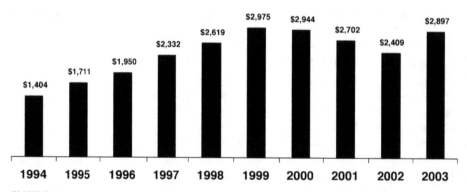

FIGURE 15-3 · Total Assets Held in Employer-Sponsored Retirement Plans (in Billions of Dollars).

The 1990s bull market helped grow retirement assets held in employer-sponsored accounts, such as 401(k)s.

Source: Investment Company Institute

While 401(k)s are popular—the vast majority of workers eligible to participate in these plans do—the fact is, your employer has to establish such a plan at the company for workers to participate. Many small businesses, for example, citing the costs of establishing 401(k) plans, don't provide this benefit to employees.

Nevertheless, tens of millions of American workers have access to 401(k)s and take advantage of them. A major reason why participation is so high may be the company match. It's a little known fact, but companies that offer 401(k)s are required to meet certain so-called "nondiscrimination tests" to ensure that highly paid workers (i.e., managers) aren't benefiting disproportionately from these plans. The upshot of it is, for corporate executives to be able to stuff certain amounts of money into these tax-favored plans, line workers—known as "non-highly-compensated workers"—must contribute a certain amount to these plans as well.

So, many companies go out of their way to encourage the rank and file to participate. One carrot used to encourage workers is the **company match**. While there are a number of ways firms match a worker's contribution, a typical match calls for the company to put in 50 cents for every $1 that a worker contributes to his or her own plan—up to around 6 percent of that worker's salary deferral.

Now, if you put in $1 and the company forks over 50 cents, you automatically have earned 50 percent returns on your investment—without taking any market risk. Moreover, when you go to invest your 401(k) money, you will be compounding your returns not on a base of $1, but rather $1.50. So the first rule of thumb for any worker eligible for a 401(k) that matches his or her contribution is to take full advantage of the match.

Tax Implications

Company-sponsored 401(k)s have two big tax benefits. First, investors fund these accounts with **pretax dollars**. In other words, the money deducted every week or month from your paycheck and invested in 401(k) accounts is not counted toward your annual income for tax purposes. So you don't pay taxes on the money before it gets sheltered in a 401(k). Moreover, once in a 401(k), money is allowed to grow **tax-deferred**. This is a big advantage: Not only do you avoid taxes along the way, but the money that would have otherwise gone toward paying taxes is allowed to compound itself within these accounts.

There are, however, a couple of disadvantages to a 401(k). First, when you retire, your withdrawals from these accounts will be taxed as **ordinary income**, even if some or most of the money accumulated as capital gains. Keep this in mind as you decide what to use these accounts to invest in. Moreover, unlike in a taxable account, *investors in a 401(k) are not allowed to realize capital losses* *to offset capital gains elsewhere in their portfolio* (which is a classic way that investors in taxable accounts can reduce their tax bill). In other words, if you lose money on investments within these accounts, you cannot take advantage of the tax rule that allows you to lower your capital gains by booking losses simultaneously.

What Belongs Inside

As our prior example indicates, investors who have access to both 401(k)s and brokerage accounts are probably better off using the 401(k) to invest in fixed-income securities. The reason, again, is that equities have become more tax efficient than bonds. And it would be a waste to use that tax efficiency inside a tax-sheltered account. So if you have access to stocks through your brokerage as well as your 401(k), it's better to use the brokerage account to invest in stocks and the 401(k) to invest in bonds.

Of course, for some investors the 401(k) represents the sum total of their investment portfolio. In that case, there's really nothing wrong with using the 401(k) to invest in stocks and bonds. But if you have some flexibility, you'd probably want to use the 401(k) to invest more in growth stock funds than value stock funds. Why? Because value stock funds tend to invest in more dividend-paying stocks. And as we discussed, dividends already receive beneficial tax treatment. Why would you want to put dividends, which are taxed at 15 percent, inside a 401(k) where withdrawals will eventually be taxed as ordinary income—and will be assessed at much higher rates?

On the other hand, growth stock funds tend to have more turnover than value funds. Indeed, according to Morningstar, the typical growth stock fund's turnover rate is around 110 percent, versus approximately 70 percent for value funds. This means that growth funds tend to be less tax efficient. Since you want to put high-tax investments inside tax shelters, growth stock funds may be a better bet for your 401(k).

Taxable Brokerage Accounts

What They Are

Taxable brokerage accounts are your basic investment accounts, available through brokerages, mutual fund companies, and even banks, which give investors access to individual securities. Every investor can open any number of brokerage accounts, either at discount shops like Schwab or E*TRADE or full-service firms like Merrill Lynch and Morgan Stanley. While taxable brokerage accounts are, by definition, the least tax-advantaged accounts, there are many reasons to open a brokerage account.

For starters, unlike a 401(k), where your employer gives you a choice of say, 10 or 15 mutual funds to select from, brokerage accounts give you access to any number of funds along with individual stocks and individual bonds. That means you have more choice. You also have more freedom with taxable accounts, since there are no government- or company-imposed restrictions on how much you can invest, how long you can keep money in these accounts, and how and when you can withdraw the funds.

Tax Implications

Investing in a taxable account exposes you to five different types of taxes: **long-term capital gains taxes**, which we noted are capped at 15 percent for most investors; **short-term capital gains**, which are taxed as ordinary income; **qualified dividend income**, capped at 15 percent; **unqualified dividends**, which are taxed as ordinary income; and **bond income**, which is taxed as ordinary income.

What Belongs

You probably would want to keep the most tax-efficient of your taxable holdings in regular brokerage accounts, so you can use your tax-deferred accounts for your least tax efficient holdings.

Within fixed income, that means putting your municipal bond holdings here. You'll recall that **muni bonds** are free from federal income tax and, depending on the bonds you select and your state of residence, they could also be state and local tax-free as well. If that's the case, why waste such tax efficiency in a tax-sheltered plan like a 401(k)? As for other bonds, they probably are best-suited for your tax-deferred accounts.

Among stocks, you also probably would want to consider the most tax-efficient holdings here as well. That could mean using your brokerage account for purchasing dividend-paying blue-chip stocks. Individual stocks that you consider your "core" holdings—shares you plan to buy and hold for years—may also be appropriate for these taxable accounts. And within the universe of mutual funds, you'd probably want to use your regular accounts to purchase value-oriented stock funds, as we discussed just a second ago.

Another type of stock fund that may be appropriate for a taxable account is a **passively managed index fund**. As you'll recall, index funds, by definition, tend to have lower turnover than actively managed funds, since these portfolios simply buy and hold all the stocks in a particular market index. As such, they tend to be tax-efficient and therefore don't require tax shelters to make them attractive. If you're thinking of investing in so-called **tax-efficient funds**, whose managers are instructed to minimize taxes by buying and holding and also by matching losses with capital gains, than those funds probably belong in a taxable account as well. Again, why waste the tax efficiency?

Though it sounds odd, you may also want to consider investing in the riskiest of your stock holdings here as well. Though taxable accounts are good for long-term buy-and-hold investments, they are also a decent place for high-risk holdings. Why? Should a high-risk gamble in your taxable account fail, you can always sell the stock, realize the loss, and use the capital loss to offset gains in your portfolio to reduce your capital gains tax bill. You cannot do this in a tax-deferred account. In other words, Uncle Sam shares some of the risks with you in a taxable account by giving you a tax break for realizing losses in your portfolio. But he won't share that same risk in a tax-deferred account, since he's already letting you off the hook for taxes.

Traditional IRAs

What They Are

Individual retirement accounts, or **IRAs**, were founded 30 years ago as a way to allow workers to save and invest for their own retirement in tax-deferred, self-directed retirement accounts. Today, more than 45 million households own some kind of an IRA, up from 29 million in 1996. The total assets in these accounts, since 1992, are shown in Figure 15-4.

The best-known type of IRA is a **traditional IRA** where contributions are tax-deductible. Once inside this type of account, money is allowed to grow tax-deferred, much like in a 401(k). Unlike a 401(k), however, where investment options are generally limited, investors can set up an IRA at any number of financial institutions. In fact, you can set an IRA up through your bank, your favorite fund company, your favorite broker, and even through an insurance company (Figure 15-5).

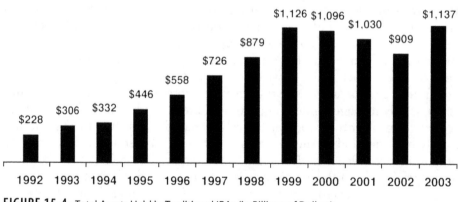

FIGURE 15-4 · Total Assets Held in Traditional IRAs (in Billions of Dollars).

Source: Investment Company Institute

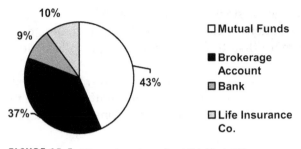

FIGURE 15-5 · Where Americans Establish Their IRAs.

Source: Investment Company Institute

One important point to understand is that an IRA is not, in and of itself, an investment. It is not an asset like a stock or bond. Surveys indicate that there is some confusion about this point. An IRA, like a 401(k) or a brokerage account, is simply a type of account through which you can buy and sell stocks, bonds, cash, mutual funds, and other assets. Think of an IRA as a bucket you can use to carry certain assets. What's nice is that you get to decide what type of bucket you want and where to purchase it. And by choosing where to buy this container, you can gain access to virtually all types of financial securities.

For example, if you only want to invest in mutual funds in your IRA, you can call up your favorite fund company and set up an account there. But if you want a greater choice of funds, you can call up a mutual fund supermarket and establish your IRA at a place that will give you access to thousands of different funds. Even better, you can set up an IRA with your bank or broker and gain access to thousands of individual stocks and bonds in addition to funds.

This is the advantage of an IRA over a 401(k). But IRAs have a big disadvantage: *The federal government now allows IRA investments of only $5,000 in 2010.* $5,000 is hardly a generous amount, especially for workers racing to set aside money for their retirement. The good news for workers 50 and older is that Uncle Sam has instituted a so-called "catch-up provision": This allows older workers the right to stuff an additional $1,000 into their IRAs in 2010.

Tax Implications

As we mentioned, money in traditional deductible IRAs is **tax-deductible**. That means they are similar to 401(k)s in that you get to fund these accounts with **pretax dollars**. But there is an **income limit** for that deductibility. In 2010, for example, the federal government allowed only those married couples earning less than $89,000 a year or singles earning under $56,000 to fully deduct their annual IRA contributions. Meanwhile, couples earning more than $91,000 and singles earning more than $57,000 could only partially deduct their contributions.

Once inside a traditional IRA, though, money is allowed to grow **tax-deferred**, which, as we discussed, gives investors the advantage of uninterrupted compounding. But upon retirement, withdrawals are taxed as ordinary income, just like in a 401(k).

What Belongs

Like a 401(k), IRAs are another place to consider buying bonds or bond funds. In reality, IRAs give investors more flexibility than 401(k)s to gain fixed-income exposure. Why? Most 401(k)s offer only limited choices among bond funds. Many only offer one bond fund, and that is typically a long- or intermediate-term general bond fund that invests in a mix of government and corporate debt. In an IRA, though, investors can establish their accounts anywhere and therefore have far greater fixed-income choices to consider.

Within the universe of bonds, the less tax-efficient a bond or bond fund is, the more suitable it is for an IRA, since the tax-deferral can shelter your investment. So high-yield bonds, which throw off the most income, are a great type of asset to shield in an IRA. But be careful here: Don't just invest in a high-yield junk bond fund just because they are appropriate for IRAs from a tax standpoint. Make sure they and other assets are appropriate for you, based on your overall asset allocation strategy.

Real Estate Investment Trusts (REITs) also make a good fit for IRAs from a tax standpoint. While REITs and REIT funds are not fixed-income securities, they do throw off a good deal of dividend income. Unfortunately, REIT income is not considered "qualified dividend income," and therefore is taxed as ordinary income, not at the beneficial 15-percent-dividend tax rate. By placing these real estate securities in an IRA, you can shield yourself from those hefty tax bills.

As far as equities go, funds that trade stocks often are candidates for IRAs. This includes small-cap funds, which on average have a significantly higher turnover rate than large-cap portfolios. It also includes growth-oriented portfolios, which also have a greater tendency to pick and roll rather than buy and hold. If you're thinking of investing in individual stocks that you don't plan to hold for years—but rather, plan to trade frequently—then those may be appropriate for an IRA, since the tax deferral will shelter you from having to pay immediate capital gains taxes. But again, make sure these are relatively stable holdings that aren't the absolute riskiest types of stocks. Remember, in an IRA, you cannot take advantage of **tax-loss harvesting**, which is a fancy term that refers to realizing capital losses to match up with gains elsewhere in one's portfolio.

Roth IRA

What They Are

Roth IRAs were first made available to investors in 1998. Since, this newfangled individual retirement account has changed the way individual investors save for their own retirement. (Figure 15-6 shows the total assets held in Roth IRAs since from 1998 to 2003.)

Like a traditional IRA, a Roth IRA is an individual retirement account that allows you to shelter money from taxes. But a Roth IRA works differently. For starters, it does not allow you to deduct your annual contributions. In other words, you fund these accounts with **after-tax dollars**, not pretax funds. Moreover, at retirement, gains withdrawn from a Roth IRA come out tax-free (you can also withdraw your principal contributions to a Roth tax-free as well, since you already paid taxes on that money).

This means that compared with a deductible IRA, a Roth IRA starts off with a disadvantage, **not tax-deductible,** but ends with a huge advantage, **tax-free withdrawals.** Because it takes some time for a Roth to overcome its early disadvantage, it tends to be more appropriate for investors who have longer time frames in which to invest in these accounts.

Having said that, Roth IRAs have **income restrictions.** As of the printing of this book, only married couples earning less than $167,000 and singles earning less than $105,000 qualify to make full contributions each year to a Roth IRA. Moreover, couples earning more than $177,000 a year and singles earning more than $120,000 can't make any contributions at all (those who fall in between are eligible for partial contributions).

Just as with traditional IRAs, Roth IRAs allow you to stuff $5,000 a year. And investors 50 or older are allowed to put in an additional $1,000 a year in catch-up contributions.

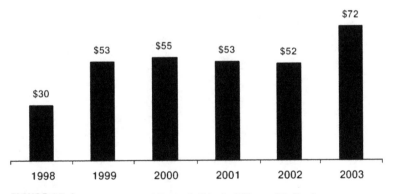

FIGURE 15-6 · Total Assets Held in Roth IRAs (in Billions of Dollars).

Source: Investment Company Institute

Tax Implications

Because a Roth IRA does not allow you to deduct any of your contributions, it is funded entirely with after-tax money. Once inside the account, the money is sheltered from all taxes. And withdrawals come out entirely tax-free.

What Belongs

Again, in general it makes sense to use your tax-deferred vehicles to invest in bonds—to maximize the tax shelter. So bonds, in particular high-income bonds, make attractive candidates for Roth IRAs. Virtually all types of investments suitable for a traditional IRA make sense in a Roth IRA as well.

But if you plan to use your tax-deferred accounts to invest some money in stocks, then a Roth IRA is the most attractive type of tax-deferred account to use for equities. Why? In a 401(k) and a traditional IRA, withdrawals are taxed as ordinary income. So an equity investor may enjoy tax-deferral. But at withdrawal he or she may be forced to convert capital gains and dividend taxes—which get the beneficial 15 percent rate—into ordinary income taxes, which are typically much higher.

This does not happen in a Roth IRA, because qualified withdrawals are completely tax-free. So instead of converting low taxes into high taxes, you are in effect converting low taxes into no taxes. So, a Roth IRA can be appropriate not only for stocks and bonds, but for all types of equities, ranging from dividend-paying stocks to high-growth and high-turnover funds.

QUIZ

1. *Asset location* refers to the mix of stocks, bonds, and cash you own in your portfolio.
   A. True
   B. False

2. Taxes can typically eliminate what percentage of an investor's annual returns?
   A. 2 percent
   B. 15 percent
   C. 25 percent
   D. 33 percent

3. Long-term capital gains are taxed as ordinary income.
   A. True
   B. False

4. Qualified dividend income is taxed as ordinary income.
   A. True
   B. False

5. A 401(k) plan allows you to . . .
   A. Pay taxes up front and withdraw money at retirement tax free.
   B. Defer taxes until you withdraw money at retirement.
   C. Eliminate taxes entire.

6. In a 401(k) plan, the investor assumes . . .
   A. All the investment risk but enjoys all the investment gains.
   B. Some of the investment risk but enjoys only some of the investment gains.
   C. Some of the investment risk but enjoys all of the investment gains.
   D. All of the investment risk but enjoys only some of the investment gains.

7. All things being equal, municipal bond funds should be held in which of the following types of accounts?
   A. IRA
   B. Roth IRA
   C. 401(k)
   D. Taxable account

8. All things being equal, REITs should be held in which of the following types of accounts?
   A. IRA
   B. Separate account
   C. Taxable account

9. The wealthy should put all their money into traditional deductible IRAs to hide their money from taxes.
    A. True
    B. False

10. Because Roth IRAs offer no up-front deductions but levy no taxes at withdrawal, these accounts are best suited for the following type of investor:
    A. A person who is in a higher tax bracket today than he or she expects to be at retirement
    B. A person who is in a lower tax bracket today than he or she expects to be at retirement
    C. A person who doesn't pay any taxes

Final Exam

1. **Saving and investing are the same thing.**
   A. True
   B. False

2. **Most workers invest because . . .**
   A. They have to.
   B. They want to.
   C. Their employer-sponsored retirement plans make them invest.
   D. Most workers don't invest.

3. **One of the most important concepts for all investors to appreciate is . . .**
   A. Compound interest.
   B. Mortgage interest.
   C. Negative interest.

4. **Which of the following investment vehicles are you likely to use at some point in your life?**
   A. 529
   B. 401(k)
   C. IRA
   D. All of the above
   E. None of the above

5. If you wanted to double your money in 10 years, what rate of interest would you have to earn annually?

A. 11.6 percent

B. 7.2 percent

C. 4.1 percent

D. 17.5 percent

6. You don't need to invest if you're eligible for Social Security and corporate pensions.

A. True

B. False

7. If you're 65 and are about to retire, your time horizon would be . . .

A. 0 years.

B. 10 years.

C. 18 years.

8. You are not an investor if you put all your money into . . .

A. Stocks.

B. Bonds.

C. Cash.

9. Before you start investing, you must . . .

A. Save and budget.

B. Diversify and allocate your assets.

C. Both.

D. Neither.

10. What is the best way to describe capital appreciation?

A. The total return your investments earn including income and price.

B. Gains in the value of one's investments over time.

C. The proper respect shown by savers to the power of saving money.

11. Which of the following is not an investment?

A. Stocks

B. Mutual funds

C. ETFs

D. Real estate

E. CDs

12. **All forms of debt are bad.**

    A. True

    B. False

13. **Which of the following is considered the most beneficial form of debt?**

    A. Credit card balances

    B. Student loans

    C. Margin debts

    D. Car loans

14. **You should always have emergency savings in place before you start investing.**

    A. True

    B. False

15. **Your emergency fund should be included as part of your investment portfolio.**

    A. True

    B. False

16. **A rainy day fund should be how large?**

    A. Enough to cover at least six months of your take-home pay

    B. Enough to cover at least six months of expenses

    C. Enough to cover one month of household bills

17. **Before you invest, you should . . .**

    A. Determine the most appropriate asset allocation strategy for you.

    B. Learn how to invest in individual stocks.

    C. Pay down all of your debt.

18. **How frequently should you check up on your investments?**

    A. Every day

    B. Multiple times a day

    C. At least once every quarter

    D. Once every four years

19. **What does it mean to have an asset allocation strategy?**
    A. Determining the appropriate mix of stocks, bonds, and cash to meet your goals
    B. Determining how much of your money belongs in investible assets and how much should go to hard assets
    C. Determining how much of your money should go into your 401(k)s, IRAs, and taxable savings

20. **Your time horizon is . . .**
    A. The amount of time you have before you need to tap your investments.
    B. The length of time you hold onto your stocks, bonds, and mutual funds.
    C. The time before you plan to retire.

21. **The longer your time horizon . . .**
    A. The more risk you can take with your portfolio.
    B. The less risk you can take with your portfolio.
    C. The less room for error you have.

22. **Which of the following pays out dividends?**
    A. Cash
    B. Bonds
    C. Stocks

23. **What is a dividend payment?**
    A. A percentage of the earnings that are paid only to preferred stock-holders
    B. Income thrown off by bonds
    C. A portion of the company's earnings returned to stockholders

24. **A company with 10 million shares outstanding and whose shares are trading for $100 a piece has a market capitalization of . . .**
    A. $1 million.
    B. $10 million.
    C. $100 million.
    D. $1 billion.

25. **Assume you purchased a stock at $15 a share and it falls to $10, at which point you sell. You would have lost . . .**
    A. 33 percent.
    B. 50 percent.

C. 25 percent.

D. 100 percent.

26. Standard deviation reflects what about a stock?

    A. Growth potential

    B. Stability

    C. Volatility

    D. Earnings

27. If an investment's beta is said to be 1.07, it is . . .

    A. 7 percent more volatile than the S&P 500 index of blue-chip stocks.

    B. 0.7 percent more volatile than the S&P 500 index of blue-chip stocks.

    C. 0.07 percent more volatile than the S&P 500 index of blue-chip stocks.

28. Rising interest rates are _____ when it comes to your existing bond funds.

    A. Good

    B. Bad

    C. Indifferent

29. Which of the following investments enjoy tax benefits?

    A. Preferred stocks

    B. Common stocks

    C. Foreign bonds

    D. Municipal bonds

30. If a bond fund has a duration of 5, its value will potentially do what if market interest rates rise 1 percentage point?

    A. Fall 5 percent

    B. Rise 5 percent

    C. Fall 0.5 percent

    D. Rise 0.5 percent

31. If you invested $1,500 every year for the next 20 years and earned 7.5 percent a year on your money, how much would you have at the end of this period?

    A. $65,000

    B. $6,500

    C. $25,000

    D. $2,500

32. **Diversifying your investments makes sense because . . .**
    A. It maximizes your total returns.
    B. It reduces volatility in your portfolio.
    C. You are not skilled at picking stocks.

33. **The losses suffered by stocks between 2000 and 2010 reinforce which lesson?**
    A. Stocks are a lousy investment.
    B. To invest in stocks, you need a time horizon of more than 10 years.
    C. Stocks always suffer bad decades after experiencing good ones.

34. **Which of the following are ways to gauge the valuation of a stock?**
    A. Price-to-earnings ratios
    B. Price-to-book value ratios
    C. Price-to-sales ratios
    D. All of the above
    E. None of the above

35. **Active investing is often a better bet than index investing.**
    A. True
    B. False

36. **A fund that has a turnover rate of 50 percent is likely to . . .**
    A. Gain 50 percent in a good year.
    B. Lose 50 percent in a bad year.
    C. Replace half its stocks in a year.

37. **A buy-and-hold investor who cares about costs is likely to invest in . . .**
    A. Actively managed funds.
    B. Index funds.
    C. Growth funds.
    D. Value funds.

38. **An investor who follows technical analysis will probably care about . . .**
    A. Earnings.
    B. Profit margins.
    C. Sales.
    D. Moving averages.

39. A fundamentally oriented investor cares about . . .

    A. The book value of a company.

    B. Recent trading trends in a company's stock.

    C. Price momentum.

40. Historically, bonds return roughly how much per year, on average?

    A. 1 percent

    B. 5 percent

    C. 10 percent

    D. 15 percent

41. The total returns generated by bonds represent income plus or minus any change in price.

    A. True

    B. False

42. Investors can reduce market risk by . . .

    A. Investing in more than 50 stocks at one time.

    B. Moving money out of stocks from time to time, as volatility rises.

    C. Concentrating their bets in fewer than 10 stocks.

43. The following represent forms of diversification:

    A. Buying stocks and bonds

    B. Dollar-cost averaging into the market

    C. Both

    D. Neither

44. Value and growth strategies are both forms of what?

    A. Index investing

    B. Active investing

    C. Both

    D. Neither

45. A value investor cares about . . .

    A. Growth.

    B. Momentum.

    C. Price.

46. There is a risk in not being in the market.
    A. True
    B. False

47. Which are good hedges against inflation?
    A. Stocks
    B. Bonds
    C. Cash
    D. Mutual funds

48. Which of the following vehicles has not been able to outpace inflation over time?
    A. Stock
    B. Bonds
    C. Cash
    D. Mutual funds

49. Small stocks have historically outpaced blue-chip stocks.
    A. True
    B. False

50. You should always have more money in small-cap stocks than in large-cap stocks.
    A. True
    B. False

51. Dividend payments and corporate profits are related.
    A. True
    B. False

52. Which of the following statements is true?
    A. Over the long term, you're better off investing only in growth stocks because they earn more in profits.
    B. You're better off investing only in domestic stocks because the United States dominates Europe and Asia when it comes to earnings growth rates.
    C. You should not expect to earn much more than 10 percent a year on average in stocks.

53. In a classic "flight to quality," money is expected to go . . .

    A. From value stocks into growth stocks because growth-oriented shares produce better profits and sales.

    B. From large stocks into small stocks.

    C. From U.S stocks into foreign stocks.

    D. From stocks into bonds.

54. A market order and a stop-loss order are the same things.

    A. True

    B. False

55. Why do investors need bonds when they return less than stocks over the long term?

    A. Because bonds beat inflation

    B. Because bonds don't always return less than stocks in the short term

    C. Because bonds are cheaper than stocks

56. Bonds help diversify a total portfolio by . . .

    A. Losing less than stocks during a bear market.

    B. Adding ballast to your stock holdings.

    C. Both A and B.

    D. Neither A nor B.

57. The best time to buy a bond fund is . . .

    A. When interest rates are falling.

    B. When interest rates are rising.

    C. When equities are performing poorly.

58. The best time to buy an individual bond is when rates are falling.

    A. True

    B. False

59. A fair way to compare the valuations of stocks and bonds is to compare a bond's yield against the earnings yield for a stock.

    A. True

    B. False

60. To calculate the earnings yield for a stock . . .

   A. Take the price of the shares and divide it by the underlying company's earnings.

   B. Take the price of the shares and divide it by the underlying company's earnings per share.

   C. Take the underlying company's earnings per share and divide it by the stock price.

61. A simple way to minimize credit risk is to . . .

   A. Buy a diversified bond fund.

   B. Buy shorter-term bonds.

   C. Ladder your individual bonds.

   D. You can't minimize credit risk.

62. A simple way to minimize interest-rate risk is to . . .

   A. Buy long-term bonds.

   B. Buy a diversified bond fund.

   C. Buy individual bonds and hold them to maturity.

   D. You can't minimize interest-rate risk.

63. A simple way to minimize inflation risk is to . . .

   A. Buy intermediate-term bonds.

   B. Buy a diversified bond fund.

   C. Buy TIPs.

   D. You can't minimize inflation risk.

64. Zero-coupon bonds are a type of bond that . . .

   A. Pays no interest.

   B. Pays the investor interest in a lump sum at maturity.

   C. Is considered tax efficient because it pays no interest income during the life of the bond and therefore generates no taxable income.

65. Which of the following are considered inflation hedges:

   A. Stocks

   B. TIPs

   C. Commodities

   D. Real estate

   E. All of the above

66. A Treasury Inflation-Protected Security is a unique type of Treasury bond that . . .

    A. Has an adjustable interest rate that keeps up with inflation.

    B. Has an adjustable par value that keeps up with inflation.

    C. Has an adjustable par value that keeps up with inflation, but also calculates its fixed annual interest payments based on the adjusted par.

67. Bonds serve what purpose in an investor's portfolio?

    A. Ballast

    B. Income

    C. Diversification

    D. All of the above

    E. None of the above

68. Cash serves what purpose in an investor's portfolio?

    A. Growth

    B. Liquidity

    C. Capital appreciation

    D. Inflation hedge

69. Cash allows you to . . .

    A. Preserve capital.

    B. Wait for good investment opportunities.

    C. Both of the above.

    D. Neither of the above.

70. Cash is a total return investment vehicle.

    A. True

    B. False

71. Which is the safest form of cash?

    A. Money market funds

    B. Money market accounts

    C. Long-term CDs

72. Money market funds will always yield more than money market accounts.

    A. True

    B. False

73. **A simple way to ladder your CDs is to . . .**
    A. Buy different lots of CDs maturing in the same year.
    B. Buy CDs of different maturities so that as one comes due, you can reinvest the money at the long end of the ladder.
    C. You can't ladder CDs.

74. **Which of the following savings products is not federally insured?**
    A. Money market funds
    B. T-bills
    C. Passbook savings accounts

75. **T-bills and Treasury notes are the same things.**
    A. True
    B. False

76. **Which type of savings vehicle offers the greatest liquidity?**
    A. Money market funds
    B. Money market accounts
    C. CDs

77. **When considering money market mutual funds, what attributes should you focus on?**
    A. Solid past performance
    B. Low fees
    C. Highest current yield

78. **A mutual fund is a . . .**
    A. Favored asset among individual investors, alongside stocks, bonds, and cash.
    B. Type of stock or bond.
    C. A company whose purpose is to invest in stocks, bonds, and/or cash.

79. **According to their placement in mutual fund style boxes, large-cap value stock funds are considered the most . . .**
    A. Appropriate for most investors.
    B. Conservative.
    C. Aggressive.

80. A large-cap value fund is a type of . . .

    A. General equity fund.

    B. Sector fund.

    C. Hybrid fun

81. Sector funds are often considered riskier than general equity funds because . . .

    A. Of the specific sectors they invest in.

    B. Sector fund managers have less experience than general domestic stock fund managers.

    C. They only invest in one sector of the economy.

82. Which of the following can lose money:

    A. Stock funds

    B. Bond funds

    C. Money market funds

    D. All of the above

    E. None of the above

83. Short-duration bonds don't expose you to interest-rate risk.

    A. True

    B. False

84. Municipal bond mutual funds are tax free when it comes to . . .

    A. Only federal taxes for in-state residents.

    B. Local taxes and in most cases state taxes.

    C. Federal taxes and in some cases local and state taxes for in-state residents.

85. Municipal bond funds are a type of federal government bond fund.

    A. True

    B. False

86. Balanced funds are allowed to invest in . . .

    A. Only stocks and bonds.

    B. A mix of stocks, bonds, and cash.

    C. Only stocks and cash.

87. No-load mutual funds are . . .

    A. The most popular type of mutual fund because they do not charge commissions.

    B. The least popular type of fund because they require investors to deal directly with the fund company.

    C. Not advisable for individual investors.

88. A-share class funds are almost always preferable to B-share class funds because it's better to get commissions out of the way.

    A. True

    B. False

89. If a fund reports a total return of 7 percent and has a total expense ratio of 2.50 percent, what it actually earned in gross market returns was . . .

    A. 9.5 percent.

    B. 4.5 percent.

    C. 9.45 percent.

90. Which fund manager is better at picking stocks: one whose fund charges 2 percent in total expenses but reports total returns of 7 percent, or one whose portfolio has expenses of 0.2 percent but net returns of 6 percent?

    A. The one with total expenses of 2 percent and total returns of 7 percent.

    B. The one with total expenses of 0.2 percent and returns of 6 percent.

    C. They performed exactly the same.

91. The total expense ratio includes these types of costs:

    A. Management fees, 12b-1 fees, and transactional costs

    B. Shareholder servicing fees, management fees, and transactional costs

    C. Management fees, 12b-1 fees, and shareholder servicing fees

92. Home ownership historically generates greater annual returns than stocks.

    A. True

    B. False

93. An investment in residential real estate is a bet on . . .

    A. The national economy.

    B. The regional economy.

    C. Your personal economy.

    D. All of the above.

94. What does *R*-squared refer to?
    A. The correlation of an investment's performance to a benchmark index
    B. The measure of an investment's volatility
    C. The measure of an investment's performance

95. A REIT is more like . . .
    A. A stock than a bond.
    B. A bond than a stock.
    C. An entirely different asset than a stock or a bond.

96. An advantage of exchange-traded funds (ETFs) over regular mutual funds is that . . .
    A. ETFs are professionally managed.
    B. ETFs are low in cost.
    C. ETFs are purchased through a brokerage account and not through a no-load fund company.

97. You can look up a company's net profits in which financial statement:
    A. Balance sheet
    B. Income statement
    C. Statement of cash flows

98. Which of the following is *not* a way to measure profits?
    A. PEG
    B. ROE
    C. Net income

99. Why are a company's sales figures important to consider?
    A. They speak to the company's profitability.
    B. They speak to the company's efficiency.
    C. They speak to the demand for the company's basic goods and services.

100. A Roth IRA and a traditional IRA differ because . . .
     A. Roth IRAs are deductible and traditional IRAs aren't.
     B. Withdrawals from Roth IRAs are taxed as ordinary income while withdrawals from traditional IRAs are tax-free.
     C. Roth IRAs are funded with after-tax money while some traditional IRAs can be funded with pretax dollars.

Answers to Quizzes and Final Exam

Chapter 1	Chapter 3	Chapter 5	Chapter 7
1. B	1. B	1. B	1. A
2. B	2. C	2. C	2. B
3. A	3. B	3. B	3. B
4. B	4. A	4. A	4. A
5. B	5. C	5. A	5. C
6. C	6. D	6. A	6. E
7. B	7. A	7. B	7. B
8. C	8. B	8. D	8. B
9. A	9. A	9. A	9. C
10. A	10. A	10. B	10. A

Chapter 2	Chapter 4	Chapter 6	Chapter 8
1. C	1. B	1. A	1. C
2. B	2. E	2. C	2. A
3. D	3. B	3. D	3. C
4. B	4. C	4. B	4. B
5. D	5. B	5. D	5. B
6. A	6. A	6. B	6. A
7. B	7. B	7. E	7. B
8. E	8. B	8. D	8. C
9. B	9. D	9. D	9. C
10. C	10. A	10. B	10. E

Chapter 9	Chapter 11	Chapter 13	Chapter 15
1. B	1. A	1. B	1. B
2. B	2. B	2. B	2. A
3. A	3. D	3. C	3. B
4. B	4. B	4. A	4. B
5. A	5. C	5. A	5. B
6. C	6. A	6. E	6. A
7. C	7. E	7. B	7. D
8. C	8. A	8. A	8. A
9. C	9. C	9. B	9. B
10. B	10. A	10. D	10. B

Chapter 10	Chapter 12	Chapter 14
1. B	1. A	1. A
2. D	2. A	2. D
3. D	3. B	3. A
4. B	4. B	4. C
5. A	5. B	5. B
6. B	6. C	6. C
7. B	7. A	7. D
8. C	8. C	8. A
9. C	9. B	9. C
10. A	10. C	10. D

Final Exam

1. B	41. A	81. C
2. A	42. A	82. D
3. A	43. C	83. B
4. D	44. D	84. C
5. B	45. C	85. B
6. B	46. A	86. B
7. C	47. A	87. A
8. C	48. C	88. B
9. A	49. A	89. A
10. B	50. B	90. A
11. E	51. A	91. C
12. B	52. C	92. B
13. B	53. D	93. D
14. A	54. B	94. A
15. B	55. B	95. C
16. B	56. C	96. B
17. A	57. A	97. B
18. C	58. B	98. A
19. A	59. A	99. C
20. A	60. C	100. C
21. A	61. A	
22. C	62. C	
23. C	63. C	
24. D	64. B	
25. A	65. E	
26. C	66. C	
27. A	67. D	
28. B	68. B	
29. D	69. C	
30. A	70. B	
31. A	71. B	
32. B	72. B	
33. B	73. B	
34. D	74. A	
35. B	75. B	
36. C	76. A	
37. B	77. B	
38. D	78. C	
39. A	79. B	
40. B	80. A	

Glossary

A share class fund. An advisor-sold fund where the brokerage commission is levied up front, before an investor puts money into the market. Also known as a **front-end load fund**.

American Depositary Receipts, or **ADRs.** ADRs allow individuals to invest directly in foreign companies, particularly in the stocks of developed markets. An ADR is a proxy of sorts that represents shares of a foreign company. The actual shares of that foreign stock are held by a bank in the United States, while the ADR itself, or the receipt of those shares, trades on the major U.S. stock exchanges, like the NYSE or Nasdaq.

Annual report. Issued by publicly traded companies once a year, the annual report communicates the firm's performance and activities during the previous year to shareholders. It includes financial highlights and a review of operations, which should provide detail on important recent developments, including new product launches, acquisitions, mergers, and sales of units.

Ask price. The price that current shareholders are willing to sell their shares for.

Asset allocation. Refers to the amount of money, in percentage terms, we invest in stocks, bonds, and cash in a portfolio. The vast majority of an investor's returns over time can be explained by his or her **asset allocation strategy**, rather than by stock selection.

Automated savings plan. A savings program where a portion of your paycheck is automatically set aside each week or month and sent to a money market fund or some other savings vehicle. A derivation of an automated savings plan is a so-called **automated investment plan**, where a small amount of an investors' money is dollar-cost averaged into a stock or bond fund every month.

B share class fund. An advisor-sold fund where the commission is deducted when the investor sells the fund, as opposed to when he or she buys it. Also known as **back-end** or **deferred load funds**. A common feature of back-end loads is that they diminish gradually over time, so the longer you hold the fund without selling, the more you delay having to pay commissions—and often, the lower the commission is.

Balanced funds. Also known as **hybrid funds**, balanced portfolios are mutual funds that are allowed to invest in a mix of both stocks and bonds. Typically, the mix is set at around 60 percent equities/40 percent bonds, but that can fluctuate.

Balance sheet. A financial statement that accounts for a company's assets and liabilities. It gauges a company's overall financial health at a particular point in time. The balance sheet is one of the three major financial statements that a publicly traded company must issue once a quarter.

Basic materials stocks. These are shares of companies that produce, mine, or distribute commodities or other raw materials used in the manufacturing process. Basic materials stocks range from chemical companies to mining stocks to steel.

Bear market. A major, sustained correction in the equity markets that causes stock values to fall more than 20 percent.

Beta. A classic mathematical measure of an investment's volatility. Stocks with a beta of 1 are said to be as volatile as the broad equity markets. Stocks with a beta of 2 are said to be twice as volatile.

Bid-ask spread. A hidden cost of sorts that you pay whenever you make a stock transaction. It is the difference between the price that a seller is willing to sell shares for and that a buyer is willing to pay for the same exact stock. The difference may be pocketed by middlemen known as **market makers**.

Bid price. The price a buyer states that he or she is willing to pay an existing shareholder for his or her stock.

Bond fund. A type of mutual fund that invests primarily in fixed-income securities. For smaller investors, this is the easiest—and cheapest—vehicle with which to gain bond exposure.

Bottom line. Slang for a company's **profit** or **net income**. It is referred to as the bottom line because it appears as the final line on an income statement.

Brokerage commission. Money paid to a broker or brokerage firm as compensation for placing and executing a transaction order.

Bull market. A major, sustained rally in the equity markets that causes stock values to rise more than 20 percent.

Buy on margin. A term that refers to purchasing stock with borrowed money. It is a form of leverage. Buying on margin is generally considered a risky strategy. Should your portfolio lose significant value based on a wrong bet, your broker may order a margin call.

C share class funds. An advisor-sold fund in which the commission may be taken partially up front, before an investor buys shares, and partially at the end, upon sale. Also known as **level load funds.** While these commissions may be somewhat lower than those charged in an A share or B share fund, C share funds tend to charge higher annual fees to compensate for the lower upfront commissions.

Callable bond. A bond that gives the issuer the right, under certain circumstances, to end the life of the contract sooner than expected.

Capital appreciation. Investing with the goal of growing your principal through price appreciation over time.

Capital gains. Gains achieved in the underlying value of an investment. Upon sale, those capital gains are said to be "realized." Prior to booking the profit, they are said to be "unrealized."

Capital gains taxes. Taxes that must be paid upon "realizing" capital gains. At present, the federal tax rate on long-term capital gains—those held for more than a year—is 15 percent.

Capital preservation. Investing with the goal of protecting the principal value of your investments by taking a conservative approach.

Cash drag. The negative impact on returns that large cash holdings have on a mutual fund's performance. Typically, cash drag occurs when funds are inundated with large cash flows, making it difficult for the fund manager to invest the money immediately in the stock market.

Certificates of Deposit, or **CDs**, as they are known. CDs are a popular savings vehicle created by banks that allow savers to lock in interest rates. Like a bond, CDs come with maturity dates, typically ranging from as little as one month to as long as five years. During that time, investors are largely restricted from having access to those funds. However, the interest rate at the time of purchase is guaranteed for the life of the CD.

Chicago Board Options Exchange. A leading exchange in futures and options contracts, which are complex financial instruments used by professionals to hedge their investment bets.

Chicago Mercantile Exchange. A leading commodities exchange that facilitates trading in a wide range of investments, from currencies, such as Eurodollars, to commodities like beef, dairy, fertilizer, and lumber.

Closing price. The last price a stock traded for in the day's session.

Commodities. Any unfinished or unprocessed good that can be traded in bulk. They can range from agricultural products such as pork bellies, coffee, and cotton, to basic materials such as copper and silver.

Commodity futures. Financial contracts tied to the delivery of commodities, such as metals or agricultural products, at some point in the future. This can be a dangerous game. Investing in futures contracts is akin to betting more than investing.

Common stock. The most basic share of ownership of a business. As an owner of common stock, you will probably receive a portion of the firm's earnings back through dividend payments, which are typically made quarterly or semi-annually.

Compound interest. The ability of your money to grow exponentially over time. It reflects the rate of return that an investment earns, along with how interest in subsequent periods is earned on that interest, generating powerful gains.

Cost of goods sold. The total costs it takes a company to manufacture and distribute goods and services sold in a given period. These costs might include labor, raw materials, shipping, marketing, insuring, and warehousing.

Coupon rate. Represents your interest rate if you purchased a bond at par. For example, if you bought a $1,000 Treasury bond with a 5 percent coupon for par value, you would earn $50 a year in interest on that bond, and your real interest rate and coupon rate would be 5 percent.

Credit quality. Refers to the amount of credit risk to which a bond issuer exposes you. The highest quality bonds—with credit ratings of AAA from Standard & Poor's and Fitch, or an Aaa rating from Moody—expose investors to virtually no credit risk, due to their strong financial health.

Credit risk. Refers to the possibility that the bond issuer, despite its promises and best intentions, may default on its obligations to pay you a certain coupon or to return your principal to you at maturity.

Currency risk. Refers to the change in the value of local currency. These fluctuations in currency values can have huge impacts on investors. They can also impact the underlying health of a stock.

Current yield. Represents the interest you enjoy on the bond if you purchased it at the current price. It can be determined with the formula:

Annual interest generated by the bond/Current price = Current yield

Day order. A transaction order for a security that is only good for the day in which it is placed.

Day traders. Investors who buy and sell stocks several times within a day, hoping to book quick intraday profits.

Default. The failure of a bond issuer to make good on its promise to pay the bond investor interest and to return the original principal investment back at an agreed upon date.

Developed markets. Refers to the equity and fixed-income markets in leading industrial nations, such as the United States, Japan, Germany, the United Kingdom, France, and Italy.

Direct-sold funds, also known as **no-load funds**. These are mutual funds bought and sold directly through fund companies. They do not come with commission charges.

Diversification. Refers to owning a mix of different assets—such as stocks, bonds, or cash—and different securities within those asset classes to minimize risk by spreading it out over numerous holdings.

Dividend payments. Refers to the occasional payouts that some publicly traded stocks make to their shareholders. These payouts represent a portion of the firm's earnings being returned to the owners of the business.

Dividend reinvestment plans, or **DRIPs.** DRIPs allow individuals to invest in stocks without having a brokerage account. With a DRIP, an investor can purchase stock directly from the publicly traded company itself.

Dividend yield. A measure of the amount of dividend income thrown off by a stock. The formula to calculate this is:

Dividend income per share/current price per share = Dividend yield

Dollar-cost averaging. A conservative investing approach that calls for putting small amounts of money to work each month, quarter, or at some other routine interval. By buying at intervals, you ensure that you will never be purchasing a security at the absolute worst possible time in the market. The idea is to diversify, or average out, based on when you purchase your securities.

Dow Jones Industrial Average, or **DJIA**. A benchmark stock index comprised of 30 of the biggest companies in the U.S. market that reflects the industrial strength of the domestic economy. Companies are added or deleted from the DJIA by editors of the *Wall Street Journal*.

Earnings yield. Refers to the amount of corporate earnings an investor is purchasing for every $1 he or she is buying in equities. It is the inverse of a stock's price to earnings ratio. The formula to calculate earnings yield is:

Earnings per share / Price of security = Earnings yield

Efficient market theory. Says that the stock market is ultimately rational and efficient, and that one reason it's difficult for professional managers to beat the major indexes is that stock prices fully reflect the sum total of all the relevant market information that exists to help price the stock.

Emerging market stocks. Stocks of companies—both large and small— head-quartered in countries whose economies are relatively young and therefore are undeveloped; among them are Brazil, China, Malaysia, Mexico, South Korea, South Africa, and Taiwan. Investment risks in these stocks include political instability, or in some cases even revolution in the countries where these companies are based.

Equities. Another term for **stock**.

FICO score. The letters stand for Fair, Isaac Co., a California company that assesses consumer credit-worthiness based on information found in credit reports maintained by the major credit bureaus: TransUnion, Equifax, and Experian. FICO scores range from 300 to 850; the higher your score, the better your credit rating.

52-week range. A range of prices for a stock that considers its highest and lowest closing prices over the past year.

529 plan. A self-directed state-sponsored college savings plan that allows families to invest tax-deferred. Investment gains withdrawn from a 529 plan that are used for qualified educational expenses—such as tuition, room, and board—are federal tax-free.

Fixed-income instruments. Another term for **bonds**.

Fixed maturity date. Refers to the date at which a bond matures and the original principal value of the bond is to be returned in full to the investor.

Flight to quality. Refers to investors flocking to high-quality stocks (such as shares of big, blue-chip companies) and bonds (typically Treasury securities) during times of heightened economic or geopolitical risks.

Forward P/E. A stock's price-to-earnings ratio, based on estimated earnings for the underlying company over the next 12 months.

401(k) plan. A self-directed company-sponsored retirement plan that allows workers to contribute pretax dollars and to invest the money tax-deferred. Typically, money held in a 401(k) is invested in mutual fund options.

Free cash flow. The money a company has remaining after all obligations and capital expenditures are met. The higher a company's free cash flow, the more financial flexibility it has.

Fund manager risk. Refers to the risk a mutual fund investor exposes him- or herself to by investing in an actively managed fund. While there is a possibility that your fund manager will outperform the market in any given year, there is also the risk that the same manager could have a bad year.

GARP stands for *growth at a reasonable price*. Refers to a school of investing that concentrates on shares of companies with the brightest growth prospects. But within that universe, GARP managers prefer to focus on those shares trading at relatively cheap prices, since lower valuations often equal lower risk.

General equity funds. Funds that invest in a cross section of different industries and sectors that make up the stock market.

General obligation bond. A type of municipal bond issued by states, counties, or cities for general purposes. Because it is issued by governments that have the authority to raise taxes, the perception is that this type of muni is relatively safe.

Gold stocks. Shares of companies whose core business is tied to the mining, processing, or distribution of gold.

Good-this-month order. A transaction order for a security that is good until the last trading day of the month.

Good through order. A transaction order for a security that allows an investor to assign a specific date at which the limit order will expire.

Good-till-canceled order. A transaction order for a security that allows the investor to keep the order open until he or she decides to cancel it.

Growth stocks. Shares of companies whose underlying profits and sales are growing faster than the overall market. Because of their growth characteristics, investors are often willing to pay higher prices for these shares, which leads growth stocks to have higher P/E ratios, in general, than value stocks.

Hidden load. Refers to **12b-1 fees**, which are charged to existing shareholders of a mutual fund to cover distribution and marketing expenses for the fund. In many cases the 12b-1 fees are used to compensate brokers or advisors for driving client assets into that fund.

High price. The highest trading price of a stock in a trading day.

High-yield bonds. Low-quality, or so-called **junk bonds** that are forced to pay higher interest rates to attract investors. High-yield bonds are typically issued by companies of questionable financial strength.

High-yield funds. Fixed-income mutual funds that focus on high-yield corporate debt.

High-yield muni bond funds. Fixed-income mutual funds that focus on high-yield municipal debt.

Holding period. Refers to how long an investor hangs onto a security before selling.

100-minus rule. An age-based formula for determining a basic investment mix. Under this simple—some would say overly simplistic—asset allocation strategy, you subtract your age from 100, and the answer tells you what percentage of your assets should be held in stocks. The remainder can be put into bonds or a combination of bonds and cash.

110-minus rule. An age-based formula for determining a basic asset allocation strategy, slightly more aggressive than the more common **100-minus rule**. Under this strategy, an investor subtracts his or her age from 110. The answer tells you what percentage of assets should be held in stocks. The remainder can be put into bonds or a combination of bonds and cash.

Income statement. Sometimes called the **statement of profit and losses**, the income statement is one of three major financial statements that publicly traded companies must issue at least once a quarter. It reflects the profitability of a company by measuring its revenues against the costs associated with generating those revenues.

Index. A **benchmark**, of sorts, that is used to gauge the performance of the stock or bond markets or a segment of them. Examples of leading indexes include the Dow Jones Industrial Average, the S&P 500 index of blue-chip stocks, and the Nasdaq composite index.

Individual retirement accounts, commonly known as **IRAs.** Self-directed retirement accounts an investor can voluntarily fund. Within them, money is tax sheltered while it grows. An investor can choose any number of different stocks, bonds, or mutual funds to invest in. There are several different types of IRAs, among them **traditional IRAs**, which are funded with pretax dollars, with the investor paying taxes on gains at withdrawal; and **Roth IRAs**, which are funded with after-tax dollars but withdrawals are tax-free.

Inflection points. Points in time when market trends reverse. For example, they might mark transitions from a bear market to a bull market, or from a rally to a correction.

Initial public offering, or **IPO.** A process that allows a company to begin trading its shares in the open market.

Interest income and expenses. A line item on a company's income statement that accounts for interest income earned during a particular period along with expenses incurred to finance projects.

Interest-rate risk. Refers to the risk a bond investor faces should interest rates rise. A basic principle of investing is that bond prices move in the opposite direction of market interest rates. So, if market rates rise, bond prices would fall. And should bond prices fall more than the security yields, the investor's portfolio would face losses.

Intermediate-term bonds. Fixed-income securities that mature in two to 10 years.

Intermediate-term bond funds. Mutual funds that invest in intermediate-term debt.

Intrinsic value. Gauges the true worth of a company by considering all the tangible and intangible value a firm possesses, including its perceived worth.

Investment-grade bonds. High-quality fixed-income securities issued by companies with strong credit histories and ratings, as graded by the major credit-rating agencies. These are the antithesis of high-yield bonds.

Junk bond. See **high-yield bonds**.

Large-cap stocks. Refers to companies whose market value is $10 billion or more. Also called **blue-chip stocks** because they are considered safer and more stable than shares of young start-ups.

Letter to Shareholders. A letter included in a company's annual report written by the chief executive and/or chairman of the corporation. This brief note tends to highlight important accomplishments, challenges, and setbacks of the company in the previous year.

Leverage. Refers to the act of borrowing money to invest it. The idea is, if you can borrow money, you can use the proceeds to bolster or leverage your investment to even greater gains than you could otherwise afford on your own.

Limit order. A transaction order for a security that allows the investor to set the price. For example, if you wanted to buy shares of Company X at $25 a share but the stock was currently trading at $30, you could put a limit order on the stock that would direct your broker to purchase shares once they fell to $25.

Liquidity. Refers to the ease with which investors can buy and sell an asset or security.

Load funds. A general term for mutual funds that are advisor-sold. As such, load funds charge investors a commission for the advice provided to purchase the fund. Within the universe of load funds, there are **front-load**, **back-end load**, and **level load funds**.

Long-term bonds. Bonds that mature in 10 years or more. They are regarded as more aggressive and risky from the standpoint of interest-rate risk than short-term bonds.

Low price. Refers to the lowest price at which a security traded for in a given day.

Lump-sum investor. An investor who puts a sizable portion of his or her money into stocks or bonds instead of dollar-cost averaging gradually into the market.

Market capitalization, or **market cap**. Refers to the company's total market value. It is calculated by multiplying the total number of shares a company has outstanding by the current price per share.

Market correction. A downturn in the markets. Among equities, a market correction refers to a loss of 10 percent or more in major stock indexes such as the Dow Jones Industrial Average or the S&P 500 index.

Market maker. Sometimes known as a **specialist**, a market maker is the middleman that facilitates trading in a given stock, in part by helping to match up buyers with sellers. Market makers are typically broker-dealer firms whose job, when there is an imbalance of buyers and sellers in the marketplace, is to facilitate trading in the security.

Market order. A transaction order for a security that requests immediate execution at the best possible price.

Market risk. The risk of potential losses investors face on their investments based on diminished prices.

Market value. Same as **market cap**. It refers to the value that Wall Street collectively assigns a company at any given moment in time, based on the company's stock price at that moment. The formula to calculate market value is:

Current price per share × *Total shares outstanding* = *Market value*

Market weighting. Refers to the way broad stock market indexes divide up their holdings. For example, the allocation between large stocks and small stocks in the Wilshire 5000 Total Stock Market index is roughly 80 to 20 percent, so a market weighting between large and small stocks would be said to be 80-20.

Maturity date. The date when a bond issuer agrees to redeem the bondholder. It is also the date when the loan contract itself—the bond—expires.

Micro-cap stocks. Refers to tiny stocks, generally in firms with market capitalization of $250 million or less.

Mid-cap stocks. Refers to medium-size stocks, companies whose market values range between $1 and $10 billion.

Money market account. A type of savings account that places a few restrictions on the number of transactions one can make but in exchange will often pay noticeably higher yields than a basic passbook account or checking account. Money market accounts are FDIC insured.

Money market mutual funds. Funds that invest in extremely short-term debt and they are considered a cash vehicle. Money market funds sometimes pay out more in interest than money market accounts, but they are not FDIC insured.

Moving averages. Recent trading patterns in a stock or stock index that help technical analysts gauge the relative appetite for a given investment. Common examples include the 50-day, the 100-day, and the 200-day moving averages. Typically, it is considered a bearish sign for a security if its price falls below its 50-, 100-, or 200-day moving averages. Conversely, it's considered bullish when a stock breaks out above its historic moving averages.

Municipal bonds. Debt issued by states, counties, municipalities, local agencies, and school districts to pay for such things as construction projects, highways, or basic obligations.

Mutual fund. A popular investment vehicle that offers investors access to a pooled, diversified portfolio of stocks, bonds—or a combination—with relatively low minimum initial investment requirements. The majority of mutual funds also give investors access to professional management.

Mutual fund supermarkets. Brokerage platforms that give investors access to thousands of different mutual funds run by hundreds of different mutual fund companies. Because fund supermarkets cater to self-directed investors, they tend to provide a large selection of no-load funds. Like food vendors dealing with grocery stores, the mutual fund companies themselves will often pay the fund supermarket for "shelf space" to sell their wares.

Nasdaq national market. A leading electronic stock exchange where some of the biggest and best-known technology and growth companies in the United States are listed.

Net asset value, or **NAV.** Represents the total market value of a mutual fund. Divided by the total number of shares that fund has outstanding, net asset value per share represents the current price of a mutual fund. In essence, net asset value is the total *market value* of all the securities in that fund—minus expenses and liabilities—divided by the total number of shares that are outstanding. The formula to calculate a fund's net asset value is:

Total Market Value of Portfolio − Liabilities/Total shares outstanding = NAV

Net income. The most common measure of a company's profitability. It takes all of the revenues and interest income enjoyed by a company in a reporting period and subtracts the costs that were required to engineer those sales. If you divide a firm's net income by the total number of shares it has outstanding, you get its **earnings per share**, or **EPS.** Because net income is the final line in an income statement, earnings are referred to as the **bottom line**.

New York Board of Trade. A leading exchange that facilitates trading in commodities such as cocoa, coffee, cotton, ethanol, and sugar.

New York Stock Exchange, the **NYSE.** Sometimes referred to as the Big Board, the NYSE is the nation's leading stock exchange. It is where some of the leading stocks in the U.S. market are traded.

No-load funds, also referred to as **direct-sold funds.** Funds purchased and sold directly through fund companies and do not come with any commission charges.

No transaction fee funds. Within mutual fund supermarkets, these are lists of direct-sold funds that can be bought or sold without being assessed a brokerage commission by the brokerage platform itself. These are by definition no-load funds, so investors won't be assessed a load either.

Open price. The price a stock starts trading for at the start of a trading session.

Par value. Refers to the face value of a bond. Since bonds are typically sold in $1,000 increments, it's likely that the par value of your individual bond is going to be $1,000. One exception might be with municipal bonds, where par might be set at $5,000 per bond.

Payout ratio. The percentage of profits returned to shareholders in the form of dividend income. The higher the payout ratio, the more appealing a stock may be to an income- or value-oriented investor.

Preferred stock. Represents an ownership unit of a company that is slightly less risky than common stock. Preferred stock holders typically receive bigger dividend payouts than common stock investors and are ahead of common stock investors in line to claim losses should the company file for bankruptcy. Typically, preferred shares do not give investors voting rights for the management of the underlying company.

Price appreciation. An increase in the underlying market value of a stock or other security. Combined with dividend income or yield, price appreciation represents a major component of an investment's total returns.

Price-to-earnings ratio, or **P/E.** The most widely used valuation measure for a stock. P/E ratios gauge the priceyness of a stock, based on its current share price and the earnings generated by the underlying company. A stock can have several different P/E ratios, based on how earnings are measured. **Trailing P/E,** for example, is the P/E ratio of a stock based on its actual trailing 12-month earnings, and **forward P/E** is the ratio based on estimated forward 12-month earnings. Sometimes a P/E ratio will be calculated based on calendar year earnings. To calculate a company's price-to-earnings ratio:

Current stock price / Earnings per share = P/E ratio

Prospectus. The official document issued by a mutual fund letting shareholders know how the fund and fund company plan to operate.

Publicly traded company. One whose shares are not held exclusively by a single person or family, but rather, trade freely among members of the general public on an open exchange. A company must first go through an initial public offering (IPO) to achieve publicly traded status.

R-squared. Refers to a mathematical estimation of how much of an investment's behavior can be explained by the movements of a benchmark. *R*-squared can be used by fund investors to gauge whether a portfolio is highly correlated to a market index, like the S&P 500, or if it diverges from that index.

Real Estate Investment Trust (REIT). A publicly traded company whose purpose is to invest in real estate in some form or fashion. Some REITs specialize in commercial properties, while others focus on residential real estate. Because of its focus on real estate, REITs are often considered a separate asset than equities. Because, by law, they must pass along to shareholders the vast majority of the income derived from their investments, they are popular vehicles for income-oriented investors. However, REIT income is not considered qualified dividend income, and therefore does not benefit from favorable tax treatment.

Rebalancing. Refers to the act of periodically resetting one's mix of stocks, bonds, and cash so market forces do not seriously upset a long-term strategic asset allocation plan. Typically, investors will rebalance once a quarter or once a year. Rebalancing is considered a strategy to reduce risk in a portfolio since it forces an investor to sell portions of an asset that have risen disproportionately in value and use those proceeds to purchase a competing asset that has not performed as well. That way, an investor books profits periodically and ensures that he or she buys low and sells high.

Redeem. Refers to the act of selling out of an investment in exchange for cash.

Return on equity, or **ROE.** A measure of a company's earnings relative to its shareholder equity. The higher the ROE, the more profitable a company is said to be. ROE is considered a fair way to compare the profitability of companies of varying sizes and industries. The formula for return on equity is:

$$Net\ income/Shareholder\ equity = ROE$$

Revenue bonds. A type of municipal debt floated by an agency of a state or local government for a specific project. While revenue bond holders are typically paid from the receipts generated from these projects—like highway or tunnel tolls—there is no explicit promise that the state or municipality will bail out these bond issuers should the projects run into financial difficulties.

Reverse mortgage. A type of loan providing homeowners, often senior citizens, with a stream of income that is backed by their homes. Unlike a traditional mortgage, a reverse mortgage does not require you to pay back the loan, so long as you continue to live in the house against which the mortgage is applied. Upon sale of the home or death, the reverse mortgage is paid off by the proceeds of the home's liquidation. A reverse mortgage can be paid out in a lump sum, in monthly payments, or in some other form of routine installments.

Roth IRA. A type of self-directed retirement account funded with after-tax dollars. Once inside, money in a Roth IRA can be invested in any number of vehicles and grows tax sheltered. At withdrawal, investment gains can be pulled out of these accounts tax-free, so long as the withdrawal meets certain requirements.

S&P 500 index. One of the three major stock indexes followed by U.S. investors. The S&P 500 is a benchmark that measures the performance of the 500 largest-capitalization stocks in the U.S. market. It is considered a better gauge of the broad domestic stock market than the Dow Jones Industrial Average, since the S&P measure the performance of 500 companies instead of the Dow's 30.

Secondary offering. An additional offering of public shares following a company's initial public offering, or IPO.

Sector funds, also known as **specialty portfolios.** These are a type of mutual fund that specializes in a particular sector of the economy. For example, there are sector funds that primarily invest in the technology, utilities, energy, or health-care sectors. Because of their niche, sector funds should not be used to make up one's core stock portfolio. Rather, they are useful to add some flavor to a diversified portfolio of stocks or stock funds.

Self-directed retirement accounts. Tax-advantaged retirement plans, such 401(k)s and Roth IRAs, that force the investor to make all the investment decisions.

Sell discipline. Refers to reasons why an investor will choose to unload a stock or bond. Typically, your sell discipline should mirror your buy discipline. For example, if you buy stocks because they are undervalued, then it probably makes sense to sell when you consider them overvalued.

Senior bond. A type of corporate debt higher up in the pecking order of claims in the event of a corporate bankruptcy. As a result of the greater assurance they provide, senior corporate debt does not necessarily have to offer as high an interest rate to pique an investor's attention.

Shareholder. An investor who owns a stake of a company of a mutual fund.

Shareholder equity. Refers to the total net worth of a company. You calculate it by subtracting a firm's liabilities from its assets:

$$Assets - Liabilities = Shareholders'\ equity\ (net\ worth)$$

Short-term bond. A form of debt that matures in only two or three years, meaning it is less susceptible to interest-rate risk. There are short-term corporate and short-term government bonds.

Short-term bond funds. Mutual funds that specialize in investing in fixed-income securities that mature in about two or three years or less.

Small-cap stocks. Shares of small companies with total market capitalization of $1 billion or less. Because of their size, small-cap stocks are considered a riskier bet than shares of big, blue-chip companies.

Standard deviation. A mathematical measure of an investment's volatility and risk. It compares a stock's or a fund's volatility to the average volatility of that same type of stock or fund over a particular period of time. A stock with a high standard deviation typically sees its price fluctuate wildly between high and low points.

Statement of cash flows. One of the three major financial statements that publicly traded companies must routinely provide to shareholders and regulators. It tracks the flow of money into and out of the company's coffers.

Stock, sometimes referred to as **equities**. Stocks represent partial ownership of a company. Stocks can be purchased directly by an investor through a brokerage account, or indirectly through a mutual fund that in turn purchases these securities.

Stock buyback. Refers to repurchasing of shares by a company. Firms will periodically repurchase their own stock in the open market to shrink the total number of outstanding shares, thereby boosting earnings per share. Moreover, stock buybacks are often a signal to other investors that a stock is trading at attractive prices.

Stock-specific risk. The risk of potentially losing money in a stock investment—not because the overall market is shaky, but because of turmoil in the underlying business.

Stock split. A common strategy among some companies to subdivide their existing shares outstanding. Often used by companies whose share price has soared recently, a stock split has the affect of cutting the current price of a single share of stock—which may make it easier for smaller investors to purchase the security. At the same time, stock splits expand the total number of shares outstanding. A common split formula is a 2-for-1, meaning if you owned one share of Company X at $30, it then became two shares at $15 each. Stock splits do not directly affect a company's market capitalization.

Stop loss order. A type of transaction order for a security that allows the investor to minimize losses by setting a floor on the price of a stock. For example, if you owned a stock trading at $10 a share, you could set a stop loss at $7, requesting that the stock automatically be sold if it falls to that level.

Strategic asset allocation. Refers to the long-term mix of stocks and bonds you feel is appropriate for a person in your age group with your level of risk tolerance. Strategic asset allocation is a basic blueprint for what percentage of your assets you plan to hold in stocks, bonds, and cash. It represents the general path that you plan to take to balance your desire for high returns and low risk.

Subordinated bonds. A type of corporate debt whose investors must wait until other lenders are made whole before making claims against the firm, should it fall into financial trouble. As a result of having to take on more credit risk, owners of subordinated debt are often compensated with a slightly higher interest rate.

Swing traders. Investors who trade stock frequently, and therefore have short holding periods. Unlike day traders, however, a swing trader may hang on to securities for days before selling, as opposed to hours.

Tactical asset allocation. Refers to short-term moves that investors can make in their asset allocation strategy—defined as their mix of stocks, bonds, and cash—that try to take advantage of short-term market trends. An investor can make tactical adjustments to an asset allocation strategy without upsetting a strategic, or long-term, allocation approach.

Taxable bond funds. Mutual funds that invest in either corporate bonds, U.S. government debt, or a combination of the two. They are distinct from municipal bond funds, which invest in debt issued by states and municipalities and often come with tax advantages.

Taxable-equivalent yield. A calculation that helps determine whether, on an after-tax basis, a tax-free municipal bond is more or less attractive than a taxable Treasury security. If the taxable equivalent yield of a muni is higher than the current yield of an equivalent Treasury, then a muni may be the better buy. The formula to determine it is:

Muni bond yield/(1 — Your tax bracket) = Taxable equivalent yield

Tax-efficient stock funds. Mutual funds that attempt to minimize the tax liabilities of its shareholders through tactical purchases and sales and relatively low turnover.

Time horizon. Refers to the length of time an investor has before he or she needs to tap the money that is being invested. The longer your time horizon, the more aggressive an investor can—and should—be with an asset allocation strategy.

TIPs, or Treasury Inflation-Protected securities. A relatively new form of government bond whose principal value is adjusted to reflect the impact of inflation over time. Thus, unlike other bonds, then, TIPs do not suffer from inflation risk.

Top line growth. Refers to a company's sales growth, as measured in its income statement. It is called "top line" because it is the first line item listed in the income statement.

Total expense ratio. These are comprised of the annual fees that fund investors must pay every year to cover the management and administrative costs of the fund. Expressed as a percentage of assets, the total expense ratio is deducted from your fund's returns.

Total return. The sum total of investment gains that an investor enjoys from a security. Within the realm of stocks, total return is calculated by adding a stock's capital appreciation to its dividend payout. Among bonds, total return is the yield plus or minus any changes in the bond's price.

Total sales, also referred to as **revenues.** Reflects the amount of goods or services a company has sold in a particular period. It is listed on the income statement on a quarterly and/or annual basis.

Total shares outstanding. The total number of ownership shares issued by the company or mutual fund. By knowing total shares outstanding, you can figure out how big a share of the company you own.

Trading range. Refers to a phenomenon in the stock market when the price of a stock or index can't seem to move above or below a certain level.

Trading volume. Refers to the number of shares of a specific stock that are traded in a given day, not the price of those shares. If a stock's price rises on unusually high volume, that is considered a bullish indicator for that security. On the other hand, if a stock's price falls on high volume, it would be regarded as bearish.

Trailing P/E. A stock's price-to-earnings ratio, based on actual trailing earnings over the past 12 months. Because corporate earnings generally rise over time, a stock's trailing P/E will often be higher than its forward P/E.

Treasury bill, or **T-bill.** A short-term cash instrument issued by the federal government and backed by the full faith and credit of Uncle Sam. T-bills pay no direct interest, unlike Treasury notes or bonds, where you are paid interest along the way. However, T-bills are purchased at a discount to par value, and investors earn money when they recoup the par value at maturity. Along with money market accounts, CDs, and money market funds, these are a popular cash vehicle.

Treasury bonds. Debt issued by the federal government that is backed by the full faith and credit of Uncle Sam. From the standpoint of credit risk, Treasury bonds are considered risk-free, since the Treasury Department can simply print more money to make an investor whole. However, Treasuries, like other bonds, are subject to interest-rate risk.

Two times factor. A back-of-the-envelope asset allocation strategy in which years away from retirement is multiplied by a factor of 2. The answer suggests what percentage of your portfolio belongs in stocks. Therefore, a 20-year-old worker 45 years from retirement should have 90 percent of his assets in equities. Note, however, that as one ages, this strategy may become too conservative for long-term investors.

Ultra-short-term bond fund. A mutual fund that invests in extremely short-term debt that typically matures in about a year or two, or sometimes even less. While ultra-short-term bonds are sometimes used as a cash vehicle, they are still fixed-income assets that can lose value under certain circumstances.

Valuation. Refers to the priceyness of a stock, as measured by formulas such as the price-to-earnings ratio, the price-to-book value ratio, or the price-to-sales ratio.

Value stock. Shares of companies that are undervalued or beaten down by investors, and therefore are considered a bargain by some investors.

Wilshire 5000. A benchmark stock index that gauges the performance of the total U.S. stock market. Unlike the S&P 500, which only tracks the 500 largest stocks in the United States, the Wilshire 5000 tracks large-cap, mid-cap, and small-cap stocks.

Zero-coupon bonds. A type of bond that by design does not pay any interest to investors during its life. Instead, these bonds agree to pay the investor all of the money that would have accrued as interest over the life of the loan in a lump sum at maturity—in addition to the principal investment that the investor is due back.

Index

DeMYSTiFieD®

Dear Student:

Our name says it all: the goal of the DeMYSTiFieD series is to help you master confusing subjects, understand complex textbooks, and succeed in your studies.

How can DeMYSTiFieD help you? **It's a no-brainer!**

- Study with the best—all DeMYSTiFieD authors are experts in their fields of study.

- Learn by doing—all DeMYSTiFieD books are packed with examples and practice opportunities.

- Grasp the critical concepts right away with highlighted chapter objectives.

- Get unstuck with help from the "Still Struggling?" feature. We all need a little help sometimes.

- Grade your own progress with a "Final Exam" at the end of each book and avoid the red pencil of doom.

- Move easily from subject to subject with a "Curriculum Guide" that gives a logical path.

DeMYSTiFieD is the series you'll turn to again and again to help you untangle confusing subjects, become confident in your knowledge, and achieve your goals. No matter what subject—algebra, college Spanish, business-school accounting, specialized nursing courses, and everything in between—DeMYSTiFieD is true to its motto:

Hard stuff made easy™

Curriculum Guide

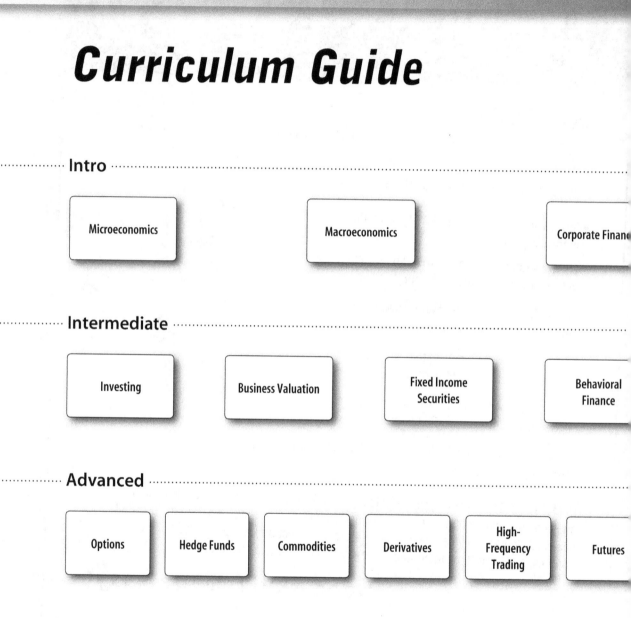

Intro

Microeconomics

Macroeconomics

Corporate Finan

Intermediate

Investing

Business Valuation

Fixed Income
Securities

Behavioral
Finance

Advanced

Options

Hedge Funds

Commodities

Derivatives

High-
Frequency
Trading

Futures

CPSIA information can be obtained
at www.ICGtesting.com
Printed in the USA
JSHW040026110321
12399JS00003B/4

9 780071 749121